Friedhelm Weick **Birds of Prey of the World**
Die Greifvögel der Welt

Friedhelm Weick **Birds of Prey of the World**
Die Greifvögel der Welt

Friedhelm Weick

Die Greifvögel der Welt

Ein farbiger Führer zur Bestimmung der Ordnung Falconiformes

Unter Mitarbeit von

Dr. Leslie H. Brown

Karen, Kenya

Mit 1144 farbigen Abbildungen und 160 Federzeichnungen

Verlag Paul Parey · Hamburg und Berlin

Friedhelm Weick

Birds of Prey of the World

A coloured guide to identification of all the diurnal species
order Falconiformes

In collaboration with

Dr. Leslie H. Brown

Karen, Kenya

With 1144 colour figures and 160 line drawings

Verlag Paul Parey · Hamburg und Berlin

For Christel and Reiner

1980021492

CIP-Kurztitelaufnahme der Deutschen Bibliothek

Weick, Friedhelm:
Birds of prey of the world: a coloured guide to identification of all the diurnal species order Falconiformes / Friedhelm Weick. In collab. with Leslie H. Brown. – Hamburg, Berlin: Parey, 1980.
   Dt. Ausg. u. d. T.: Weick, Friedhelm: Die Greifvögel der Welt.
   ISBN 3-490-08518-3

Foreword by Leslie H. Brown

This book is a true labour of love. Inspired by Peter Scott's key to the waterfowl of the world, and his own long-time interest in birds of prey, the author and artist has laboured for more than a decade, without certainty of reward, to produce a much-needed guide to identification of all the world's diurnal birds of prey, in the order Falconiformes.

Birds of prey are often difficult to identify in the field, because they are shy, swift, often solitary, and may live in wild country. Shown here are not only every species, but every distinctive race, in adult and immature plumage, often with several colour phases. A brief tabulated text accompanying each plate gives essential measurements, field characters and distribution. With this book in hand, there should be no serious difficulty in identifying any bird of prey anywhere in the world. And, since identification is the first step towards knowledge, it should serve as a springboard for research on some of the most magnificent and interesting of all the world's birds.

In the early part of the book there are keys to genera, and to identification in the field by certain characters, such as long legs, long tails or crests of different shapes and sizes. While these are not arranged in systematic order – purposely – they will often help to narrow the field of search for a hitherto unknown species, of which perhaps the observer had just a fleeting impression before it flew, or which he saw while travelling in a car, and could not stop sufficiently quickly. If it had some such distinctive feature he can then say "It might be such an one"; and then look it up in the key and make certain. I know from experience how many people see a bird of prey and notice only some such distinguishing character, perhaps not even its colour; and that this often enables one who knows the birds and their habits to say what it probably was. Well – if they have this book, they can do it themselves.

The author and artist learned how important accuracy was when doing illustrations for the Handbook of Central European Birds. Nowhere is his accuracy better displayed than in the beautiful drawings which accompany his description of genera. He has also been to special trouble, in the main illustrations, to ensure accuracy in the colour of the eyes, cere, and legs – so often among the first characters to strike an observer, but often inaccurately described in guides, and even handbooks, because the original collector did not correctly describe them when preparing his specimen. If every artist would take as much trouble to be accurate, we should all be better informed.

In order to keep the book of moderate size, and to keep the number of plates down for reasons of cost, some plates will appear to the reader overpopulated with similar birds. It may appear that these are not drawn to scale; but careful examination will show that this is an optical illusion. They are correctly sized, as I found when I went into this in detail myself. The birds are all shown in one position, but the artist has carefully thought out which is the best and most likely position for such a bird; and has sometimes shown them with wings partly open, or tail spread to bring out diagnostic characters.

He has worked largely from museum skins, or birds kept in zoos or collections, when he has been unable to see the bird in the field himself. Although he acknowledges the help he has obtained from such sources, he rightly condemns the increasingly prevalent practice of keeping birds of prey captive for spurious reasons, such as attempts to breed them in captivity or study of disease, without adequate facilities for such purposes. I agree wholeheartedly with him in deploring the capture of a magnificent bird, which then languishes in unsuitable surroundings, and eventually dies without ever reproducing its own kind. Birds of prey, especially those species whose numbers have been reduced by the action of chemical pesticides, should only be kept for such purposes when the facilities and finance are adequate, and there is a good chance of success. In saying this I am not decrying genuine falconers, or those few institutions which are now successfully breeding falcons and hawks, so reducing the toll on wild birds.

The author is the last person to blow his own trumpet; but in fact he has done an immense amount of skilled, detailed, meticulously accurate work which is a real advance on anything of the sort previously attempted. All raptor-lovers will carry this book world-wide, and use it daily to identify unfamiliar species. Friedhelm Weick pays graceful tribute to those who have helped him, including myself and my wife. If we have helped in a small way – and it was a small way only – to make the text or pictures more accurate and useful, it has been a pleasure to further the work of one whom we hope will have a deserved success with his labour of love – and find that love sometimes pays dividends.

Vorwort von Leslie H. Brown

Dieses Buch ist wahrhaftig aus Leidenschaft geboren. Angeregt durch das Bestimmungsbuch für die Wasservögel der Welt von Peter Scott, und erfüllt von seinem langjährigen Interesse für die Greifvögel, hat der Autor und Künstler weit über ein Jahrzehnt, ohne sichere Aussicht auf materiellen Erfolg, intensiv daran gearbeitet, einen dringend benötigten Führer zur Bestimmung der Greifvögel, der Ordnung Falconiformes, zu erstellen.

In der freien Natur sind Greifvögel häufig schwer zu bestimmen, da sie scheu und flink, auch oft einzelgängerisch sind und nicht selten in schwer zugänglichen Gebieten leben. Hier wurden nicht nur alle Arten, sondern auch jede gut unterscheidbare Rasse im Adult- und Immaturkleid, häufig in verschiedenen Farbphasen, dargestellt. Jeder Farbtafel ist ein kurzer, tabellarisch angeordneter Text gegenübergestellt mit Angaben über Maße, Feldkennzeichen und Verbreitung. Mit diesem Buch in der Hand sollte es keine Schwierigkeiten mehr geben, irgendeinen Greifvogel irgendwo auf der Welt zu bestimmen. Und, weil sichere Bestimmung der erste Schritt dazu ist, sich Wissen zu erwerben, sollte es zur weiteren Erforschung einiger der prächtigsten und interessantesten Vögel der Welt dienen.

Der erste Teil des Buches enthält eine Gattungsübersicht sowie Schlüssel zu augenfälligen Merkmalen wie langen Beinen, langen Schwänzen oder Hauben verschiedener Form und Größe, die als Feldkennzeichen dienen. Da diese Schlüssel absichtlich nicht nach der systematischen Ordnung erstellt sind, werden sie gerade dadurch helfen, den gesuchten Zuordnungsbereich einer bisher unbekannten Art einzugrenzen, von der der Beobachter vielleicht nur einen flüchtigen Eindruck vor dem Abflug gewann. Falls er einige dieser Merkmale erkannt hat, kann er dann sagen: „Es könnte möglicherweise diese Art sein", im Schlüssel nachschauen und genau bestimmen. Ich weiß aus Erfahrung, daß viele Leute beim Anblick eines Greifvogels wohl solche Merkmale, aber möglicherweise nicht einmal dessen Farben erkennen, und daß dies trotzdem einem Vogelkenner oft zur Bestimmung der Art genügt. Wer also dieses Buch besitzt, kann das dann auch selber herausfinden.

Wie wichtig Genauigkeit ist, lernte der Autor und Künstler bei der Illustration der Vögel Mitteleuropas. Nirgends zeigt sich diese Sorgfalt besser als bei den Zeichnungen, welche die Gattungsübersicht ergänzen. Bei den Farbtafeln war es sein besonderes Anliegen, für die Farben der Augen, der Wachshaut und der Beine Gewähr zu bieten – wie oft bemerkt ein Beobachter gerade sie als erstes, findet sie aber häufig in Feldführern und sogar in Handbüchern nur unzulänglich beschrieben, da schon die Originalbeschreibung des Präparators unge-

nau war. Wenn jeder Illustrator sich so um Exaktheit bemüht hätte, wären wir alle besser informiert.

Um das Format des Buches und die Anzahl der Farbtafeln aus Kostengründen in einem vernünftigen Rahmen zu halten, werden dem Betrachter einige Tafeln mit ähnlichen Vögeln überladen erscheinen. Auch mag es so aussehen, als seien diese nicht maßstabgerecht gezeichnet. Sorgfältige Nachprüfung im Detail zeigte mir jedoch, daß dies eine optische Täuschung ist: Die Maße stehen im richtigen Verhältnis zueinander. Die Vögel wurden alle in derselben Ansicht dargestellt, doch wurde vom Illustrator sorgfältig bedacht, welches die beste und zudem wahrscheinliche Haltung ist. Um charakteristische Merkmale besser zu zeigen, werden manche Vögel mit leicht geöffneten Schwingen oder gespreiztem Schwanz gezeigt.

Vögel, die nicht im Felde zu beobachten waren, wurden nach Bälgen oder in Zoos und Vogelparks gehaltenen Tieren gemalt. Der Autor erkennt zwar die Hilfe, die er von diesen Stellen erhalten hat, dankend an; zurecht verurteilt er aber die zunehmend geübte Unsitte, Greifvögel in Gefangenschaft zu halten, wobei ernsthafte Gründe wie die Bemühungen um Gefangenschaftszucht oder um die Erforschung von Krankheiten vorgetäuscht werden, ohne daß die hierzu erforderlichen Einrichtungen vorhanden sind. Aus vollem Herzen stimme ich seiner Klage über den Fang solch prächtigen Vogels zu, der dann in ungeeigneter Umgebung dahinsiecht und wahrscheinlich stirbt, ohne dem Erhalt seiner Art gedient zu haben. Greifvögel, insbesondere die Arten, deren Individuenzahl durch chemische Pestizide stark zurückgegangen ist, sollten zu solchen Zwecken nur gehalten werden, wenn die Anlagen und die finanziellen Mittel dazu in ausreichendem Maße vorhanden sind. Mit dieser Feststellung möchte ich natürlich nicht die echten Falkner oder jene wenigen Einrichtungen in Verruf bringen, die erfolgreich Falken und Habichte züchten, um den Aderlaß bei den Wildvögeln zu verringern.

Der Autor ist gewiß der letzte, der für sich die Trommel schlägt; doch hat er in der Tat ein enormes Maß an fachmännischer, präziser, peinlich genauer Arbeit geleistet, die immer einen echten Fortschritt bewirkt, gleichgültig was man anpackt. Alle Greifvogelfreunde werden dieses Buch in der ganzen Welt mit sich führen und täglich zum Bestimmen wenig vertrauter Arten benutzen. Friedhelm Weick zollt allen dankbares Lob, die ihm geholfen haben, so auch meiner Frau und mir. Wenn wir ein klein wenig dazu beigetragen haben – und es war nur ein klein wenig –, Texte oder Abbildungen noch genauer und brauchbarer zu machen, so war es uns ein Vergnügen, die Arbeit eines Menschen zu fördern, für den wir hoffen, daß er mit diesem Werk seiner Leidenschaft den verdienten Erfolg erzielt – damit wir feststellen können, daß sich Liebe manchmal auszahlt.

Preface

When, in 1967, I first saw Peter Scott's "Coloured Key to the Waterfowl of the World" I was filled with admiration. I felt at once that the same was needed for the birds of prey.

The fascinating Order Falconiformes has interested me for more than the last twenty-five years, and its spell holds me to this day, occupying most of my spare time. The continual persecution of birds of prey in many parts of the world is a depressing fact. Reduction of their numbers by indiscriminate use of chemicals combined with the destruction of their habitat is still further accelerated by the activities of almost fanatical collectors – for profit or for show, for private collectors or for clubs and organisations. While it is still possible, this book is dedicated to capture these fabulous birds with brush and pen.

In 1969 I was lucky enough to work as an illustrator on the „Handbuch der Vögel Mitteleuropas" under Professor Doktor U. N. Glutz von Blotzheim. Valuable experience was gained at this time.

The plates shown here are intended as straightforward colour sketches based on the Peterson Field Guide technique. To show true comparisons between the species it was necessary to show all birds in similar positions, often with slightly spread wings and tail to illustrate all salient points.

This book is primarily the work of a bird artist and should be used as such. The text has been compressed to the permissible minimum, using as guidelines Brown and Amadon's "Eagles, Hawks and Falcons of the World" and Grossman and Hamlet's "Birds of Prey of the World".

Plates and tables have been arranged so as to complement one another. Information on an individual bird is found exactly opposite its illustration. Wherever possible, related species and genera have been shown on one and the same plate. Illustrations of flight patterns have been deliberately omitted since they are amply covered in other publications.

Various subspecies have only been illustrated when distinct differences exist. In addition, juvenile and immature plumages, and different colour phases are shown, together with sexual differences within a species. Limited space has meant that immature and subadult plumages cannot all be shown. Great emphasis has been placed on the correct rendering of iris colour, and of bare skin or soft parts, which have often in other works been neglected, and are misleading. Races not illustrated are listed in smaller print in the tables.

The German bird names of the European species are derived from Peterson. All others are based on the book „Greifvögel und Eulen" by D. and G. Lloyd. English common bird names have been drawn from the English language literature.

Scientific names have been given completely, with the authority and date when first described. Synonyms are given in the index of scientific names. Full details of synonymy have had to be curtailed for reasons of space. An enormous volume of world literature on birds of prey had to be studied for information. This was only possible through the very generous library system of the Badische Landesbibliothek, Karlsruhe. A bibliography of literature sources is given.

Thanks are due to all those who over the years have encouraged, advised and helped me in many various ways, – and in view of new editions I hope for their support to set this book in the actual state of knowledge. I should like to single out conservationist Diplomingenieur Günther Müller of Karlsruhe and thank him most sincerely for allowing me to use his vast library, as well as for his continued encouragement.

I must also acknowledge the helping hand of Dr. Leslie H. Brown (of Karen, Kenya) one of the most competent bird of prey experts, and his polyglot wife. His critical perusal of manuscript and tables, and his advice combined with his comprehensive knowledge of birds of prey were invaluable and indispensable. He has critically checked the English translation of the text.

Finally, my sincere thanks go to Verlag Paul Parey. Only their understanding, cooperation, and expert working team have made this book possible.

One of the main objects of this book will be fulfilled if, by illustrating the variety and beauty of an endangered bird species, a better understanding and increased measures to protect it is achieved.

Bruchsal, Spring 1980   Friedhelm Weick

Vorwort

Als mir im Jahre 1967 erstmals Peter Scotts „Farbiger Bestimmungsschlüssel für das Wassergeflügel der Welt" zu Gesicht kam, war ich davon begeistert. Der Gedanke drängte sich mir auf, daß man etwas Ähnliches auch für die Greifvögel erstellen müsse.

Dieser faszinierenden Ordnung Falconiformes gilt mein Interesse und ein großer Teil meiner Freizeit schon seit über fünfundzwanzig Jahren. Sie hält mich noch immer in ihrem Bann.

Die stetige, anscheinend unaufhaltsame Dezimierung der Greifvögel in nahezu allen Teilen unserer Erde ist ein deprimierender Vorgang. Der Rückgang ihres Bestandes als Folge wahllosen Gebrauchs chemischer Mittel zur Schädlingsbekämpfung im Verein mit der Zerstörung ihrer natürlichen Lebensräume wird noch beschleunigt durch die gewissenlose Wegnahme von Eiern und Aushorstung von Greifvogelgelegen.

An dieser Stelle sollte ein Wort gesagt werden zu den Bemühungen, Greifvögel in Gefangenschaft zu halten. Dieser schwierigen Aufgabe sollten sich nur Fachleute unterziehen, denen die Kenntnisse und die Mittel dafür zu Gebote stehen. Von echten Falknern betriebene Falkenhöfe und andere qualifizierte Zuchtstätten haben beachtliche Zuchterfolge vor allem bei stark bedrohten Arten vorzuweisen. Groß aber ist die Zahl der Greifvögel, und sie wächst beständig, die in unwürdiger Gefangenschaft dahinvegetieren und schließlich verenden, ohne der Erhaltung ihrer Art gedient zu haben. Aufklärung über die Biologie und die Ökologie der Greife sollte dieser Entwicklung entgegenwirken.

Vor diesem Hintergrund entstand mein Buch aus dem Bedürfnis heraus, diese einzigartige Vogelgruppe mit Pinsel und Zeichenfeder festzuhalten, solange sie in der freien Natur, in Zoos, Falkenhöfen und wo sonst noch immer zu sehen sind.

Dabei kam es mir sehr zustatten, daß ich dank der Fürsprache des unvergessenen Professor Doktor Stresemann im Jahr 1969 als Illustrator für das von Professor Doktor U. N. Glutz von Blotzheim herausgegebene „Handbuch der Vögel Mitteleuropas" tätig werden und so wertvolle Erfahrungen sammeln konnte.

Die Vogeltafeln wollen keine Gemälde sein, sondern Farbskizzen zur Bestimmung von Arten und Rassen in Anlehnung an das vielfach bewährte „Petersonsche" Darstellungsschema. Unter diesem Aspekt sollten sie betrachtet werden. Um echte Vergleiche zwischen den dargestellten Arten anstellen zu können, war es nötig, alle Vögel in derselben Ansicht, oft mit gewollt leicht gespreiztem Flügel und Schwanz, letzteren etwas zum Betrachter „gedreht", darzustellen. Nur so war es möglich, alles Wesentliche zu zeigen.

Da dieses Buch in erster Linie als Arbeit eines Vogelmalers und -zeichners verstanden sein will, wurde der Text knapp gehalten. Er beschränkt sich auf Tabellen, Bestimmungsschlüssel und eine systematische Übersicht der Gattung. Die systematische Richtschnur sowohl in der Beschreibung der Gattung als auch in der Reihenfolge der Arten bildeten ausschließlich die Werke von L. H. Brown und D. Amadon „Hawks und Falcons of the World" sowie von M. L. Grossmann und I. Hamlet „Birds of Prey of the World".

Die Tabellen sollen nicht nur Lücken aufzeigen, sondern auch zum Ergänzen anregen: Ihr Aufbau entspricht dem der Farbtafeln. Vögel, welche im oberen Teil der Tabelle aufgeführt sind, finden sich auch im oberen Teil der gegenüberliegenden Farbtafel.

Um möglichst übersichtlich und umfassend verwandte Arten und Formen zu zeigen, wurden diese wenn möglich auf einer Farbtafel zusammengefaßt. Dies ließ sich aus Platzgründen in einigen Fällen nicht realisieren. So mußten zum Beispiel zusammen mit Fischadler und Sekretär oder mit den Dickfuß- und einigen Waldadlern diese weniger nahestehenden Arten auf jeweils einer Tafel untergebracht werden.

Auf eine Abbildung von Flugbildern wurde bewußt verzichtet. Diese sind zum Beispiel in „Birds of Prey of the World" oder für Europa im „Handbuch der Vögel Mitteleuropas" beziehungsweise in „Flight-Identification of European Raptors" in reichlichem Maße abgebildet.

Abbildungen von Rassen wurden auf den Farbtafeln nur dort berücksichtigt, wo deutliche Unterscheidungsmerkmale im Habitus gegeben sind, nicht aber, wenn diese nur auf Unterschiede in den Maßen basieren.

Darüberhinaus sind Juvenil- und Immaturkleider sowie Farbphasen dargestellt oder beide Geschlechter bei deutlichem Sexualdimorphismus in der Färbung. Der Wunsch, möglichst die ganze Vielfalt an Formen und Kleidern der Greifvögel darzustellen, war aus verschiedenen Gründen unausführbar. Als Beispiel seien hier nur die über Jahre dauernden, komplizierten Mauserstadien von Immatur- und Subadultkleidern vieler Großgreife erwähnt. Hier wurden mir Grenzen gesetzt, die aus Platzgründen, aber auch um nicht zu sehr Verwirrung zu stiften, eingehalten werden mußten. Großer Wert wurde auf die Wiedergabe von Irisfarben und nackten Körperteilen gelegt, da es gerade hierbei in vielen Feldführern häufig zu fehlerhaften Darstellungen kam. Rassen, die nicht abgebildet wurden, kann man in den Tabellen sofort daran erkennen, daß deren Namen in gewöhnlicher, magerer Schrift gesetzt wurden.

Die deutschen Vogelnamen der europäischen Arten sind weitgehend aus Petersons „Die Vögel Europas" übernommen. Für die außereuropäischen Arten fanden die Namen aus dem Büchlein „Greifvögel und Eulen" von D. und G. Lloyd Verwendung. Die englischen Trivialnamen sind der englischsprachigen Greifvogelliteratur entnommen. Die wissenschaftlichen Bezeichnungen wurden in der üblichen Art durch die Autorennamen und das Datum der Erstbeschreibung ergänzt. Synonyme für Gattungsnamen sind im Verzeichnis der wissenschaftlichen Namen mit aufgeführt. Auf die unübersehbare Zahl der Art- beziehungsweise Rassensynonyme mußte verzichtet werden. Die Sichtung der äußerst umfangreichen Weltliteratur über Taggreife, ohne deren Kenntnis eine solche umfassende Arbeit nicht zustande kommen konnte, ermöglichte zu einem beachtlichen Teil das unbürokratische Verleihsystem der Badischen Landesbibliothek, Karlsruhe. Ein Verzeichnis der benutzten Literatur ist im Anhang aufgeführt.

Ein Wort des Dankes gilt all jenen, die mich im Laufe der Jahre durch Ratschläge, Anregungen, Literaturhinweise oder durch Beschaffung von Literatur sowie unzähligen Vorlagen aller Art unterstützt haben, – und auf deren Unterstützung ich auch in Zukunft hoffe, um das Werk bei Neuauflagen auf dem neuesten Stand zu halten.

Stellvertretend für sie möchte ich an dieser Stelle Herrn Hauptkonservator Diplomingenieur Günther Müller, Karlsruhe, auf das herzlichste danken. Seine Hilfe, das Benutzen seiner reichhaltigen Bibliothek und seine stetige Ermutigung haben wesentlichen Anteil an der Vollendung dieser Arbeit.

Besonderer Erwähnung bedarf die menschlich und sachlich ungewöhnliche Hilfsbereitschaft von Doktor Leslie H. Brown (Karen/Kenya), eines der kompetentesten Greifvogelkenner, und seiner sprachkundigen Frau. Seine kritische Durchsicht von Manuskript und Farbtafeln, seine Ratschläge und Verbesserungsvorschläge wirkten im Verein mit seiner immensen Sachkenntnis befruchtend auf die gesamte Arbeit. Die englische Fassung ist sein Werk.

Herzlichen Dank möchte ich auch dem Verlag Paul Parey aussprechen. Sein Entgegenkommen und Verständnis in allen Belangen ließen meine Arbeit erst zu dem Buch werden, das mir vorschwebte.

Wenn dieses Buch durch Aufzeigen der Schönheit und Vielfalt einer äußerst bedrohten Vogelordnung einen Beitrag leisten könnte zu mehr Verständnis, mehr Rücksicht und zu dem Willen, sie auch außerhalb der oft weitmaschigen und trägen Gesetzesmaschine zu schützen, dann wäre der Sinn meiner Arbeit erfüllt.

Bruchsal, Frühjahr 1980   Friedhelm Weick

Inhalt Content

Zum Gebrauch des Bestimmungsschlüssels

Auf jeder der vierzig Farbtafeln sind verwandte Arten zu Gruppen zusammengefaßt. Zur schnellen Orientierung sind Hinweise auf verschiedene Kennzeichen wie Größe, Gestalt, Farbe, Schnabel-, Hauben- und Schwanzformen etc. mit dem Verweis auf die Tafelseite gegeben.

Bestimmte anatomische und äußerliche Merkmale der verschiedenen Gattungen sind in kurzer Übersicht zusammengefaßt und können ebenfalls zur Orientierung hinzugezogen werden.

Vergleichsgrößen einiger Greifvögel

How to use this key

On each of the forty colour-plates related forms are united in groups. As a quick guide, indications of such different characters as size, build, colour, shape of bill, crest and tail etc., cross-referenced to number of the colour-plate are given.

Marked anatomical or external characters of all genera are gathered in a compressed review, and should also help in identification.

Comparison in size of some diurnal birds of prey

sehr groß
very large | Vultur

ziemlich groß
rather large | Hieraaëtus

mittelgroß
medium-sized | Buteo

groß
large | Aquila

sehr klein
very small | Microhierax

klein
small | Elanus

Topographie eines Greifvogels
(Heterospizias)

Topography of a diurnal bird of prey
(Heterospizias)

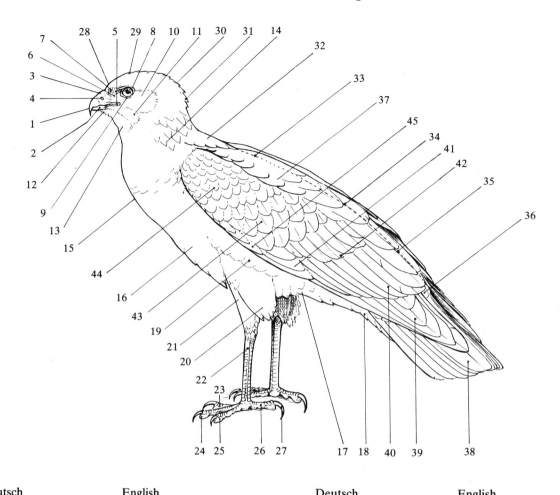

	Deutsch	English		Deutsch	English
1	Oberschnabel	upper mandible	23	Innenzehe	inner toe
2	Unterschnabel	lower mandible	24	Mittelzehe	middle toe
3	Wachshaut	cere	25	Außenzehe	outer toe
4	Nasenloch	nostril	26	Hinterzehe	hind toe
5	Schnabelspalt	gape	27	Kralle	claw
6	Zügel	lore	28	Stirn	forehead
7	Borsten	bristles	29	Scheitel	crown
8	Auge	eye	30	Hinterkopf	occiput
9	Augenring	orbital ring	31	Genick	nape
10	Ohrdecken	ear-coverts	32	Nacken	hind neck
11	Wange	cheek	33	Vorderrücken	upper back
12	Kinn	chin	34	Hinterrücken	lower back
13	Kehle	throat	35	Bürzel	rump
14	Hals	neck	36	Oberschwanzdecken	upper tailcoverts
15	Brust	chest or breast	37	Schulterfedern	scapulars
16	Bauch	belly	38	Schwanz	tail
17	Aftergegend	vent	39	Handschwingen	primaries
18	Unterschwanzdecken	under tailcoverts	40	Armschwingen	secondaries
19	Weichen, Flanken	flanks	41	Handdecken	primary-coverts
20	Hose	thigh	42	Große Flügeldecken	greater wing coverts
21	Schenkel	tibia	43	Mittlere Flügeldecken	median wing coverts
22	Lauf	tarsus	44	Kleine Flügeldecken	lesser wing coverts
			45	Afterflügel	bastard wing, alula

Dieses Diagramm zeigt, welche Maße in den Tabellen gegenüber den Tafeln Verwendung fanden und deren gebräuchliche Meßmethoden.

This diagram shows the measurements used in the tables opposite the colour plates, and the standard methods used.

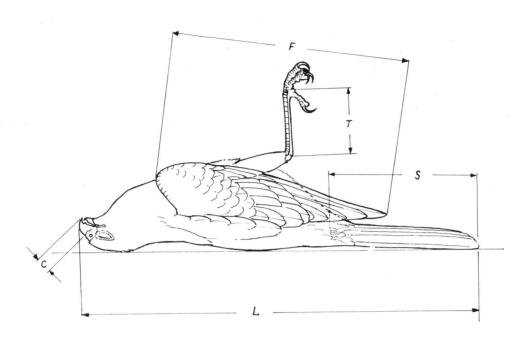

L. Gesamtlänge in cm, von der Schnabel- bis zur Schwanzspitze bei gestrecktem Hals; dieses Maß ist zur Rassenbestimmung ungeeignet, da die Methoden zur Präparierung von Bälgen zu unterschiedlich sind. Museumsbälge können z. B. durch Strekkung mehr oder weniger lang sein als der lebende oder frischtote Vogel. So kann dieses Maß nur bei gefangenen Vögeln Verwendung finden und hat keine wissenschaftliche Bedeutung.

L. Total length in centimetres (cm), from the tip of the bill to the tip of the tail with outstretched neck; this measurement cannot be used for racial determination because of varying methods for preparation of study skins. Museum skins may be stretched, and more or less longer than in the flesh, so that unless this measurement was recorded when the specimen was taken, it has no scientific value.

F. Flügellänge in mm, vom Bug des gefalteten Flügels zur Spitze der Handschwingen; kann mit dem Maßstab bzw. Maßband oder (häufiger) durch festes Andrücken des Flügels auf eine Unterlage mit Maßeinteilung gemessen werden. Bei letzterer Meßmethode muß der Flügel flach auf der Unterlage liegen, um das Maximalmaß zu erreichen. Dieses Maß zeigt bei Greifvögeln deutlich den häufigen Sexualdimorphismus auf und ist maßgebend bei der Rassenbestimmung.

F. Length of wing in mm, from the bend of the folded wing to the tip of primaries; may be measured with a rule or, alternatively, (usually), the wing is pressed flat against a scale to give the longest obtainable measurement. This measurement shows the sexual dimorphism usual in birds of prey and is definitive in describing a race or subspecies.

S. Schwanzlänge in mm, vom Ansatz der mittleren Schwanzfedern bis zur Spitze der längsten Schwanzfedern.

S. Length of tail in mm, from the fold of skin between the central tail-feathers and the tip of the longest tail-feathers.

Gewicht in Gramm, frischtoter oder lebender Vögel, möglichst ohne Kropfinhalt.

Weight in grams, of freshly killed or living birds, if possible without crop contents.

T. Lauflänge (tarsometatarsus) in mm, vom oberen Ende des Laufes (dicht unter der Vertiefung zwischen Lauf und Fersengelenk) bis zur Gelenkvertiefung zwischen Lauf und Mittelzehe oder bis zum Rande des untersten ungeteilten Laufschildes.

C. Schnabellänge in mm, vom Ende der Wachshaut bis zur Schnabelspitze in gerader Linie (ohne Berücksichtigung der Firstkrümmung). Manchmal wird dieses Maß, von der Schnabelwurzel inclus. der Wachshaut bis zur Schnabelspitze gemessen, angegeben. Dann sind die Werte in Klammern ( ) angegeben.

T. Length of tarsus (tarsometatarsus) in mm, from the top of the tarsus (just below the tibio-tarsal joint, or „heel") to the joint at the base of the middle toe, or the last undivided scute on the front of the leg at the base of the toes.

C. Length of the bill (culmen) in mm, from the end of the cere to the billtip along the straight line. This measurement is sometimes made from the base of the cere to the bill tip; if so it is shown in brackets( ).

Symbole und Abkürzungen

adult = ausgewachsener, geschlechtsreifer Vogel im Alterskleid.
sub-adult = Vogel in Übergangsstufe zum Alterskleid.
immat. = unreifer, unausgefärbter Vogel, hat schon geraume Zeit das Nest verlassen.
juvenile = jugendlicher Vogel, Jugendkleid, hat erst kürzlich das Nest verlassen.
♂ = Männchen
♀ = Weibchen
E = Ost-, S = Süd-, W = West-, N = Nord-.

Symbols and abbreviations

adult = fully developed bird in adult plumage
sub-adult = a bird in subadult plumage about to become adult.
immature = a bird in immature plumage, but not just out of the nest.
juvenile = a bird in juvenile plumage, recently out of the nest.
♂ = male
♀ = female
E = East-, S = South-, W = West-, N = North-.

Die verschiedenen Maßstäbe auf den Tafeln

Zum Zeichnen der Tafeln wurden sieben verschiedene Maßstäbe verwendet. Dies war erstens wegen der unterschiedlichen Anzahl der Individuen pro Tafel, zweitens wegen der unterschiedlichen Körperproportionen der einzelnen Arten notwendig. So konnten die kleinen Habichts- oder Falkenarten nicht in demselben Maßstab wie zum Beispiel Geier oder Seeadler dargestellt werden.

Auf folgenden Farbtafeln wurde jeweils derselbe Maßstab benutzt:

a) Tafel   16, 17, 18
b) Tafel   14, 15, 19, 20, 21, 35, 36, 37, 38, 40
c) Tafel   39
d) Tafel   3, 4, 5, 11, 12, 13, 23, 33, 34
e) Tafel   22, 24, 25, 26, 27, 29, 30
f) Tafel   1, 2, 6, 9, 10, 28, 31, 32
g) Tafel   7, 8

The different size-scales on plates

In drawing the plates seven different scales were used. This was necessary, firstly because of the varying number of specimens per plate, and secondly because the species differ in size. Small accipiters and falcons could not, for instance be shown on the same scale as vultures or sea eagles.

The following size-scales were used on plates numbered as below:

a) Plate   16, 17, 18
b) Plate   14, 15, 19, 20, 21, 35, 36, 37, 38, 40
c) Plate   39
d) Plate   3, 4, 5, 11, 12, 13, 23, 33, 34
e) Plate   22, 24, 25, 26, 27, 29, 30
f) Plate   1, 2, 6, 9, 10, 28, 31, 32
g) Plate   7, 8

Bestimmungsschlüssel

Key for identifying

	Größe	**Size**	*Tafel/ Plate*
	sehr groß	**very large**	
Gymnogyps californianus	Nackter Kopf u. Hals; Gefieder einfarbig schwärzlich, an den Flügeln wenig weiß.	Head and neck naked; plumage uniform blackish, some white on wings.	*1*
Vultur gryphus	Nackter Kopf und Hals; Männchen mit fleischigem Kamm; kontrastreiches Gefieder, schwarz, weiß und grau.	Head and neck naked; male with fleshy comb; plumage strongly contrasting, black, white and grey.	*1*
Sagittarius serpentarius	Sehr hochbeinig; schlank; die mittleren Steuerfedern stark verlängert; am Hinterkopf lange, spatelförmige Federn; kontrastreiches Gefieder grau und schwarz.	Very long-legged; slender; central-tail feathers greatly elongated; an occipital crest of long spatulate feathers; plumage contrasting, grey and black.	*2*
Haliaeëtus pelagicus	Extrem hoher, schmaler und beilförmiger Schnabel; Immaturgefieder düster graubraun; Adultgefieder schwärzlich mit weissem Schwanz, weißen Hosen, Unterbauch, manchmal auch Flügel und Stirn weiß.	Beak strongly arched, narrow, laterally compressed; immature dark grey-brown; adult blackish with white tail, thighs, abdomen, „shoulders" and (sometimes) forehead.	*6*

Harpia harpyja

Gypaëtus barbatus	Langer, gestreckter Körper; langer, spatelförmig-gerundeter Schwanz; langer, stark gekrümmter Schnabel, mit borstigem Bart; Gefieder oben dunkel, unten weiß, rostfarben überflogen.	Body long, slim; tail long, diamond-shaped; bill long, strongly hooked, with „beard" of bristles; plumage dark above, below white, washed rufous.	*7*
Torgos tracheliotus	Kopf und Hals nackt, mit großen faltigen Lappen; gewaltiger Hakenschnabel; Gefieder einfarbig braunschwarz, an Unterseite mit vielen weißen Dunen.	Head and neck bare, with large folded lappets; very powerful, deep hooked bill; plumage uniform blackish, with much white down below.	*7*
Aegypius monachus	Kopf und Hals nackt, Oberkopf durch Dunen bedeckt; gewaltiger und klobiger Hakenschnabel; Gefieder düster schwarzbraun.	Head and neck naked, downy on crown; powerful hooked bill; plumage uniform dull blackish-brown.	*7*

	Größe	**Size**	*Tafel/ Plate*
	sehr groß	**very large**	
Gyps himalayensis	Gänsegeiertypus; langer, nackter Hals mit weißen Dunen bedeckt, weiße Halskrause, Bürzel weiß; Schnabel lang und hoch; Gefieder hellbeige, rostbraun und dunkelbraun.	Typical „griffon" vulture; long bare neck, covered with white down; ruff white; bill long, deep; body plumage sandy, rufous or dark brown.	8
Harpia harpyja	Dicker Kopf mit zweigeteilter Haube; kurze, breite Flügel; langer Schwanz; gewaltige, langkrallige Fänge; kontrastreiches Gefieder grau und weiß.	Head large, feathered, with forked crest; short broad wings; long tail; legs powerful, talons long, strong; contrasting grey and white plumage.	28
Pithecophaga jefferyi	Extrem hoher, seitlich zusammengedrückter und beilförmiger Schnabel. Kopf und Hals mit aufrichtbaren lanzettartigen Federn; Flügel kurz und breit; Schwanz lang; kräftige Fänge; Gefiederoberseite dunkelbraun, Unterseite weißlich.	Bill extremely arched, highly compressed, deeply hooked; head, neck with erectile lanceolate feathers; wings short and broad; tail long; feet powerful; plumage above dark brown, below whitish.	28
	groß	**large**	
Haliaeëtus leucocephalus	Kräftiger, hoher Hakenschnabel; Gefieder Adultvogel kontrastreich dunkelbraun mit weißem Kopf, Hals und Schwanz; Immaturvogel einfarbig braun.	Strong, deeply hooked bill; adult plumage contrasting dark brown with head, neck and tail white; immature uniform brown.	6
Haliaeëtus albicilla	Ähnlich *H. leucocephalus*; Kopf jedoch nur gelblich grau-weiß aufgehellt; Schwanz im Alter weiß; Immaturkleid einfarbig braun.	Resembles *H. leucocephalus*, but head, neck buff to pale brown, or greyish-white; tail white in adult; brown in immature.	6
Sarcogyps calvus	Kopf und Hals nackt und lappig; Halskrause und Gefieder düster braun; Vorderbrust weißlich.	Head and neck bare, wattled; ruff, body plumage dark brown, chest whitish.	7
Gyps species ohne except himalayensis	Schnabel lang, hoch und kräftig; Kopf und der lange Hals nackt, spärlich bedunt; Immaturkleid meist dunkler braun als Adultkleid; im Alter weiß-dunige Halskrause.	Bill long, deep, powerful; head and long neck naked except for sparse down; immatures darker brown than adults; ruff usually white in adults.	8
Harpyopsis novaeguineae	Dicker Kopf, kurze und runde Haube; kurze, breite Flügel; langer Schwanz; Oberseite braun mit hellen Säumen; Unterseite weißlich.	Head large, with short, full crest; wings short, broad; tail long; above brown, edged paler; below whitish.	28
Stephanoaëtus coronatus	Schnabel kräftig, mäßig lang, hoch; zweigeteilte Haube; kurze, breite Flügel; langer Schwanz; Jugendkleid sehr hell; Adultkleid oberseits schwarz-braun, unterseits weiß oder beige, schwarz gefleckt und gebändert.	Bill moderately long, deep; crest double; wings short, broad; tail long; juvenile plumage mainly white/grey; adult, above black-brown; below white or buff blotched and barred black.	28
Polemaëtus bellicosus	Dicker Kopf, kurze Haube; lange, breite Flügel; Schwanz kurz; junge Vögel sehr hell; alte Vögel oberseits dunkelbraun-grau, unterseits weiß mit schwärzlichen Flecken.	Head large, crest short; wings long, broad; tail short; immature plumage mainly white/grey; adult dark brownish grey above, below white, spotted blackish.	28
Aquila chrysaëtos	Gefieder in verschiedenen Brauntönen, an Nacken und Hals heller, lanzettartige Federn goldbraun bis fuchsbraun; Jungvögel mit weißer Schwanzwurzel und weißem Flügelfleck.	Plumage brown to dark brown, variable; nape and neck paler, lanceolate feathers light rufous to yellowish; juvenile has base of tail and wing patch white.	32

Größe		Size	Tafel/Plate
groß		**large**	
Aquila verreauxii	In Größe und Gestalt ähnlich Steinadler; Gefieder Alterskleid schwarz mit weißem Rücken; Jugendkleid braun und schwarz.	Size similar to Golden Eagle; adult black, with white back; juvenile brown and black.	*32*
Aquila audax	Steinadlertypus, jedoch mit Keilschwanz und klobigerem Schnabel. Gefieder düster schwarzbraun, aufgehellt an Nacken, Hinterhals und Oberflügeldecken.	Resembles Golden Eagle, but tail wedge-shaped, bill heavier; plumage dark blackish-brown, paler on nape, hindneck and upper wing coverts.	*32*

Gyps rueppellii

	ziemlich groß	**rather large**	
Cathartes species	Langer, nur wenig gekrümmter Schnabel; Kopf und Hals nackt; Gefieder dunkelbraun bis schwarz.	Long, slightly hooked bill; head and neck bare; plumage dark brown to black.	*1*
Coragyps atratus	Langer, schwach gekrümmter Schnabel; Gefieder schwarz; ziemlich hochbeinig; Schwanz eckig.	Long, scarcely hooked bill; plumage black; legs rather long; tail square.	*1*
Sarcoramphus papa	Nackter Kopf und Hals, prächtig gefärbt; Schnabel klobig. Gefieder: Alterskleid kontrastreich gelblich-weiß und schwarz; Jugendkleid einfarbig dunkelbraun.	Head and neck naked, brightly coloured; bill heavy; adult plumage contrasting creamy white and black; juvenile uniform dark brown.	*1*
Pandion haliaëtus	Kurze Haube; Augen nach vorne gerichtet; Gefieder kontrastreich braun-weiß. Fänge grau-blau.	Short crest; eyes directed forward, plumage contrasting brown and white; feet bluish-grey.	*2*
Milvus migrans linaëtus	Großer Schwarzmilan, unterscheidet sich von der Nominatform durch dunkleren Scheitel, helleren Bauch und Unterschwanzdecken.	Large Black Kite, differing from nominate race in having darker crown, lighter abdomen and lower tail coverts.	*5*
Haliaeëtus leucogaster	Kräftiger Schnabel; Gefieder: Altvogel graubraun und weiß; Jungvogel braun und beige.	Bill strong; adult, grey-brown and white, juvenile brown and buff.	*6*

Größe		Size	Tafel/
			Plate
ziemlich groß		**rather large**	

Haliaeëtus sanfordi	Schnabel und Gestalt ähnlich *leucogaster*; Gefieder jedoch hell rötlichgelb bis dunkelbraun. Immaturgefieder ähnlich dem von *leucogaster*.	Bill and body shape resembling *leucogaster*; plumage buff to dark brown; edged paler; immature plumage resembles *leucogaster*.	6
Haliaeëtus vocifer	Schnabel schwächer und Schwanz kürzer als bei *leucogaster*; Gefieder beim Altvogel sehr kontrastreich weiß, schwarz und rotbraun. Jugendkleid bräunlich; Subadultkleid mit weniger Weiß als beim Altvogel.	Bill weaker and tail shorter than in *leucogaster*; adult plumage strongly contrasting white, black and chestnut; juvenile brownish; subadults less white than adults.	6
Haliaeëtus vociferoides	Altvogel entspricht im Gefieder einem subadulten *vocifer* mit weißem Kopf und Schwanz; Immaturkleid mit rötlichweißem Kopf und hellerem Bauch als im Alterskleid.	Adult resembles subadult *vocifer*, with white head and tail; immature has buffy-white head and is paler brown than adult.	6
Haliaeëtus leucoryphus	In Gestalt und Schnabelform zwischen den schwarzschnäbligen, kleineren *Haliaeëtus*-Arten und den größeren, hellschnäbligen nördlichen Arten *albicilla* und *leucocephalus*. Kopf und Vorderrücken rahmgelb bis rötlichgelb, weiße Schwanzbinde, sonst braun bis dunkelbraun. Immaturkleid: heller, Kopf und Hals dunkler gefärbt; ziemlich langschwänzig.	Bill shape and build intermediate between smaller dark-billed *Haliaeëtus* species and larger pale billed northern *albicilla* and *leucocephalus*. Body brown to dark brown, with head and mantle buffish-white to buff; tail with white bar. Immature: paler, more dusky head and neck; tail rather long.	6
Ichthyophaga species	Adultkleid: Kopf und Hals grau; Hosen und Bauch weiß, Schwanz weiß oder braun. Immaturkleid heller und scheckiger.	Adults, grey head and neck; thighs and belly white; tail brown or white. Immatures paler and more mottled.	6
Neophron percnopterus	Nacktes Gesicht, umrahmt von langer, zerschlissener Mähne; Alterskleid weißlich, hellgrau und gelblich mit schwarzen Handschwingen; Immaturkleid dunkelbraun.	Face bare, surrounded by lanceolate feathers; adult whitish, light grey and buff with black primaries; immature dark brown.	7
Necrosyrtes monachus	Nacktes Gesicht, Hinterkopf und Hals hell bedunt; im Alters- und Jugendkleid dunkelbraun.	Face bare, light down on occiput and nape; adult and juvenile plumage dark brown.	7

Cathartes aura

Größe	Size	Tafel/Plate
ziemlich groß	**rather large**	

	Größe	Size	Tafel/Plate
Trigonoceps oc-cipitalis	Kopf und Hals weiß bedunt; Schnabel klobig, rosa bis rot; Gefieder dunkelbraun, Altvogel auf Brust und Armschwingen weiß.	Head and neck downy, white; bill heavy, brightly coloured red or pink; plumage dark brown, adult with white secondaries and chest.	7
Pseudogyps africanus	Kleinerer Gänsegeiertypus. Kopf und Hals teilweise bedunt; Altvogel auf dem Unterrücken weiß; Immaturvogel ohne weißen Unterrücken, mit weißen Flecken auf Flügeldecken und Unterseite.	Smaller griffons; head, neck, sparsely covered with down; adult with lower back white; immature lacks white back, streaked whitish below and on wing coverts.	8
Pseudogyps ben-galensis	Gestalt ähnlich *Pseudogyps africanus*, aber mit viel dunklerem Gefieder. Altvogel mit grau-überflogenen Armschwingen.	Resembles *africanus* in build, but much darker; adult has grey-washed secondaries.	8
Circaëtus species	Kopf dick, eulenhaftes Aussehen; vorherrschende Gefiederfarben sind verschiedene Brauntöne, manchmal mit viel weiß auf der Unterseite; Jungvögel heller als Adultvögel.	Large head, owl-like appearance; chiefly various shades of brown, sometimes with much white below; juveniles paler than adults.	9
Terathopius ecaudatus	Adultvogel: dickköpfig, mit extrem kurzem Schwanz; rote Wachshaut; kontrastreiches Gefieder, schwarz, rotbraun, hellbraun und weiß. Immaturvogel goldbraun bis dunkel graubraun, hell gefleckt.	Adult, big-headed, with extremly short tail; cere red; contrasting black, chestnut, pale brown and white plumage. Immature golden-brown to dark grey-brown, mottled paler.	9
Eutriorchis astur	Runder Schopf; kurz- und rundflügelig; Schwanz lang; Gefieder mit dunklem bis hellem Goldbraun und mit Weiß.	Full, round crest, wings short, rounded; tail long; plumage dark to paler golden brown and white.	9
Spilornis species	Ohne *klossi, elgini* und die kleineren Formen von *cheela*; dickköpfig, mit runder Haube. Adultkleid: vorwiegend schwarz, dunkel- oder heller braun, häufig mit weißen Tupfen auf Brust und Bauch. Jungvögel heller.	Excepting *klossi, elgini*, and small races of *cheela*; big-headed with full, bushy crest. Adults predominantly black, dark or lighter brown, often spotted white on chest and belly. Juveniles paler.	10
Harpyhaliaëtus species	Große Bussardverwandte, mit mehr oder minder langem Schopf; Gefieder überwiegend dunkel, auf Oberschwanzdecken und Schwanz weiß.	Large buteonines, more or less crested, long-legged; plumage mainly dark, with white on tail and upper tail-coverts.	23
Geranoaëtus melanoleucus	Großer, kurzschwänziger Bussardverwandter, mit kontrastreichem weiß-, grau- u. schwarzem Alterskleid. Immaturkleid mehr scheckig.	Large, short-tailed buteonine, with contrasting white, grey and black adult plumage. Immature more mottled.	24

Spilornis cheela

	Größe	**Size**	*Tafel/ Plate*
	ziemlich groß	**rather large**	
Buteo rufinus, hemilasius, regalis	Große, ziemlich langläufige Bussarde. Gefieder sehr variabel. Jede Art hat eine dunkle Phase.	Large, rather long-legged buzzards with very varied plumage; melanistic phases occur.	27
Morphnus guianensis	Dickköpfig, mit langer Haube; Flügel kurz und breit; Schwanz lang; Jugendkleid überwiegend weiß und grau; Alterskleid kontrastreich weiß, grau, dunkelgrau; diese Art hat eine dunkle gebänderte Phase.	Big-headed and long-crested; wings short, broad; tail long. Juvenile mainly white and grey; adult contrasting grey, dark grey and white; a barred phase occurs.	28
Oroaëtus isidori	Waldbewohnender Haubenadler; sehr breitflügelig; starker Schnabel und kräftige Fänge; Alterskleid kontrastreich rotbraun, schwarz, grau und weiß. Juvenil- und Immaturkleider viel heller, mit zahlreichen Zwischenstufen.	A forest-dwelling eagle; crested, broad-winged; feet and bill powerful; adult plumage contrasting black, chestnut, grey and white; juvenile and immature much paler, moulting to adult plumage in several stages.	28
Spizaëtus tyrannus	Schlanker, langschwänziger Haubenadler; Gefieder hauptsächlich schwarzbraun und schwarz.	Long-tailed, slender; plumage mainly blackish-brown or black.	29
Spizaëtus nipalensis, philippensis, lan- ceolatus, cirrhatus	Manchmal mit Haube; kurzflügelig, lang-schwänzig. Oberseite rahmbraun bis dunkelbraun; Unterseite hell, mehr oder weniger gefleckt und gebändert. *Spizaëtus cirrhatus limnaëtus* mit dunkler Phase.	Sometimes crested; short-winged, long-tailed. Above ochre-brown to dark-brown; below usually whitish, more or less spotted and barred. Melanistic phase occurs in *Spizaëtus cirrhatus limnaëtus*.	29
Hieraaëtus fasciatus	Kräftiger Schnabel, starke Fänge. Läufe befiedert. Alterskleid: Euro-Asiaten oberseits dunkelbraun, unten weiß mit Flecken und Streifen, Afrikaner oberseits braunschwarz und grau, unten weiß mit schwarzen Flecken. Immaturvögel an Kopf, Hals und Unterseite hell-rötlichbraun und weiß.	Beak strong, feet powerful, tarsi feathered. European and Asian adults dark-brown above, white below, spotted and streaked. African adults brownish-black and grey above, white below spotted blackish. Immatures pale brown and white on head, neck and underparts.	30
Aquila rapax, clanga, pomarina, heliaca, gurneyi	Schnabel und Fänge mehr oder minder kräftig, Läufe befiedert. Gefieder von hell-rahmfarben bis schwarzbraun; Immaturkleid mit viel weiß auf Rücken, Flügeln, Bürzel und Hosen. *A. heliaca* im Adultkleid mit weißen Flecken auf Flügel und Rücken.	Beak and feet more or less strong, feathered tarsi. Plumage creamy to blackish-brown; immatures with much white mottling on back, wings, rump and thighs. Adult *A. heliaca* have white patches on bend of wing and mantle.	31/32
Ictinaëtus malayensis	Schlank, langflügelig; Läufe befiedert; Krallen nur schwach gekrümmt. Gefieder: Alterskleid tief schwarz mit Weiß auf Oberschwanzdecken und unter dem Auge; Immaturkleid an Kopf, Hals, Unterseite mit viel Hellocker und Weiß.	Slender, long-winged; tarsi completely feathered, claws not sharply curved; adult wholly black with some white on upper tail-coverts and below eye; immature, head, neck, underparts sepia to golden brown and white.	32

Haliaaëtus vocifer

Größe		Size	Tafel/Plate
sehr klein		**very small**	
Gampsonyx swainsonii	Kopfplatte und Oberseite schwärzlich; Halsring, Brust und Bauch weiß, Hinterhals rotbraun; Stirn, Wangen: gelblichbeige; Hosen rostbraun.	Crown, upperparts blackish; collar, breast and belly white, hind-neck chestnut; forehead, cheeks yellow-buff; thighs rufous.	4
Polihierax semitorquatus	Oberseite grau, ♀ mit kastanienbraunem Rücken; Schwanz schwarz mit weißen Flecken; Halsring und Unterseite weiß.	Grey above, back of ♀ chestnut; tail black, spotted white; collar and underside white.	35
Polihierax insignis	Oberkopf und Vorderrücken beim ♂ grau, beim ♀ kastanienbraun, Schwanz abgestuft und länger als bei *P. semitorquatus*; Immaturvögel auf Unterseite gestreift.	Crown and mantle grey in ♂, chestnut in ♀, tail graduated, longer than in *P. semitorquatus*; immatures streaked below.	35
Microhierax species	Sperlingsgroß; kontrastreiches, schwarzweißes Gefieder, bei manchen Arten rotbraun auf dem Bauch; Wachshaut und Fänge grau.	Sparrow-sized; plumage contrasting black and white, belly chestnut in some species; cere and feet grey.	35
Falco sparverius subspecies ♂	Kleine Rüttelfalken; Gefieder hauptsächlich beige, kastanienbraun, blaugrau und weißlich gefärbt.	Small kestrels; plumage variable, buff, chestnut, blue-grey and whitish.	35
Falco araea ♀	Kleiner Rüttelfalke mit Turmfalkenhabitus; Unterseite jedoch ungefleckt.	Small, resembling European Kestrel, but underside unspotted.	36

Gampsonyx swainsonii

	klein		**small**	
Aviceda leuphotes		Langer, spitzer Schopf; Gefieder schwarz, mit weißen und braunen Abzeichen.	Long, pointed crest; plumage black, marked white and brown.	3
Elanus species		Gefieder weiß und grau; Schulterfleck schwarz. Immaturkleid mehr beige und braun gefärbt.	Plumage grey and white; black shoulders; immatures marked buff and brown.	4
Chelictinia riocourii		Gefieder grau und weiß; tiefer Gabelschwanz; Füße klein, Schnabel kurz.	Plumage grey and white; tail deeply forked; feet small, bill short.	4
Harpagus species		Gefieder, Oberseite grau-braun-schwärzlich; Unterseite weiß-rotbraun; Schwanz gebändert; Schnabel gezahnt.	Above grey-brown-blackish; below white-rufous; tail banded; bill toothed.	5
Melierax gabar		Sperbertypus; Gefieder grau und weiß; manchmal schwarz; Immaturvögel braun und weißlich.	Resembles sparrowhawks; plumage, grey and white; sometimes black; immatures brown and whitish.	14
Accipiter species		Hierher ein großer Teil der Gattung *Accipiter*; Gefieder meist bunt und kontrastreich. Kurzflügelig, langschwänzig, Läufe meist lang und schlank.	Many members of genus *Accipiter*; plumage often brightly coloured, usually contrasting. Short-winged, long tailed, tarsi usually long, slender.	16,17,18 19,20,21

	Größe	Size	Tafel/Plate
	klein	**small**	

<table>
<tr><td>Kaupifalco mono-grammicus</td><td>Gefieder kontrastreich, grau und weiß; auf der Unterseite feine weiß-braune Bänderung; Kehle weiß mit schwarzem Mittelstreifen.</td><td>Plumage contrasting, grey and white; below finely barred white and brown; throat white with median black streak.</td><td>22</td></tr>
<tr><td>Buteo magnirostris
Buteo ridgwayi</td><td>Kleine, ziemlich variabel gefärbte Bussarde; Gefieder braun, grau, rostgelb, rotbraun und weiß.</td><td>Small, very variable buzzards; plumage brown, grey, buff, rufous and white.</td><td>24</td></tr>
<tr><td>Micrastur ruficollis
subspecies</td><td>Hierher meist Männchen; kurzflügelig; sehr langschwänzig; oberseits grau-braun-schwärzlich; unten weißlich, mehr oder weniger gesperbert.</td><td>Male usually small; short-winged; very long-tailed; above grey-brown-blackish; below whitish, more or less barred.</td><td>34</td></tr>
<tr><td>Micrastur plumbeus</td><td>Langschwänzig und kurzflügelig, ähnlich Micrastur ruficollis; oben grau oder braun; unten weiß und grau gesperbert.</td><td>Long-tailed, short-winged, like Micrastur ruficollis; above, grey or brown; below, barred white and grey.</td><td>34</td></tr>
<tr><td>Spiziapteryx circum-cinctus</td><td>Braungrauer „Kleinfalke"; Augenbrauen, Kehle, Hosen und Oberschwanzdecken weiß.</td><td>A brown and grey „Pygmy Falcon"; eyebrow, throat, thighs, rump, white.</td><td>35</td></tr>
<tr><td>Falco species</td><td>Hierher viele kleine Falken, einschließlich der meisten Rüttelfalken mit überwiegend rötlichem, geflecktem oder gestreiftem Gefieder oder grauen bis graublauen Farbtönen; die Merline mit etwas gedrungenem Körperbau; die Baumfalken meist schlank, langflügelig mit Backenstreif; die Männchen von Falco hypoleucos (grau) und von Falco deiroleucus und Falco fasciinucha; zwei bunten Wanderfalkenverwandten.</td><td>Many small falcons in this size-range include kestrels, usually reddish, spotted and streaked or bluish-grey to grey; merlins with rather stout build; hobbies usually slender and long-winged, with a moustachial stripe; and males of Falco hypoleucos (grey), and of Falco deiroleucus, Falco fasciinucha which are colourful relations of the Peregrine.</td><td>35,36
37
37
38
40</td></tr>
</table>

Harpagus bidentatus

	mittelgroß	**medium-sized**	

<table>
<tr><td></td><td>Hierher die restlichen Greifvögel.</td><td>This size-range includes all remaining birds of prey.</td><td>3</td></tr>
<tr><td>Aviceda species</td><td>Ohne leuphotes; mit spitzem Schopf; Unterseite gebändert (adult) oder gefleckt (immatur).</td><td>Except leuphotes; with pointed crest, underside barred (adults) spotted (immatures).</td><td>3</td></tr>
<tr><td>Leptodon cayanensis</td><td>Gefieder grau oder braun und weiß.</td><td>Plumage grey or brown and white.</td><td>3</td></tr>
<tr><td>Chondrohierax species</td><td>Mit hohem Hakenschnabel und sehr variablem Gefieder.</td><td>Exaggerated, deeply hooked bill; plumage very variable.</td><td></td></tr>
<tr><td>Pernis & Henicopernis species</td><td>Mit verhornten Federn auf Zügelgegend; schlanker, gestreckter Körper; Gefieder sehr variabel; manchmal mit Haube am Hinterkopf.</td><td>Lores covered with scale-like feathers; slender, elongated build; plumage very variable; head sometimes crested.</td><td>4</td></tr>
</table>

	Größe	**Size**	*Tafel/Plate*
	mittelgroß	**medium-sized**	
Elanoides forficatus	Gefieder weiß und schwarz; tiefgegabelter Schwanz; Fänge klein; Schnabel kurz.	Plumage white and black; tail deeply forked; feet small; bill short.	*4*
Machaerhamphus alcinus	Dunkles Gefieder; kurzer Schopf; große, gelbe Augen; kleiner Schnabel, jedoch tiefe Schnabelspalte.	Plumage dark; short crest; large yellow eyes; bill slight, with very wide gape.	*4*
Ictinia species	Gefieder schiefergrau und weiß; langflügelig; Schwanzende eckig oder leicht ausgebuchtet.	Plumage slate-grey and white; long winged; tail square or notched.	*5*
Rostrhamus species	Schlanker, sichelförmiger Schnabel; Gefieder dunkelgrau oder braun und weiß.	Bill slender, with very long curved hook; plumage dark grey or brown and white.	*5*
Lophoictinia isura	Schwanzende eckig. Gefieder rostfarben bis dunkelbraun, mit aufgehelltem Kopf.	Tail square. Plumage rufous to dark brown, head paler.	*5*
Milvus species	Mehr oder minder tief gegabelter Schwanz. Gefieder rostfarben bis dunkelbraun, Kopf und Hals heller.	Tail more or less forked. Plumage rufous to dark brown, head paler.	*5*
Hamirostra & Haliastur species	Mit plumperer Gestalt als *Milvus*; Schwanzende eckig oder gerundet.	More heavily built than *Milvus*; tail square or rounded.	*5*
Gypohierax angolensis	Gefieder schwarz und weiß; nackte Hautteile im Gesicht.	Plumage black and white; bare skin on face.	*7*
Dryotriorchis spectabilis	Kurzflügelig, langschwänzig, runde Haube, Kehl- und Backenstreifen.	Short-winged, long tailed, with rounded crest; moustachial and median throat-stripe.	*9*
Spilornis species	Hierher die kleineren Arten und die Zwergformen von *Spilornis cheela*.	Smaller species and smaller races of *Spilornis cheela* in this size-range.	*10*
Polyboroides species	Nacktes Gesicht; Adultkleid grau, weiß und schwarz; Immaturkleid braun und weiß. Doppelgelenkige, lange Beine.	Face bare; adult plumage grey, white and black; immatures with brown and white plumage. Double jointed, long legs.	*11*
Geranospiza caerulescens	Leicht gebaut und schlank. Hochbeinig und doppelgelenkig (wie *Polyboroides*). Gefieder grau und weiß oder schwarz und weiß.	Light bodied, slender; long-legged, double-jointed (as in *Polyboroides*). Plumage grey or black and white.	*11*
Circus species	Schlanker, gestreckter Körperbau; Gesichtsschleier; lange und dünne Läufe. Sexualdimorphismus, Männchen meist grau oder schwarz, Weibchen und Junge braun und weiß.	Slender, elongated build; facial ruff; long, slender tarsi. Dimorphic, males often grey or black, females and immatures brown and white.	*12,13*
Melierax species	(ohne *Melierax gabar*); schlank, langschwänzig und langläufig. Adultkleid grau und weiß, Immaturkleid braun und weiß.	(except *Melierax gabar*); slender, long-tailed, long-legged. Adult plumage grey and white, immatures brown and white.	*14*
Urotriorchis macrourus	Sehr langer, stufiger Schwanz. Sonst wie ein Habicht.	Very long graduated tail, otherwise like an *Accipiter*.	*14*
Megatriorchis doriae	Typisch habichtsartig; kurzflügelig, sehr langschwänzig; kräftige Fänge und starker Schnabel.	Typically accipitrine; short-winged, very long-tailed; feet and bill strong.	*14*
Erythrotriorchis radiatus	Langflügelig und ziemlich langschwänzig, entspricht *Accipiter*; Gefieder überwiegend rostfarben bis braun.	Long-winged; rather long-tailed; resembling *Accipiter*; plumage mainly rufous-brown.	*14*
Accipiter species	Hierher die größeren Habichte und Sperber. Meist kurzflügelig, langschwänzig; Gefieder sehr unterschiedlich in Färbung und Zeichnung.	Larger goshawks and sparrowhawks are in this size-range. Shortwinged, long-tailed; plumage very variable in colour and markings.	*15,16,17 18,19,20 21*

23

Größe		Size	Tafel/Plate
mittelgroß		**medium-sized**	
Butastur species	Bussardverwandte, Gefieder meist rostfarben-grau-braun; Kehle weiß, mit oder ohne Kehlstreif.	Related to *Buteo*; plumage usually rufous-grey-brown; throat white, with or without median stripe.	22
Leucopternis species	Bussardverwandte; Gefieder überwiegend weiß, weiß und grau oder weiß und schwarz gefärbt. Kontrastreich.	Related to buzzards; plumage mostly white, white and grey or white and black, strongly contrasting.	22
Heterospizias meridionalis	Hochbeiniger „Savannen-Bussard"; Gefieder überwiegend rostfarben, braun und graubraun.	Long-legged „savanna-buzzard"; plumage usually red-brown and grey-brown.	23
Busarellus nigricollis	Fuchsroter, weißköpfiger „Fischbussard", mit schwarzem Brustlatz.	Foxy-red, white-headed „fishing-buzzard", with a black breast-band.	23
Parabuteo unicinctus	Gefieder dunkelbraun, kastanienbraune Schultern, Unterflügeldecken und Schenkel; Ober- und Unterschwanzdecken und Schwanzspitze weiß. In Gestalt zwischen Habichts- und Bussardtypus.	Plumage dark brown, chestnut shoulders, underwing-coverts, thighs; tail tipped white, rump white. In build between goshawk and buzzard types.	23
Buteogallus species	Große, hochbeinige Bussarde mit kräftigem Schnabel. Adultgefieder schwarz, oder schwarz und braun (eine Art); Immaturkleid scheckig beige, rostfarben und dunkelbraun.	Large, longlegged, strong-billed „buzzards". Adult plumage black, or black and brown (one species); immatures sandy, rufous and dark brown.	23
Buteo species	Ohne die kleinen *magnirostris* und *ridgwayi* und die ziemlich großen *rufinus, hemilasius, regalis*. Breitflügelig, breitschwänzig, relativ kurzer Schnabel, Gefieder sehr variabel.	Excepting small *magnirostris* and *ridgwayi* and rather large *rufinus, hemilasius, regalis* are in this size-range. Broad winged, broad tailed, bill rather short. Plumage mostly variable.	24,25 26,27
Spizaëtus species	Hierher die kleineren Haubenadler (*ornatus, alboniger, bartelsi, nanus, africanus* sowie kleine Formen von *cirrhatus*). Kurzflügelig, langschwänzig. Oben rahmbraun bis dunkelbraun, unten meist weißlich, mehr oder weniger gefleckt und gebändert, Gefieder kontrastreich. Mit und ohne Haube.	Smaller species (*ornatus, alboniger, bartelsi, nanus, africanus* and some races of *cirrhatus*) are in this size-range. Short-winged, long-tailed. Above ochre-brown to dark brown; below usually whitish, more or less spotted and barred, plumage contrasting. Some crested.	29,30

Parabuteo unicinctus

	Größe	Size	Tafel/Plate
	mittelgroß	**medium-sized**	
Lophaëtus occipitalis	Schwarzbraun, mit langem, flatterndem Schopf; Läufe befiedert wie bei *Spizaëtus*, aber langflügeliger und kurzschwänziger.	Blackish-brown, with long waving crest; feathered tarsi as in *Spizaëtus*; longer-winged, shorter-tailed.	30
Spizastur melanoleucus	Klein, weiß und schwärzlich; die kurze dunkle Haube bildet Kontrast zu weißem Kopf und Hals; Läufe befiedert.	Small, crested, white and blackish; short dark crest contrasts with white head and neck; tarsi feathered.	30
Hieraaëtus species	Ohne *fasciatus*, kleine (meist bussardgroße) Adler mit kräftigen Fängen und befiederten Läufen. Hinterkopffedern bilden manchmal kleine Haube; die meisten Arten mit heller und dunkler Phase.	Except *fasciatus*, small (buzzard-sized) eagles with feathered tarsi. Nape sometimes with short crest; light and dark phases in most species.	30
Aquila wahlbergi	Kleiner Adler mit kurzer Haube, heller und dunkler Farbphase und „schneidiger Jagdweise".	A small eagle with short crest, light and dark colour-phases; active predator.	31
Daptrius species	Waldbewohnende, insekten- und fruchtfressende „Falken". Gefieder überwiegend schwarz; Gesicht und Kehle nackt.	Forest-dwelling, fruit and insect-eating aberrant „falcons". Plumage mainly black; face and throat bare.	33
Polyborus species	Großer Schnabel; nackte Zügel; hohe Läufe; Schopf, Gefieder: braun, schwarz und weiß.	Bill large; lores bare; long-legged; crested; plumage brown, black and white.	33
Phalcoboenus species	Nacktes Gesicht; Adultkleid hauptsächlich schwarz und weiß; Immaturkleid braun und weiß.	Face bare; adult plumage mainly black and white; immatures brown and white.	33
Milvago species	Gestreckter Körper; schwacher Schnabel, schwache Füße; Gefieder dunkelbraun und rahmfarben bis zimtbraun.	Slender build; bill and feet weak. Plumage dark-brown and sandy to rufous-buff.	33
Herpetotheres cachinnans	Dickköpfiger, großäugiger „Waldfalke". Flügel kurz und breit; Gefieder dunkelbraun bis lohgelb.	Big headed, large eyed forest falcon; wings short, broad; plumage dark brown and pale buff or sandy.	34
Micrastur species	(ohne *Micrastur ruficollis* und *Micrastur plumbeus*). Langläufige, sehr langschwänzige Waldfalken. Flügel kurz und breit; Gefieder: weiß und schwarz, weiß und grau oder orangebraun, schwarz und weiß.	(except *Micrastur ruficollis* and *Micrastur plumbeus*) long legged, very long tailed forest falcons; wings short, broad; plumage black and white, white and grey or orange-brown, black and white.	34
Falco species	Hierher die Großfalken (*cherrug, biarmicus, jugger, mexicanus, rusticolus, subniger, peregrinus, pelegrinoides, kreyenborgi*), die Weibchen von *hypoleucos* und *deiroleucus*, sowie die langschwänzigeren *berigora* und *novaezeelandiae*.	Large falcons (*cherrug, biarmicus, jugger, mexicanus, rusticolus, subniger, peregrinus, pelegrinoides, kreyenborgi*) in this size-range; also females of *hypoleucos* and *deiroleucus* and longer-tailed *berigora* and *novaezeelandiae*.	38,39 40

Falco rusticolus

25

Langer Hals / Long neck

Alle Neuweltgeier; mit nacktem Kopf und Hals	All New-World-Vultures; with naked head and neck.	*1*
Sagittarius serpentarius; schlanke Gestalt; hochbeinig; kurzzehig; spatelförmige Nakkenfedern.	*Sagittarius serpentarius*; slender build; long-legged; short-toed; spatulate nape feathers.	*2*
Einige *Haliaeëtus-* und *Ichthyophaga-Arten* haben überdurchschnittlich lange Hälse.	Some *Haliaeëtus* and *Ichthyophaga* species have longer than average necks.	*6*
Alle Altweltgeier mit befiedertem Kopf (z. B. *Gypaëtus*), nacktem Gesicht und Kropf (z. B. *Neophron*), beduntem oder teilweise beduntem Kopf und Hals (z. B. *Trigonoceps* und *Gyps*) und mit nacktem Kopf und Hals (z. B. *Torgos* und *Sarcogyps*).	All Old-World-Vultures with: feathered head (e.g. *Gypaëtus*), bare face and crop (e.g. *Neophron*), head and neck covered or partly covered with down (e.g. *Trigonoceps* and *Gyps*) and naked head and neck (e.g. *Torgos* and *Sacrogyps*).	*7* *8*

Lange Läufe (hochbeinig) / Long tarsi (long-legged)

Sagittarius serpentarius. Außergewöhnlich hochbeinig, sehr kurze Zehen.	*Sagittarius serpentarius*, exceptionally long legs, very short toes.	*2*
Die Höhlenweihen der Gattungen *Polyboroides* und *Geranospiza*. Beine „doppel-gelenkig“.	Harrier-hawks and Crane-hawks, *Polyboroides* and *Geranospiza*. Legs „double-jointed“.	*11*
Alle Weihen *Circus* species.	All harriers *Circus* species.	*12/13*
Die Habichtsverwandten *Melierax* und *Megatriorchis* species.	*Melierax* species and *Megatriorchis*, related to *Accipiter*.	*14*
Einige Habichte und Sperber der Gattung *Accipiter*.	Some goshawks and sparrowhawks of genus *Accipiter*.	*15–21*
Die Bussardverwandten *Leucopternis princeps, Heterospizias meridionalis, Buteogallus urubitinga* und *Harpyhaliaëtus* species.	*Leucopternis princeps, Heterospizias meridionalis, Buteogallus urubitinga* and *Harpyhaliaëtus* species, all allied to *Buteo* species.	*22–23*
Die Aasfalken der Gattung *Polyborus* und die Waldfalken *Micrastur mirandollei, buckleyi* und *semitorquatus*.	Caracaras *Polyborus* species and Forest-falcons *Micrastur mirandollei, buckleyi* and *semitorquatus*.	*33,34*

Nackte, bunte Hautteile am Kopf / Areas of bare skin on head

Sagittarius serpentarius. Umgebung der Augen bei Adultvogel orange-rot, bei Immaturvogel gelb.	*Sagittarius serpentarius*. Orbital region in adult orange; yellow in immature.	*2*
Gypohierax angolensis. Zügel, Kinn, Umgebung der Augen und Wangenfleck rot.	*Gypohierax angolensis*. Lores, chin, orbital region and cheeks red.	*7*
Terathopius ecaudatus. Wachshaut, Zügel bei Adultvogel rot; bei Immaturvogel grünblau.	*Terathopius ecaudatus*. Cere and lores red in adult, bluish-green in immature.	*9*
Spilornis species. Wachshaut, Zügel bei Adultvogel gelb bis grüngelb.	*Spilornis* species. Cere and lores in adult yellow to green.	*10*
Polyboroides species. Gesicht gelb bis gelbgrün, bei Erregung aber rosa.	*Polyboroides* species, sides of face yellow-green, flushing in pink in emotion.	*11*
Die Aasfalken *Polyborus, Milvago* und *Phalcoboenus* species mit bunter Gesichtshaut.	Caracaras *Polyborus, Milvago* and *Phalcoboenus* species with brightly coloured face.	*33*

Kopf und Hals nackt oder nur teilweise bedunt	Head and neck naked, or partly covered with down	Tafel/Plate
Cathartes aura: nackte Haut, rot bis gelb bei Adultvogel; bräunlich bei Immaturvogel.	*Cathartes aura*: bare skin red to yellow in adult, brownish in young-bird.	*1*
Cathartes burrovianus und *melambrotus*: nackte Haut rot, orange, gelb und bläulich.	*Cathartes burrovianus* and *melambrotus*: bare skin red, orange, yellow and bluish.	*1*
Coragyps atratus. Kopf, Hals: grau, mit schwarzen Borsten.	*Coragyps atratus*. Head, neck grey with black bristles.	*1*
Sarcoramphus papa. Karunkel auf Wachshaut, runzelige Kopfseiten. Nackte Haut, violett, orange, weiß.	*Sarcoramphus papa*. Cere with caruncle, corrugated skin on sides of head. Bare skin violet, orange, white.	*1*
Gymnogyps californianus. Kopf, Hals: gelb bis orange im Alter; graubraun in der Jugend.	*Gymnogyps californianus*. Head, neck yellow to orange in adult, grey-brown in juvenile.	*1*
Vultur gryphus. Kopf, Hals Adultvogel: fleischfarben bis bläulich. ♂ mit Kamm; Juvenilvogel grau-braun, dunig.	*Vultur gryphus*. Head and neck in adult: flesh-coloured to bluish-grey; juvenile grey-brown, downy.	*1*
Neophron percnopterus. Adultvogel: Vorderkopf und Kropf gelb; Jungvogel grau bis weißgrau.	*Neophron percnopterus*. Adult forehead and face, also crop yellow; juvenile grey to whitish-grey.	*7*
Necrosyrtes monachus. Adultvogel: Vorderkopf und Kropf grau bis violett; Juvenile blaßgrau und violett; bedunt.	*Necrosyrtes monachus*. Adult face and crop grey to violet; juvenile pale grey and violet; downy.	*7*
Sarcogyps calvus. Adultvogel: Kopf, Hals karminrot, Immaturvogel rosa.	*Sarcogyps calvus*. Adult head and neck crimson, immature pink.	*7*
Torgos trocheliotus. Adultvogel: Kopf, Hals fleischfarben. Immaturvogel rosa bis blaßblau.	*Torgos trocheliotus*. Adult head and neck flesh-coloured, immature pink to pale bluish.	*7*
Aegypius monachus. Adultvogel: Kopf, Hals blaugrau; schwarz und braun bedunt. Jungvogel und Immaturvogel stärker bedunt.	*Aegypius monachus*. Adult head and neck bluish-grey, covered with brown and black down; juvenile and immature densely covered with down.	*7*
Gyps und Pseudogyps. Mit zunehmendem Alter werden Kopf und Hals kahler.	*Gyps* and *Pseudogyps*. With age head and neck become more naked.	*8*
Daptrius species. Gesicht und Vorderhals nackt, gelb oder rot.	*Daptrius* species. Face and foreneck bare, yellow or red coloured.	*33*

Schnabel gelb   Bill yellow

	Schnabel gelb	Bill yellow	Tafel/Plate
Chondrohierax uncinatus wilsoni	Mittelgroß; mit großem, stark gekrümmtem Hakenschnabel; Gefieder grau-weiß oder braun-weiß.	Medium sized; with a large, strongly curved, hooked bill. Plumage grey-white or brown-white.	*3*
Haliastur indus flavirostris	Mittelgroß; Gefieder weiß und rotbraun.	Medium-sized; plumage white and chestnut.	*5*
Milvus migrans parasitus, M. m. aegyptius adult	Mittelgroß; Gefieder dunkelbraun, Gabelschwanz.	Medium-sized; plumage dark brown, tail forked.	*5*
Haliaeëtus leucocephalus adult	Groß; Kopf, Hals und Schwanz weiß; Rest schwarzbraun.	Large; head, neck and tail white; remainder blackish brown.	*6*
Haliaeëtus albicilla adult	Groß; Schwanz weiß; Kopf weißgrau; Rest graubraun.	Large; tail white; head grey-white; remainder grey brown.	*6*
Haliaeëtus pelagicus adult	Sehr groß; Schwanz weiß; meist auch Stirn, Schultern und Hosen. Rest braun bis schwarzbraun.	Very large; tail white, frequently also forehead, shoulders and thighs. Remainder brown to blackish-brown.	*6*

	Schnabel rot	Bill red	Tafel/Plate

Trigonoceps oc-cipitalis

Schnabel rot / **Bill red**

Beim Altvogel starker Kontrast zwischen dem roten Schnabel, der blauen Wachshaut und dem weißen Kopf. Beim Immaturvogel Schnabel matter rosa.

In adult, red bill contrasts with blue cere and white head; in immature, bill duller pink. — 7

Auffällige Schnabelformen
Conspicuous shapes of Bill

lang, mit kleinem Haken
Long, little hooked

Cathartes und _Coragyps_ mit durchgehenden Nasenlöchern.

Cathartes and _Coragyps_ with perforated nostrils. — 1

Gypaëtus barbatus mit schwarzem Borstenbart.

Gypaëtus barbatus with a „beard" of black bristles. — 7

Neophron percnopterus mit nacktem Gesicht.

Neophron percnopterus with a bare face. — 7

Necrosyrtes monachus mit dunigem Oberkopf und Hinterhals.

Necrosyrtes monachus; crown, occiput and hindneck covered with down. — 7

Gewaltiger, klobiger Hakenschnabel
Powerful, clumsy hooked bill

Sarcoramphus papa, große Karunkel auf Wachshaut.

Sarcoramphus papa, large caruncle on cere. — 1

Vultur gryphus, ♂ mit fleischigem Kamm.

Vultur gryphus, large, fleshy comb in male. — 1

Gymnogyps californianus, nackter Kopf und Hals.

Gymnogyps californianus, bare head and neck. — 1

Die Altweltgeier _Gyps, Pseudogyps_. Die Schnäbel von _Trigonoceps, Torgos, Aegypius_ und _Sarcogyps_ noch schwerer und höher

Old World Vultures _Gyps, Pseudogyps_; of _Trigonoceps, Torgos, Aegypius_ and _Sarcogyps_ heavier and deeper. — 7 / 8

Schnabel mit papageiartigem Haken
Exaggeratedly hooked bill

Chondrohierax species, gelbe oder gelbgrüne Wachshaut und Augenring.

Chondrohierax species, yellow or yellow green cere and orbital ring. — 3

Schnabel schlank, dünn, sichelförmig
Bill slender, narrow, with long curved hook

Rostrhamus species, rote Wachshaut, roter Augenring.

Rostrhamus species, red cere and orbital ring. — 5

Extrem hoher, seitlich flachgedrückter Hakenschnabel
Exaggerated highly arched, compressed, deep hooked bill

Haliaeëtus pelagicus, sehr groß.

Haliaeëtus pelagicus, very large. — 6

Pithecophaga jefferyi, sehr groß, mit besonders schmalem Schnabel.

Pithecophaga jefferyi, very large, with highly compressed bill. — 28

Überdurchschnittlich hoher und kräftiger Hakenschnabel
Strong, and deeper than average, highly arched hooked bill

Haliaeëtus species, ohne _pelagicus_, vor allem _H. albicilla_ und _leucocephalus_.

Haliaeëtus species, except _pelagicus_, especially _H. albicilla_ and _leucocephalus_. — 6

Einige Arten der Gattung _Aquila_, vor allem _A. audax_.

Some _Aquila_ species, especially _A. audax_. — 31/32

	Wachshaut blau oder blaugrün	**Cere blue or bluish-green**	*Tafel/ Plate*
Pandion haliaëtus	Ziemlich groß. Gefieder weiß-braun. Schopf. Beine graublau.	Rather large. Plumage white-brown. Crest. Legs grey-blue.	2
Elanoides forficatus	Mittelgroß; Gefieder schwarz-weiß; tiefer Gabelschwanz.	Medium sized. Plumage black-white; deeply forked tail.	4
Trigonoceps occipitalis	Ziemlich groß; Kopf und Hals weiß bedunt. Schnabel rot.	Rather large; head and neck covered with white down. Bill red.	7
Terathopius ecaudatus immat.	Ziemlich groß aber kurzschwänzig; braun; dicker Kopf.	Rather large but very short-tailed; brown; big-headed.	9
Accipiter virgatus	Sperbergroß; deutlicher Kehlstreif; ♂ mit rostroter Unterseite.	Size of a large sparrowhawk; a distinct median throat stripe; ♂ bright rufous below.	16
Leucopternis albicollis	Mittelgroß; Gefieder überwiegend weiß, wenig Schwarz auf Rücken, Flügel und am Schwanz.	Medium-sized; plumage usually white with little black on back, wings and tail.	22
Leucopternis occidentalis	Mittelgroß; Gefieder weiß-grau-bleigrau. Graue Schwanzbinde.	Medium-sized; plumage white-grey-plumbeous. Grey tailband.	22
Buteogallus urubitinga ridgwayi	Mittelgroß; hochbeinig; Gefieder Adultvogel: überwiegend schwarz; Immaturvogel: braun, ockerbeige, weißlich – mehr scheckig.	Medium-sized; long-legged; adult plumage usually black; immature brown, ochre-buff, creamy-mottled appearance.	23
Pithecophaga jefferyi	Sehr groß; schmaler und sehr hoher Schnabel, buschige Haube; Gefieder braun, gelbbraun und weißlich.	Very large; unusually large, deeply hooked, narrow beak; full, bushy crest; plumage brown, buff and whitish.	28
Polemaëtus bellicosus	Sehr groß; dicker Kopf; kurze Haube. Gefieder braun und weiß.	Very large; big, short-crested head; plumage brown and white.	28
Daptrius americanus	Mittelgroß; Gefieder schwarz, Hosen und Bauch weiß. Gesicht und Vorderhals nackt.	Medium-sized. Plumage black, thighs and abdomen white. Face and fore neck bare.	33
Milvago chimango	Gestreckter, leichter Körper. Mittelgroß. Gefieder braun-rahmfarben.	Stretched, light build. Medium-sized. Plumage brown-creamy.	33
Phalcoboenus australis juv.	Gefieder dunkel rußbraun. Mittelgroß.	Plumage sooty-brown. Medium-sized.	33
Falco berigora	Mittelgroßer, langschwänziger Falke. Überwiegend braun.	Medium-sized, long-tailed, mainly brown.	38
Falco species	Hierher die Jungvögel sowie einige adulte Exemplare von *Falco cherrug, Falco biarmicus, Falco jugger, Falco mexicanus, Falco peregrinus* und *Falco novaezeelandiae*.	Juveniles and some adults of *Falco cherrug, Falco biarmicus, Falco jugger, Falco mexicanus, Falco peregrinus, Falco novaezeelandiae*.	38 39 40
	Wachshaut orangerot oder rot	**Cere orange-red or red**	
Sarcoramphus papa	Ziemlich groß; Kopf und Hals nackt; im Alter Karunkel auf Wachshaut und runzelige Kopfseiten.	Rather large, head and neck naked; in adult with caruncle on cere and corrugated sides of head.	1
Rostrhamus species	Mittelgroß; sichelförmiger, stark gekrümmter und dünner Schnabel.	Medium-sized; very long narrow, deeply hooked bill.	5
Sarcogyps calvus	Groß; Kopf, Hals nackt. Gefieder düsterbraun, Brust weißlich.	Large; head and neck naked; plumage blackish, white on cheek.	7
Terathopius ecaudatus adult	Ziemlich groß, extrem kurzschwänzig; Gefieder: schwarz, weiß, kastanienbraun.	Rather large, exceptionally short-tailed; plumage black, white, chestnut.	9
Melierax species	Klein bis mittelgroß; Gefieder grau-weiß oder braun-weiß.	Small to medium-sized; plumage grey and white or brown and white.	14
Accipiter poliocephalus	Kleiner Habicht. Gefieder bei Adultvogel grau und weiß.	Small goshawk. Adult plumage grey and white.	18

	Wachshaut orangerot oder rot	Cere orange-red or red	Tafel/ Plate
Accipiter princeps	Mittelgroßer Habicht. Gefieder grau-weiß. Selten.	Medium-sized goshawk. Plumage grey-white. Rare.	18
Accipiter trinotatus, adult.	Kleiner, bunter Habicht mit deutlichen, kleinen Schwanzflecken. Lange Läufe.	Small, brightly-coloured goshawk with spotted tail. Long tarsi.	18
Accipiter badius, adult.	Kleiner Sperber. Wachshaut beim ♀ mehr orange-gelb.	Small sparrowhawk. Cere in female more orange-yellow.	18
Kaupifalco mono- grammicus	Kleiner Bussardverwandter. Gefieder grau und weiß. Beine orangerot.	Small buteonine; plumage grey and white, with orange legs.	22
Leucopternis species	Mittelgroß. Ohne *albicollis* und *occidentalis*, diese mit blauer Wachshaut.	Medium-sized. Except *albicollis* and *occidentalis*, which have blue ceres.	22
Phalcoboenus species adult.	Mittelgroße, überwiegend schwarze Aasfalken; Bauch und Hosen weiß oder rotbraun.	Medium-sized, usually black caracaras; belly and thighs white or sienna-brown.	33
Polyborus plancus	Mittelgroßer, großschnäbliger Aasfalke; hochbeinig; mit Schopf; Gefieder: schwarz und weiß oder braun und weiß.	Medium-sized. Heavy-billed caracara; long-legged and crested; plumage black and white or brown and white.	33
Polihierax semitor- quatus	Sehr klein; Gefieder grau, weiß und kastanienbraun (Weibchen). Beine leuchtend rot.	Very small; plumage grey, white and chestnut (female). Legs bright red.	35
Falco vespertinus	Klein, ♂ blaugrau, Hosen rotbraun, ♀ grau, hellbraunrot und weiß. Beine rot.	Small. ♂ blue-grey, thighs chestnut; ♀ grey, light rufous and white; legs red.	36

Terathopius ecaudatus

	Iris weiß	**Iris white**	
Sarcoramphus papa	Mit rotem Augenring.	With a red orbital ring.	1
Gypaëtus barbatus	Mit roter Augenhaut.	Sclerotic ring red.	7
Chondrohierax species	Mit gelbgrünem Augenring.	With a yellow-green orbital ring.	3
Butastur teesa adult	Mittelgroßer Bussardverwandter, braun, mit schwarzem Kehlstreif.	Medium sized, related to *Buteo*, brownish with median black throat-streak.	22
Gyps coprotheres	Nur im Adultkleid.	Only in adult-plumage.	8
	Iris weiß-grau	**Iris greyish-white**	
Melierax species juvenile	Auge oft grau-weiß bis weiß.	Eyes are almost greyish-white or white.	14
Morphnus guianensis adult	Dicker Kopf, lange Haube; kurze Flügel; langer Schwanz.	Big head; long crest; short wings; long tail.	28
Falco rupicoloides	Auge hell-grau bis weiß.	Eyes pale-grey to white.	35
	Iris grau oder graublau	**Iris grey or bluish-grey**	
Spilornis cheela juvenile	Heller als Vögel im Alterskleid.	Paler than birds in adult plumage.	10
Pithecophaga jefferyi	Gefieder oben dunkelbraun, unten weißlich.	Plumage above dark brown, below whitish.	28

	Iris rot	**Iris red**	*Tafel/ Plate*
Vultur gryphus adult	Rot beim ♀; beim ♂ brauner.	Red in ♀; browner in ♂.	*1*
Gymnogyps californianus	Beim Jungvogel brauner.	Iris browner in juvenile.	*1*
Rostrhamus sociabilis	Orangerot bis rot.	Orange-red to red.	*5*
Gampsonyx adult	Jungvogel mit braunerer Iris.	Iris browner in juvenile.	*4*
Elanus species adult	Das rote Auge bildet Kontrast zum hellen Kopf.	Red eye strongly contrasts with grey head.	*4*
Elanoides & Chelictinia	Mit tiefgegabelten Schwänzen.	With deeply forked tails.	*4*
Ictinia species	Mit eckigem oder leicht ausgebuchtetem Schwanz.	With a square or a notched tail.	*5*
Harpagus species	Klein; bunt gefärbt; Schnabel doppelt gezahnt.	Small; bright-coloured; double-toothed beak.	*5*
Geranospiza c. nigra & livens adult	Mit tiefgrauem bis grauschwarzem Gefieder.	With a dark-grey to greyish-black plumage.	*11*
Melierax species	Auch Wachshaut und Beine rot.	Cere and legs also red.	*14*
Accipiter species	Viele Arten der Gattung *Accipiter* haben eine rote Iris; bei einigen verfärbt sich die gelbe oder orangefarbene Iris im Alter tiefrot.	Many *Accipiter* species have red eyes; in some a yellow or orange eye becomes red with age.	*15–21*
	(*Accipiter gentilis, melanoleucus, meyerianus, brachyurus, striatus, imitator, haplochrous, novaehollandiae, superciliosus, bicolor* etc.)		
Kaupifalco monogrammicus	Auch Wachshaut und Beine rot.	Cere and legs also red.	*22*

	Beine grau, graublau oder weißgrau	**Legs grey, blue-grey, or whitish grey**	
Pandion haliaëtus	Kurze Haube; Gefieder weiß und braun.	Short crest; plumage white and brown.	*2*
Aviceda subcristata	Spitze Haube; Brust blaugrau; Unterseite gebändert oder gefleckt.	Pointed crest; breast blue-grey; barred or spotted below.	*3*
Henicopernis species	Langschwänzig; schlank. Zügel mit verhornten Borsten bedeckt.	Long-tailed; slender. Lores covered with imbricated bristles.	*4*
Elanoides forficatus	Schlank, mit tiefgegabeltem Schwanz; kleine Füße und Schnabel.	Slender, with deeply forked tail, small feet and bill.	*4*
Machaerhamphus species	Gefieder rußbraun; kleiner Schopf; große Augen.	Plumage sooty brown; small crest; large eyes.	*4*
Gypaëtus barbatus	Sehr groß; Keilschwanz; am Schnabel Borstenbart.	Very large; wedge tailed; beak with a bristly „beard".	*7*
Gyps & Pseudogyps species			*8* *7*
Neophron percnopterus immat.	Farbe der Beine variiert von grau-weiß bis dunkelgrau.	Legs varying from greyish-white to dark grey.	*7*
Necrosyrtes monachus			*7*
Torgos & Aegypius			
Circaëtus gallicus, cinereus & pectoralis	Beine hell blaugrau bis braungrau.	Legs light blue-grey to brownish-grey.	*9*
Terathopius ecaudatus immat.	Gefieder braun, mit undeutlichen helleren Abzeichen.	Plumage brown, with indistinct paler markings.	*9*
Megatriorchis doriae	Beine hell braungrau bis grauweiß.	Legs light brownish grey to greyish white.	*14*

	Beine grau, graublau oder weißgrau	**Legs grey, blue-grey, or whitish grey**	*Tafel/ Plate*
Busarellus nigricollis	Zehensohlen mit rauhen, dornigen Schuppen bedeckt.	Soles of feet covered with roughly spicules and scales.	23
Hieraaëtus morphnoides	Einige mit blaßgelben, andere mit grauen oder grau-weißen Beinen.	Some have pale yellow legs, others grey or greyish white.	30
Milvago chimango	Beine bläulichweiß bis blaugrau.	Legs bluish-white to bluish-grey.	33
Microhierax species	Alle Arten mit grauer Wachshaut und grauen Beinen.	All species have grey legs and cere.	35
Falco species	Hierher die Jungvögel von *Falco novaezeelandiae, biarmicus, mexicanus, jugger, cherrug, rusticolus* und *peregrinus*. Im Jugend- und Alterskleid *F. berigora* und *F. subniger*.	Juveniles of *Falco novaezeelandiae, biarmicus, mexicanus, jugger, cherrug, rusticolus* and *peregrinus*. Adults and juveniles of *F. berigora* and *F. subniger*.	38 39 40 38

	Beine rot	**Legs red**	
Terathopius ecaudatus	Wachshaut und Gesichtshaut rot.	Cere and facial skin red.	9
Geranospiza caerulescens	Farbe variiert von orange bis rot.	Colour varying from orange to red.	11
Melierax species adult	Wachshaut und Augen ebenfalls rot.	Cere and eyes also red.	14
Accipiter poliocephalus & princeps	Oberseite grau, Unterseite weiß.	Above grey, below white.	18
Kaupifalco monogrammicus	Kleiner Bussardverwandter, Wachshaut ebenfalls rot.	Small buteonine; cere also red.	22
Leucopternis schistacea plumbea & semiplumbea	Beine orangerot.	Legs more orange-red.	22
Polihierax semitorquatus	Sehr kleiner „Zwergfalke"; Wachshaut ebenfalls rot.	Very small „Pygmy Falcon"; cere also red.	35
Falco vespertinus	Kleiner Falke. ♂ blaugrau und kastanienbraun.	Small falcon. ♂ blue-grey and chestnut.	36

	Dicker Kopf, große Augen	**Big head, large eyes**	
	Circaëtus species; Augen groß, gelb bis orange.	*Circaëtus* species; large eyes, yellow to orange.	9
	Spilornis species; Augen groß, gelb bis orange; runde Haube.	*Spilornis* species; large eyes, yellow to orange; round crest.	10
	Herpetotheres cachinnans; Augen groß, dunkel; Maske.	*Herpetotheres cachinnans*; large, dark eyes. Black mask.	34

	Gesichtsschleier	**Facial ruff**	
	Alle Arten von *Circus*. Mittelgroß; lange, schmale Flügel, langer Schwanz; Läufe lang und schlank. *Offenes Gelände*.	All *Circus* species. Medium-sized with long narrow wings, long tail; tarsi long and slender. *Open country*.	12–13
	Micrastur species. Schleier weniger deutlich als bei *Circus*; langläufig, oft sehr langschwänzig. *Wälder*.	*Micrastur* species. Ruff less distinct than in *Circus*; long-legged, often very long-tailed. *Forests*.	34

Verschiedene Schopfformen	Different shapes of crest	Tafel/ Plate

a) Hinterkopf und Nackenfedern bilden eine aufrichtbare, breite und runde, manchmal zweigeteilte Haube, z. B. *Circaëtus, Terathopius, Spilornis* etc.

a) Feathers of back of head and nape erectile into a broad round cowl or sometimes double crest e. g. *Circaëtus, Terathopius, Spilornis* etc.

9,10

b) Hinterkopf und Nackenfedern lanzettförmig verlängert und bei Erregung aufstell- bzw. abspreizbar, z. B. *Neophron, Pithecophaga, Aquila audax* etc.

b) Feathers of back of head and nape elongated, lanceolate; erectile into a flaring cowl or „fright mask" e. g. *Neophron, Pithecophaga, Aquila audax* etc.

7,28
32

c) Scheitelfedern zu kurzer, spitzer Haube oder Schopf verlängert. Dieser wird normalerweise nicht aufgestellt und ist im Felde meist nicht zu erkennen, z. B. *Hieraëtus dubius, Aquila wahlbergi, Polemaëtus bellicosus* etc.

c) Feathers of crown elongated into short pointed crest. Such crests are not normally erected and may be invisible in the field, e. g. *Hieraëtus dubius, Aquila wahlbergi, Polemaëtus bellicosus* etc.

31,30
28

d) Kurze, aber häufig aufgerichtete Haube, z. B. *Pandion haliaëtus*.

d) Short, readily erectile crest, e. g. *Pandion haliaëtus*.

2

e) Langer, spitzer Schopf, mehr oder minder aufrichtbar, z. B. *Aviceda* species, *Pernis* species etc.

e) Longish, pointed, more or less erectile crest, e. g. *Aviceda* species, *Pernis* species etc.

3

f) Lange Scheitelfedern bilden einen lockeren, langen, oft im Winde flatternden Schopf, z. B. *Lophaëtus occipitalis, Spizaëtus cirrhatus* (Subsp.) *Spizaëtus ornatus* etc.

f) Long crown-feathers forming a loose crest often blown about by wind, e. g. *Lophaëtus occipitalis, Spizaëtus cirrhatus* (subspec.), *Spizaëtus ornatus* etc.

29, 30

g) Aufrichtbare, zweiteilige Haube, mehr oder minder groß, mit gerundeten Spitzen, z. B. *Stephanoaëtus, Harpia, Morphnus*.

g) Erectile double crest, more or less exaggerated, rounded at tips e. g. *Stephanoaëtus, Harpia, Morphnus*.

28

h) Sehr lange, spatelförmige Nackenfedern, aufrichtbar, z. B. *Sagittarius*.

h) Very long nape feathers, spatulate, erectile as a crest, e. g. *Sagittarius*.

2

	Auffällige Schwanzformen	**Conspicuous tail shapes**	*Tafel/ Plate*
	a) Ungewöhnlich kurz, eckig; z. B. *Terathopius*.	a) Unusually short, square; e. g. *Terathopius*.	9
	b) Auffallend lang, eckig oder leicht gerundet; z. B. *Accipiter, Circus*.	b) Markedly long, more or less square-ended; e. g. *Accipiter, Circus* etc.	*12,13 15–21*
	c) Auffallend lang, gerundet oder abgestuft; z. B. *Eutriorchis, Megatriorchis, Urotriorchis, Micrastur*.	c) Markedly long, rounded or graduated; e. g. *Eutriorchis, Megatriorchis, Urotriorchis, Micrastur*.	*9 14,34*
	d) Lang, keilförmig; z. B. *Neophron, Gypaëtus, Aquila audax*.	d) Long, wedge-shaped; e. g. *Neophron, Gypaëtus, Aquila audax*.	*7 32*
	e) Lang, leicht gegabelt; z. B. *Milvus*.	e) Long, shallowly forked, e. g. *Milvus*.	5
	f) Lang, sehr tief gegabelt; z. B. *Elanoides, Chelictinia*.	f) Long, very deeply forked e. g. *Elanoides, Chelictinia*.	*4*
	g) Mittlere Schwanzfedern stark verlängert; z. B. *Sagittarius*.	g) Central tail feathers greatly elongated; e. g. *Sagittarius*.	2

	Gefieder überwiegend weiß	**Plumage largely white**	*Tafel/ Plate*
Elanus species adult	Grau u. weiß; schwarze Schulter- oder Flügelflecke.	Grey and white; black shoulder or wing-patches.	*4*
Neophron perc- nopterus adult	Weiß, am Kopf gelblich, auf dem Flügel grau und schwarz.	White, head and neck buff, wings grey and black.	*7*
Circus cyaneus, pygargus & mac- rourus ♂	Grau bis blaugrau und weiß; Flügelspitzen schwarz.	White to blue-grey and withe; black wing tips.	*13*
Accipiter gentilis buteoides& albidus, (hell/pale)	Weiß; mit wenig kontrastierenden Flek-ken, Strichen und Bändern.	White with inconspicuous spots, streaks and bars.	*15*
Accipiter n. novaehollandiae & n. leucosomus	Weiß; Wachshaut, Beine gelb; Auge orange bis rot.	White; cere and feet yellow; eyes orange to red.	*20*
Leucopternis albidus	Weiß; mit wenig Schwarz auf Flügeln und Schwanz.	White, with a little black on wings and tail.	*22*
Buteo nitidus pallidus adult	Weiß oder grauweiß; Schwanz schwarz und weiß.	White or grey and white; tail black and white.	*24*
Buteo b. buteo hell/pale)	Es gibt manchmal fast weiße Exemplare.	Some specimens are almost pure white.	*26*
Falco rusticolus (hell/pale)	Gelblichweiß oder weiß, mit wenigen dunklen Abzeichen.	Creamy white or white, with a few dark markings.	*39*

Leucopternis albidus

	Gefieder kontrastreich hell-dunkel	**Plumager contrasting, light and dark**	
Sarcoramphus papa adult	Schwarz und lohgelblich-weiß; Kopf und Hals bunt.	Black and buffy-white; head and neck brightly coloured.	*1*
Pandion haliaëtus adult	Braun und weiß; Wachshaut und Beine blaugrau.	Brown and white; cere and legs blue or grey.	*2*
Sagittarius serpen- tarius adult	Schwarz, grau und weiß; hochbeinig, lang-schwänzig.	Black, grey and white. Long-legged, long-tailed.	*2*
Elanus forficatus	Schwarz und weiß. Auge rot. Wachshaut, Beine bläulich.	Black and white; cere and legs bluish.	*4*
Gypaëtus barbatus adult	Dunkelbraun und rostfarben; Kopf weiß und schwarz. Iris weiß.	Dark brown and rufous; head white and black. Iris white.	*7*
Gypohierax angolen- sis adult	Schwarz und weiß; nackte Gesichtshaut rot.	Black and white; bare red facial skin.	*7*
Accipiter albigularis adult	Dunkelgrau und weiß.	Dark-grey and white.	*19*
Accipiter melanoleucus & meyerianus	Schwarz und weiß. Auge rot.	Black and white. Eye dark red.	*15*

Gefieder kontrastreich hell-dunkel	**Plumage contrasting, light and dark**	*Tafel/* *Plate*
Accipiter poliocephalus & princeps	Grau und weiß. Auge rot, Beine orange.	Grey-white. Eye red, legs orange.	18
Accipiter imitator & haplochrous adult	Dunkelgrau und weiß. Auge rot, Beine gelb.	Dark-grey and white. Eye red, legs yellow.	19
Accipiter poliogaster adult	Schwarz, grau-weiß.	Black, grey and white.	21
Leucopternis species	Schwarz oder dunkelgrau und weiß. Bunte Wachshaut und Beine.	Black or darkgrey and white. Brightly coloured cere and legs.	22
Spizastur melanoleucus	Schwarzbraun und weiß. Wachshaut orange.	Blackish-brown and white. Cere orange.	30
Hieraaëtus fasc. spilogaster adult	Schwarzbraun und weiß. Füße und Wachshaut gelb.	Blackish-brown and white. Feet and cere yellow.	30
Micrastur buckleyi & semitorquatus	Schwarz oder grau und weiß. Lange Läufe, langschwänzig.	Black or grey and white. Long-legged, long-tailed.	34

Pandion haliaëtus

Gefieder schwarz oder nahezu schwarz	**Plumage black or mainly black**	
Cathartidae	Mit Ausnahme von *Sarcoramphus papa* adult.	With the exception of *Sarcoramphus papa* adult.	1
Chondrohierax species	Dunkle Phase. Wachshaut und Gesicht gelbgrün.	Dark phase. Cere and facial skin yellow-green.	3
Henicopernis infuscata adult	Wenig hell auf Flügel, Kopf und Schwanz.	Dark phase. A little light marking on head, wing and tail.	4
Pernis a. torquatus	Dunkle Phase. Wenig hell auf Hosen und Bauch.	Dark phase. A little light on thighs and abdomen.	4
Machaerhamphus alcinus	Dunkle Phase. Wenig weiß am Nacken.	Dark phase. A little white on nape.	4
Haliaeëtus pelagicus „niger"	Weißer Schwanz.	White tail.	6
Geranospiza c. nigra	Grau und schwarz mit weißen Schwanzbinden.	Grey and black, with white tail bands.	11
Circus ae. spilothorax	Dunkle Phase. Wachshaut und Beine gelb.	Dark phase. Cere and legs yellow.	12
Circus maurus adult & *Circus buffoni*	Dunkle Phase. Mit Blaugrau und Weiß auf Flügeln und Schwanz.	With some blue-grey and white on wings and tail.	13
Melierax gabar	Dunkle Phase. Klein. Mit drei grauen Schwanzbinden.	Dark phase. Small, with three grey tail-bands.	14
Accipiter melanoleucus adult	Dunkle Phase. Mit wenig Weiß auf Kehle und Bauch.	Dark phase. With a little white marking on throat and belly.	15

	Gefieder schwarz oder nahezu schwarz	**Plumage black or mainly black**	*Tafel/ Plate*
Accipiter meyerianus & bürgersi adult	Dunkle Phase. Mit wenig Weiß am Nakken.	Dark phase. With a little white on nape.	15
Accipiter ovampensis adult	Dunkle Phase. Wenig Grau auf dem Schwanz.	Dark phase. With a little grey on tail.	16
Accipiter tachiro subsp.	Dunkle Phase. Wenig Grau auf dem Schwanz.	Dark phase. With a little grey on tail.	17
Accipiter albogularis adult	Dunkle Phase. Wachshaut, Augenring, Beine gelb.	Dark phase. Cere, orbital skin and legs yellow.	19
Buteogallus anthracinus & urubitinga subsp. adult	Mit Weiß auf Bürzel und Schwanz.	White on rump and tail.	23
Buteo swainsoni adult	Dunkle Phase. Wenig Weiß an Kopf und Unterbauch, weiße Schwanzspitze.	Dark phase. With a little white on head and abdomen. Tail with white edging.	25
Buteo albonotatus adult	Wenig Weiß an der Stirn, weiße Schwanzbinden.	A little white on forehead, white tail-bands.	25
Buteo ventralis & jamaicensis	Dunkle Phase. Gelbe Wachshaut und Beine.	Dark phase. Cere and legs yellow.	26
Buteo leucorrhous adult	Mit weißen Oberschwanzdecken, aschbrauner Schwanzbinde, rostfarben auf den Hosen.	White rump, ashy-brown single tail-band, rufous on thighs.	24
Buteo platypterus adult & *Buteo brachyurus* adult	Dunkle Phase. Einfarbig ruß-schwarz, Schwanzbinden etwas heller.	Uniform sooty-black, tail-bands a little lighter.	24
Buteo hemilasius adult	Dunkle Phase. Wenig Weiß auf Flügel, grau am Schwanz.	Dark phase. A little white on wings, grey on tail.	27
Buteo rufofuscus augur	Dunkle Phase. Wenig Weiß auf Rücken und Flügel, roter Schwanz.	Dark phase. A little white on wings and lower back, red tail.	27
Spizaëtus tyrannus adult	Weiße Abzeichen auf Schopf, Flügelbug, Schenkeln und Unterbauch.	White markings on crest, bend of wing, thighs and abdomen.	29
Spizaëtus cirrhatus limnaëtus	Dunkle Phase. Mehr rußschwarz. Schwanz heller.	Dark phase. Sooty-black. Tail lighter.	29
Lophaëtus occipitalis	Langer, wehender Schopf, auffällige weiße Flügelflecke im Fluge sichtbar, weiße Laufbefiederung.	Long waving crest, conspicuous white spots on wings in flight, white thighs.	30
Aquila verreauxi adult	Mit Weiß auf Rücken und Bürzel.	White on back and rump.	32
Ictinaëtus malayensis adult	Wenig Weiß unter dem Auge und auf Oberschwanzdecken.	A little white beyond the eyes and on upper tail coverts.	32
Micrastur semitorquatus adult	Dunkle Phase. Wenig Weiß auf Unterbauch, Unterschwanzdecken und am Schwanz.	Dark phase. A little white on abdomen, lower tailcoverts and on tail.	34

Meliërax gabar

	Gefieder schwarz oder nahezu schwarz	**Plumage black or mainly black**	*Tafel/ Plate*
Falco concolor & eleonorae, adult	Dunkle Phase. Wachshaut und Beine gelblich.	Dark phase. Cere and legs yellowish.	37
Falco subniger adult	Mehr ruß-schwarz. Heller an Kehle und Wangen.	Sooty-black; paler on throat and cheeks.	38
Falco rusticolus „obsoletus"	Dunkle Phase. Auf Unterseite mit etwas Weiß.	Dark phase. Has a few white markings on underside.	39

	Gefieder sehr bunt	**Plumage brightly coloured**	
Gampsonyx swainsonii	Schwarz, weiß, rostfarben und lohgelb; Augen rot; Beine gelb.	Black, white, rufous and buff; eyes red; legs yellow.	4
Haliastur indus	Weiß, rotbraun; Wachshaut, Beine gelb.	White and chestnut. Cere and legs yellow.	5
Haliaeëtus vocifer adult	Weiß, rotbraun, schwarz; Wachshaut, Beine gelb.	White, chestnut and black. Cere and legs yellow.	6
Terathopius ecaudatus adult	Schwarz, weiß und rotbraun, manchmal rahmgelb auf dem Rücken; Gesichtshaut, Beine rot.	Black, white and chestnut, sometimes creamy on back; legs, face red.	9
Urotriorchis macrourus adult	Dunkelgrau, weiß und rotbraun; sehr langschwänzig.	Dark-grey, white and chestnut; very long-tailed.	14
Accipiter melanochlamys	Schwarz und rotbraun. Wachshaut und Beine orange.	Black and chestnut; cere and legs orange-yellow.	19
Accipiter species ♂ adult	Die meisten ♂♂ der auf den Tafeln 16 und 17 abgebildeten Arten.	Most of the ♂♂, painted on plate 16 and 17.	16,17
Accipiter trinotatus ♀ adult	Braun, hellgrau, weiß, fuchs- bis kastanienrot.	Brown, grey, white, foxy-red to chestnut.	18
Accipiter albigularis adult	Weiß, grau, kastanienbraun.	White, grey and chestnut.	19
Accipiter rufitorques adult	Oberseite grau, Unterseite blaß weinrot, braun, Kehle weiß.	Grey above, vinaceous brown below; throat white.	19
Accipiter novaehollandiae subspec. adult	Sehr variabel, von weiß bis hellgrau oder dunkelgrau und rostgelb, rostrot oder kastanienbraun; Beine und Wachshaut blaßgelb bis gelborange.	Very variable, from white to light or dark grey, and buff, rufous or chestnut; legs and cere pale yellow to yellow-orange.	20
Accipiter bicolor ♂ adult	Grau, braun, weiß, kastanienbraun, in vielen Schattierungen.	Grey, brown, white, chestnut; in many shades.	21
Busarellus nigricollis	Rahmweiß, beige, hellrostrot bis kastanienbraun; schwarzer Latz, auf Flügeln und Schwanz schwarz.	Creamy, sandy, bright rufous-chestnut; black on upper throat, wings and tail.	23

Busarellus nigricollis

	Gefieder sehr bunt	**Plumage brightly coloured**	*Tafel/ Plate*
Buteo lineatus adult	Rostrot bis braun, mit schwarzen und weissen Zeichnungen.	Rufous-brown, marked black and white.	24
Buteo polyosoma & poecilochrous adult	Verschiedene Kombinationen von Grau, Weiß und Kastanienbraun. Zahlreiche Farbphasen.	Many combinations of grey, white and chestnut; several phases.	25
Buteo rufofuscus subsp. dult	Oberseite schwarzgrau; Unterseite weiß, rostbraun oder dunkelbraun und schwarz.	Blackish grey above; white rufous or dark brown and black below.	27
Oroaëtus isidori dult	Schwarz und dunkelkastanienbraun mit etwas Grau; Füße und Wachshaut gelb.	Black and dark chestnut, with some grey; feet and cere yellow.	28
Spizaëtus ornatus adult	Schwarz, braun, fuchsrot und weiß. Füße und Wachshaut gelb.	Black, brown, foxy-red and white. Feet and cere yellow.	29
Hieraaëtus kienerii adult	Schwarz, braun, kastanienbraun, weiß. Füße und Wachshaut gelb.	Black, brown, chestnut and white. Feet and cere yellow.	30
Micrastur buckleyi & semitorquatus adult	Verschiedene Kombinationen von Schwarz, Weiß, Grau und Hell-Rostbraun; zahlreiche Farbphasen.	Various combinations of black, white, grey and pate rufous; several phases.	34
Polihierax species	Grau, schwarz und weiß; ♀♀ auch mit Kastanienbraun.	Grey, black and white; ♀♀ with chestnut also.	35
Falco sparverius ♂	Unterschiedlich, blau oder graublau, rostbraun und kastanienbraun, mit Weiß.	Variable, blue or blue-grey, rufous and chestnut, with white.	35
Falco chicquera adult	Blaugrau oder grau, schwarz und weiß, Kopf hell rostrot.	Blue-grey or grey, black and white, with head bright rufous.	37
Falco fasciinucha adult	Schwarz, dunkel- und hellgrau, rostrot und weiß.	Black, dark and pale grey, rufous and white.	40
Falco deiroleucus adult	Schwarz, beige bis kastanienbraun und weiß.	Black, buff to chestnut and white.	40
Falco peregrinus peregrinator adult	Dunkelbraun, rostrot und schwarz.	Darkbrown, rufous and black.	40

Hieraaëtus kienerii

Übersicht über die Ordnung Falconiformes

Compendium of the order Falconiformes

Unter-Ordnung Cathartae
Super-Familie Cathartoidea
Familie Cathartidae

Sub-Order Cathartae
Super-Family Cathartoidea
Family Cathartidae

Gattung Cathartes Illiger 1811

Ziemlich große Geier von leichtem Körperbau. Kopf und Hals nackt, Kopf ohne größere Karunkeln. Schnabel schlank, Stoß gerundet. Mit einigem Geruchsvermögen.

Rather large vultures of slender proportions. Head and upper neck naked, without caruncle. Beak slender, tail rounded, has some sense of smell.

Coragyps Geoffroy 1853

Ziemlich große, stämmige Geier. Kopf und größtenteils auch Hals nackt und runzlig. Hinterhals befiedert. Kopf ohne Karunkeln. Schnabel schlank. Stoß kurz und eckig. Ziemlich hochbeinig.

Rather large, stockily proportioned vultures. Head and most of neck bare, hind neck feathered. Skin corrugated, without caruncle. Beak slim; tail short, square; legs rather long.

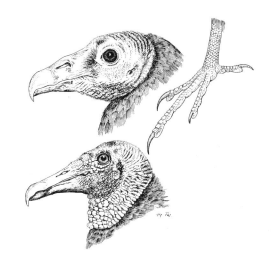

Sarcoramphus Duméril 1806

Ziemlich große, breitflügelige, kurzschwänzige Geier. Schnabel ziemlich hoch und kräftig. Kopf und Hals fast vollständig nackt, prächtig gefärbt. Runzeln an Kopfseiten, große fleischige Karunkel auf der Wachshaut. Außenzehe länger als Innenzehe.

Rather large, broad-winged, short-tailed vultures. Bill rather deep. Head and neck mostly bare, brightly coloured. Head corrugated, cere with large, fleshy caruncle. Outer toe longer than inner.

Gymnogyps Lesson 1842

Sehr große Geier. Kopf und Hals nackt, ohne Karunkelbildung, nur mit kleinem Hautlappen am Unterhals. Stoß kurz und eckig.

Very large vultures. Head and neck bare, with no caruncle, a small wattle on lower neck. Tail short, square.

Vultur Linnaeus 1758

Sehr große Geier. Männchen etwas größer als Weibchen. Lang- und breitflügelig. Stoß ziemlich lang. Kopf und Hals nackt, nur mit einigen Borsten bedeckt. Männchen mit fleischigem Kamm auf der Stirn. Weiße, dunige Halskrause. Außen- und Innenzehe annähernd gleichlang.

Very large vultures; wings long, broad; tail rather long. Head and neck bare, with some bristles; male rather larger than female, with fleshy comb-like caruncle on top of head. White, downy ruff round neck. Outer and inner toe about equal.

Sub-Order Accipitres
Super-Family Accipitroidea
Family Pandionidae

Pandion Savigny 1809

Mittelgroße Greifvögel. Flügel lang, ziemlich schmal. Federn ohne Afterschaft. Nasenlöcher schräg und schlitzförmig, die beliebig verschlossen werden können. Augen mehr nach vorne gerichtet als bei anderen Greifvögeln. Lauf kürzer als Mittelzehe mit Kralle, ganz mit Schildern bedeckt, die sich oft schuppenartig übereinanderschieben. Außenzehe nach hinten wendbar, Unterseite der Zehen mit spitzen Dornen bedeckt. Krallen schlank und spitz, nur die mittlere mit abgeflachter Innenseite.

Medium sized raptors. Wings long, rather narrow. Feathers with no aftershafts. Nostrils oblique, slit-shaped, can be closed at will. Eyes directed more forward than in other birds of prey. Tarsus shorter than middle toe and claw combined, covered with projecting sales. Outer toe reversible, soles of feet covered with spicules. Claws long, slender, all except middle toe oval in section, rounded below.

Super Familie Sagittarioidea
Familie Sagittariidae

Super Family Sagittarioidea
Family Sagittariidae

Sagittarius Hermann 1783

Große, ungewöhnlich hochbeinige Greifvögel. Am Hinterkopf Schopf aus langen, spatelförmigen Federn. Schwanz stufig, die beiden mittleren Steuerfedern stark verlängert. Schnabel ziemlich kurz und stark gekrümmt, Nasenlöcher oval, schräg gestellt. Umgebung der Augen nackt. Lauf 3–4 mal so lang wie Mittelzehe, vorn mit Gürteltafeln, hinten mit zwei Reihen Quertafeln bedeckt. Zehen kurz, an der Wurzel durch kleine Spannhäute verbunden. Krallen stumpf.

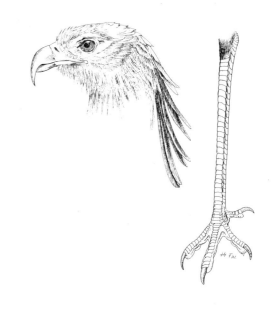

Large, exceptionally long-legged raptors. Long crest of spatulate feathers. Tail graduated, central tail feathers much elongated. Bill rather short, curved; nostrils oblique, oval. Sides of face bare. Tarsus 3–4 times as long as middle-toe, covered in front with girdle scales, behind with to rows of transverse scutes. Toes short, connected by small basal webs; blunt claws.

Familie Accipitridae

Family Accipitridae

Aviceda Swainson 1836

Kleine bis mittelgroße „Kuckucksaare". Oberschnabel mit Doppelzahnung, Nasenlöcher schlitzförmig. Nackenfedern mehr oder weniger verlängert zu Schopf. Beine kurz und kräftig, Lauf kürzer als Mittelzehe, teilweise befiedert. Alle Arten mit Ausnahme von *A. leuphotes* bilden wahrscheinlich Superspecies.

Small to medium-sized kites (Cuckoo Falcons). Upper mandible with two teeth. Nostril slit-shaped. Nape feathers more or less elongated in a crest. Legs short, stout, tarsus shorter than middle-toe, partly feathered. All except *A. leuphotes* comprise a superspecies.

Leptodon Sundevall 1835

Mittelgroße Greifvögel; Schwanz lang, gerundet. Oberschnabel mit einem Zahn; Nasenlöcher schräg, schlitzförmig. Beine kurz und kräftig, Lauf kürzer als Mittelzehe, etwa zur Hälfte befiedert, Rest mit regelmäßigen Schildern bedeckt.

Medium-sized kites; tail long, rounded. Upper mandible with one tooth; nostrils oblique, slit-shaped. Legs short, stout, tarsus shorter than middle-toe, about half covered with feathers, the rest with hexagonal scales.

Chondrohierax Lesson 1843

Mittelgroße „Hakenweihen". Schnabel ungewöhnlich groß, seitlich zusammengedrückt, mit übergroßem, papageiartigem Haken. Nasenlöcher fast senkrecht, schlitzförmig. Zügel und Umgebung der Augen nackt. Flügel und Schwanz lang, gerundet.

Medium-sized „hook-billed kites". Bill unusually large, compressed, exaggeratedly hooked, parrot-like. Nostrils vertical, slit-shaped. Lores and face round eye bare. Wings and tail long, rounded.

Pernis Cuvier 1816

Langschwänzige, bussardgroße „Wespenbussarde". Schnabel schwach und nur mäßig gekrümmt. Nasenlöcher schlitzförmig. Zügel mit schuppenförmigen Federn bedeckt. Nackenfedern häufig zu aufrichtbarer, kurzer oder langer Haube verlängert. Lauf so lang wie Mittelzehe oder etwas kürzer, mit sechseckigen Schildchen bedeckt, Krallen schlank und wenig gebogen. *Pernis apivorus, P. orientalis, P. ptilorynchus* und *P. philippensis* sind wahrscheinlich conspezifisch.

Long-tailed, Buteo-sized „honey-buzzards". Bill weak, slightly curved. Nostrils at an angle slit-shaped. Lores covered with scale-like feathers. Nape feathers often elongated into an erectile short or long crest. Tarsus as long as or slightly shorter than middle-toe, covered with hexagonal scales. Claws slender, slightly curved. *Pernis apivorus, P. orientalis, P. ptilorynchus* and *P. philippensis* perhaps all conspecific.

Henicopernis Gray 1859

Mittelgroße „Wespenbussarde". Flügel und Schwanz sehr lang. Am Oberschnabel Zahn nur angedeutet. Zügel befiedert, aber mit mehr lanzettförmigen (verhornten) Federchen als *Pernis*. Nackenfedern etwas verlängert. Läufe kräftig, an der Vorderseite mit Quertafeln bedeckt.

Medium-sized „honey-buzzards", wings and tail very long. A suggestion of a tooth on upper mandible. Lores feathered, with more lanceolated feathers than in *Pernis*. Feathers of nape slightly elongated. Tarsi stout, covered in front with transverse scutes.

Elanoides Vieillot 1818

Mittelgroße, schlanke, leichtgebaute „Aare". Flügel lang und spitz; Schwanz lang, tief gegabelt. Schnabel klein, Nasenlöcher rundlich bis oval. Kropflos. Lauf ziemlich stämmig und kurz, aber länger als Mittelzehe, obere Hälfte befiedert, sonst mit kleinen Schildchen bedeckt.

Medium-sized, slender, lightly-built kites. Wings long, pointed; tail long, very deeply forked. Bill small, nostrils round to oval; no crop. Tarsus longer than middle-toe but stout, short; upper half feathered, lower covered with reticulate scales.

Machaerhamphus Westermann 1851

Mittelgroße „Fledermausaare", Gestalt falkenähnlich, Flügel lang, spitz. Schnabel klein, seitlich zusammengedrückt, mit tiefer Schnabelspalte. Nasenlöcher fast waagerecht. Zügel dick, samtartig befiedert; kurzer Schopf. Zehen lang, schlank, insbesondere die Mittelzehe, Krallen sehr scharf.

Medium-sized „bat hawk"; proportions falcon-like; long pointed wings. Bill small, compressed, with very wide gape. Nostrils almost horizontal. Lores covered with thick velvety feathers; a short crest. Toes long, slender, especially middle toe, claws very sharp.

Gampsonyx Vigors 1825

Sehr kleine „Zwergaare". Schnabel kurz, stark gekrümmt, Oberschnabel ohne Zahn. Die gefalteten Flügel reichen nahezu bis Schwanzende, Schwanz gerundet. Fänge im Verhältnis zur Körpergröße groß. Lauf länger als Mittelzehe, obere Hälfte befiedert, untere Hälfte mit kleinen Schildchen bedeckt.

Very small „pygmy kites". Bill short, strongly hooked, upper mandible with no teeth. Folded wings almost reach tail-tip; tail rounded. Feet large, related to body-size; tarsus longer than middle toe, upper half feathered, lower half reticulated.

Elanus Savigny 1809

Kleine „Aare" mit spitzen Flügeln. Schnabel klein, schmal an der Spitze, breit an der Basis. Zügel mit starken Borsten bedeckt. Lauf kurz, zu drei Viertel befiedert, Rest mit runden Schildchen bedeckt. Krallen an Unterseite gerundet. Ein Paar Puderdunen an jeder Seite des Hinterrückens.

Small kites, with pointed wings. Bill small, narrow at tip, wide at base. Lores covered with strong bristles. Tarsi short, three quarters feathered, remainder with rounded scales. Talons rounded below. A pair of powder-down patches on each side of rump.

Chelictinia Lesson 1843

Kleine „Aare" mit langen, spitzen Flügeln, sehr langem und sehr tief gegabeltem Schwanz, die beiden äußersten Federn sind die längsten. Fänge kurz und kräftig, Krallen stark gekrümmt.

Small kites, with long, pointed wings, long, very deeply forked tail, outermost feathers prolonged. Legs short, stout, talons strongly curved.

Rostrhamus Lesson 1830

Mittelgroße „Milane", Flügel breit und ziemlich lang, Schwanz mittellang bis kurz, schwach ausgebuchtet oder gegabelt. Schnabel schlank, Oberschnabel mit außergewöhnlich langem und stark gekrümmtem Haken. Nasenlöcher schmal und oval. Lauf kürzer als Mittelzehe, obere Hälfte befiedert, untere Hälfte vorn, bisweilen auch hinten mit Quertafeln bedeckt. Krallen lang und scharf.

Medium-sized kites, wings broad, rather long, tail medium to short, slightly notched or forked. Bill slender, upper mandible with exaggerated long, sharply curved hook. Nostrils narrow, oval. Tarsus shorter than middle toe, upper half feathered, lower covered frontally, sometimes also behind, with transverse scutes. Talons long, sharp.

Harpagus Vigors 1824

Kleine „Milane". Größenunterschied zwischen den Geschlechtern stärker als bei den meisten Milanen. Oberschnabel mit zwei deutlichen Zähnen. Nasenlöcher schmal, oval, mit zentralem Zäpfchen. Flügel kurz, reichen im Sitzen nur knapp bis zur Schwanzmitte. Lauf länger als Mittelzehe, Krallen stark gekrümmt und scharf.

Small kites; size difference between sexes greater than in most kites. Upper mandible with two distinct teeth. Nostrils narrow ovals, with central tubercle. Wings short, when folded hardly reaching centre of tail.

Ictinia Vieillot 1816

Kleine bis mittelgroße „Milane". Flügel lang und spitz. Schwanzende eckig oder leicht ausgebuchtet. Schnabel mittelgroß, Oberschnabel schwach gezahnt. Nasenlöcher oval und durch Häutchen teilweise bedeckt. Läufe mit befiederter oberer Hälfte, sonst mit großen Quertafeln bedeckt. Zehen und Krallen kurz, doch letztere stark gekrümmt.

Small to medium sized kites. Wings long, pointed; tail square or slightly notched. Bill moderately strong, slightly toothed on upper mandible. Nostrils oval, part covered by a membrane. Tarsi with upper half feathered, rest covered with large transverse scales. Toes and talons short, but talons strongly curved.

Lophoictinia Kaup 1847

Mittelgroße, langflügelige Milane; Schwanz lang und leicht ausgebuchtet. Schnabel schlanker als bei *Milvus*. Beine kurz; Laufvorderseite mit kleinen Schildchen bedeckt.

Medium-sized, long-winged kites; tail long; slightly notched. Bill more slender than in *Milvus*. Legs short; front of tarsus covered with reticulate scales.

Hamirostra Brown 1846

Mittelgroße, schwergebaute Milane. Flügel breit, bussardartig, Schwanz kurz und breit. Schnabel groß und klobig, Zügel nackt, mit wenigen Borsten bedeckt. Läufe grob und stark, länger als bei *Milvus*, mit kleinen Schildchen bedeckt.

Medium-sized, heavy-bodied kites; wings broad, Buteo like; tail short, broad. Bill large, heavy; lores bare, covered with some bristles. Tarsi coarse, heavy, longer than in *Milvus*, with reticulate scales.

Haliastur Selby 1840

Mittelgroße Milane. Flügel lang, reichen im Sitzen bis oder etwas über Schwanzspitze. Schwanz lang, leicht gerundet bis leicht keilförmig. Nasenlöcher rundlich und schrägstehend, mit knochigem Rand, Läufe etwas kürzer als Mittelzehe, oberer Teil befiedert, der untere Teil auf Vorderseite mit breiten Quertafeln bedeckt, sonst hexagonale Schilder. Zehensohlen mit kleinen, scharfen Schuppen bedeckt. Aussenzehe länger als die innere, Krallen mittellang und gekrümmt.

Medium sized Kites. Wings long, when folded reaching near or beyond tip of tail. Tail square or slightly wedge-shaped. Nostrils round and oblique, with bony margin. Tarsi rather shorter than middle-toe, feathered at top, lower bare part with broad transverse scutes in front, hexagonal scales elswhere. Soles of feet with small sharp spicules. Outer toe longer than inner, talons moderately long, curved.

Milvus Lacépède 1799

Mittelgroße Milane; Flügel lang (mit deutlichem Knick am Handgelenk); Schwanz lang, mehr oder minder tief gegabelt. Beine kurz, Lauf auf Vorderseite mit großen Quertafeln, hinten mit kleinen Schildchen bedeckt. Krallen schwach gekrümmt, aber scharf.

Medium-sized kites; wings long, distinctly bent at carpal joint; tail long, more or less forked. Legs short, tarsus with transverse scutes in front, reticulate scales behind. Claws not strongly curved, sharp.

Haliaeëtus Savigny 1809

Große bis sehr große Greifvögel (Adler). Flügel lang, breit; Schwanz kurz bis ziemlich kurz, 12-federig, mit Ausnahme von *H. pelagicus* mit 14 Schwanzfedern (daher von einigen Autoren in Gattung *Thalassoaëtus* Kaup 1844). Schnabel groß, kräftig, manchmal hoch gewölbt, seitlich zusammengedrückt. Läufe ziemlich kurz, nur am oberen Ende befiedert, auf Vorderseite mit großen Tafeln bedeckt, sonst mit kleinen Schildchen. Zehen und Krallen groß und sehr kraftvoll, erstere mit dornigen Schuppen bedeckt. Die Gattung bildet ein Bindeglied zwischen *Haliastur* und *Ichthyophaga*.

Large to very large birds of prey (eagles). Wings long, broad; tail short to rather short, of 12 feathers except *H. pelagicus* with 14 (therefore placed by some authors in *Thalassoaëtus* Kaup 1844). Bill large, strong, sometimes deeply arched, compressed laterally. Tarsi rather short, feathered at base only, covered with large scutes in front, behind with reticulate scales. Toes and talons large and very powerful, feet with spicules. The genus forms a link between *Haliastur* and *Ichthyophaga*.

Ichthyophaga Lesson 1843

Ziemlich große Adler. Beine nackt, vorne und hinten mit Schildern bedeckt. Auf Zehensohlen dornige Schuppen ähnlich *Pandion*; Krallen sehr lang, gekrümmt. Außenzehe ist Wendezehe, jedoch weniger beweglich als beim Fischadler. Federn haben Afterschäfte, und auch sonst hat diese Gattung mehr Ähnlichkeit mit *Haliaeëtus*.

Rather large eagles. Legs bare, tarsus in front and behind scutellate. Resemble *Pandion* in having spicules on soles of feet; talons very long, curved; outer toe partially reversible; but feathers have aftershafts and otherwise genus resembles *Haliaeëtus*.

Gypohierax Rüppell 1835

Mittelgroßer „Geierseeadler", an Zügel, Umgebung der Augen und Streifen an der Schnabelwurzel nackt, rot. Flügel ziemlich kurz, sehr breit; Schwanz kurz, leicht gerundet, etwa halb so lang wie Flügel. Kräftiger, adlerartiger, seitlich zusammengedrückter Schnabel, Nasenlöcher oval. Beine nackt, mit sechseckigen Schildchen bedeckt. Krallen ziemlich kurz, aber krumm und scharf.

Medium-sized „Vulturine Fish Eagle", with lores, skin round eye, and streak below base of bill bare, red. Wings rather short, very broad; tail short, slightly rounded, about half length of wing. Powerful, eagle-like compressed bill, nostrils oval. Bare legs with reticulate scales. Talons rather short, but curved and sharp.

Neophron Savigny 1809

Mittelgroße Geier, langflügelig, mit langem, 14-fedrigem, keilförmigem Schwanz. Nackenfedern zerschlissen lanzettförmig. Schnabel lang, schlank, an der Spitze leicht hakig gekrümmt; Nasenlöcher länglich und waagerecht stehend. Gesicht und Kehle nackt. Lauf mittellang, Krallen lang, Außen- und Mitelzehe an Basis durch Spannhaut verbunden.

Medium-sized vultures, long-winged, with long, wedge-shaped tail of 14 feathers. Nape feathers lanceolate. Bill long, slender, slightly hooked at tip; nostril elongated, horizontal. Face and throat bare (nape feathered). Tarsus moderately long, claws long, outer and middle toe joined at base with partial web.

Gypaëtus Storr 1784

Schnabel lang, bis unter das Auge gespalten, weniger hoch als bei *Gyps, Aegypius* etc. An jeder Oberschnabelseite tiefe Kerbe. Wenig nackte Hautteile, Wachshaut unauffällig und wie der gesamte Schnabelgrund mit schwarzen Borsten bedeckt, ebenso am Kinn roßhaarartiger „Bocksbart". Nasenlöcher länglich oval, völlig von Borsten bedeckt. Am Auge ist die Augenhaut (Sclera) als leuchtend roter, wulstiger Ring sichtbar. Füße klein, aber trotzdem gute Greiforgane. Schwanz sehr lang, keil- oder spatelförmig, 12-fedrig; Flügel sehr lang.

Beak long, gape extending to below eye, less deep than in *Gyps, Aegypius* etc.; a deep depression on either side of upper mandible. Little bare skin; at base of bill a black tuft of bristles; a similar bristly „beard" on the chin. Nostrils long ovals, completely covered by bristles. Eye surrounded with red sclerotic ring. Feet small, but nevertheless powerful grasping organs. Tail very long, wedge or diamond-shaped, 12 feathers; wings very long.

Necrosyrtes Gloger 1841

Mittelgroße Geier, in einigem *Neophron* ähnlich, aber Unterschiede in Form der Nasenlöcher, Kopfbefiederung und Anzahl der Schwanzfedern (12). Schnabel lang und schlank; Kopf und Kehle nackt, Hinterkopf und Nacken mit kurzen, wolligen Dunen bedeckt. Schwanz kurz, leicht gerundet. Flügel breit und gerundet.

Medium-sized vultures, somewhat resembling *Neophron*, different in shape of nostril, head feathering and number of tail-feathers (12). Bill long and slender; head and throat naked, occiput and nape with short woolly down. Tail short, slightly rounded. Wings broad, rounded.

Torgos Kaup 1828

Sehr große Geier; Gefieder besitzt wollige Unterdunen; Flügel breit, Schwanz stufig. Mächtiger Schnabel, höher als breit, Nasenlöcher länglich und senkrecht stehend. Kopf und Hals mit fleischigen Falten und Hautlappen bedeckt, die seitlich herunterhängen, mit Borsten bewachsen, sonst nahezu nackt. Lauf und Zehen ziemlich lang.

Very large vultures; plumage with underlying woolly down, wings broad, tail graduated. Bill powerful, deeper than wide, nostrils oblong, vertical. Head and neck bristly, nearly naked, with large hanging lappets of skin. Tarsus and toes rather long.

Sarcogyps Lesson 1842

Große Geier; Kopf und Hals nackt, Halsseiten mit auffallenden Lappen. Oberkopf spärlich mit Borsten besetzt und warzig. Schnabel hoch, aber schwächer als bei *Torgos* oder *Aegypius*, Nasenlöcher mehr rundlich als bei *Torgos*. Lauf nackt, nur am Gelenk befiedert, Schenkelinnenseite nackt.

Large vultures; head and neck bare, sides of neck with pronounced lappets. Crown sparsely covered with bristles, and with small caruncles. Bill deep, less powerful than in *Torgos* or *Aegypius*; nostrils rounder than in *Torgos*. Tarsus bare, feathered at joint; inner face of tibia naked.

Aegypius Savigny 1809

Sehr große Geier. Der gewaltige Schnabel ist höher als breit. Nasenlöcher rund bis eckig. Der breite Kopf und die Halsunterseite mit langem Flaum bedeckt. Der übrige Hals nackt, mit mäßig großer Krause, die bis auf den Rücken reicht. Unter dem Gefieder weicher Flaum. Schwanz 12-federig, gerundet. Lauf länger als Mittelzehe, an der oberen Hälfte befiedert. Krallen auf der Unterseite mit Riefen.

Very large vultures. Powerful bill deeper than broad; nostrils round or square. Broad head and underside of neck with long down; rest of neck naked with a moderate ruff at base reaching up to its back. Whitish down underlies feathers. Tail rounded, of twelve feathers. Tarsus longer than middletoe, feathered on upper half, claws keeled on underside.

Trigonoceps Lesson 1842

Ziemlich große Geier. Schnabel groß mit starkem Haken. Kopf mit weißen Dunen bedeckt, diese länger an Hinterkopf und Nacken; Vorderhals und Kehle nackt. Lauf länger als Mittelzehe, oberes Drittel befiedert.

(*Torgos*, *Sarcogyps* und *Trigonoceps* werden neuerdings in der Gattung *Aegypius* vereinigt, da in den Gattungsmerkmalen und im Verhalten große Ähnlichkeit besteht.)

Rather large vultures. Bill large, strongly hooked. Top of head covered with white down, longer on nape; throat and front of neck bare. Tarsus longer than middle toe, upper third covered with feathers. (By common consent *Torgos*, *Sarcogyps* and *Trigonoceps* are now merged with *Aegypius*, as the generic differences are so slight, and they all have similar habits.)

Gyps Savigny 1809

Ziemlich große bis große Geier; Schwanz 14-fedrig. Schnabel klobig, ziemlich lang, an der Spitze stark gekrümmt. Nasenlöcher schmal oval oder schlitzförmig, senkrecht stehend. Kopf und langer Hals nackt, mehr oder weniger mit Dunen bedeckt. Halskrause aus lanzettförmigen Federn, vorne unterbrochen. An den Brustseiten je ein nackter, auffällig gefärbter Hautfleck. Lauf deutlich kürzer als Mittelzehe.

Rather large to large vultures; tail of 14 feathers. Bill heavy, rather long, much hooked at tip. Nostrils narrow oval or slit-shaped vertical. Head and long neck bare, more or less covered with down. A ruff of lanceolate feathers, interrupted in front. On either side of chest a bare, coloured patch of skin. Tarsus distinctly shorter than middle toe.

Pseudogyps Sharpe 1873

Ziemlich große Geier, Schwanz 12-fedrig. Schnabel kürzer als bei *Gyps*, Oberschnabel mit stärkerer Ausbuchtung. Die beiden Arten *africanus* und *benghalensis* bilden wahrscheinlich Superspecies, eventuell conspezifisch (nach einigen Autoren).

Rather large vultures, tail of 12 feathers. Bill shorter than in *Gyps*, with a sharper cutting edge on upper mandible. The two species *africanus* and *benghalensis* form a superspecies if not conspecific (acc. some authors).

Terathopius Lesson 1830

Nur mittelgroße „Adler", aber von kräftiger Gestalt. Kopf mit kurzer, runder Haube, Kopfseiten nackt und farbenprächtig; Beine nackt, rundlich beschuppt. Flügel sehr lang und spitz; Schwanz extrem kurz, meist gerade abgeschnitten, von den gefalteten Flügeln weit überragt. Verwandtschaft mit *Circaëtus* im Jugendkleid am deutlichsten.

Medium-sized but stout-bodied eagles. Head with short, full crest, sides of face bare, brightly coloured; legs bare, heavily scaled. Wings very long, pointed. Tail extremely short, almost square; folded wings protrude far beyond tail tip. Relationship to *Circaëtus* is clear in juvenile plumage.

Circaëtus Vieillot 1816

Ziemlich große bis mittelgroße „Adler", mit langen Flügeln, mittellangen Schwänzen und dicken Köpfen mit grossen Augen; nahe verwandt mit *Spilornis*. Nasenlöcher jedoch immer länglich und aufrecht, fast senkrecht stehend. Reichlich Kinn- und Schnabelwinkelborsten, Stirn- und Kinnbefiederung zu steifen Borsten verlängert. Nackenfedern schmal und spitz. Läufe lang, nackt und ganz mit hexagonalen Schildern bedeckt. Zehen kurz, die äußere als Wendezehe ausgebildet. Krallen kurz.

Rather large to medium-sized „eagles" with long wings, moderately long tails and large heads with large eyes; allied to *Spilornis*. Nostril always elongated and upright, almost vertical. Feathers around base of bill, forehead and chin elongated into stiff bristles; neck feathers narrow and pointed. Tarsus long, bare, and covered all round with hexagonal scales. Toes short, the outer partly reversible; claws short.

Spilornis Gray 1840

Mittelgroße bis ziemlich große Schlangen„adler". Die breiten, verlängerten Nackenfedern bilden aufgerichtet eine runde Haube. Flügel relativ kürzer als bei *Circaëtus*, meist gerundet. Nasenlöcher rund oder oval. Die nackten Gesichtsseiten mehr oder weniger durch Borsten bedeckt. Lauf länger als Mittelzehe, mit großen hexagonalen Schildern bedeckt. Krallen kurz, krumm und scharf.

Medium sized to rather large snake„eagles". Nape feathers broad and elongated, forming a full crest when erect; wings relatively shorter than in *Circaëtus*, most rounded. Nostril round or oval; sides of face naked, more or less covered with bristles. Tarsus longer than middle toe covered with large hexagonal scales. Claws short, hooked and sharp.

Dryotriorchis Shelley 1874

Mittelgroß. Flügel kürzer und runder als bei *Circaëtus* oder *Spilornis*; Schwanz lang, gerundet, hat mehr als dreiviertel Flügellänge. Nasenlöcher länglich oval, schmal, fast senkrecht stehend. Kopf groß, mit kurzer, lanzettfedriger Haube; Augen groß, Beine gleichen *Circaëtus* und *Spilornis*.

Medium-sized, with shorter rounder wings than in *Circaëtus* or *Spilornis*; tail long, rounded, about three quarters of winglength. Nostrils narrow ovals, nearly vertical. Head large, with a short, lanceolate crest; eyes large. Tarsi and feet resemble *Circaëtus* and *Spilornis*.

Eutriorchis Sharpe 1875

Ähnlich *Dryotriorchis*, Schwanz jedoch noch länger, nahezu so lang wie Flügel; die gefalteten Flügel erreichen kaum die Schwanzwurzel. Nasenlöcher durch haarähnliche Borsten bedeckt. Die breiten Hinterkopffedern bilden deutliche Haube und lassen auf Verwandtschaft mit *Spilornis* schließen.

Resembling *Dryotriorchis*, but tail still longer, almost as long as wing; folded wings scarcely exceed base of tail. Nostrils hidden by hairlike bristles. Crown feathers broad, forming a distinct crest, suggesting relationship to *Spilornis*.

Polyboroides A. Smith 1829

Mittelgroße, leichtgebaute Greife. Flügel lang und breit, Schwanz lang und gerundet. Schnabel schwach, Nasenlöcher schlitzförmig und waagerecht. Seiten des Gesichts und unterhalb der Schnabelspalte nackt. Kurze, buschige Haube. Lauf lang, mit vieleckigen Schildern bedeckt. Lauf im Fersengelenk nach vorn und hinten beweglich (Doppelgelenk), nach hinten etwa um 30°. Kurze Spannhaut zwischen Mittel- und Außenzehe. Krallen schlank.

Medium-sized, lightly built raptors. Wings long, broad, tail long, rounded. Bill weak; nostril slit-shaped, horizontal. Sides of face and below gape naked. A short, bushy crest. Tarsus long, covered with polygonal scales. Tibiotarsal joint can bend either way (,,double-jointed") backwards through about 30 degrees. A slight web between middle and outer toes; talons slender.

Geranospiza Kaup 1847

Mittelgroße, schlanke und leichtgebaute Greifvögel. Flügel lang und gerundet, mit langen Armschwingen; Schwanz lang gerundet. Nasenlöcher rundlich oder oval, ohne Zäpfchen. Schenkelbefiederung kurz, Lauf lang, vorn und hinten mit Quertafeln bedeckt, vorne zu Längsschienen verschmolzen. ,,Doppelgelenkig" wie bei *Polyboroides*, das heißt, Lauf kann ca. 30° nach hinten geknickt werden.

Medium-sized, slim and slightly built birds of prey. Wings short, rounded, with long primaries. Tail long, rounded. Nostrils round or oval, without tubercle. Thigh-feathers short, tarsus long, with transverse scutes in front and behind, those in front continuing onto middle toe. "Double-jointed" like *Polyporoides*; tarsus can bend 30° behind vertical.

Circus Lacépède 1799

Mittelgroße, schlanke Greifvögel mit ausgeprägtem Geschlechtsdimorphismus, die Weibchen unterschiedlich gefärbt und erheblich größer als die Männchen. Flügel lang, schmal; Schwanz lang. Lockeres, weiches Gefieder, Gesicht mit eulenartigem Schleier, Schnabelborsten. Läufe lang, schlank, mit hexagonalen Schildern oder die Vorderseite mit Tafeln bedeckt. Alle Arten mit einer Ausnahme (*assimilis*) sind Bodenbrüter.

Middle sized, slender, dimorphic, females differently coloured and much larger than males. Wings long narrow, tail long. Plumage soft, loose, face with an owl-like ruff, lores with bristles. Tarsi long, slender, sometimes reticulated scales all round, sometimes with frontal scutes. All but one species (*assimilis*) nest on ground.

Melierax Gray 1840

Mittelgroße bis kleine ,,Habichte". Flügel mittellang, etwas gerundet, Schwanz lang (mehr als 2/3 der Flügellänge), gerundet. Nasenlöcher rund, mit Zäpfchen; Wachshaut bis zur Schnabelwurzel prächtig gefärbt. Läufe lang, Front- und Rückseite mit eckigen Tafeln bedeckt. Die Art *gabar* ist in Größe und Proportionen sehr verschieden zur *canorus-metabates*-Gruppe und daher häufig in separate Gattung *Micronisus* Gray 1840 gestellt.

Middle sized or small,,goshawks". Wings medium long, rather rounded; tail more than 2/3 wing length, rounded.

Nostril round, with tubercle; cere to base of beak brightly coloured. Tarsus long, with square plates on front and back. The species *gabar* is very different in proportions and size from *canorus-metabates* group, and is often separated in genus *Micronisus* Gray 1840.

Megatriorchis Salvadori & d'Albertis 1876

Mittelgroße Habichte mit sehr kurzen, gerundeten Flügeln und sehr langem, gerundetem Schwanz. Schnabel kräftig, seitlich etwas zusammengedrückt. Läufe lang, kräftig auf der Vorderseite teils befiedert, teils mit Tafeln bedeckt. Zehen und Krallen lang und schlank. Weibchen erheblich größer als Männchen.

Medium-sized hawks, with very short, rounded wings and very long, rounded tail. Bill strong, rather compressed. Tarsi long, strong, partly covered with feathers, scutellate in front. Toes and talons long and slender. Female much larger than male.

Erythrotriorchis Sharpe 1875

Mittelgroße Habichte, ähnlich *Megatriorchis*, aber Flügel bussardartig lang und breit; Schwanz lang, wenig abgestuft. Läufe und Zehen sehr kräftig, die lange Mittelzehe typisch für den Vogeljäger. Die Zehen auf Unterseite mit charakteristischen „Haltebeeren", gut zum Greifen geeignet. Weibchen erheblich größer als Männchen.

Medium-sized hawks, resembling *Megatriorchis*, but with buzzard-like longer, broad wings; tail long, somewhat graduated. Tarsi and toes very strong, long middle-toe typical of bird-hunter. Toes have characteristic lumps below, perhaps prehensile with prey. Female much larger than male.

Accipiter Brisson 1760

Kleine bis mittelgroße Greifvögel, langschwänzig, meist langbeinig, mit kurzen gerundeten Flügeln. Schnabel kurz mit Einkerbung am Oberschnabel. Nasenlöcher rund oder oval ohne Zäpfchen. Lauf auf Vorder- und Rückseite mit breiten Quertafeln bedeckt, manchmal zu geschlossenen Schienen verschmolzen. Weibchen größer oder erheblich größer als Männchen. Die meisten Arten sind gebüsch- oder waldbewohnende Vogeljäger.

Small to medium-sized raptors, long-tailed and most long-legged, with short, rounded wings. Bill short, with cutting edge on upper mandible. Nostril circular or oval without tubercle. Tarsus with broad transverse scutes in front, and behind, sometimes fused, resulting in a "booted" formation. Females larger or much larger than males. Most are forest or woodland bird-hunters.

Urotriorchis Sharpe 1874

Mittelgroße Habichte mit auffallend langem, abgestuftem Schwanz (dieser länger als Kopf und Rumpf zusammen); Flügel kurz und gerundet. Nasenlöcher rundlich mit Knochenzäpfchen. Läufe kräftig, an Vorderseite zur Hälfte befiedert; Zehen kräftig.

Medium-sized hawks with exceptionally long tail (more than head and body combined) graduated; wings short, rounded. Nostrils circular, with bony tubercle. Tarsi powerful, half covered with feathers in front; talons strong.

Butastur Hodgson 1843

Mittelgroße Bussardverwandte, Flügel lang, breit und
ziemlich spitz, reichen im Sitzen fast bis zum Schwanzende.
Schnabel relativ schwach, Nasenlöcher rundlich ohne Zäpfchen. Läufe mäßig lang, auf der Vorderseite mit Quertafeln, auf Seiten und Sohlen mit hexagonalen Schildern bedeckt. Zehen ziemlich schwach.

Medium-sized „buteonines" (related to buzzards). Wings
long, broad, somewhat pointed, when folded exceeding tail
tip. Bill rather weak. Nostrils circular, with no tubercle.
Tarsi moderately long, with transverse scutes in front, sides
with reticulate scales; toes rather weak.

Kaupifalco Bonaparte 1854

Kleine Bussardverwandte; Flügel ziemlich lang und spitz.
Schwanz etwa 2/3 der Flügellänge, gerundet bis eckig, überragt die angelegten Flügel um seine halbe Länge. Lauf kurz,
zur Hälfte befiedert, auf der Vorderseite mit Tafeln, auf der
Rückseite mit sechsseitigen Schildchen bedeckt. Verwandtschaftlich wohl *Leucopternis* und *Buteo* species nahestehend.

Small „buteonines"; wings rather long and pointed. Tail 2/3
winglength, rounded or square extending for half its length
beyond folded wing tips. Tarsus short, half covered with
feathers, scutellated in front and with reticulated scales behind. Probably allied to *Leucopternis* and *Buteo* species.

Heterospizias Sharpe 1874

Mittelgroßer Bussardverwandter, mit langen schlanken
Beinen und kurzen Zehen. Flügel lang und spitz (hauptsächlich im Fluge sichtbar); Schwanz mittellang; Flügelspit-
zen reichen im Sitzen fast bis zum Schwanzende. Federn
des Hinterhalses lanzettförmig verlängert, bilden schwa-
chen Schopf. Nasenloch rund mit Zäpfchen. Jugendkleid
und Alterskleid sehr unterschiedlich. Wahrscheinlich mit
Buteogallus verwandt.

Medium-sized buteonine, with long, slender legs and short
toes. Wings long, pointed (chiefly noted in flight); tail
medium; folded wings extend to near tip of tail. Feathers
of hind neck prolonged into a slight crest. Immature plumage very different from adult. Nostril round with tubercle;
probably related to *Buteogallus*.

Busarellus Lafresnaye 1842

Mittelgroßer Bussardverwandter, mit langen, sehr breiten
Flügeln und kurzem Schwanz. Hinterkopffedern etwas zugespitzt und zu leichter Haube verlängert. Jugendkleid dem
Alterskleid sehr ähnlich. Schnabel ziemlich lang, Oberschnabel mit starker Krümmung; Nasenlöcher rundlich mit
Zäpfchen, Schenkelbefiederung kurz; Lauf länger als Mittelzehe, auf der Vorderseite mit breiten Gürteltafeln bedeckt, hinten eine Reihe breiter Tafeln, seitlich Schildchen.
Zehen gespalten, aber die Sohlen mit rauhen Schuppen
und dornigen Warzen bedeckt, ähnlich *Pandion*.

Medium-sized buteonine, with long, very broad wings and
short tail. Feathers of crown and nape somewhat pointed,
forming slight crest. Immature plumage not very different
to adult. Bill rather long, upper mandible strongly hooked;
nostril circular with tubercle. Thigh feathers short; tarsus
longer than middle-toe, covered in front with broad fused
scales, behind with row of scutes, sides with reticulate
scales. Toes unwebbed, but soles covered with spicules and
rough scales, resembling *Pandion*.

Leucopternis Kaup 1847

Kleine bis mittelgroße Bussardverwandte, wohl der Gattung *Buteogallus* nahestehend, aber mit kürzeren Läufen und schmaleren Flügeln. Nasenlöcher rundlich bis oval; Zügel und Beine prächtig gefärbt. Jungvögel ähneln sehr den Adultvögeln. Mit Ausnahme von *L. albicollis* und *L. princeps* ist die Schenkelbefiederung nicht zu „Hosen" verlängert.

Small to medium-sized hawks, probably related to *Buteogallus*, but with shorter tarsi and narrower wings. Nostrils circular to oval; lores and legs brightly coloured. Immatures resemble adults. Excepted *L. albicollis* and *L. princeps* the thigh feathers do not form „flags".

Buteogallus Lesson 1830

Bussardgroße, langbeinige Neuweltgreife. Sehr breitflügelig, mit fünf gekerbten Handschwingen und kurzem, eckigem Schwanz. Oberkopf- und Nackenfedern etwas verlängert zu kurzem Schopf. Immatur- und Alterskleid meist sehr unterschiedlich, etwas einheitlicher bei *B. aequinoctialis*. Nasenlöcher oval bis rund, mit Zäpfchen nahe dem oberen Rande. Zügel und Umgebung nackt in unterschiedlicher Form.

Buzzard-sized, long-legged New World raptors. Very broad-winged, with five emerginated primaries, and short, square tail. Top of head and nape elongated into a short crest. Immature and adult plumages normally very different, more alike in *B. aequinoctialis*. Nostrils oval or round with a tubercle near upper border. Face and lores more or less naked.

Harpyhaliaëtus Lafresnaye 1842

Große Bussardverwandte, mit mehr oder weniger ausgeprägtem Schopf am Hinterkopf. Flügel lang, breit; Schwanz kurz bis mittellang (etwa halbe Flügellänge). Schnabel mittelgroß, Nasenlöcher rund bis oval; Zügel mit einigen Borsten. Lauf länger als Mittelzehe, mit unregelmäßigen Schildern bedeckt. Jugendkleid und Alterskleid sehr unterschiedlich.

Large buteonines, more or less crested on occiput. Wings long, broad; tail short to medium (half wing length). Bill moderately powerful, nostril round or oval; lores with some bristles. Tarsi longer than middle toe, covered with irregular plates. Immature plumage very different to adults.

Parabuteo Ridgway, 1899

Mittelgroßer, kräftig gebauter Bussardverwandter, lange Flügel und langer, gerundeter Schwanz. Nackenfedern etwas zugespitzt; Zügel fast nackt; Nasenlöcher rund mit Knochenzäpfchen nahe dem oberen Rande. Läufe lang, etwa zur Hälfte befiedert, sonst mit Schuppen bedeckt. Zehen und Krallen im Verhältnis zur Körpergröße lang u. kräftig.

Medium-sized, heavily built buteonine, with long wings and long, rounded tail. Feathers of nape somewhat pointed; lores nearly bare; nostrils round with bony tubercle near upper margin. Tarsi strong, about half covered with feathers, otherwise with scutellate scales. Toes and talons long and powerful related to body-size.

Geranoaëtus Kaup 1844

Bussardverwandte von Adlergröße, mit langen, breiten Flügeln und sehr kurzem, leicht gerundetem Schwanz; Weibchen bedeutend größer als Männchen. Schnabel groß, seitlich ziemlich zusammengedrückt, an der Spitze stark gekrümmt, tiefer Schnabelspalt; Nasenlöcher schräg bis horizontal (ähnlich der Gattung *Aquila*). Zügel spärlich befiedert, Oberkopf- und Nackenfedern lanzettförmig. Lauf etwa zu einem Drittel befiedert, sonst mit Schildern bedeckt. Zehen kurz und kräftig. Immaturkleid sehr unterschiedlich zum Alterskleid und mit längerem Schwanz.

Large „eagle-sized" buteonines, with long, broad wings and very short, somewhat rounded tail; females much bigger than males. Bill large, rather compressed, deeply hooked, with a wide gape; nostril obliquely horizontal (resembling genus *Aquila*). Lores sparsely feathered, crown and nape feathers lanceolate. Tarsus covered about one third with feathers, otherwise with shield like scales. Toes short and strong. Immature plumage very different to adult, with longer tail.

Buteo Lacépède 1799

Kleine bis mittelgroße, wenig spezialisierte Greife mit breiten Flügeln und breiten Schwänzen, ausgesprochene Segler. Läufe meist nackt (a), ausnahmsweise befiedert (b). Schnäbel von unterschiedlichen Dimensionen, doch meist kurz; Nasenlöcher (mit einer Ausnahme) ohne Zäpfchen. Zehen und Krallen von unterschiedlicher Größe, aber meist ziemlich kurz. Die meisten Arten mit 4 tief eingekerbten Handschwingen, bei einigen amerikanischen Arten des offenen Geländes sind nur 3 Handschwingen eingekerbt (*swainsoni, galapagoensis, albicaudatus, polyosoma, poecilochrous*). Einige Neuwelt-Bussarde sind zur Untergruppe der Waldbussarde zusammengefaßt; von diesen sind die Arten *albidus* und *magnirostris* Bindeglieder zwischen *Buteo* einerseits und *Leucopternis* und *Buteogallus* andererseits. *B. nitidus* wird auf Grund eines anderen Mauserverlaufes als Gattung *Asturina* Vieillot betrachtet, während *B. magnirostris* zu anderen *Buteo*-Arten Unterschiede in Mauser und Anatomie zeigt und daher auch als Gattung *Rupornis* Kaup betrachtet wird.

(a)

Small to medium-sized unspecialised hawks, with broad wings and broad tail well adapted to soaring. Tarsi normally bare (a), but occasionally feathered (b). Beaks of average proportions, normally rather short; nostrils (with one exception) without tubercle. Toes and claws of moderate size, usually rather short. Most species have four outer primaries emarginated, but some American species of open country have only three emarginated primaries (*swainsoni, galapagoensis, albicaudatus, polyosoma, poecilochrous*). Some New World *Buteos* are included in a sub-group of „Woodland buteos"; *B. albidus* and *B. magnirostris* link *Buteo* with *Leucopternis* and *Buteogallus*. *B. nitidus* on account of different moult pattern is sometimes placed in the genus *Asturina* Vieillot; while *B. magnirostris*, differing from other *Buteo* in moult and osteology is often placed in *Rupornis* Kaup.

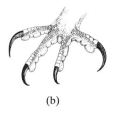

(b)

Morphnus Dumont 1816

Ziemlich große, habichtsartige Adler, mit breiten, runden Flügeln und besonders breiten Armschwingen. Schwanz lang und gerundet. Die angelegten Flügel reichen nicht bis zur Schwanzmitte. Hinterkopffedern zu breitem Schopf verlängert. Nasenlöcher schlitzförmig und schräg stehend. Lauf länger als Mittelzehe, oberer Teil etwas befiedert, sonst vorn und hinten mit breiten Tafeln bedeckt. Fänge und Schnabel im Verhältnis zur Körpergröße bedeutend schwächer als bei *Harpia*; Alterskleid sehr variabel.

Rather large, Accipiter-like eagle, with broad rounded wings, especially broad secondaries; tail long, rounded. The folded wings do not reach centre of tail. Crown feathers elongated to form a full crest. Nostril oblique, slit-shaped. Tarsus longer than middle-toe, upper part covered with feathers, with scutes in front and behind on rest. Claws and beak related to body-size much weaker than in *Harpia*; adult plumage very variable.

Harpia Vieillot 1816

Sehr große, sehr kraftvolle Adler, ähnlich *Morphnus*, aber mit viel kürzerem, dickerem Lauf, nur etwa so lang wie Mittelzehe. Flügel breit, gerundet; Schwanz lang, etwa 2/3 der Flügellänge. Lange, aufrichtbare Doppelhaube. Mächtige Zehen, Krallen lang und stark gekrümmt. Weibchen bedeutend größer als Männchen.

Very large, very powerful eagles, resembling *Morphnus* but with much shorter stout tarsus about as long as middle toe. Wings broad, rounded; tail long about 2/3 of wing length. A long erectile double crest. Toes very powerful, talons very long, strongly curved. Female much larger than male.

Harpyopsis Salvadori 1875

Große Adler, mit kurzen, runden Flügeln und langen, gerundeten Schwänzen, in Gestalt ähnlich *Morphnus*. Nackenfedern zu voller, runder Haube verlängert. Schnabel hoch, seitlich zusammengedrückt, Nasenlöcher rund. Läufe lang, mit je einer Reihe großer Schilder auf Vorder- und Rückseite bedeckt. Zehen lang und ziemlich schlank, Krallen lang und stark gekrümmt.

Large eagles, with short rounded wings and long rounded tails, resembling *Morphnus* in build. Nape feathers elongated into a round, full crest. Bill deep, compressed; nostril round. Tarsi long, with one row of scutes in front and another behind. Toes long and rather slender, talons long, strongly curved.

Pithecophaga Ogilvie-Grant 1896

Sehr große Adler, in Größe und Stärke der Läufe ähnlich *Harpia*. Hinterkopf- und Nackenfedern lang und lanzettförmig, zu buschiger Krone aufrichtbar. Flügel kurz und gerundet, Schwanz lang, eckig oder leicht gerundet. Schnabel extrem hoch, gebogen, seitlich stark zusammengedrückt; Nasenlöcher schlitzförmig, senkrecht. Zügel und Wangen durch Federborsten bedeckt. Lauf ziemlich kurz, dick und kräftig; Zehen kraftvoll mit langen, stark gekrümmten Krallen.

Very large eagles, similar in size, strength of legs to *Harpia*. Feathers of crown and nape lanceolate, erectile into a crest or crown all round head. Wings short, rounded, tail long and almost square or slightly rounded. Bill exceptionally deep, arched, laterally compressed; nostrils slit-like, vertical. Lores and checks covered with bristles. Tarsus rather short, very stout and powerful; feet powerful with long, strong curved talons.

Polemaëtus Heine 1890

Große Adler; Flügel lang, breit; Schwanz kurz; kurze Haube. Schnabel groß, seitlich leicht zusammengedrückt, Spitze stark gekrümmt. Läufe lang, stark, befiedert; Zehen sehr lang, Krallen lang, stark gekrümmt, scharf.

Large eagles; wings long, broad, tail short; a short crest. Bill large, compressed, deeply hooked. Tarsi long, stout, feathered, toes very long, talons long, strongly hooked, sharp.

Oroaëtus Ridgway 1920

Große, kräftige Waldadler; Flügel ziemlich lang, sehr breite Armschwingen; Schwanz lang, gerundet, weniger deutlich als bei *Spizaëtus*. Haube lang, spitz. Mächtiger Schnabel, Oberschnabel mit zahnähnlicher Einkerbung und stark gekrümmter Spitze, Nasenlöcher oval. Kräftige, befiederte Läufe, starke Zehen mit langen, scharfen Krallen. Ähnlich *Spizaëtus*, aber langflügeliger und mit mächtigeren Fängen.

Large, heavily built forest eagles; wings rather long, very broad secondaries; tail long, rounded, less so than in *Spizaëtus*. Crest long, pointed. Bill powerful, with tooth-like curved upper cutting edge, strongly hooked, nostril oval. Tarsi strong, feathered, toes strong, with long, sharp talons. Similar in proportions to *Spizaëtus*, but longer winged, more powerful feet.

Stephanoaëtus W. Sclater 1922

Große, kraftvolle Waldadler, vergleichbar mit *Harpia*. Flügel kurz, gerundet, breit; Schwanz lang, breit. Mit langer, aufrichtbarer Doppelhaube. Schnabel mäßig lang, seitlich zusammengedrückt, hoch und stark gekrümmt; Nasenlöcher schlitzförmig, fast senkrecht stehend. Mächtige Fänge, Läufe befiedert; Zehen ziemlich kurz und dick, Krallen lang, stark und scharf. *Spizaëtus* nahestehend, aber viel größer und kräftiger.

Large, powerful forest eagles, comparable to *Harpia*. Wings short, rounded, broad, tail long, broad. A long double crest, erectile. Bill moderately long, laterally compressed, powerfully arched and hooked; nostril-slit shaped, nearly vertical. Legs very powerful, feathered; toes rather short, thick, talons long, strong, sharp. Closely allied to *Spizaëtus* but much larger, more powerful.

Spizaëtus Vieillot 1816

Mittelgroße bis ziemlich große Waldadler. Körperproportionen sehr unterschiedlich, meist schlank. Flügel kurz, gerundet, Schwanz lang, gerundet; die meisten Arten mit langer, spitzer oder buschiger Haube; einige ohne. Schnabel kurz, mit stark gekrümmter Spitze; Läufe befiedert, Zehen lang, meist kräftig; Krallen lang und scharf. Eine Art (*cirrhatus*) mit melanistischer Phase.

Medium-sized to rather large eagles, mainly in forest. Proportions variable, usually slender. Wings short, rounded, tail long, rounded; usually with long, pointed or bushy crest; a few crestless. Bill short, deeply hooked; tarsi feathered, toes long, often strong; talons long, sharp. One species (*cirrhatus*) has melanistic phase.

Spizastur Gray 1841

Bussardgroße Adler mit ziemlich kurzen, gerundeten Flügeln, langem Schwanz und deutlicher Haube. Handschwingen weniger stark gekerbt als bei *Hieraaëtus*. Schnabel schlank, ziemlich lang, Zone um Unterschnabelwinkel nackt; Nasenlöcher oval, aufrecht gestellt. Läufe befiedert, Zehen lang und relativ groß, Krallen schlank, stark gekrümmt.

Buteo-sized eagles with rather short, rounded wings, long tail and distinct crest. Primaries less emarginated than in *Hieraaëtus*. Bill slender, rather long, area along rear edge of lower mandible bare; nostril oval, vertical. Legs feathered, toes long and strong related to body-size, talons slender, deeply curved.

Lophaëtus Kaup 1847

Mittelgroße Adler, Flügel mäßig lang, aber breit, gerundet; breiter, leicht gerundeter Schwanz von etwa halber Flügellänge. Haube lang, aus 6 oder mehr biegsamen Federn. Schnabel kurz, Schnabelspalte tief, Nasenlöcher rund. Läufe befiedert; Zehen und Krallen relativ schwach.

Medium-sized eagles, with moderately long, broad, rounded wings; broad, rather rounded tail, about half wing length. Crest of six or more feathers, long, flexible or pendent. Bill short, gape wide, nostril round. Legs feathered; feet and talons rather weak.

Hieraaëtus Kaup 1844

Mittelgroße bis ziemlich große „schneidige" Adler, *Aquila* und *Spizaëtus* nahestehend. Schlanker Körperbau, Flügel ziemlich lang und spitz, Schwanz mäßig lang. Kopf manchmal mit Haube. Oberschnabel von der Wurzel an gekrümmt, mit starker Einkerbung. Nasenlöcher immer länglich, aufrecht gestellt. Läufe befiedert, Zehen und Krallen lang, stark gekrümmt, scharf.

Medium-sized to rather large, swift eagles, allied to *Aquila* and *Spizaëtus*. Slender; wings long, pointed, tail moderately long. Head sometimes crested. Bill curved from base, with marked curve on cutting edge of upper mandible. Nostril oval, vertical. Legs feathered; toes and talons long, strongly curved, sharp.

Aquila Brisson 1760

Mittelgroße bis große Adler, eng mit *Hieraaëtus*, etwas weitläufiger mit *Spizaëtus* verwandt. Flügel lang, ziemlich breit, Schwanz mittellang bis sehr lang, eckig, gerundet oder keilförmig. Nacken- und Halsfedern meist lanzettförmig, jedoch nur eine Art (*wahlbergi*) mit Haube. Schnabel mehr oder weniger lang, First hinten gerade, vorn mehr oder minder stark gekrümmt; Nasenlöcher rundich oder oval, aufrecht stehend. Kräftige Beine, Läufe bis zu den Zehen befiedert; Zehen meist kräftig, manchmal etwas schwächer, mit langen, gekrümmten Krallen.

Medium-sized to large eagles, closely related to *Hieraaëtus*, less so to *Spizaëtus*. Wings long, rather broad, tail medium to very long, square, rounded, occasionally wedge shaped. Nape feathers usually lanceolate „hackles", but only one species crested (*wahlbergi*). Bill more or less long, with straight upper-edge, more or less deeply hooked; nostrils circular or oval, vertical. Legs normally powerful, feathered to toes; toes normally strong, sometimes rather weak, with long curved talons, variable.

Ictinaëtus Blyth 1843

Ziemlich große, jedoch leichtgebaute Adler, in mancher Beziehung'an *Milvus* erinnernd. Flügel und Schwanz lang, die äußeren Handschwingen tief eingekerbt. Nackenfedern lanzettförmig zugespitzt, bilden leichten Schopf. Schnabel ziemlich kurz, Oberschnabel stark gekrümmt; Wachshaut ausgedehnt; Nasenlöcher oval. Läufe befiedert; Krallen lang, schwach gekrümmt, Außenzehe sehr kurz.

Rather large, slenderly built eagles, in some respects kite-like. Wings and tail long, the outer primaries of the wing emarginated very deeply. Nape feathers pointed, forming a slight crest. Bill rather short, upper mandible deeply curved, cere extended; nostrils oval. Tarsi feathered; talons long, but little curved; outer toe very short.

Unter-Ordnung Falcones
Familie Falconidae
Unter-Familie Daptriinae

Sub-Order Falcones
Family Falconidae
Sub-Family Daptriinae

Daptrius Vieillot 1816

Mittelgroße, leichtgebaute, waldbewohnende Mitglieder der Falkenfamilie (wenig Ähnlichkeit mit echten Falken). Flügel lang, Schwanz lang gerundet. Gesichtshaut und Kehle nackt, prächtig gefärbt, mit wenigen Borsten bestanden. Schnabel schwach, Oberschnabel schwach gekrümmt mit leichter Ausbuchtung. Ausgedehnte Wachshaut, Nasenlöcher rundlich. Läufe kurz, zum Teil befiedert oder mit hexagonalen Schuppen bedeckt, Zehen mit Schildern. Krallen lang, schwach gekrümmt, aber scharf. Immaturkleid dem Adultkleid sehr ähnlich.

Medium-sized, slightly built forest dwelling members of falcon family (not resembling true falcons). Wings long, tail long and rounded. Face and throat bare, brightly coloured, with a few bristles. Bill weak, little hooked; a slight curve in edge of upper mandible; cere extended, nostril circular. Tarsi short, part covered with feathers, with hexagonal scales, becoming scutes on toes. Talons long, gently curved, but sharp. Immature plumage resembles adult.

Phalcoboenus d'Orbigny 1834

Mittelgroße, hochlandbewohnende Aasfalken. Leicht gebaut, Flügel lang und spitz. Gesicht, und bei einer Art auch Kehle, mehr oder weniger nackt. Oberkopffedern gekräuselt oder zugespitzt, kappenartigen Schopf bildend. Schnabel schwach, wenig gekrümmt; Nasenlöcher rund. Beine ziemlich schwach, Krallen dünn, wenig gekrümmt. Im Alterskleid schwarz und weiß. Immaturkleid unterschiedlich, brauner; *Ph. carunculatus* weicht von den übrigen Arten in Aussehen und Verhalten ab.

Medium-sized, upland dwelling caracaras. Lightly built, wings long, pointed. Face, and in one species throat, more or less bare; crown feathers curled or pointed, forming a small crest. Bill weak, little hooked; nostril round. Legs weak; talons thin, little curved. Adults black and white, immatures different, browner; *Ph. carunculatus* differs from other species in appearance and social habits.

Polyborus Vieillot 1816

Mittelgroße, *Phalcoboenus* nahestehende Aasfalken. Flügel lang, spitz; Schwanz mittellang, schwach gerundet; Oberkopf- und Nackenfedern zugespitzt und zu Haube verlängert. Schnabel groß, leicht zusammengedrückt, nur schwach gekrümmt; Oberschnabel mit schwacher Ausbuchtung. Wachshaut ausgedehnt, fleischig, Nasenlöcher länglich und schräg gestellt. Kopfseiten und Kinn nackt, borstenbedeckt. Lauf lang, der untere Teil mit Schildern bedeckt, Zehen kurz, mit Quertafeln bedeckt; Krallen lang, aber nur leicht gekrümmt und stumpf.

Medium-sized caracaras, related to *Phalcoboenus*. Wings long, pointed; tail moderately long, somewhat rounded; crown and nape feathers pointed forming a crest. Bill large, somewhat compressed, but little hooked; slight curve in edge of upper mandible. Cere large, fleshy, nostril oval, oblique. Sides of face and chin naked, bristly. Tarsus long, with scutellate scales on lower part; toes short, covered with transverse scutes; talons long, but little curved and blunt.

Milvago Spix 1824

Kleine und leichtgebaute Aasfalken, Flügel lang und gerundet, Schwanz gerundet. Kopf ohne Nacktstellen, aber Zügel und Kehle nur spärlich befiedert. Schnabel schwach, mit deutlicher Ausbuchtung; Wachshaut klein, Nasenlöcher rund, nackte Augenringe. Lauf dünn, auf Vorderseite Doppelreihe länglicher Tafeln sowie eine Reihe von Schildern auf den Zehenoberseiten. *Milvago* steht den echten Falken verwandtschaftlich näher als die übrigen Aasfalken.

Small, slightly built caracaras, with long, rounded wings and rounded tail. Head lacking bare patches, but feathers sparse on lores and throat. Bill weak, but with distinct notch; cere small, nostril circular, orbital ring bare. Tarsus slender, with two rows of longitudinal scutes in front; toes covered above with single row of longitudinal scutes. *Milvago* more closely resembles true falcons than the other caracaras.

Unter-Familie Herpetotherinae
Sub-Family Herpetotherinae

Herpetotheres Vieillot 1817

Mittelgroße, waldbewohnende Falken, eulenhaftes Aussehen durch dicken Kopf und große Augen. Flügel ziemlich kurz und gerundet; Schwanz mäßig lang, fächerförmig und stark gerundet. Schnabel stämmig, mit Auskerbung am Unterschnabel und Ausbuchtung am Oberschnabel. Nasenlöcher rund mit knochigem Rand. Zügel mit spärlichen Borsten, Augenring nackt, Augenlider mit starken Borsten. Läufe kurz und stämmig, am unteren Teil nackt. Läufe und Zehen mit kleinen, rauhen, meist hexagonalen Schuppen bedeckt, Zehenunterseite rauh mit einigen kleinen Dornen.

Medium-sized, forest loving falcons; owlish appearance due to large eyes and head. Wings rather short, rounded; tail moderately long, fan-shaped, strongly rounded. Bill stout, notched on lower, curved on upper mandible; nostrils circular with bony margin. Lores densely bristled, patch round eye bare, eyelids with strong bristles. Legs rather short, stout, bare on lower part. Tarsi and toes covered with small, rough, hexagonal scales, undersurface of toes rough, with some small spicules.

Unter-Familie Micrasturinae
Sub-Family Micrasturinae

Micrastur Gray 1841

Kleine bis mittelgroße, leichtgebaute Waldfalken. Flügel kurz, stark gerundet. Schwanz lang bis sehr lang, gerundet oder abgestuft. Schnabel kräftig, stark gebogen, falkenähnlich, jedoch ohne Zahn. Nasenlöcher rundlich, mit knochigen Zäpfchen. Zügel und Augenring nackt, mit wenigen Borsten bedeckt. Oberkopffedern wenig zugespitzt; Federn der Ohrgegend bilden leichten Schleier; Ohröffnung groß. Läufe lang und kräftig. Zehen lang, habichtsähnlich, aber mit unregelmäßigen, hexagonalen Schuppen bedeckt. Am Boden schnelle und geschickte Läufer.

Small to medium-sized, lightly-built forest falcons. Wings short, very rounded; tail long to very long, rounded or graduated. Bill stout, strongly curved, falconlike, but not toothed. Nostrils circular with bony tubercle. Lores and orbital ring bare, with some bristles. Crown feathers somewhat pointed; feathers round ear curled, forming a slight ruff; ear opening large. Tarsi long, strong; toes long, resembling *Accipiter* but covered with irregular hexagonal scutes. Runs very fast on ground.

Unter-Familie Falconinae
Sub-Familiy Falconinae

Tribus Polihieracini
Tribe Polihieracini

Spiziapteryx Kaup 1852

Kleine Falken, Flügel gerundet; Schwanz lang, gerundet, etwa 3/4 der Flügellänge; die äußersten Schwanzfedern sind erheblich kürzer als die folgenden. Die angelegten Flügel reichen nicht bis zum Schwanzende. Schnabel ohne Zahn, aber mit deutlicher Ausbuchtung. Nasenlöcher rundlich mit zentralem Zäpfchen; Augenringe nackt. Lauf und Zehen kräftig, der erstere länger als die (sehr kurze) Mittelzehe; Lauf zu einem Viertel befiedert, sonst große hexagonale Schilder auf Vorder- und Rückseite, seitlich mit kleineren Schildchen bedeckt. Gefieder in beiden Geschlechtern annähernd gleich; wahrscheinlich mit *Polihierax* verwandt.

Small falcons, wings rounded; tail long, rounded, about 3/4 of wing length, with outer tail feathers much shorter than central; folded wings do not reach tail-tip. Bill moderately notched, not toothed; nostrils round with central tubercle; orbital rings bare. Tarsi strong, toes strong, first longer than middle (very short); about one-fourth covered with feathers, with large hexagonal scales in front and behind, small on sides. Plumage similar in both sexes; perhaps allied to *Polihierax*.

Polihierax Kaup 1847

Kleine bis sehr kleine „Zwergfalken"; Flügel kurz, ziemlich spitz, Schwanz eckig oder abgestuft. Schnabel deutlich gezahnt, Nasenlöcher rundlich bis oval, ohne Zäpfchen. Lauf im oberen Teil befiedert, sonst mit runden Schuppen bedeckt. Krallen sehr scharf. Geschlechter sind in Gefiederfärbung verschieden, Weibchen mit Kastanienrot.

Small or very small „Pygmy" falcons; wings short, rather pointed, tail square or graduated. Bill distinctly toothed, nostril round to oval without tubercle. Tarsi covered with feathers at top. otherwise with round scales. Talons very sharp. Sexes differ in plumage, females with chestnut.

Microhierax Sharpe 1874

Zwergenhafte Falken; Flügel kurz, aber spitz; Schwanz mässig lang und gerundet. Schnabel kräftig, seitlich leicht zusammengedrückt, mit Doppelzahn. Beine groß und kräftig im Verhältnis zur Körpergröße. Lauf kürzer als Mittelzehe, zur Hälfte etwa befiedert, sonst auf der Vorderseite und auf den Zehen mit breiten Schildchen bedeckt. Immaturkleid ähnlich dem Adultkleid.

Tiny falcons; wings short pointed; tail moderately long, rounded. Bill stout, slightly compressed, double-toothed. Legs long and powerful related to body-size; tarsi shorter than middle-toe, half covered with feathers, in front and on toes covered with broad scutes. Immature plumage resembles adult.

Tribus Falconini
Tribe Falconini

Falco Linnaeus 1758

Kleine bis mittelgroße Greifvögel, mit langen, spitzen Flügeln; Weibchen immer größer als Männchen. Kurzer, kräftiger, stark gekrümmter Oberschnabel mit deutlichem Zahn, passend zu entsprechender Einkerbung am Unterschnabel. Nasenlöcher rund, mit zentralem Zäpfchen. Flügel und Schwanz variieren in Länge, Lauf in Stärke und Länge. Die Gattung bildet einige mehr oder minder deutlich abgegrenzte Gruppen.
(1) Turm- oder Rüttelfalken und Rotfußfalken; hauptsächlich Kleinnager- und Insektenjäger. Schwanz ziemlich lang, gerundet. Lauf an oberer Hälfte befiedert, so lang oder etwas länger als Mittelzehe. Außen- und Innenzehe meist nahezu gleichlang, bei wenigen Arten Doppelzahnung. Hierzu folgende Arten: *tinnunculus, moluccensis, cenchroides, newtoni, punctatus, araea, sparverius*; etwas entfernter sollen die Arten *naumanni, rupicoloides* und *alopex* stehen. Die Arten *ardosiaceus, zoniventris, dickinsoni* und *vespertinus* ähneln in einigem dieser Gruppe, *vespertinus* unterscheidet sich durch deutlicheren Sexualdimorphismus, bei den drei anderen Arten handelt es sich wahrscheinlich um Primitivformen.
(2) Merlinfalken. Mit den Arten *columbarius* und *chicquera*, auf Grund einiger Unterschiede in Form und Verhalten zwischen Rüttel- und Hobbyfalken vermittelnd.
(3) Hobby- oder Baumfalken. Schlanke, langflügelige Vogel- und Insektenjäger (im Fluge); lang- und spitzflügelig, relativ kurzer oder mittellanger Schwanz. Hierher: *subbuteo, cuvieri, severus, longipennis, eleonorae, concolor, rufigularis, femoralis*; wahrscheinlich auch *hypoleuos* und *subniger*. Etwas primitivere Formen vermutet man in den Arten *berigora* und *novaezeelandiae*, mit deutlich längerem Lauf als Mittelzehe. *F. berigora* ist sehr langschwänzig und jagt mehr als alle anderen Falken vom Ansitz aus (Habichtsfalke).

(4) Großfalken. Wie die Baumfalken gute Flieger, aber mit größerer Beute. Lauf etwa zur Hälfte befiedert, kaum so lang wie Mittelzehe. Zehen relativ kürzer und schwächer als die der nächsten Gruppe. Hierzu: *mexicanus, biarmicus, jugger, cherrug* und *rusticolus*.
(5) Wanderfalken und Verwandte. Spezialisten auf fliegende Beute, vor allem Vögel, welche sie durch ‚Binden' in der Luft oder durch ‚zu Boden schlagen' erbeuten. Lauf kräftig, Zehen lang, Außenzehe länger als Innenzehe. Hierher: *peregrinus, pelegrinoides, deiroleucus, fasciinucha* und evtl. die etwas fragwürdige Art *kreyenborgi*.

Small to middle-sized birds of prey with long, pointed wings; females always larger than males. Short, strong, hooked upper mandible with marked tooth, fitting into depression in lower mandible. Nostril round with central tubercle. Wings and tail vary much in length, tarsus in strength and length; the genus subdivides into more or less distinct groups.

(1) Kestrels and Red-footed Falcons; mainly small mammal- and insect-eaters. Tail rather long, rounded. Tarsus feathered on upper half, as long as or slightly longer than middle toe. Outer and inner toes almost equal. Double-toothed in some species. Includes the following species: *tinnunculus, moluccensis, cenchroides, newtoni, punctatus, araea, sparverius*; species *naumanni, rupicoloides* and *alopex* differ somewhat of these. Species *ardosiaceus, zoniventris, dickinsoni* and *vespertinus* somewhat resemble this group; *vespertinus* shows strong sexual dimorphism, the other three possibly are more primitive forms.

(2) Merlins; includes the species *columbarius* and *chicquera*, on grounds of some differences of form and (hunting) habits, intermediate between Kestrels and the Hobby group.

(3) The Hobby Group. Slim, long-winged, mostly hunting insects or birds in flight; long pointed wings, relatively short or medium-long tail. These include: *subbuteo, cuvieri, severus, longipennis, eleonorae, concolor, rufigularis, femoralis*; possibly also *hypoleucos* and *subniger*. Somewhat more primitive members of this group include *berigora* and *novaezeelandiae*, with the tarsus markedly longer than the middle toe. *F. berigora* is also very longtailed and hunts more from perches than other falcons, like an *Accipiter*.

(4) The Great Falcons. Like the Hobby group fine fliers, but taking larger prey. Tarsus about half covered with feathers, almost the same length as middle toe. Toes relatively shorter and weaker than in the next (5) group. These include: *mexicanus, biarmicus, jugger, cherrug* and *rusticolus*.

(5) Peregrine and allies; specialists in hunting flying prey, chiefly birds, caught in the air and carried or struck dead to fall to ground. Tarsus powerful, toes long, outer toe longer than inner toe. These include: *peregrinus, pelegrinoides, deiroleucus, fasciinucha* and doubtfully, the little-known *kreyenborgi*.

Farbtafeln der Greifvögel der Welt

Colourplates of the birds of prey of the world

Aus Platzgründen konnten die ergänzenden Hinweise auf den Farbtafeln nicht alle zweisprachig wiedergegeben werden. Die dazugehörigen Übersetzungen lauten:

In order to save place not all supplementary remarks on the colourplates are reproduced in both languages. The corresponding translations read as follows:

Deutsch	English
Augenfarbe	eyecolour
braun (selten)	brown (rare)
dunkel	dark
erregt	excited
Form	phase
Fortschrittskleid	progressive plumage
gelbbraun	buffy
grau-weiß	grey and white
hell	pale
helläugig	pale-eyed
hellgrau	pale grey
hellrot	pale-rufous
hellrückig	creamy-backed
Jahr	year
Kragen	collar

Deutsch	English
mit weißer Stirn	with white forehead
mittel	intermediate
Nackenband	nape-band
normal	normal
oder gelb	or yellow
rot	red, rufous
rotrückig	red-backed
schwarz	black
südl. Südamerika	southern South-America
Stirn	forehead
Typ	phase, type
Unterseite rotbraun gestreift	rufous barred below
weiß	white
weiß-grau	white and grey
weißkehlig	white throat

Benennung	Nomenclature	Verbreitung	Distribution	Länge Length cm	Flügel Wing mm	Schwanz/Tail mm	Gewicht Weight g	Tarsus mm	Culmen mm () = mit Wachshaut with cere
Cathartes aura (Linnueus, 1758) Truthahngeier	Turkey Vulture								
C. a. septentrionalis Wied. 1839 (brauner als *aura*, vor allem Säume der Flügeldecken)	(browner than *aura*, especially on edges of wing covert)	Östl. Nordamerika (Plains i., W Florida i. S) N des 39. Breitengrades Zugvogel. Winters: Florida, Louisiana	Eastern N America, west to the plains, south to Florida, north of 39° S migrating. Winter: Florida, Louisiana		♂ 518–550 ♀ 527–559	♂ 252–285 ♀ 270–298	1200–2000	68	78
C. a. aura (Linnaeus, 1758) (Habitus ähnl. *ruficollis*, aber etwas brauner im Gefieder)	(similar to *ruficollis*, plumage rather browner)	Westl. Nordamerika (v. S Kanada) südl. bis Costa-Rica, evtl. Panama. Bahamas, Kuba, Insel de Pinos. Auf Hispaniola ausgerottet, auf Puerto Rico eingebürgert	Western N America (from S Canada south to Costa-Rica, possibly W Panama) Extreme S Florida, Bahamas, Cuba, Isle of Pines, Haiti extinct; Puerto Rico introduced	66–76	458–538	253–270 (evtl.unter250)		59	
C. a. ruficollis Spix, 1824 (schwärzer als *aura*, braune Säume fehlen fast vollständig. Gefiederglanz blau u. purpur! Am Hinterkopf gelb.)	(blacker than *aura*, brown edgings reduced or absent, plumage with blue or purplish gloss, yellow bare skin on nape)	Von Panama u. S Amerik. Tiefland bis Nord-Argentinien; Trinidad	From Panama and tropical lowland, South America south to N Argentina, Trinidad		485–530	270			
C. a. jota (Molina, 1782) (dunkler als *aura*, nackte Kopfhaut tiefer rot)	(darker than *aura*, bare skin on head brillant red without yellow)	Andenregion v. Kolumbien südlich, aber auch Küste SW Ecuadors und S Perus, Patagonien, Falkland-Inseln	Andean region from Colombia south, also coastal lowland from S W Ecuador, Peru, Patagonia, Falkland Islands		470–550	295		74	65
Cathartes burrovianus Cassin, 1845 Kleiner Gelbkopfgeier (grüner Gefiederschimmer, bunter Kopf)	Lesser yellow-headed Vulture (plumage more glossed with green, many-coloured head)	Küsten v. Guayana u. Surinam, NW Venezuela, N u. W Kolumbien, Brasilien, Paraguay, Uruguay bis Nord-Argentinien	Coastal region of Mexico, Panama, Guiana and Surinam. NW Venezuela, N and W Colombia, Brazil, Paraguay, Uruguay to N Argentina	56–66	480–515	215–300	950–1550	59–68	70
Cathartes melambrotus Wetmore, 1964 Großer Gelbkopfgeier (Kehle gelb bis orange)	Greater yellow-headed Vulture (throat yellow to orange)	S E Kolumbien, Venezuela (Orinoco Region), Guayana u. Surinam bis E Peru, N E Bolivien u. N Brasilien	S E Colombia, Venezuela (Orinoco region), Guianas and Surinam to E Peru, N E Bolivia and N Brazil	71–81	♂ 488–530 ♀ 510–512	♂ 252–275 ♀ 272–285		68–75	
Coragyps atratus (Bechst. 1793) Rabengeier	Black Vulture								
C. a. atratus (Bechstein, 1793) (Kopf u. Hals schwarz, nicht bunt wie bei *Cathartes*)	(black head and neck, lacks bright colour)	USA – Nord-Mexiko	USA to N Mexico		414–445	172–212		70–83	72
C. a. brasiliensis (Bonaparte, 1850) (Habitus wie *atratus*)	(plumage similar to *atratus*)	Trop. Amerika v. Zentral-Mexiko bis Peru u. Brasilien	Tropical America from Central Mexico to Peru and Brazil	56–66	386–413		1180–1940		
C. a. foetens (Lichtenstein, 1817) (Habitus wie *atratus*)	(plumage similar to *atratus*)	Südl. Teile v. Paraguay, Argentinien u. Chile, im N bis Anden Ecuadors	Southern parts of Paraguay, Argentina and Chile, north to Andes of Ecuador		412–437	213			79–85
Sarcoramphus papa (Linn. 1758) Königsgeier (bunter Kopf u. Hals. Rücken, Flügeldecken u. Unterseite blaßrosa bis blaßgelblich beim Altvogel)	King Vulture (adult with brillantly coloured head and neck; back, wing coverts and under-surface light vinaceous buff to pinkish-white)	Von Zentral-Mexiko südl. bis Nord-Argentinien, Trinidad	From Central Mexico south to N Argentina. Trinidad	76–81	482–508	228–257	3000–3780		53
Gymnogyps californianus (Shaw, 1797) Kaliforn. Kondor (Kopf, Hals bunt, weißgraue Teile an d. Armschwingen)	California Condor (coloured head and neck, greyish-white edges of secondaries)	Kalifornien (Santa Barbara- u. Mittel-Ventura-Bezirk, sowie San Joaquin-Valley, gelegentl. bis Sierra Nevada) Früher v. Sierra Nevada bis Stiller Ozean	California (Santa Barbara and Central Ventura district; San Joaquin Valley and casually Sierra Nevada) Formerly from Sierra Nevada to the Pacific Ocean)	100–116	760–915	380–450	8170–14070	110–140	70–87
Vultur gryphus Linnaeus, 1758 Kondor (♂ mit Kamm. Altvögel mit viel Weiß am Flügel)	Andean Condor (♂ with comb-like caruncle, adult with much ashy-white on upper wingcoverts, secondaries and primaries)	S Amerikanische Anden o. Kordilleren von W Venezuela u. Kolumbien bis zur Magellanstraße u. Feuerland. Aber auch Küsten Perus (Pazifik) u. Küsten v. Argentinien bis Feuerland (Atlantik)	South America. Andes and Cordilleras from W Venezuela and Colombia south to Straits of Magellan and Tierra del Fuego. Occurs also Pacific Coast of Peru and Atlantic Coast of Argentina south to Tierra del Fuego	♂ 96–116 ♀ 94–102?	♂ 800–850 ♀ 785–800	♂ 354–380 ♂ 330–370	♂ 11000–12000 ♀ 9210	♂ 115–120	♂ 69

Plate 1

juv.
Cathartes aura
septentrionalis
adult

Cathartes aura
jota adult

ruficollis
adult

Cathartes
melambrotus
adult

Cathartes burrovianus

adult   juv.

juv.   adult

Coragyps atratus

Sarcoramphus papa
adult

juv.

♂ juv.

♀ juv.

Vultur gryphus

♂ immat.

♀ adult

Vultur gryphus
♂ adult

Gymnogyps californianus

adult   juv.

1973/76
F. Weick

Benennung	Nomenclature	Verbreitung	Distribution	Länge Length cm	Flügel Wing mm	Schwanz/Tail mm	Gewicht Weight g	Tarsus mm	Culmen mm () = mit Wachshaut with cere
Pandion haliaëtus (Linnaeus, 1758) Fischadler	Osprey								
P. h. haliaetus (Linnaeus, 1758) (♂ auf Brust u. Kopf meist dunkler)	(♀ usually rather darker on head and breast)	Europa, N Afrika u. Asien; im Winter in Afrika (bis Kap) u. Indien, Sri Lanka, Malaya, Gr. Sunda-Inseln u. Philippinen	Europe, N Africa and Asia Winter: Africa (south to Cape) India, Sri-Lanka, Malaya, Greater Sunda Islands, Philippines		♂ 450–510 ♀ 470–510	170–240	♂ 1120–1740 ♀ 1208–2050	58–69	30–35
P. h. carolinensis (Gmelin, 1788) (kein braunes Brustband, nur wenige Flecken, Haube weiß, kleiner)	(lacks brown pectoral band, only few spots, white crest, smaller size)	N Amerika, v. NW Alaska, südl. bis Nieder-Kalifornien, östl. bis zur Golfküste der USA	N America, from NW Alaska south to lower California and east to Gulf Coast of the USA	55–61	♂ 462–506 ♀ 488–518				
P. h. ridgwayi (. J. Maynard, 1887 (Brust weiß, Haube m. wenigen Flecken, Hinteraugstreif oft nur undeutlich, kleiner als *carolinensis*)	(still whiter on breast, some spots on crest, streak behind eye often missing or slight smaller than in *carolinensis*)	Bahamas, Honduras u. Kuba	Bahamas, Honduras, Cuba		♂ 433–483 ♀ 455–495				
P. h. cristatus (Vieillot, 1816) (hinter dem Auge helleres Band, nur wenige Flecken auf d. Haube)	(clear white head, with a pale band behind eye, sometime few spots on crest)	Australien, südl. bis 20° S und Tasmanien	Australia south to 20° S, Tasmania		♂ 426–431 ♀ 425–490				
P. h. melvillensis Mathews, 1912 (Haube weiß, Band hinter d. Auge noch heller als bei *cristatus*; noch kleiner als *cristatus*)	(white crest, band behind eye still paler, smaller than *cristatus*)	Australien, nördl. des 20° S u. die Inseln i. N bis zu den Philippinen, i. E bis Salomonen u. i. W bis Sumatra	Australia north of 20° S, and islands north to Philippines east to Solomons, west to Sumatra		♂ 384–428 ♀ 410–464	170–193		49–58	30,5
Sagittarius serpentarius (Miller, 1779) Sekretär	Secretary Bird								
(♂ oft etwas heller, mit längeren Schopffedern u. längerem Stoß als ♀) (Die braune Färbung bei Jungvögeln ist atypisch)	(♂ often rather paler, with longer crest and tail than ♀) (the brownish immature-variant is atypical)	Afrika, südl. d. Sahara, v. Senegal bis Somaliland u. i. S bis zum Kap	Africa south of Sahara, from Senegal to Somalia and south to Cape Province	112–127	♂ 630–675 ♀ 610–660	♂ 670–854 ♀ 570–705	♂ 3809 ♀ 3405	278–342	45–54

Plate 2

Pandion h. haliaëtus juv. →

Pandion h. cristatus juv. adult

Pandion h. haliaëtus adult ♀

♂

P. h. melvillensis adult

Pandion h. carolinensis adult

Pandion h. ridgwayi adult

Sagittarius serpentarius ♂ adult

♀ adult

♂ adult erregt

Sagittarius serpentarius immat. normal

braun (selten)

F. Weick

Benennung	Nomenclature	Verbreitung	Distribution	Länge Length cm	Flügel Wing mm	Schwanz/Tail mm	Gewicht Weight g	Tarsus mm	Culmen mm () = mit Wachshaut with cere
Aviceda cuculoides Swainson, 1837 Afrikakuckucksaar (brauner Hinterkopffleck, vor allem bei gespreiztem Schopf sichtbar)	African-Cuckoo, Falcon (chestnut nape-patch, conspicuous mainly when crest erected)								
A. c. cuculoides Swainson, 1837 (graue Brust kontrastiert mit weiß-braun gespertem Bauch.)	(grey breast contrasting with chestnut and white barring of belly)	West-Afrika (Sierra Leone bis Kamerun)	W Africa (Sierra Leone to Cameroon)	38–41	289–295	186		30–35	30
A. c. verreauxi Lafresnaye, 1846 (Habitus, wie cuculoides, aber größer)	(plumage similar to cuculoides, but larger)	Angola, Zaire, Uganda bis Kap-Provinz u. Natal.	Angola, Zaire, Uganda, Maputo to Natal, Cape Province		293–328	200–207		35–38	30–32
Aviceda madagascariensis (A. Smith, 1834) Madagaskarkuckucksaar (von Buteo brachypterus durch Haube u. ausgebuchteten Schwanz unterschieden)	Madagascar Cuckoo Falcon (distinguishable from Buteo brachypterus by crest and a notched tail)	Östl. Madagaskar von 0–2000 ü. M.	Eastern Madagascar (from sea level to 6000 feet)	40–45	315–331	197–230		35–42	29–31
Aviceda jerdoni (Blyth, 1842) Schopfkuckucksaar	Jerdon's Baza								
A. j. jerdoni (Blyth, 1842) (♂ m. dunklerem Brustband u. Kopfgefieder als ♀)	(♂ with darker head and chestband than ♀!)	N Indien, Burma, Thailand, Malaya, Sumatra	North-India, Burma, Thailand, Malayan Peninsula, Sumatra		323–332	228–240			35
A. j. ceylonensis (Legge, 1876) (Habitus wie jerdoni, nur etwas kleiner u. heller)	(similar to jerdoni, but rather smaller and paler!)	Sri Lanka u. SW Indien	Sri Lanka and S W India	43–48	297–305	190			38
A. j. borneensis (Brüggemann, 1876) (Kopf- u. Halsseiten rotbraun)	(head and sides of neck rufous)	Borneo	Borneo	♂ 291–					26
A. j. magnirostris (Kaup, 1847) (Kopfseiten, Kehle, Oberbrust grau)	(sides of head, throat and chest grey)	Philippinen (Luzon, Mindanao)	Philippines (Luzon, Mindanao)	♂ 292–311 ♀ 298–324			♂ 353		31–38
A. j. celebensis (Schlegel, 1873) (Kopf, Brust, Nacken mehr rotbraun als borneensis)	(still more rufous on head, chest and nape than borneensis)	Sulawesi, Banggai, Sula-Inseln	Sulawesi, Banggai, Sula Islands	280–305		200			32
Aviceda subcristata (Gould, 1838) Haubenkuckucksaar	Crested Baza								
A. s. subcristata (Gould, 1838) (Unterseitenbänderung kann auch mehr graubraun sein)	(barring of lower surface also may be more greybrown)	Australien (haupts. Küstennähe)	Australia (chiefly near coasts)	♂ 325–348 ♀ 335–358	♂ 195 ♀ 225			37	31
A. s. njikena Condon & Amadon, 1954 (viel dunkler auf Ober- u. Unterseite als subcristata)	(much darker above and below than subcristata)	NW Australien	N W Australia	♂ 310 ♀ 320–348					
A. s. megala (Stresemann, 1913) (O.-Seite dunkler, U.-Seite weniger rotbraun überflogen als bei subcristata)	(darker upper-surface, below less washed with rufous than subcristata)	E Neuguinea, Japen, Fergusson- u. Goodenough-Inseln	E New Guinea, Japen, Fergusson and Goodenough Islands	♂ 285–316 ♀ 314–334					
A. s. stenozona (Gray, 1858) (Habitus ähnlich subcristata, viel kleiner)	(plumage resembles subcristata, much smaller)	W Neuguinea, Aru, Misool- u. Salawati-Inseln	W New Guinea, Aru, Misol, Salawati Islands	♂ 290–303 ♀ 296–314					
A. s. waigeuensis Mayr, 1940 (O.-Seite heller, Unterseite weniger deutlich gebändert als bei subcristata)	(paler upper-surface, below less distinctly barred than subcristata)	Waigeo	Waigeu	38–43	♂ 308 ♀ 314–319				
A. s. gurneyi (Ramsey, 1882) (Unterseite fast fleckenlos)	(under-surface nearly unmarked or with much reduced barring)	Salomonen (San Cristobal, Ugi, Santa Anna, Malaita, Guadalcanar)	Solomon Islands (San Cristobal, Ugi, Santa Anna, Malaita, Guadalcanal)	♂ 288–304 ♀ 301–317	♂ 175–185 ♀ 185–197				
A. s. robusta Mayr, 1945 (Habitus ähnl. gurneyi, U.-Seite aber dichter gebändert u. mehr rostfarben überflogen)	(like gurneyi, more heavily barred below, with stronger rufous wash)	Salomonen (Choiseul u. Isabel)	Solomon Islands (Choiseul und Ysabel)	♂ 300–322 ♀ 309–324	♂ 179–189 ♀ 191–205	♂ 300–325 ♀ 306–411			
A. s. proxima Mayr, 1945 (Habitus ähnlich robusta, kleiner)	(similar to robusta, but smaller)	Salomonen (Bougainville und Shortland-Inseln)	Solomon Islands (Bougainville and Shortland Islands)	290–297	♂ 174–181 ♀ 182–188				
A. s. bismarkii (Sharpe, 1888) (Habitus: groß u. dunkel, O.-Rücken schiefergrau, U.-Seite dicht schwarz gebändert, U.-Schwanzdecken rostfarben)	(large size and darker colour, slaty on upperback, heavily barred blackish below, rufous abdomen)	Neubritannien, Neuirland, Neuhannover (Lavongai)	New Britain, New Ireland, New Hanover (Lavongai?)	♂ 299–320 ♀ 306–329	♂ 169–195 ♀ 185–203	♂ 273–310 ♀ 320–411			
A. s. coultasi Mayr 1945 (Habitus ähnl. bismarckii, Oberbrust heller, weniger dicht gebändert)	(similar to bismarcki, paler chest and less heavily barred)	Admiralty-Inseln (Manus)	Admiralty Islands (Manus)	♂ 304–307 ♀ 317	♂ 176, 178 ♀ 184				
A. s. obscura Junge, 1956 (Habitus dunkler als angrenzende Rassen, ähnlich njikena)	(darker plumage than adjacent races, similar njikena)	Insel Biak	Biak Island	♂ 278–294 ♀ 287–300					
A. s. stresemanni (Siebers, 1930) (ähnl. subcristata, aber Unterseite dunkler gebändert u. U.-Schwanzdecken mehr rostbraun)	(similar to subcristata, but blacker barring below, more rufous under tail coverts)	Insel Buru	Buru Island	♂ 302–308 ♀ 316–325					
A. s. rufa (Schlegel, 1866) (Roter als jede andere Rasse)	(much redder than any other race!)	Obi u. N Molukken	Obi and N Moluccas	310–317					
A. s. reinwardtii (Müller u. Schlegel, 1843) (Habitus: Oberseite dunkel, U.-Seite dicht gebändert, ähnlich njikena)	(similar njikena, dark above, heavily barred below)	Ceram, Amboina, Haruku	Ceram, Amboina, Haruku	285–307	184			32	31
A. s. pallida (Stresemann, 1913) (Oberseite u. Brust sehr hell)	(very pale upper-surface and chest)	Kei- u. Goram Inseln	Kei and Goram Islands	♂ 285–295 ♀ 300–319					
A. s. timorlaoensis (Meyer, 1893) (Habitus: zieml. hell, U.-Seite stark rostfarben, auch graue Brust rot überflogen)	(rather pale above, below strongly rufous; chest with rufous wash)	Kleine Sunda-Inseln (v. Lombok bis Timor, Damar, Barbar, Timorlaut u. d. Tukang-Besi-Inseln)	Lesser Sunda Islands (from Lombok east to Timor, Damar, Babar, Timorlaut and Tukang Besi Islands)	♂ 295–306 ♀ 316–325					
Aviceda leuphotes (Dumont, 1820) Zwergschopfaar	Black Baza								
A. l. leuphotes (Dumont, 1820) (rotbraun an Kopf u. U.-Seite)	(chestnut on head and under-surface)	N u. SW Indien	N and S W India	28–33	227–243	130–145		26–27	20–22
A. l. syama (Hodgson, 1836) (nur wenig Braun auf der Bauchgegend, am Kopf fehlend)	(much less chestnut on under surface, lacking on head)	Burma, Assam bis Nepal	Burma, Assam to Nepal		221–246	130–149		26–30	20–23
Leptodon cayanensis (Latham, 1790) Cayennemilan	Grey headed o. Cayenne Kite								
Grey headed o. Cayenne Kite (L. forbesi ist nur Variante des Immaturkleides)	(L. forbesi is only a variant of immature plumage)	Zentrales E Mexiko, südl. bis E Brasilien, N Argentinien, Paraguay u. S Brasilien. Trinidad	Central and E Mexico, south E and S Brazil, N Argentina, Paraguay. Trinidad	43–51	♂ 290–338 ♀ 303–365	♂ 208–250 ♀ 220–263	♂ 415–455 ♀ 416–474 (1♀ 605)	46–54	
Chondrohierax uncinatus (Temminck, 1822) Hakenweih, Langschnabelweih	Hook-billed Kite								
Ch. u. uncinatus (Temminck, 1822) (Durch große Variationsbreite des Gefieders sind leicht Verwechslungen mit ähnl. Greifvögeln möglich)	(because of the great variation in plumage, confusion with similar Birds of Prey is possible)	Mittelamerika (Süd-Mexiko) bis E Peru, Bolivien, N Argentinien, Paraguay. Trinidad	Central-America (S Mexico) to E Peru, Bolivia, N Argentina, Paraguay, Trinidad	♂ 265–301 ♀ 268–321	♂ 173–210 ♀ 191–228	♂ 247–274 ♀ 235–300	31–37	40–64
Ch. u. aquilonis Friedm. 1934 (Oberseite etwas dunkler)	(somewhat darker above than uncinatus)	Mexiko, S Texas (1 ×)	Mexico, Texas (1 ×)	♂ 291 ♀ 293					
Ch. u. mirus Friedmann, 1934 (Habitus: ♂ an Unterseite keine graubraunen Binden u. Spitzenflecke ♀ an Unterseite lohfarbene Querbinden)	(♂ with no greyish edges or ventral barring, ♀ more tawny below)	Insel Grenada	Grenada Island	40–46	3 ♂ 250–265 2 ♀ 269, 270				
Ch. u. wilsonii (Cassin, 1847) (Schnabel stärker u. gelb, Kragen auf d. Rücken deutlich gespert)	(rather stronger and yellow bill, barred collar)	E Kuba (selten)	E Cuba (rare)	2 ♂ 240, 244 ♀ 250–262	195			53

Plate 3

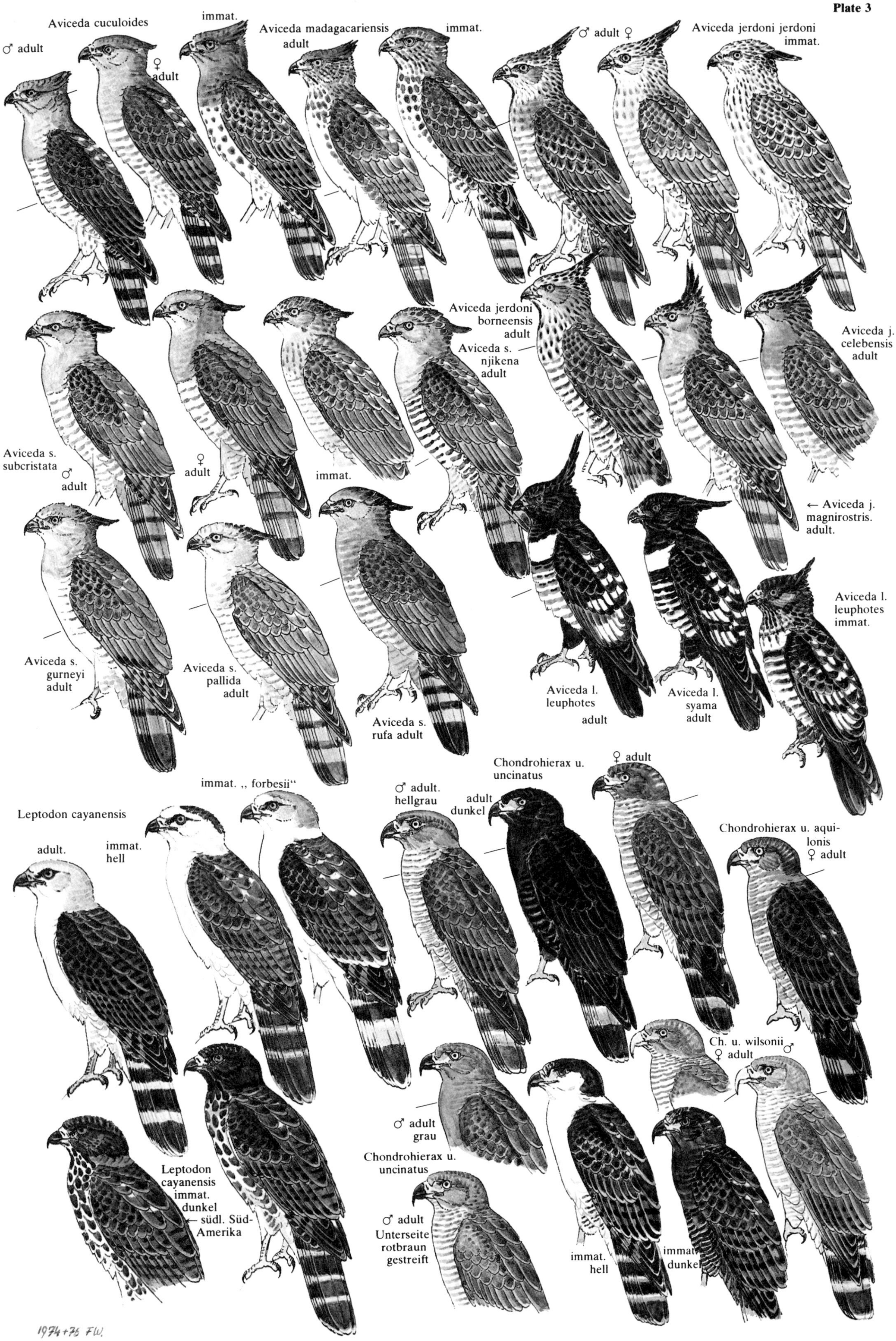

Aviceda cuculoides

♂ adult

immat.

Aviceda madagacariensis
adult

immat.

♂ adult ♀

Aviceda jerdoni jerdoni
immat.

♀ adult

Aviceda jerdoni
borneensis
adult

Aviceda s.
njikena
adult

Aviceda j.
celebensis
adult

Aviceda s.
subcristata
♂
adult

♀
adult

immat.

← Aviceda j.
magnirostris.
adult.

Aviceda s.
gurneyi
adult

Aviceda s.
pallida
adult

Aviceda s.
rufa adult

Aviceda l.
leuphotes
adult

Aviceda l.
syama
adult

Aviceda l.
leuphotes
immat.

immat. „forbesii"

♂ adult.
hellgrau

adult
dunkel

Chondrohierax u.
uncinatus

♀ adult

Chondrohierax u. aqui-
lonis
♀ adult

Leptodon cayanensis

adult.

immat.
hell

Ch. u. wilsonii ♂
♀ adult

Leptodon
cayanensis
immat.
dunkel
← südl. Süd-
Amerika

♂ adult
grau

Chondrohierax u.
uncinatus

♂ adult
Unterseite
rotbraun
gestreift

immat.
hell

immat.
dunkel

1974+75 FW.

Benennung	Nomenclature	Verbreitung	Distribution	Länge Length cm	Flügel Wing mm	Schwanz/Tail mm	Gewicht Weight g	Tarsus mm	Culmen mm () = mit Wachshaut with cere
Henicopernis longicauda (Garnot, 1828) Papuawespenbussard (bei Adultv. nur 3 sichtbare helle Schwanzbinden)	Long-tailed Honey-Buzzard (in adult only three visible light tail bars)	Neuguinea, sowie umliegende Inseln: Biak, Batanta, Salawati, Misool, Japen, Aru	New Guinea, off lying islands: Biak, Batanta, Salawati, Misol, Japen, Aru	51–56	331–439 (kleine Maße – Inselvögel)	290–365	♂ 447– ♀ 730	50–58	22,5 (35)
Henicopernis infuscata Gurney 1882 Schwarzer Wespenbussard (Immaturvögel ähnl. Alterskleid)	Black Honey-Buzzard (immature birds differ little from adults)	Neubritannien	New Britain Island	48–51	340–358	250–265		53–57	
Pernis apivorus (Linnaeus, 1758) Wespenbussard	Honey-Buzzard								
Pernis a. apivorus (Linn. 1758) (keine Haube, ♂ am Kopf grauer ♀ an Oberseite mehr braun statt graubraun, Schwanzzeichnung)	(crestless, ♂ on forehead, lores and around eye greyer than ♀. Above female more brown than greyish-brown. Tail-banding.)	Europa und N Asien im N bis 63° N, im S bis Spanien, Portugal, Italien, Griechenland, Kl. Asien; im E bis W Sibirien, Surgut, Tobolsk, Novosibirsk. Winter: bis S Afrika (Natal)	Europe and N Asia as far north about 63° N, as far south to Spain, Portugal, Italy, Greece, Asia Minor; in E as far as western Siberia, Surgut, Tobolsk, Novosibirsk. Wintering: S Africa (Natal)		♂ 370–441 ♀ 372–447 Europa 395–475 W-Sibirien	♂ 210–276 ♀ 240–269 Europa 248–270 W-Sibirien	♂ 440–800 ♀ 625–1050	46,5–55	19–23
Pernis a. orientalis Taczanowski, 1891 (meist heller an Ober- u. Unterseite als apivorus, schwarzer Kehllatz. Stärkere Fänge. Meist ohne Haube)	(paler above and below in adult than apivorus, black gorget across throat. Feet stronger. Most individuals lack a crest.)	E Sibirien, N China, Mandschurei, Korea, Japan Winter: Burma, S E Asien, Taiwan, Philippinen, Borneo, Java, Sumatra	E Siberia, N China, Manchuria, Korea, Japan Migrant in Winter to Burma, SE Asia, Taiwan, Philippines, Borneo, Java, Sumatra		♂ 414–475 ♀ 413–495	242–290	♂ 819–1180 ♀ 950–1490	50–60	23–26
P. a. ruficollis Lesson, 1830 (kürzere Flügelspitze als orientalis. Am Hals mehr rostfarben. Haube kurz oder fehlend)	(length of wing tip proportionaly shorter than in orientalis. More rufous on neck. Crest short or absent)	Indien, Sri Lanka, Assam, Burma, N-Thailand, Jünnan	India, Sri Lanka, Assam, Burma, N Thailand, Yunnan	51–61	♂ 363–417 ♀ 388–445	♂ 245–262 ♀ 250–290		♂ 48–57 ♀ 50–60	(36–42)
P. a. torquatus Lesson, 1831 (noch bunter als ruficollis, purpurner Schimmer an Oberseite, Schwanzbänderung im Immaturkleid ähnelt dem Adultkleid. Haube bis 64 mm)	(more richly coloured than ruficollis purplish gloss above, Tail-banding in immature like adult plumage. Crest about 64 mm)	Malaya, Thailand, Sumatra, Borneo	Malaya, Thailand, Sumatra, Borneo		398–455				
P. a. ptilorhyncus (Temminck, 1821) (weniger gebändert als torquatus. Haube 64–100 mm)	(below more uniformly coloured, less barred than in torquatus. Crest 64–100 mm)	Java	Java		♂ 380–390 ♀ 405–418	241–263		44–49	30–36
P. a. palawanensis Stresemann, 1940 (ähnl. torquatus, aber Haube nur 30–35 mm)	(similar to torquatus but crest only 30–35 mm)	Palawan	Palawan		♂ 397				
P. a. philippensis Mayr, 1939 (ähnl. hell wie orientalis, aber mit größerem Schnabel u. relat. längerem Schwanz. Ohne Haube	(paler than other island-forms, similar to orientalis but with a larger bill and relatively longer tail. Crestless)	Philippinen (Mindanao, Cebu u. Luzon)	Philippines (Mindanao, Cebu and Luzon)		415–436	275–289			
Pernis celebensis Walden, 1872 Malaienwespenbussard	Barred Honey Buzzard								
P. c. celebensis Walden, 1872 (kräftige, schwarze Unterseitenbänderung, ohne Haube)	(strongly, barred black below, crestless)	Sulawesi, Muna u. Peling Ins.	Sulawesi, Muna and Peling Islands		♂ 348–374 ♀ 365–392	245–283		45–55	
P. c. steerei W. L. Sclater, 1919 (Unterseite fahler gebändert als celebensis. Haube bis 70 mm)	(barring below paler than in celebensis. Crest about 70 mm)	Philippinen, m. Ausnahme von Palawan	Philippines, not Palawan	51–56					
Elanoides forficatus (Linnaeus, 1758) Schwalbenweih	Swallow-tailed Kite								
E. f. forficatus (Linn. 1758) (Adultvogel mit kastanienrotem bis purpurnem Glanz auf Schultern u. Oberrücken)	(adult with maroon or purplish gloss on shoulders and upper-back)	Südl. USA bis N Mexiko	Southern USA to N Mexico	60–63	♂ 418–436 ♀ 436–445	♂ 317–343 ♀ 343–368	500	33	
E. f. yetapa (Vieillot, 1818) (Adultvogel mit grünl. Glanz auf Schultern u. Oberrücken)	(adult with greenish gloss on shoulders and upper-back)	S Mexiko bis Bolivien, Paraguay, S Brasilien u. NE Argentinien	S Mexico to Bolivia, Paraguay, S Brazil and N E Argentina		383–447	320–330		♂ 390–407 ♀ 372–435	
Machaerhamphus alcinus Westermann, 1851 Fledermausaar	Bat Hawk, Pern								
M. a. alcinus Westermann, 1851 (sehr dunkel m. wenig Weiß an Kehle, über u. unter d. Auge)	(whole plumage very dark, except some white on throat, above and below eye)	Südl. Tenasserim, Malaya, Sumatra, Borneo	S Tenasserim, Malaya, Sumatra, Borneo	41–47	371–412	171–177 (198 Swann)		58–63	(34)
M. a. papuanus Mayr, 1940 (kurzer Schopf, weißes Halsband, wenig Weiß auf Unterbauch)	(short crest, white nuchal collar, some white on abdomen)	SE Neuguinea	SE New-Guinea		♂ 338–348 ♀ 374–378	♂ 171		♂ 58	♂ 20
M. a. anderssoni (Gurney, 1865) (brauner u. mehr Weiß auf Kehle, Brust u. Nacken als alcinus)	(generally browner with more white on throat, upper-breast and nape than in alcinus)	W u. E Afrika, südl. Sahara, im S bis Damaraland u. Natal, Madagaskar	W and E Africa, south of Sahara, south to Damaraland and Natal. Madagascar		♂ 323–338 ♀ 336–362	154–188		57–64	25
Gampsonyx swainsonii Vigors, 1825 Perlaar	Pearl Kite								
G. s. leonae Chubb, 1918 (klein, kontrastreiches Gefieder)	(small size and contrasting plumage are distinctive for field indentification)	Nicaragua u. S Amerika südl. bis Amazonas	Nicaragua and South America, south to the Amazon		♂ 141–154 ♀ 150–163	♂ 94–98 ♀ 95–102	♂ 94	28–32	13
G. s. swainsonii Vigors, 1825 (Flanken weiß)	(sides white, without rufous wash)	S Amerika südl. Amazonas bis Paraguay u. N Argentinien	South America, south of Amazon to Paraguay and N Argentina	20–23	♂ 145–158 ♀ 158–169	♂ 90–95 ♀ –100		29	
G. s. magnus Chubb, 1918 (Habitus wie leonae, aber größer)	(like leonae, but larger)	Küstengebiet Perus u. Ecuadors, W Bolivien	Coastal N Peru, Ecuador and W Bolivia		♂ 170–175 ♀ 174–178	♂ 104–108 ♀ –115		32	14
Elanus leucurus (Vieillot, 1818) Weißschwanzgleitaar	White-tailed Kite								
E. l. majusculus Bangs & Penard 1920 (Habitus wie leucurus, aber größer)	(resembles leucurus, but larger)	USA und E Mexiko	USA and E Mexico	34–41	302–328	174–186		36–39	
E. l. leucurus (Vieillot, 1818) (kein schwarzer Hinteraugfleck)	(no black spot behind eye)	S Amerika von Kolumbien, Venezuela bis Paraguay, Uruguay u. N Argentinien	South-America, from Colombia, Venezuela to Paraguay, Uruguay and N Argentina		292–308	151–175		♂ 250, 297 ♀ 307	35
Elanus caeruleus (Desfontaines, 1789) Gleitaar	Black-shouldered Kite								
E. c. caeruleus (Desfont. 1789) (Brustseiten u. Flanken grau überflogen. Flügelunterseite mit schwarzen oder grauen Handschwingen)	(sides of breast and flanks with grey wash. Under wing with black or greyish primaries)	Portugal, Afrika (NW Afrika, Arabien u. Afrika südl. Sahara), Süd-Asien	Portugal, Africa (NW Africa, Arabia and Africa south of Sahara). S Asia		♂ 255–280 ♀ 258–290	♂ 110–129 ♀ 100–135	♂ 232,5 ♀ 235	♂ 30–37 ♀ 32–40	15,5–18 16–18,5
E. c. sumatranus Salomonsen, 1953 (große schiefergraue Flecke auf Unterflügeldecken)	(large, slate grey spots on underwing coverts)	Sumatra	Sumatra	28–35	300–306				
E. c. hypoleucus Gould, 1859 (reinweiße Brustseiten u. Flanken, Flügelunterseite mit schwarzen oder hellen Innenfahnen der Handschwingen)	(clear white sides of breast and flanks. Underwing with black or light inner web of primaries)	Java, Lombok, Sumba, Borneo, Sulawesi, Sulu-Inseln, Kalao u. Philippinen	Java, Lombok, Sumba, Borneo, Sulawesi, Sulu Islands, Kalao and Philippines		289–303	138–152		36–38,5	19–20
E. c. wahgiensis Mayr & Gilliard, 1954 (ähnl. hypoleucus, aber mit grauen Brustseiten, Handschwingen auf Unterseite m. schwarzer Innenfahne)	(similar to hypoleucus but with grey wash on sides of breast primaries below black on inner web)	Hochland von E u. Zentral-Neuguinea	Highlands of East and Central New Guinea		♂ 275 ♀ 297	♂ 126			
Elanus notatus Gould, 1838 Schwarzschultergleitaar (auf Rücken u. Flügel mehr Silberweiß als scriptus)	Australian Black-shouldered Kite (back and wings more silverwhite coloured than in scriptus)	Australien (ohne Tasmanien)	Australia (except Tasmania)	33–35	♂ 280–302 ♀ 280–310	♂ 142–153 ♀ 142–154	250–270	36–39 (45)	
Elanus scriptus Gould, 1842 Schwarzachselgleitaar (Kopf weißer, Rücken u. Flügel mehr bräunlichgrau als bei notatus)	Letter-winged Kite (more whitish on head, back and wing more brownish-grey than in notatus)	Zentral- u. S Australien, Queensland	Central- and South-Australia and Queensland	30–35	♂ 292–296 ♀ 302–313	♂ 146–150 ♀ 156–165		33–37	
Chelictinia riocourii (Vieillot, 1822) Schwalbengleitaar (schlank, grau-weiße Färbung, langer Gabelschwanz bei Altvogel)	African Swallow-tailed Kite (slim, greyish-white, with deeply forked tail in adult)	Afrika, von Senegal u. Gambia bis N-Kenia. In W Afrika Zugvogel	Africa from Senegal and Gambia to N Kenya. Seasonal migrant in West Africa	36–38	♂ 225–246 ♀ 227–254	Außenfeder 170–216 Innenfeder 92–100		28–33	16

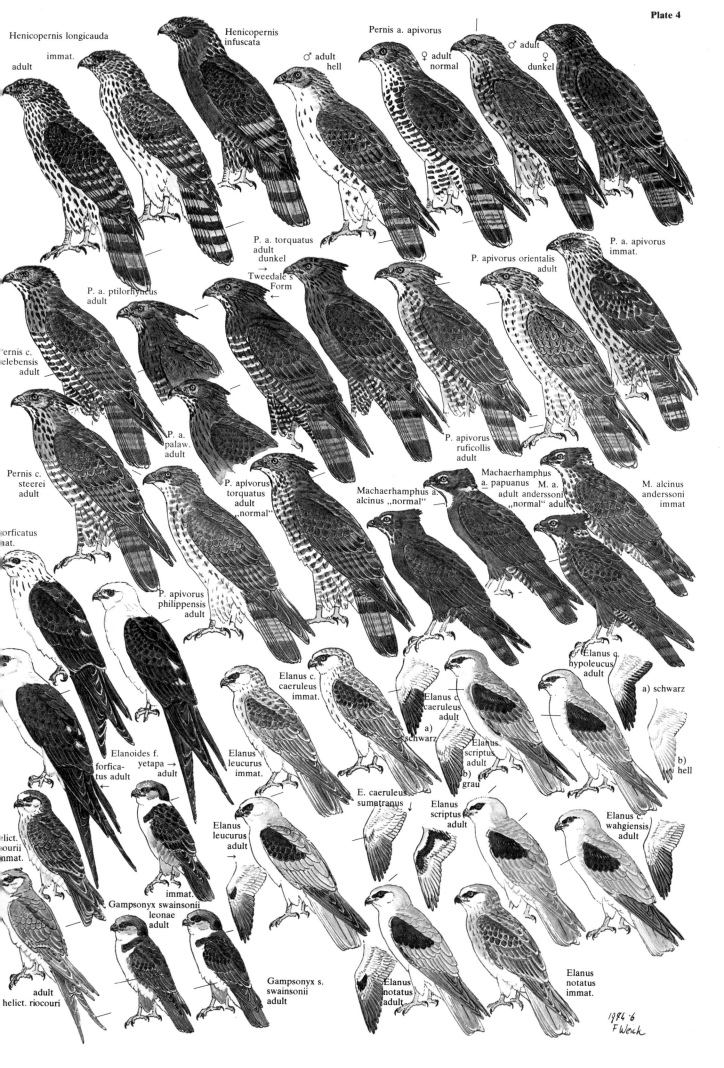

Plate 4

Henicopernis longicauda
immat.
adult

Henicopernis infuscata

♂ adult hell

Pernis a. apivorus
♀ adult normal
♂ adult
♀ adult dunkel

P. a. ptilorhyncus adult

P. a. torquatus adult dunkel
→ Tweedale's Form ←

P. apivorus orientalis adult

P. a. apivorus immat.

Pernis c. celebensis adult

Pernis c. steerei adult

P. a. palaw. adult

P. apivorus ruficollis adult

P. apivorus torquatus adult „normal"

Machaerhamphus a. alcinus „normal"

Machaerhamphus a. papuanus adult anderssoni „normal" adult

M. a. alcinus anderssoni immat

M. alcinus anderssoni immat

forficatus nat.

P. apivorus philippensis adult

Elanus c. hypoleucus adult

a) schwarz

lict. ourii nmat.

Elanoides f. forficatus adult ←

yetapa → adult

Elanus c. caeruleus immat.

Elanus c. caeruleus adult
a) schwarz

Elanus scriptus adult
b) grau

b) hell

Elanus leucurus immat.

E. caeruleus sumatranus ↓

Elanus scriptus adult

Elanus c. wahgiensis adult

adult helict. riocouri

Gampsonyx swainsonii leonae adult

Elanus leucurus adult →

immat.

Gampsonyx s. swainsonii adult

Elanus notatus adult

Elanus notatus immat.

1986·6
F Weick

Tafel 5

Benennung	Nomenclature	Verbreitung	Distribution	Länge Length cm	Flügel Wing mm	Schwanz/Tail mm	Gewicht Weight g	Tarsus mm	Culmen mm () = mit Wachshaut with cere
Rostrhamus sociabilis (Vieillot, 1817) Schneckenmilan	Everglade o. Snail Kite								
R. s. plumbeus Ridgway, 1874 (Habitus: wie *sociabilis*, wenig größer)	(resembles *sociabilis*, slightly larger)	Everglade-Sümpfe v. Florida. Selten, fast ausgerottet	Everglades of Florida, rare, nearly extinct		♂ 340–368 ♀ 345–373	170–193		51–57	(30.4–30.9)
R. s. levis Friedmann, 1933 (Habitus: wie *sociabilis*, größer)	(resembles *sociabilis*, larger)	Kuba u. Insel de Pinos	Cuba, Isle of Pines	35–42	350–371				25–26 (33–35.5)
R. s. major Nelson & Goldmann, 1933 (Habitus wie *sociabilis*, deutlich größer, besonders d. Oberschnabel)	(resembles *sociabilis*, distinctly larger, with longer bill)	E Mexiko, N Guatemala	East-Mexico and N Guatemala		365–382	198			29.5–33
R. s. sociabilis (Vieillot, 1817) (In allen Kleidern weiße, breite Stoßbinde)	(rump and base of tail white in all plumages)	Nicaragua bis Uruguay und N Argentinien	Nicaragua to Uruguay and N Argentina		325–350	200	♂ 304–385 ♀ 384, 413	50	24–26,5 (31–33)
Rostrhamus hamatus (Temminck, 1821) Schlankschnabelmilan	Slender-billed Kite								
(Adultvogel Schwanz ungebändert, Immaturvogel Schwanz mit weißen Binden)	(tail of adult uniform, Immature showing some white tailband)	Lokale Verbreitung: Surinam, Venezuela, Kolumbien, W E Peru, Brasilien (Amazonas) E Panama?	Local but common in Surinam, Venezuela, Colombia, W E Peru, Brazil (Amazon), E Panama?	34–38	276–288 (310 Swann)	125–142 (bis170Swann)	♂ 377–448 ♀ 367–485	41–46 (51 Swann)	
Harpagus bidentatus (Latham, 1790) Doppelzahnweih, Zwischenweih	Double-toothed Kite								
H. b. fasciatus Lawrenze, 1868 (Unterseite deutlicher gebändert als bei *bidentatus*)	(more distinctly barred below than *bidentatus*)	S Mexiko bis W Kolumbien und Ecuador, Panama	S Mexico to W Colombia, Ecuador, Panama		♂ 198–210 ♀ 222–226	141–158	♂ 175–198 ♀ 190–229	41–45	
H. b. bidentatus (Latham, 1790) (Unterseitenfarben verwaschener)	(below less clearly barred, markings more washed with olive-grey and amberbrown)	Guayana, Venezuela, E u. Z Peru, E Bolivien, Brasilien (Amazonas), Trinidad	Guianas, Venezuela, E and Central Peru, E Bolivia, Brazil (Amazon), Trinidad	30–36	♂ 192–222 ♀ 204–232	♂ 158– ♀ 170	♂ 161–185 ♀ 196–207	1 ♂ 37 1 ♀ 40	22
Harpagus diodon (Temminck, 1823) Braunschenkelweih	Rufous-thighed Kite								
(Unterseite bei Adultvogel licht grau)	(adult with pale-grey under-surface)	Guayana, Surinam, E Brasilien, N Paraguay, N Argentinien	Guiana, Surinam, E Brazil, N Paraguay, N Argentina	30–36	♂ 200–210 ♀ 210–220	135–160		37–40	20
Ictinia plumbea (Gmelin, 1788) Grauschwebeweih	Plumbeous Kite								
(Flügelspitzen überragen d. Schwanz)	(folded wings at rest exceed tail-tip)	Tropen d. Neuen Welt, Guayana, Venezuela, Kolumbien, Ecuador, Peru, S bis Bolivien, Paraguay, Brasilien, N Argentinien (Sommer: S Mexiko-Panama)	Tropical zone of New World, Guianas, Venezuela, Colombia, Ecuador, Peru, south to Bolivia, Paraguay, Brazil, N Argentina. Summer: S Mexico to Panama	36–38	♂ 270–313 ♀ 274–321	123–167	♂ 190–267 ♀ 232–280	34–43	22
Ictinia misisippiensis (Wilson, 1811) Mississippi- o. Schwebeweih	Mississippi Kite								
(Flügelspitzen erreichen das Schwanzende)	(folded wings at rest do not exceed tail-tip)	Z u. S USA. Winter: Florida, Mexiko, Guatemala, Costa Rica (selten), Paraguay, Argentinien	Central and southern USA. Winter: Florida, Mexico, Guatemala, Costa Rica (rare), Paraguay, Argentina	34–36	♂ 266–305 ♀ 300–317	149–172	♂ 216–269 ♀ 278–339	35–41	25
Lophoictinia isura (Gould, 1838) Schopfmilan	Square-tailed Kite								
(Immaturvogel viel heller als Adultvogel)	(immature-bird much paler than adult)	Australien (ohne SE u. Tasmanien)	Australia (except SE and Tasmania)	48–51	♂ 445–470 ♀ 470–480	♂ 245–260 ♀ 280		48–50	36
Hamirostra melanosternon (Gould, 1841) Schwarzbrustmilan, Haubenmilan	Black-breasted Kite								
(Habitus bussardähnlich)	(broad wings and tail, heavy body, result in Buteolike proportions)	N u. Z Australien (am häufigsten in N-Queensland u. Nord-Territorium)	N and Central Australia (commonest in N-Queensland and N Territory)	53–61	♂ 437–463 ♀ 440–477	♂ 201–208 ♀ 215–224		64–68	♂ 51 ♀ 63
Milvus migrans (Boddaert, 1783) Schwarzmilan	Black Kite								
M. m. migrans (Boddaert, 1783) (Im größten Teil seines Verbreitungsgebietes, in welchem neben M. migrans auch M. milvus vorkommt, kann er aufgrund seines dunkleren, matteren Gefieders u. der geringeren Schwanzgabelung von diesem unterschieden werden)	(in most of its range, where M. migrans occurs with M. milvus, it can be distinguished by darker and duller colouring and less deeply forked tail)	Europa, N bis Finnland u. N Rußland, Asien E bis Ural, Belutschistan, Persien, Mittl. Osten, Mittelmeerländer (ohne Ägypten) N W Afrika	Europe, N to Finland and N Russia, Asia east to Ural, Baluchistan, Persia. Middle East, Mediterranean countries (except Egypt) NW Africa	46–61	♂ 417–475 ♀ 430–480	♂ 230–281 ♀ 220–300	♂ 630–928 ♀ 750–1076	50–62	22–28
M. m. aegyptius (Gmelin, 1788) (Kopf u. Hals braun, Unterseite u. Schwanz mehr rotbraun)	(head and neck browner, under-surface and tail rather more rufous)	Ägypten, Küsten d. Roten Meeres, Arabien, Somalia, Küste Kenias	Egypt, Red Sea coasts, Arabia, Somalia, Kenya (coast)		♂ 418–443 ♀ 425–465	254–290			
M. m. parasitus (Daudin, 1800) (Unterseite mehr zimtbraun, stärker gestreift)	(below more cinnamon and more heavily streaked)	Afrika, S Sahara bis Kapstadt. Komoren, Madagaskar	Africa, south of Sahara to Cape Town. Comoros and Madagascar		♂ 415–425 ♀ 425–450		♂ 567–650 ♀ 617–682		
M. m. lineatus (JE Gray, 1831) (Kehle, Wangen hell, Ohrdecken dunkel)	(throat and cheeks light, ear-coverts dusky)	W Sibirien, E bis Japan, Taiwan, Hainan, Kaschmir, SE China	W Siberia, east to Japan, Taiwan, Hainan, Kashmir, SE China	61–66	♂ 433–505 ♀ 460–529	288–345	♂ 782, 855 ♀ 980, 1186	58–67	24–32
M. m. govinda Sykes, 1832 (Habitus: Kopf mit mehr rostrot u. deutl. gestreift als lineatus, Skapularen u. Oberflügeldecken beige gesäumt, Schwanz deutl. gebändert)	(head and neck more rufous and more distinctly streaked than lineatus, scapulars and upper wing coverts edged buff, tail more distinctly barred)	Belutschistan, Indien, Sri Lanka, Burma S Indochina, vereinzelt bis Malaya	Baluchistan, India, Sri Lanka, Burma, S Indo-China, straggling to Malaya		♂ 410–453 ♀ 420–482	♂ 246–289 ♀ 244–290		49–58	(32–38,5)
M. m. affinis Gould, 1838 (Habitus: dunkler als govinda, kleine u. mittlere Flügeldecken bilden helleres Feld)	(darker than govinda, but lesser and median wing coverts form a more conspicuous wingpatch!)	Lombok, Sumba, Timor, Sulawesi, Neuguinea, Australien (nördl. 20° S)	Lombok, Sumba, Timor, Sulawesi, New-Guinea, Australia (north of 20° S)		♂ 383–402 ♀ 414–420		429		
Milvus milvus (Linnaeus, 1758) Rotmilan	Red Kite								
M. m. milvus (Linnaeus, 1758) (Schwanz nur verwaschen gebändert oder ungebändert)	(tail indistinctly barred, bars decreasing towards central pair)	S Schweden, W Rußland, S bis M Europa, Spanien, Italien, Sizilien, Bulgarien, Serbien, Kl. Asien, Palästina bis N Iran, W Mittelmeer, NW Afrika, W Kanaren. Winter: NW Afrika, NW Indien	S Sweden, W Russia, south to Central Europe, Spain, Italy, Sizily, Bulgaria, Serbia, Asia Minor, Palestine to N Iran, western Mediterranean, NW Africa, W Canaries. Winter: NW Africa, NW India	56–61	♂ 483–525 ♀ 495–535	♂ 300–380 ♀ 310–390	♂ 757–1221 ♀ 960–1600	51–64	25,1–29,9
M. m. fasciicauda Hartert, 1914 (Vermittelt im Habitus z. M. migrans)	(in plumage intermediate between M. milvus and M. migrans)	Kapverdische Inseln	Cape Verde Islands		♂ 420–470 ♀ 452–481	♂ 285–300 ♀ 310–320			
Haliastur indus (Boddaert, 1783) Brahminenmilan	Brahminy Kite								
H. i. indus (Boddaert, 1783) (Schwanz gerundet, nicht keilförmig wie bei *sphenurus*)	(tail rounded not wedge-shaped as in H. *sphenurus*)	Indien, Sri Lanka, trop. Asiat. Festland ohne Malaya	India, Sri Lanka, tropical continental Asia, except Malayan Peninsula		♂ 359–394 ♀ 379–403	180–207		51–59	(34–38)
H. i. intermedius Blyth, 1865 (wie indus, Schaftstriche etwas undeutlicher)	(similar to indus, but shaft-streaks less distinct)	Malaya, Philippinen, Borneo, Indonesien	Malayan Peninsula, Philippines, Borneo, Indonesia	43–51	♂ 375–398 ♀ 405–425	203–215	♂ 587 ♀ 566	48,5–55	♂ 26,5
H. i. girrenera (Vieillot, 1825) (Immaturvogel m. weißem Bauch u. „Hosen")	(immature birds with white on belly and thighs)	Australien, Molukken, Neuguinea, Bismarck-Louisiaden-Admiralty Ins.,	Australia, Moluccas, New-Guinea, Bismarck-, Louisiade and Admiralty Islands		♂ 343–378 ♀ 353–378	♂ 178	♂ 409 ♀ 434–500	♂ 43	
H. i. flavirostris Condon & Amadon, 1954 (Wachshaut u. Schnabel gelb u. etwas stärker als bei girrenera)	(cere and bill entirely yellow and distinctly heavier than in girrenera)	Salomon-Inseln	Solomon Islands		♂ 357–384 ♀ 371–390		♂ 625–650 ♀ 900		
H. sphenurus (Vieillot, 1818) Pfeifmilan	Whistling Eagle								
(Schwanz keilförmig, Immaturvögel am Kopf heller u. sandfarbener als Adultvogel, sonst dunkler, Stoß gebändert)	(tail wedge-shaped, immatures with paler and more sandy coloured head and neck as in adult, elswhere rather darker, tail banded)	Australien (ohne Tasmanien) E Neuguinea u. Neukaledonien	Australia (except Tasmania) E New Guinea, New Caledonia	51–56	♂ 370–417 ♀ 400–448	♂ 225–272 ♀ 249–290	♂ 650 ♀ 761–921	58–60	44

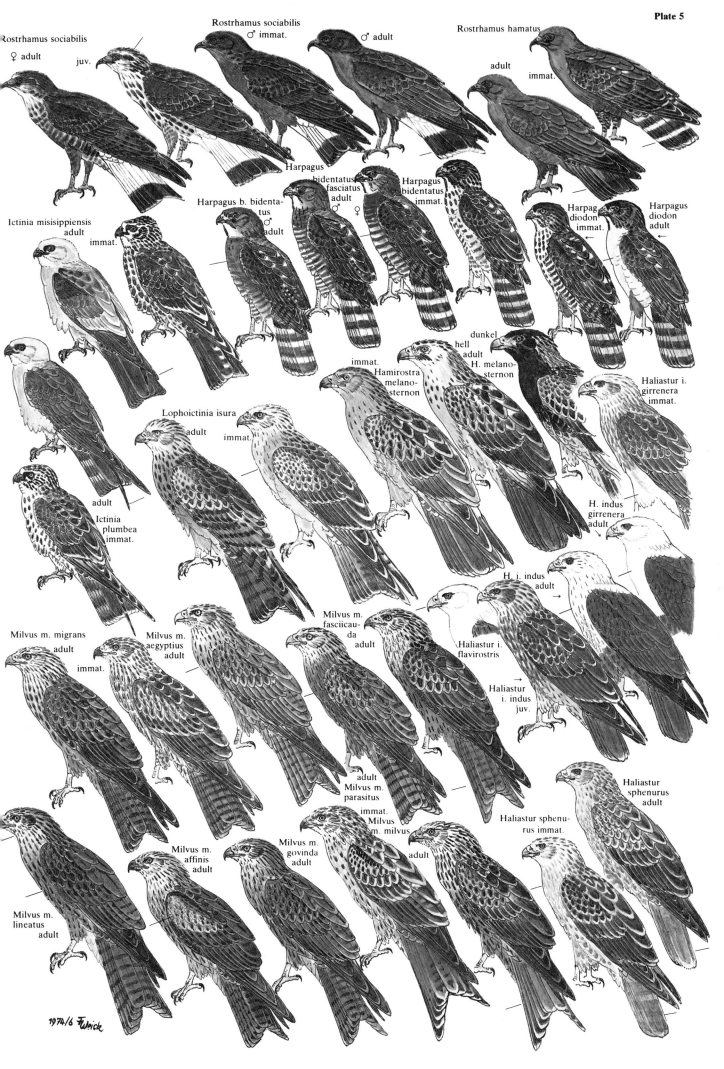

Plate 5

Rostrhamus sociabilis ♀ adult

juv.

Rostrhamus sociabilis ♂ immat.

♂ adult

Rostrhamus hamatus adult

immat.

Harpagus bidentatus fasciatus adult ♀

Harpagus b. bidentatus ♂ adult

Harpagus bidentatus immat.

Harpag diodon immat.

Harpagus diodon adult

Ictinia misisippiensis adult

immat.

immat. Hamirostra melano-sternon

dunkel hell adult H. melano-sternon

Haliastur i. girrenera immat.

Lophoictinia isura adult

immat.

H. indus girrenera adult

adult

Ictinia plumbea immat.

H. i. indus adult

Milvus m. fasciicau-da adult

Haliastur i. flavirostris

Milvus m. migrans adult

immat.

Milvus m. aegyptius adult

Haliastur i. indus juv.

adult Milvus m. parasitus

immat. Milvus m. milvus

adult

Haliastur sphenurus adult

Haliastur sphenu-rus immat.

Milvus m. affinis adult

Milvus m. govinda adult

Milvus m. lineatus adult

1974/6 F. Weick

Benennung	Nomenclature	Verbreitung	Distribution	Länge Length cm	Flügel Wing mm	Schwanz/Tail mm	Gewicht Weight g	Tarsus mm	Culmen mm () = mit Wachshaut with cere
Haliaeëtus leucogaster (Gmelin, 1789) Weißbauchseeadler (Schwanz keilförmig)	White-bellied Sea Eagle (tail wedge-shaped)	Küstengewässer Indiens u. Sri Lankas im E bis S China, im S bis Australien u. Tasmanien, Neuguinea, Bismarckarchipel	Coasts of India and Sri-Lanka, east to S China, south to Australia and Tasmania, New Guinea, Bismarckarchipelago	60–69	♂ 526–589 ♀ 588–606	208–260	♂ 1750–2200 ♀ 2475–2800	92–99 (102 ♂ 107 ♀ Swann)	48–55 (66)
Haliaeëtus sanfordi Mayr, 1936 Salomonenseeadler (Stoß keilförmig)	Sanford's Sea Eagle (tail wedge shaped)	Salomon-Inseln	Solomon Islands	64–71	♂ 525–547 ♀ 535–575	♂ 259 ♀ 245–283 (290–310 juv)	2300–2500	91–102	
Haliaeëtus vocifer (Daudin, 1800) Schreiseeadler (Schwanz rund)	African Fish Eagle (River Eagle) (tail rounded)	Afrika, von Senegal u. Gambia bis S Sudan u. Äthiopien, südwärts bis Kap. Fehlt in Somalia u. N Äthiopien	Africa, from Senegal and Gambia to S Sudan and Ethiopia south to Cape-Province. Not in Somalia and N Ethiopia	58–74	♂ 485–540 ♀ 533–605	230–275	3 ♂♂ 1986–2497–2782 2♀♀ 3170–3630	80–90	38–44,5 (63)
Haliaeëtus vociferoides (Des Murs, 1845) Madagaskarseeadler (Schwanz rund)	Madagascar Fish Eagle (tail rounded)	Madagaskar, v. allem W Küste u. an einigen Binnenseen	Madagascar, chiefly western coast and some inland waters	58–66	♂ 484–494 ♀ 514–529	♂ 229–273 ♀ 269–295 (180–220 nach Hartlaub)		♂ 92–100 ♀ 99–106	(63)
Haliaeëtus leucoryphus (Pallas, 1771) Bindenseeadler (Schwanz rund, relativ länger als bei *albicilla*)	Pallas' Sea Eagle (tail rounded and relatively longer than in *albicilla*)	Zentral-Asien, v..Kirgisensteppe E bis Im S bis Irak, Pamir, im N bis Indien und Burma. Winter: Irak, N Indien, Teile Indochinas	Central Asia; from Kirghiz Steppe east to Manchuria, Tibet, eastern Mongolia. South to Iraq, N India. Casually Indo China	68–81,5	♂ 545–585 ♀ 558–623 ♂ juv–597 ♀ juv–628	♂ 271–287 ♀ 274–291 ♂ juv–325 ♀ juv–365	♂ 2620–3278 ♀ 2900–3700	♂ 97–103 ♀ 98–111	♂ 42–45,5 ♀ 47–53,5
Haliaeëtus leucocephalus (L. 1766) Weißkopfseeadler **H. l. leucocephalus (Linnaeus, 1766)** (Schwanz rund, relativ länger als bei *albicilla*)	Bald Eagle (tail rounded and relatively longer than in *albicilla*)	Südl. USA–Mexiko	Southern USA to Mexico	76–92	(487,4 Bent) ♂ 515–545 ♀ 548–588 (520 Bent)	♂ 232–264 ♀ 247–286		95–107	47–54
H. l. alascanus Townsend, 1897 (Habitus: wie *leucocephalus*, aber größer)	(similar to *leucocephalus*, but larger)	Bering-Ins. NW Alaska, N Mackenzie u. N Quebec. S bis Brit. Kolumbien u. Große Seen. Winter: Washington, Montana, Connecticut	Bering Islands, NW Alaska, N Mackenzie and N Quebec. South to British Columbia and the Great Lakes Winter: Washington, Montana, Connecticut		♂ 570–612 ♀ 605–685 (705 Dement.)	♂ 290–322 ♀ 300–365	♂ 4000–4600 ♀ 5800–6300	95–124	50–57
Haliaeëtus albicilla (Linnaeus, 1758) Seeadler (Schwanz keilförmig)	White-tailed Sea-Eagle Grey Sea Eagle (tail wedge-shaped)	Grönland u. lokale Vorkommen in Paläarktis (in weiten Gebieten ausgerottet) von N Norwegen S bis Mittelmeer, Irak u. Iran, E bis Anadyrland, Mandschurei, Hokkaido u. Kurilen. Winter bis Indien, S W China u. Taiwan, Korea, Japan, seltener Afrika	Greenland and locally in Palearctic region, (in great areas extinct) from northern Norway south to Mediterranean, Iraq and Iran, east to Anadyrland, Manchuria, Hokkaido and Kurile Islands Winter: southwards to India, SW China and Taiwan, Korea, Japan. Rarely Africa	62–97	♂ ad 570–660 ♂ juv 612–672 ♀ ad 610–704 ♀ juv 634–715	♂ ad 225–295 ♂ juv 296–303 ♀ ad 260–335 ♀ juv 305–380	♂ 3075–4985 ♀ 3650–7500	♂ 89–107 ♀ 93–115	♂ 44–57 ♀ 52–62,7
Haliaeëtus pelagicus (Pallas, 1811) Meeradler, Riesenseeadler (Schwanz keilförmig. Die als *niger* beschriebene Form stellt wahrscheinlich nur eine dunkle Farbphase dar. Diese evtl. schon im Aussterben begriffen.)	Steller's Sea Eagle (tail wedge-shaped. *H. p. niger* of Korea may be only a colour phase, now very rare, nearly extinct)	Koryakland, S bis Kamtschatka, Küsten des Ochotskischen- u. Bering-Meeres, Shantar und N Sachalin, N Korea Winter: Ussuriland, Japan, Korea, aber auch bis Pribilof-Inseln, Anadyrland, Kodiak u. Riu-Kiu-Inseln, im Inland bis Jakutsk u. Peking	Koryakland south to Kamschatka, coast of Sea of Okhotsk and Bering Sea, Shantar and north Sakhalin Island, northern Korea Winter: Ussuriland, Japan, Korea. Straggles to Pribilof Islands, Anadyrland, Kodiak Islands and Riu Kiu Islands, inland as far as Yakutsk and Peking	89–104	♂ 560–630 ♂ juv 645–662 ♀ ad 610–620 ♀ juv 650–680	♂ ad 320–345 ♂ juv–385 ♀ ad 340–360 ♀ juv–400	♂ 5000–6000 ♀ 6800–8970	95–100 (–124 Swann) (–115 Kobayashi)	66–75
Ichthyophaga nana (Blyth, 1842) = humilis (Müller, 1841) Braunschwanzfischadler **J. nana nana (Blyth, 1842)** (Schwanz gerundet u. relativ lang)	Lesser-Fishing Eagle (tail rounded, rather long)	Siam, Tenasserim, Malaya, Sumatra, Borneo	Siam, Tenasserim, Malaya, Sumatra, Borneo	51–64	354–397	174–205 (195–222 Swann)		66–73	51
J. nana plumbea (Jerdon, 1871) (Habitus: wie *nana*, jedoch größer)	(similar to *nana*, but larger)	Kaschmir, Assam, N Burma u. N Indochina, Hainan	Kashmir, Assam, northern Burma and N Indo-China, Hainan		426–495	215–248		78–91	40–46
Ichthyophaga ichthyaëtus (Horsfield, 1821) Weißschwanzfischadler (Altvogel weißschwänzig, mit dunkler Subterminalbinde)	Grey-headed Fishing Eagle (in adult plumage tail white, with a single dark subterminal band)	Große Teile Indiens, Sri-Lanka im E bis Indochina, Borneo, Sumatra, Java, Philippinen	Great parts of India, Sri-Lanka east to Indo-China, Borneo, Sumatra, Java and the Philippines	61–74	♂ 420–455 ♀ 445–518	232–252 (280 Baker)	♂ 1590 ♀ 2270–2700	85–100	45–57

Plate 6

Haliaeëtus leucogaster adult

immat. 2. Jahr

Haliaeëtus leucogaster immat.

Haliaeëtus sanfordi
adult   immat.
immat. 2. Jahr

Haliaeëtus vocifer juv.

Haliaeëtus vocifer adult
immat. 2. Jahr

Haliaeëtus vociferoides adult   immat.

m. weißer Stirn adult
Haliaeëtus pelagicus

Haliaeëtus leucoryphus adult
immat.

Haliaeëtus leucocephalus adult

immat.

Haliaeëtus pelagicus „niger" adult
immat.

Haliaeëtus albicilla immat. 1. Jahr

immat. 3. Jahr

Haliaeëtus albicilla adult

Ichthyophaga ichthyaëtus adult
immat.

immat. Ichthyophaga n. nana adult

74 F. Weick

Benennung	Nomenclature	Verbreitung	Distribution	Länge Length cm	Flügel Wing mm	Schwanz/Tail mm	Gewicht Weight g	Tarsus mm	Culmen mm () = mit Wachshaut with cere
Gypaëtus barbatus (Linnaeus, 1758) Bartgeier	Bearded Vulture								
G. b. aureus (Hablizl, 1783) (mit „goldenstem" Anflug an Hals u. Brust aller Rassen)	(with the most golden wash on neck and breast of all races)	Europa (Rhodos, Kreta, Griechenland, Albanien, Jugosl., Sardin., Korsika, Pyrenäen) Asien (China, bis Pamir, Hindukusch, Altai, S bis NE Assam, Bhutan, Nepal, Kaschmir, W Pakistan, Iran bis Kaukasus, Kleinasien, Zypern, Sinai, Libanon, NE Ägypten	Europe (Rhodes, Crete, Greece, Albania, Yugoslavia, Sardinia, Corsica, Pyrenees) Asia (China to Pamir, Hindukush, Altais, south to NE Assam, Bhutan, Nepal, Kashmir, W Pakistan, Iran to Caucasus, Asia Minor, Cyprus, Sinai Peninsula, Lebanon, NE Egypt)	94–117	♂ 464–580 ♀ 472–580		4568 7100	♂ 90–100 ♀ 85–115	♂48–51 ♀48–52 (90–95) (–102)
(G. b. hemalachanus Hutton, 1838) (Die Unterschiede zu *aureus* bei Überschneidung der Variationsbreiten, sind nach Vaurie, Glutz v. Blotzheim u. Brown/Amadon zur Abtrennung als Rasse ungenügend.)	(after Vaurie ,Glutz v. Blotzheim and Brown/Amadon the variation is clinal and not sufficient to separate a race)				♂ 760–860 ♀ 780–890 ♂ 750–850 ♀ 810–915				
G. b. barbatus (Linnaeus, 1758) (wenige dunkle Flecke auf Brust und Kopfseiten)	(few black spots on breast and sides of head)	N.-W. Afrika im S bis Sahara im E bis Ägypten (Maghreb)	NW Africa south to Sahara east to Egypt (Maghreb)		♂ 715–760 ♀ 750–805				
G. b. meridionalis Keyserling & Blasius, 1840 (Lauf distal 20 mm unbefiedert)	(lower part of tarsus unfeatherd about 20 mm)	Yemen, Äthiopien, E u. S Afrika	Yemen, E and S Africa south to Drakensberg Massif, formerly Cape Province.		♂ 720–760 ♀ 735–790		432–445 (Roberts)	101	49 (–95)
Gypohierax angolensis (Gmelin, 1788) Palmgeier	Palm Nut Vulture								
(wirkt im Fluge breit- und rundflügelig)	(in flight, wings broad, rounded)	Afrika, v. Kenia u. S Sudan durch W Afrika bis Gambia, im S bis Oranje u. N Kapland	Africa, from Kenya to S Sudan through W Africa to Gambia, south to Orange River and N Cape-Province	56–62	397–445 (♀ 480 Swann)	188–210 (♀ 230 Swann)	1361–1830	75–85 (♀ 90 Swann)	40–46
Neophron percnopterus (Linnaeus, 1758) Schmutzgeier	Egyptian Vulture								
N. p. percnopterus (Linnaeus, 1758) (Beinfarbe variiert v. blaßgelb bis blaßlila)	(colour of feet varying from pale yellow to whitish-lilac)	Europa: Iber. Halbinsel, S Frankreich, S Italien, S Balkanhalbinsel, Balearen, Sizil.) Afrika: N Afrika, Inseln Rotes Meer, Kanaren, Kapverden, Mali, E Afrika bis Tansania, S Afrika bis Oranje. Naher u. mittlerer Osten v. Türkei bis Iran, Afghanist., NW Indien	Europe: Iberian Peninsula, S France, S Italy, S Balkan Peninsula, Balearic Islands, Sicily Africa: N Africa, Islands of the Red Sea, Cape Verde and Canary Islands, Mali, E Africa to Tanzania, S Africa to Orange River (now very rare), Near and Middle East, from Turkey to Iran, Afghanistan and NW India	53–66	♂ 470–536 ♀ 460–545	♂ 220–251 ♀ 240–267	1584–2180 (2400 Glutz)	♂ 75–84,5 ♀ 78–88	28,5–34,5
N. p. ginginianus (Latham, 1790) (Schnabel kann auch Brauntöne zeigen)	(bill sometimes may be brownish-coloured)	Indien (v. Fuße d. Himalaja bis Kap Komorin) fehlt in Sind, Assam u. Nieder-Bengalen. Irrgast auf Sri Lanka	India (from Himalayan foothills to Cape Comorin. Absent from Sind, Assam and Lower Bengal). Rare straggler to Sri-Lanka		♂ 393–490 ♀ 455–505	228–251		82–85	
Necrosyrtes monachus (Temminck, 1823) Kappengeier	Hooded Vulture								
N. m. monachus (Temminck, 1823) (einfarbig, braunes Gefieder, kurzer gerader Schwanz u. dünner Schnabel sind Feldkennzeichen)	(uniform brown plumage, short square tail and slim bill are field marks)	West-Afrika, im E bis Sudan, Nördl. Grenze des Guinea-Urwaldes	West Africa, east to Sudan, northern border of Guinean forest		455–490	220–253		82–94	(76)
N. m. pileatus (Burchell, 1824) (Habitus dunkel, Nacktteile bläulicher, nur schwer unterscheidbar vom sehr ähnlichen *monachus*)	(darker plumage, bare skin more bluish, only doubtfully separable from very similar *monachus*)	Ost-Sudan, Äthiopien, E u. S Afrika bis Natal u. Oranje-Fluß, S W Afrika bis Steppen S Angolas	E Sudan, Ethiopia, E and S Africa as far as Natal and Orange River, SW Africa to the steppes of southern Angola	61–66	460–542	235–285	1524–2102	78–95	29,5–33,5 (68)
Trigonoceps occipitalis (Burchell, 1824) Wollkopfgeier	White-headed Vulture								
(Bei Altvogel kontrastiert das dunkle Brustband m. dem weißen Kopf u. Bauch auffällig.)	(in adult the dark chest contrasts strongly with the white crop and belly)	Trockengebiete Afrikas, Von Senegal i. W bis Sudan u. N Äthiopien im N, S bis Oranje-Fluß, fehlt in Arabien	Drier parts of Africa; from Senegal in W to N Ethiopia in the N. south to Orange River Not in Arabia	76–81	610–643 (582 Swann)	265–295 (310 Swann)	2476–4820	95–110 (125 Swann)	48–54 (90)
Torgos tracheliotus (J. R. Forster, 1796) Ohrengeier	Lappet-faced Vulture								
(auffällig die hellen „Hosen" u. der nackte, wulstige Kopf)	(notice the whitish thighs and the naked wattled head)	Trockenere Teile Afrikas, von NW Sahara bis N Äthiopien u. S bis Kapland. S Israel	Drier parts of Africa, from NW Sahara to N Ethiopia and south to Cape-Province. S Israel	102–112	715–795	340–380	♀ 6800	122–146	68–71
Sarcogyps calvus (Scopoli, 1786) Lappen- o. Kahlkopfgeier	Indian Black or King Vulture								
(Altvogel m. weißen Flankenflecken)	(adult has white thigh patches)	Indien, Burma, Thailand, Laos, Süd-Jünnan, N Malaya	India, Burma, Thailand, Laos, S Yunnan, N Malaya	76–84	570–625	226–257 (278 Swann)	3700–5400	105–116	63 (74–80)
Aegypius monachus (Linnaeus, 1766) Mönchs- o. Kuttengeier	European Black or Cinereous Vulture								
(Kopfbedunung nimmt mit zunehmendem Alter ab)	(blackish head down reduced with age)	Von Spanien bis N Marokko, im E bis Afghanistan, Belutschistan, Turkestan, N E Mongolei (bis 64° N) Ural u. bis Assam Im Winter in N Indien, Burma, S China, Korea, Japan u. Afrika bis Sudan	From Spain to Morocco and east to Afghanistan, Baluchistan, Turkestan, Tibet, NE Mongolia (north to 64° N), Ural. Possibly along the Himalaya to Assam. Winter: N India, Burma, S China, Korea, Japan, Africa to Sudan	107–113	715–887	290–412	♂ 7000–11500 ♀ 7500–12500 (Extreme 6310 u. 14000)	107–146	52–66,5 (80–88)

Plate 7

Gypaëtus. b.
barbatus ad.

Gypaëtus b.
aureus
adult
←

Gypaëtus b.
hemalachanus
adult →

Gypaëtus b.
meridionalis
adult

Gypaëtus b.
aureus →
immat.

Gypohierax
angolensis
adult

immat.

Neophron p.
percnopterus
adult

immat.

adult
Trigonoceps occi-
pitalis
juv.

adult   immat.
Necrosyrtes m. monachus

Necrosyrtes m.
pileatus
adult

oder gelb!

Neophron p.
ginginianus
adult

adult
„helläugig"

adult „normal"

immat.

Sarcogyps calvus

immat.

Torgos tracheliotus.
adult

juv.

immat.

Aegypius monachus
adult

74 F.Weick

Benennung	Nomenclature	Verbreitung	Distribution	Länge Length cm	Flügel Wing mm	Schwanz/Tail mm	Gewicht Weight g	Tarsus mm	Culmen mm () = mit Wachshaut with cere
Gyps fulvus (Hablizl, 1783) Gänsegeier	Griffon Vulture								
G. f. fulvus (Hablizl, 1783) (Halswurzel vor allem zur Balzzeit blau)	(base of neck bluish, especially in display)	S Europa bis Mittlerer Osten, E Altai u. Persien, Maghreb (vor allem Marokko), N Algerien, S Tunesien	Southern Europe to Middle East, E Altai and Persia, Maghreb (chiefly Morocco), N Algeria, S Tunisia	99–104	♂ 684–735 ♀ 690–750	♂ 310–395 (280) ♀ 325–375	♂ 6200–8500 ♀ 6500–8300 (Extr. 4250)	♂ 100–113 ♀ 102–114 (125)	♂ 50–55 ♀ 50–54
G. f. fulvescens Hume, 1869 (Gefieder rötlicher, ins zimtfarbene gehend)	(more golden rufous or cinnamon)	Belutschistan, Afghanistan u. N W Indien im S bis Haiderabad	Baluchistan, Afghanistan and NW India, south to Hyderabad		675–747	302–330 (Extr. 340)		100–120 (Extr. 132)	71–74?
Gyps coprotheres (J. R. Forster, 1798) Fahlgeier	Cape Vulture								
(an Halsvorderseite u. Wangen nackte, blaue Haut sichtbar)	(front of neck and cheeks shows bare bluish skin)	S-Afrika, S v. Damaraland u. S W Simbabwe m. Ausn. der Kalahari-Wüste. Irrgast bis S E Zaire	S Africa, south of Damaraland and SW Zimbabwe, except Central Kalahari. Straggling to S E Zaire	99–104	675–702	300–345		90–105	51–60
Gyps himalayensis Hume, 1869 Schneegeier	Himalayan Griffon								
(Oberflügeldecken weiß bis lichtbeige, Halswurzel m. roten Flecken; weißer Unterrücken)	(upper wing coverts whitish to pale yellowish-brown, base of neck with red spots)	Bergregionen Zentralasiens von Afghanistan bis Bhutan, Tianshan, Pamir, Himalaja, Tibet, Sikiang, Ku-ku-nor	Mountainious regions of Central Asia, from Afghanistan to Bhutan, Tianshan, Pamir, Himalaya, Tibet, Sikiang, Kokonor	104–109	755–805	365–402	8000– 12000	110–126	71–77
Gyps rueppellii (AE. Brehm, 1852) Sperbergeier	Rüppell's Griffon								
G. r. rueppellii (AE. Brehm, 1852) (schuppiges, bzw. geflecktes Erscheinungsbild kennzeichnet Altvögel)	(adult is distinguished by a scaly or spotted appearance)	In den trockeneren Gebieten Afrikas, Senegal, E bis Sudan, S bis Tanganjika, Kenia, Uganda	Drier parts of Africa, Senegal east to Sudan, south to Tanganyika, Kenya, Uganda	89–94	612–700	275–300	7710– 9000	108–115	(90)
G. r. erlangeri Salvadori, 1908 (kleiner u. heller als *rueppellii*; Unterseite rahmfarben)	(smaller and paler than *rueppellii*; below more buffy-white)	Äthiopien, Somalia	Ethiopia, Somalia		625–665		6384		
Gyps indicus (Scopoli, 1786) Indiengeier	Indian Griffon								
G. i. indicus (Scopoli, 1786) (nackthalsig u. m. relativ längerem Schnabel als andere *Gyps*-Arten)	(bare skin on head and neck and a relatively longer bill distinguish from other species of *Gyps*)	N Indien u. östlich und südl. der Ganges-Ebene, ohne Sind u. Sri Lanka	N India and further east, south of Indo-Gangetic plain except Sind and Sri-Lanka	81–86	560–750	238–310		90–109	66–74
G. i. tenuirostris G. R. Gray, 1844 = nudiceps Stuart Baker 1927 (Schnabel länger u. schmaler, Kopf u. Hals noch nackter als bei *indicus*)	(bill still more elongated, head and neck quite naked, than in *indicus*)	Gangesebene nördl. bis u. längs Himalaya, v. Kaschmir bis Nepal, Bengalen, Assam	Indo-Gangetic plain north to and along Himalayas, from Kashmir through Nepal, Bengal and Assam		590–630	237–256		110	66–68
Pseudogyps bengalensis (Gmelin, 1788) Bengalengeier	Indian white backed Vulture								
(auffällig das dunkle Gesamtcolorit, u. die silbergrau überflogenen Armschwingen)	(generally dark colour contrasts strikingly with silvery washed secondaries)	Indien, E bis Burma, Indochina, im Sommer bis Afghanistan	India, east to Burma, Indo-China. Summer: to Afghanistan	76	535–578 (Extr. 608)	217–238	4763–5660	108–124	(71–81) 62
Pseudogyps africanus (Salvadori, 1865) Zwerggänsegeier	African white-backed Vulture								
(♀♀ sind noch lichter gefärbt als ♂♂, Vorderhals fast nackt; Oberkopf u. Hinterhals weiß bedunt)	(♀♀ still paler than ♂♂; front of neck rather naked, crown and hind-neck covered with white down)	Afrika, v. N Äthiopien, Sudan u. Senegal, S bis Transvaal, Zululand u. Kalahari	Africa from N Ethiopia, Sudan and Senegal south to Transvaal, Zululand and Kalahari	76	550–640	240–275	5050–7711	86–118	46–50

Plate 8

Gyps fulvus
immat.
adult

Gyps coprotheres
adult
immat.

Gyps f. fulvescens
adult

Gyps himalayensis
adult
immat.

Gyps r. rueppellii
adult

immat.

Gyps rueppellii
erlangeri
adult

Gyps i. indicus
adult
immat.

Gyps i.
tenuirostris
adult

adult
Pseudogyps africanus
immat.

Pseudogyps bengalensis
adult
immat.

74 F. Weick

Benennung	Nomenclature	Verbreitung	Distribution	Länge Length cm	Flügel Wing mm	Schwanz/Tail mm	Gewicht Weight g	Tarsus mm	Culmen mm () = mit Wachshaut with cere
Circaëtus gallicus (Gmelin, 1788) Schlangenadler	Short-toed or Serpent Eagle								
Circaëtus g. gallicus (Gmelin, 1788) (Altvögel können noch helleres o. dunkleres Kleid zeigen, als dargestellt)	(adults can be still darker or paler than those painted)	S u. E Europa u. vom E Mittelmeer über Iran, Kasachische SSR, Afghanistan, Pakistan, Indien u. N Mongolei, N Afrika	S and E Europe and from Mediterranean through Iran, SSR of Kazakhstan, Afghanistan, Pakistan, India and N Mongolia, N Africa		♂ 510–585 ♀ 520–605	♂ 246–306 ♀ 255–330	♂ 1500–2000 ♀ 1513–2324	♂ 87–98 ♀ 86–105	♂ 32–38 ♀ 33–39
Circaëtus g. beaudouini Verreaux & des Murs, 1862 (Schwanz eckig u. gerade abgeschnitten, dunkles Brustband, Bauch fein gespert)	(tail square, dark breastband, belly finely barred)	Trop. W Afrika, v. Senegal E bis Kordofan, S bis N Nigeria, N Kamerun, Uganda, W Kenia (vermischt sich dort mit *C. g. pectoralis*) und W Äthiopien	Tropical W Africa from Senegal east to Kordofan, south to N Nigeria, N Cameroons, Uganda, W Kenya (where intergrades and interbreeds with *pectoralis*) and W Ethiopia	60–81	475–502 (Swann –520)	266–278		93	(48)
Circaëtus g. pectoralis Smith, 1830 (Schwarzbrustschlangenadler) (Altvögel m. fleckenlosem Bauch- u. Schenkelgefieder)	(adult with immaculate belly and thighs)	E u. S Afrika v. E Sudan u. Äthiopien, durch Kenia, Simbabwe bis S Afrika, im W bis Gabun	E and S Africa from E Sudan and Ethiopia through Kenya, Zimbabwe to S Africa; west to Gabon		♂ 490–534 ♀ 563–570	255–315	1 ♂ 2187	85–100	32–37
Circaëtus cinereus Vieillot, 1818 Brauner Schlangenadler (Juv. unterscheidet sich leicht durch Schwanzzeichnung von *cinerascens*)	Brown Harrier Eagle, Brown Snake Eagle (juvenile bird is distinguished from that of *cinerascens* by different tail-banding)	Afrika, S der Sahara besonders im E u. NE Afrikas, aber auch W u. SW Afrika, im S bis Transvaal	Africa south of Sahara, especially E and NE Africa, but also W and SW Africa and south to Transvaal	74–78	♂ 485–550 ♀ 490–567	♂ 245–273 ♀ 280–295		92–108	42–45
Circaëtus fasciolatus Kaup, 1850 Streifenschwanzschlangenadler (Adultvogel mit hellbrauner Brust u. dichter Bänderung v. Bauch u. Hosen)	Southern Banded Snake Eagle (adult with pale-brownish breast, belly and thighs clearly barred)	Trop. Küsten Afrikas v. N Kenia bis Tanganjika, S bis Natal	Tropical coastal Africa from N Kenya – Tanganyika – Natal	58–61	♂ 363–380 (Swann –385) ♀ 371–390 (Swann –400)	245–270	2 ♂ 960 1 ♀ 1100	76–87	27–32,5
Circaëtus cinerascens S. W. v. Müller, 1851 Weißbandschlangenadler (Schwanz m. einer breiten, weißen Binde)	Smaller Banded or Cinereous Snake-Eagle (single broad white band across the tail)	Afrika, v. Sierra Leone im E bis S Äthiopien, im S bis SW Afrikas u. Sambesi	Africa from Sierra Leone east to S Ethiopia, south to South-West Africa and Zambesi river	63–66	367–408	220–231 (Swann –248)		80–84 (Swann –87)	31–33 (50)
Terathopius ecaudatus (Daudin, 1800) Gaukler (extrem kurzer Schwanz, jedoch langflügelig)	Bateleur (very short tail, but long wings)	Afrika, S der Sahara, Wanderungen bis S Arabien	Africa south of Sahara, wandering to South-Arabia	56–64	♂ 485–550 ♀ 500–550	♂ 98–116 ♀ 105–127	1927–2950	65–75 (Swann 82)	35–37,5
Dryotriorchis spectabilis (Schlegel, 1863) Kongoschlangenhabicht	Congo Serpent Eagle or Beautiful Wood-Hawk								
Dryotriorchis sp. spectabilis (Schlegel, 1863) (langschwänzig, kurze Haube, Altvogel mit rotbraunem Nackenband)	(longtailed with a short crest, adult bird with a rufous nape-band)	W Afrika, Ghana bis Kamerun	West Africa, Ghana to Cameroons		295–315	245–268		63–70	(48)
Dryotriorchis sp. batesi Sharpe, 1904 (Oberseite brauner und nur auf den Flanken gefleckt)	(browner above and spots confined to flanks)	W Afrika (S Kamerun, Gabun bis Zaïre)	West Africa (south Cameroons, Gabon to Zaire)	56–58	♂ 282–307 ♀ 300–307				
Eutriorchis astur Sharpe, 1875 Madagaskarschlangenhabicht (Immaturkleid evtl. mit Adultkleid weitgehend identisch)	Madagascar Serpent Eagle (immature-plumage undescribed, possibly similar to that of adult)	N und E Madagaskar	Northern and eastern Madagascar	58–66	1 ♂ 301 1 ♀ ? 341	♂ 280–292 1 ♀ ? 335		90–92	(44)

Plate 9

Circaëtus gallicus

immat.

Circaëtus g.
beaudouini
adult

immat.

adult
„hell"

adult
„dunkel"

Circaëtus g.
pectoralis
← adult   juv. →

immat.
Circaëtus
cinereus
adult

Circaëtus cinerascens
immat.   adult
←   →

adult
Circaëtus fasciolatus
immat.

immat.
Terathopius
ecaudatus
♂ adult

Terathopius
ecaudatus
♀ adult
„hellrückig"
adult ♀
„normal"

Dryotriorchis s. batesi
adult

Dryotriorchis
s. spectabilis
adult

Dryotriorchis s.
spectabilis
immat.

adult

Eutriorchis astur
immat. ?

1974/6
F.Weick

Benennung	Nomenclature	Verbreitung	Distribution	Länge Length cm	Flügel Wing mm	Schwanz/Tail mm	Gewicht Weight g	Tarsus mm	Culmen mm () = mit Wachshaut with cere
Spilornis holospilus (Vigors, 1831) Philippinenschlangenhabicht (Haubenfedern bei Adultvogel rostfarben gesäumt, Unterseite hell rostbraun mit vielen großen Flecken)	Philippine Serpent Eagle (crest-feathers with rufous edges, below light rufous with many clear oval white spots)	Philippinen	Philippines	58–64	♂ 317–341 ♀ 332–367	230–263	♂ 603–762 ♀ 691–1604	77–94	36–40
Spilornis rufipectus Gould, 1857 Celebesschlangenhabicht	Celebes Serpent Eagle								
Spilornis r. rufipectus Gould, 1857 (Altvogel m. schwarzem Kopf, Unterseite gebändert)	(adult with black head, clear white barring below)	Sulawesi	Sulawesi	41–48	♂ 322–345 ♀ 328–370	218–250		69–76	37
Spilornis r. sulaensis (Schlegel, 1866) (kleiner u. deutlich heller)	(smaller, much paler)	Sula-Ins.	Sula Islands		♂ 309 ♀ 325–345				
Spilornis cheela (Latham, 1790) Schlangenhabicht	Crested Serpent Eagle								
Spilornis c. cheela (Latham, 1790) (graue Wangen, Brust fein gewellt, Bauch deutlich abgesetzt)	(grey cheeks, breast narrowly barred, belly clearly contrasting with breast)	W Pakistan u. N Indien	West-Pakistan and northern India		♂ 468–510 ♀ 482–532	♂ 295–305 ♀ 299–315		♂ 100–105 ♀ 102–115	(42–50)
Spilornis c. melanotis (Jerdon, 1844) (Kopf u. Brust viel dunkler, Armschwingenband grauer, Kehle heller als bei cheela)	(much darker on head and below, band on secondaries greyer, less black on throat than in cheela)	Südl. Indische Halbinsel (S 25° N)	Southern Peninsular India (south of lat. 25° N)		♂ 357–440 ♀ 424–481	♂ 211–279 ♀ 260–315		91–109	(40–48)
Spilornis c. burmanicus Swann, 1920 (mit undeutlicher Brust- u. Bauchzeichnung als bei cheela. Kehle u. Brust, dabei sehr hell)	(less clearly spotted and barred on breast and belly than cheela)	Burma, Shan-Staaten, Tenasserim, Siam, Thailand, Indochina (ohne Nördl. N Vietnam)	Burma, Shan States, Tenasserim, Siam, Thailand, Indo-China (except Northern N Vietnam)		♂ 405–455 ♀ 436–474				
Spilornis c. ricketti W. L. Sclater, 1919 (noch heller als burmanicus, Rückenfärbung mehr aschbraun)	(paler than burmanicus, back more ashy-brown)	S E China, Nördl. N Vietnam, Jünnan	South-east China, Northern N Vietnam, Yunnan		♂ 430–455 ♀ 470–490		~ 900		
Spilornis c. malayensis Swann, 1920 (viel dunkler als burmanicus und mit deutlicherer weißer Fleckung, Armschwingen ohne weiße Spitzen)	(distinctly darker than burmanicus, more clearly marked with white spots and bars, secondaries lack white tips)	S Tenasserim, Malaya, Anambasinseln u. N Sumatra	Southern Tenasserim, Malaya, Anambas Islands, northern Sumatra		♂ 348–380 ♀ 368–394				
Spilornis c. spilogaster (Blyth, 1853) (hellgraue Kehlfärbung, Wangen u. Ohrdecken hell graubraun)	(throat light-grey, cheeks and ear-coverts pale greyish-brown)	Sri Lanka	Sri Lanka		♂ 355–389 ♀ 384–402	♂ 222–240 ♀ 240–254		83	(38–44)
Spilornis c. davisoni Hume, 1873 (ähnl. spilogaster, Oberseite brauner, Brust deutl. gebändert)	(similar to spilogaster, browner above, distinctly barred breast)	Andamanen	Andaman Islands		374–407				
Spilornis c. rutherfordi Swinhoe, 1870 (dunkler als burmanicus, Abzeichen deutlicher)	(darker than burmanicus, more distinctly marked)	Hainan	Hainan		♂ 393–411 ♀ 405–430				
Spilornis c. hoya Swinhoe, 1866 (sehr ähnlich cheela, Kehle u. Ohrdecken schwarzbraun, Brust nahezu einfarbig braun, mit wenig Zeichnung, Unterseite dunkler zimtbraun als cheela)	(very like cheela, throat and ear-coverts blackish-brown, breast plain-coloured, below darker cinnamon than cheela)	Taiwan	Taiwan		470–481				
Spilornis c. perplexus Swann, 1922 (sehr hell, großer Kontrast zwischen Kopf- u. Rückenfärbung, Unterseite viel heller als bei pallidus)	(very pale, dark head contrasts strongly with light head, undersurface much paler than in ‚pallidus')	Südl. Riu Kiu-Ins. (Ishigaki, Iriomote)	Southern Riu Kiu Islands (Ishigaki and Iriomote)	41–76!	♂ 338–360 ♀ 354–372	♂ 215–221 ♀ 227–237		70– 78,5	27,5– 30
Spilornis c. pallidus Walden, 1872 (hell, Unterseite rostfarben überflogen, Wangen u. Kehle grau, Brust einfarbig braun)	(very pale, below with a rufous wash, grey cheeks and throat, uniform brown breast)	Tiefland Borneos	Lowland Borneo		♂ 335–355 ♀ –362				
Spilornis c. kinabaluensis W. L. Sclater, 1919 (zusammen mit bido dunkelste cheela-Rasse, Nacken amberbraun)	(together with bido darkest form of cheela, rich umber-brown nape band)	Bergland Borneos	Mountainious region of Borneo		370–390				
Spilornis c. natunensis Chasen, 1934 (sehr hell u. kurzschwänzig)	(very pale above and very short tail)	Natuna, Bunguran u. Billiton	Natuna, Bunguran and Billiton Islands (West of Sumatra)		♂ 295–309 ♀ 313–324				
Spilornis c. sipora Chasen & Kloss, 1926 (ähnlich kinabaluensis, aber viel kleiner)	(like kinabaluensis, but much smaller)	Mentawei- u. Sipora-Ins. (W v. Sumatra)	Mentawei and Sipora Islands (West of Sumatra)		290–318	215			
Spilornis c. batu Meyer de Schauensee & Ripley, 1940 (heller als sipora, größer als asturinus)	(paler than sipora, larger than asturinus)	Batu u. S Sumatra	Batu Islands and southern Sumatra		♂ 329–352 ♀ 340–354	♂ 204–217 ♀ 218–221			
Spilornis c. asturinus A. B. Meyer, 1884 (graue Kopfseiten, hell u. kurzschwänzig)	(sides of head grey, very pale above and with a short tail)	Nias	Nias Island		290–308	179–190	♂ 420 ♀ 565	72	29
Spilornis c. abbotti Richmond, 1903 (Oberseite purpurbraun, braunweiße Schwanzbinde zieml. schmal)	(above purplish-brown, narrow brownish-white tailband)	Simalur Insel (W von Sumatra)	Simalur Island (West of Sumatra)		♂ 330–345 ♀ 343–362				
Spilornis c. bido (Horsfield, 1821) (zieml. dunkelbraun aber deutlicher weißbefleckt als kinabaluensis, Kehle, Ohrdecken, Brust schwärzlich)	(rather dark brown but clearer white spotting than kinabaluensis; throat, sides of head, breast blackish)	Java, Bali	Java, Bali		384–392				
Spilornis c. baweanus Oberholser, 1917 (weiße Stoßbinde sehr schmal, Binde an Schwanzwurzel braun, Kehle, Brust tiefbraun)	(white tail band rather narrow, brownish band on base of tail! throat and breast deeply brown!)	Bawean, Insel N von Java	Bawean Island (north Java)		♂ 310–324 ♀ 328–342	208– 231		72– 76,5	24,5– 27,5
Spilornis c. palawanensis W. L. Sclater, 1919 (ähnl. spilogaster, jedoch Brust rotbraun gebändert, weiße Fleckung groß u. deutlich)	(like spilogaster, but barred rufous on breast, clear white spots)	Palawan, Busuanga, Calamian u. Balabac-Inseln	Palawan, Busuanga, Calamianes and Balabac Islands		380–410				
Spilornis c. minimus Hume, 1873 (helle Kopffärbung, helle Schwanzbinden)	(light colouring on sides of head, two light tailbands)	Nikobaren-Ins. (Kamorta, Trinkat, Nancoury, Katschall)	Central Nicobar Islands (Kamorta, Trinkat, Nancoury, Katschall)		♂ 280–291 ♀ 293–304	191–192		75–77	35–37
Spilornis klossi Richmond, 1902 Nikobarschlangenhabicht (Oberseite zieml. hell, Unterseite einfarbig hell zimtbraun)	Nicobar Serpent Eagle (rather pale above, below uniform pale cinnamon)	Große Nikobar-Insel	Great Nicobar Island	38–41 (–46Ripley)	♂ 257–260 ♀263,275, 289	♂ 165–169 ♀ –197		65– 75	33
Spilornis elgini (Tytler, 1863) Andamanenschlangenhabicht (dunkelste aller Spilornis-Arten)	Andaman Serpent Eagle (darkest species of genus Spilornis)	Andamanen Nikobaren Ins. (?)	Andaman Islands, possibly Nicobar Islands?	54–56	♂ 344–374 ♀ 370–407	♂ 215–226 ♀ 213–241	♂ 790–1024 ♀ 1024–1450	81– 88	36– 41

Plate 10

immat.

Spilornis holospilus
adult

Spilornis r.
sulaensis

Spilornis klossi
adult

immat.

adult

Spilornis elgini
adult

immat.

Spilornis
rufipectus
immat.

S. c. ricketti ad.

Sp. ch. burmani-
cus adult

S. c.
melanotis
adult

S. c.
malayensis
adult

S. c. spilogaster
adult

Spilornius c.
perplexus adult

Spilornis c.
cheela
adult

immat.

Spilornis c.
kinabaluesis
adult

Spilornis c.
pallidus
adult

Spilornis c.
natunensis
adult

Spilornis c.
sipora adult

Spilornis c.
baweanus
adult

S. c.
asturinus
adult

S. c.
minimus
adult

S. c.
abotti
adult

Spilornis c.
bido adult

74 F. Weick

Benennung	Nomenclature	Verbreitung	Distribution	Länge Length cm	Flügel Wing mm	Schwanz/Tail mm	Gewicht Weight g	Tarsus mm	Culmen mm () = mit Wachshaut with cere
Polyboroides typus A. Smith, 1829 Afrikahöhlenweihe	African Harrier Hawk								
Polyboroides t. typus A. Smith, 1829 (gelbe Gesichtshaut und Schwanz mit einziger, weißer Binde)	(yellow fascial skin, and tail crossed with single broad white band)	Afrika: v. Äthiopien u. Zentral-Sudan bis Sambesi u. Gambia	Africa from Ethiopia and Central Sudan to Zambesi and Western Gambia		♂ 443–463 ♀ 457–483	280–320	etwa 570	83–100	22–26
Polyboroides t. pectoralis Sharpe, 1903 (dichter gebändert, auf Unterseite dunkle Sperberung, etwa so breit wie die weißen Zwischenräume)	(more heavily barred below, dark bars equal to white bars)	Trop. W Afrika (Gabun–Gambia)	Tropical W Africa (Gabon to Gambia)	51–68	377–434	257–294			
Polyboroides t. graueri (Swann, 1921) (kleiner u. dunkler als typus, dunkle Sperberung der Unterseite, breiter als die weißen Zwischenräume, als Rasse unsicher)	(smaller and darker than typus, black bars wider than white bars, race is not generally recognized)	Zentral-Äquatorial-Afrika (Zaïre, Uganda)	Central-Equatorial Africa (Zaïre, Uganda)		445–450				
Polyboroides radiatus (Scopoli, 1786) Madagaskarhöhlenweihe (Oberseite heller silbergrau als typus)	Madagascar Harrier Hawk (much paler silvery grey above than typus)	Madagaskar (v. Meereshöhe bis ca. 1500 m)	Madagascar (from sea level to 5000 feet)	58–61	♂ 369–398 ♀ 392–418	♂ 292–321 ♀ 314–327		86–99	28–30
Geranospiza caerulescens (Vieillot, 1817) Sperberweihe	Crane Hawk								
Geranospiza c. nigra (Du Bus, 1847) (dunkler als livens, Weiß an Kinn u. Hosen deutlicher)	(darker coloured and with more distinct white barring on chin, thighs and tail than livens)	Mexiko (ausgen. N W) S bis Kanalzone v. Panama	Mexico (except NW) south to Panama (canal zone)		♂ 282–318 ♀ 315–340	♂ 224–247 ♀ 234–254	2 ♂ 340,358	78–98	
Geranospiza c. livens (Bangs & Penard, 1921) (mehr grau als grauschwarz)	(dark grey rather than greyish-black)	N W Mexiko	N W Mexico		♂ 320–334 ♀ 334–349				
Geranospiza c. balzarensis (W. Sclater, 1918) (im Jugendkleid ausgedehntere rostgelbe Unterseitenzeichnung als bei livens, Alterskleid sehr ähnl. livens)	(immature birds with more extended buffy-white marks than in livens. Adult similar to livens)	Pazifische Küste v. E Panama bis NW Peru	Pacific slope from E Panama to NW Peru	41–51	♂ 285–293 ♀ 298–308				
Geranospiza c. caerulescens (Vieillot, 1817) (nur wenig o. keine weiße Sperberung auf Unterseite u. Hosen)	(whitish barring on belly and thighs reduced or absent)	E Kolumbien u. Ecuador, Venezuela, Guayana, Brasilien bis zum Amazonas i. S	E Colombia and Ecuador, Venezuela, the Guianas, Brazil south Amazon Valley		♂ 225–295 ♀ 273–328	200–220	♂ 235–298 ♀ 273–353	70–79	
Geranospiza c. gracilis (Temminck, 1821) (Unterseitenbänderung kann auf Kehle u. Brust fehlen)	(throat and chest sometimes unbarred)	NE Brasilien, i. S bis Bahia	N E Brazil south to Bahia		285–316				
Geranospiza c. flexipes Peters, 1935 (größer u. heller als gracilis, Weiß auf Flügel ausgedehnter als bei gracilis)	(larger and paler than gracilis with more extended white barring on wings)	S Brasilien, Gran Chaco v. Paraguay, N Argentinien, Bolivien	S Brazil, Chaco of Paraguay, N Argentina, Bolivia		312–370				

Plate 11

Polyboroides t. typus
adult

immat.
2. Jahr

juv.

Polyboroides
t. graueri adult

Polyboroides t.
pectoralis adult

Polyboroides
radiatus
adult

immat.

Geranospiza c.
nigra adult

G. c.
livens
adult

Geranospiza c. caerulescens
adult

Geranospiza c.
gracilis adult

Geranospiza c.
flexipes ad.

Geranospiza c.
nigra immat.

Geranospiza c.
gracilis
immat.

Geranospiza
c. balzarensis
immat.

Geranospiza
c. caerulescens
immat.

juv.
Geranospiza c. caerulescens

75 F. Weick

Benennung	Nomenclature	Verbreitung	Distribution	Länge Length cm	Flügel Wing mm	Schwanz/Tail mm	Gewicht Weight g	Tarsus mm	Culmen mm () = mit Wachshaut with cere
Circus assimilis Jardine & Selby, 1828 Austral- o. Fleckenweihe (Altvogel vorwiegend blaugrau auf Oberseite, rotbraun an Unterseite, Jungvogel mehr rostbraun mit auffälligem Flügelfleck)	Spotted Harrier (adult blue-grey above, chestnut below, immature birds with more rufous appearance and prominent rufous wing patch)	E N u. W Australien, Celebes, Timor, Taliabu u. Sumba	East-, North and West Australia, Celebes, Timor, Taliabu and Sumba	48–61	♂ 368–410 ♀ 414–460	♂ 252–273 ♀ 281–286	♂ –400 ♀ –440	90–105	
Circus aeruginosus (Linnaeus, 1758) Rohrweihe **C. a. aeruginosus (Linnaeus, 1758)** (alte ♀♀ sind im Gefieder ♂♂ ähnlicher als bei anderen Circus-Arten)	Marsh Harrier (adult female generally more like the male in plumage than in most other harriers)	Europa; Zentral-Asien, E bis Tomsk, Krasnojarsk, Baikalsee, S bis Mittelmeergebiet, Kaukasus u. Israel	Europe, Central-Asia, east to Tomsk, Krasnojarsk, Lake Baikal, south to Mediterranean, Caucasus and Israel		♂ 375–415 ♀ 390–440	♂ 210–245 ♀ 223–258	♂ 405–667 ♀ 672,685 800; 1105	♂ 81–92 ♀ 87–97	♂ 19–23 ♀ 19,5–25
C. a. harterti Zedlitz, 1914 (♀ ad. sind heller als ♀ von aeruginosus)	(adult female rather paler than in aeruginosus)	Marokko u. Algerien	Morocco and Algeria		♂ 384–400 ♀ 415–435				
C. a. spilonotus Kaup, 1847 (♂ entspricht im Farbschema weitgehend dem ♂ v. aeruginosus, ist jedoch viel stärker weiß gezeichnet)	(male in colour patches very similar to those of aeruginosus, but ground colour much more white)	Asien, E v. Tomsk, Krasnojarsk u. Baikalsee bis N China, Mandschurei u. N Korea Winter: Japan, Taiwan, Borneo, Philippinen u. S E Asiat. Festland	Asia east of Tomsk, Krasnojarsk and Lake Baikal to North China, Manchuria, North-Korea Winter: Japan, Taiwan, Borneo, Philippines and south east continental Asia		♂ 378–410 ♀ 395–423	♂ 224–240 ♂ 244–256	4♀ 370–780 (1♀1370 Winter)	80–99	20–27
C. a. macrosceles A. Newton, 1863 (♂ ähnl. spilonotus, jedoch oberseits schwärzer, auf Unterseite kräftiger gestreift)	(male similar to spilonotus, but blacker above and more heavily streaked below)	Madagaskar u. Komoren	Madagascar and Comoro Island		♂ 392–426 ♀ 424–444				
C. a. maillardi Verreaux, 1863 (♂ u. ♀ viel dunkler als die von spilonotus)	(male and femal much darker than in spilonotus)	Insel Réunion	Reunion Island	48–58	♂ 340–357 ♀ 380–390				
C. a. spilothorax Salvadori & d'Albertis, 1875 (♂ mit mehr braun an Kopf, Nacken u. Unterschwanzdecken)	(male with more brown on head, neck and under-tail coverts)	Zentral- u. E Neuguinea	Central and eastern New Guinea		♂ 380 (?♂434 AmBrown)	♂ 185		♂ 61	
C. a. approximans Peale, 1848 (♂♂ dieser Rasse ähneln sehr den ♀♀ von macrosceles)	(male of this form very similar to female of macrosceles)	Wallis Insel, Loyalty-Inseln, Neukaledonien, Fidji-, Tonga-, Society-Inseln, Neue Hebriden. Selten auf Samoa, Chatam u. Kermadec-Inseln.	Wallis Island, Loyalty Islands, New Caledonia, Fiji, Tonga, Society Islands, New Hebrides, straggling to Samoa, Chatham and Kermadec Islands		♂ 392–415 ♀ 418–430		1♀ 798		
C. a. gouldi Bonaparte, 1849 (dunkler u. dichter gestreift als approximans)	(darker above and more heavily streaked below than approximans)	S E Neuguinea, E u. S Australien, Tasmanien, Neuseeland, Irrgast auf der Norfolkinsel	S E New Guinea, E and S Australia, Tasmania, New Zealand straggling to Norfolk Island		♂ 367–425 ♀ 400–444	♂ 223–248 ♀ 250		88–98	
Circus ranivorus (Daudin, 1800) Froschweihe (Bei alten ♀♀ fehlt das Silbergrau auf Flügeln u. Schwanz.)	African Marsh-Harrier (adult female lacks silvery-grey on wing and tail)	E u. S Afrika, v. Uganda und Kenia bis Angola u. S Afrika	E and S Africa from Uganda and Kenya to Angola and Cape-Province	46–51	♂ 340–368 ♀ 365–395	210–248	1♂ 423 1 imm 606	72–82	19–22

Plate 12

Circus a. aeruginosus

♀ adult

♀ adult

♂ adult

Circus assimilis

adult

juv.

C. a. aeruginosus

immat.

immat.

immat.

Circus a. spilonotus
♀ adult

Circus a.
harterti ad.

Circus a.
spilonotus
♂ adult

Circus a.
maillardi
adult
♀

♂

Circus a.
macrosceles
♂ adult

adult ♀

Circus a.
gouldi
♂ adult

♂ „dunkel"
Circus a. spilothorax
♂ adult

♀ (adult?)

Circus a.
approximans
adult

immat.

immat.

Circus ranivorus

adult

1974 Weick.

Benennung	Nomenclature	Verbreitung	Distribution	Länge Length cm	Flügel Wing mm	Schwanz/Tail mm	Gewicht Weight g	Tarsus mm	Culmen mm () = mit Wachshaut with cere
Circus cyaneus (Linnaeus, 1766) Kornweihe **C. c. cyaneus (Linnaeus, 1766)** (die ♀♀ v. cyaneus sind am Unterbauch u. den Hosen meist kräftiger u. deutlicher gestreift als ♀♀ von hudsonius)	Hen Harrier (female of cyaneus, more heavily and distinctly streaked on belly than in hudsonius)	Paläarktis (Europa u. Asien bis E Sibirien im E, im S bis Portugal, Spanien, Italien, Karpaten u. Kaukasus. N Turkestan, N Tibet, Mongolei; Winter: Korea, Japan, China, Indochina, Burma, Indien, Borneo, Persien, Mittelmeerraum, N Afrika bis Nubien)	Palearctic region (Europe and Asia east to E Siberia, south to Portugal, Spain, Italy, Carpathian and Caucasus mountains, N Turkestan, N Tibet, Manchuria Winter: Korea, Japan, China, Indo China, Burma, India, Borneo, Persia, Mediterranean basin, N Africa to Nubia.		♂ 330–362 ♀ 360–390	♂ 200–225 ♀ 210–247	7♂ 362–388 2♀ 370–560	♂ 65–73 ♀ 71,5–80	♂ 15–16,5 ♀ 16–19
C. c. hudsonius (Linnaeus, 1766) (♂ an Oberseite wenig brauner überflogen, kleine Flecke auf Unterseite. Wahrscheinlich sep. Art)	(♂ above browner than in cyaneus, small spots below. Possibly a distinct species)	Nordamerika (Alaska bis Niederkalifornien, N Texas, N Virginia Winter: bis Mittelamerika u. Kuba, Kolumbien u. Venezuela	North America (Alaska to Lower California, N Texas, N Virginia). Winter: to Central America, Cuba, Colombia and Venezuela	46–56	♂ 328–352 ♀ 335–405		♂ 472– ♀ 570	♂ 71–79,5 ♀ 80–89	
Circus cinereus Vieillot, 1816 Grauweihe (♂ sehr ähnl. der Rasse hudsonius, aber an Unterseite rotbraune Sperberung auf weiß)	Cinereous Harrier (male similar to hudsonius, but with rufous barring below on white ground)	Falklandinseln u. südliches Südamerika im N bis S Brasilien und Paraguay im W bis Ecuador u. Kolumbien	Falkland Islands and southern S America north to S Brazil and Paraguay in the east, to Ecuador and Colombia in the west	46–51	♂ 297–342 ♀ 345–371	♂ 204–253 ♀ 230–282		66– 76	(31)
Circus macrourus (Gmelin, 1771) Steppenweihe (Kopfseiten u. der weiße Bürzel, dieser mehr grauweiß gebändert)	Pallid Harrier (sides of head clear white, lacks conspicuous white rump patch, which is barred grey and white)	Rumänien, i. E bis S Rußland u. SW Sibirien bis Tianshan u. Ferghana. Weiter westlich gelegentlich bis Schweden und S Deutschland Winter: Afrika S bis Kapland, Indien, Sri Lanka und Burma	Rumania east to S Russia and SW Siberia, Tianshan, Ferghana; occasional irruptions west to Sweden and Central Europe Winter: Africa south to Cape-Province; India, Sri-Lanka and Burma	43–51	♂ 310–356 ♀ 345–391	♂ 197–232 ♀ 215–255	♂ 235–416 ♀ 255–550	♂ 63–72 ♀ 67–78	♂ 15–17,5 ♀ 18,5–19,
Circus pygargus (Linnaeus, 1758) Wiesenweihe (♂ dunkler an Oberseite als c. cyaneus oder macrourus, schmalflügliger u. mit dunklem Fleckenband auf den Armschwingen, Bauch, Hosen gestreift)	Montagu's Harrier (male darker above than c. cyaneus and macrourus, wings more pointed, black bar on secondaries, belly, abdomen, thighs streaked rufous)	Großbritannien ostwärts durch Mitteleuropa, Mittelrußland, in Asien v. Ob bis Krasnojara. Brütet im S bis N Afrika, Kaukasus, Transkaspien, Pamir und Tarbagatai. Winter: Afrika, v. Senegal bis Äthiopien, S bis Kapland und Indien, Sri Lanka, seltener Burma	Great Britain east through Central Europe, Central Russia; in Asia from Ob river to Krasnojara. South to N Africa, Caucasus, Transcaspia, Pamir, Tarbagatai Winter: Africa, Senegal to Ethiopia south to Cape Province. India, Sri Lanka, Burma (Burma rare)	41–46	♂ 342–389 ♀ 350–395	♂ 200–236 ♀ 217–250	♂ 227–305 ♀ 254–445	♂ 52–65 ♀ 60–70	♂ 14–17 ♀ 15–18
Circus melanoleucus (Pennant, 1769) Schwarzweißweihe (Altvögel bekommen auf Flügeln u. Schwanz grauen Anflug)	Pied Harrier (adult birds with greyish wash on wings and tail)	Von E Sibirien i. S bis Mongolei, N Korea u. Burma Winter: Indien u. Sri Lanka bis Indochina u. S bis Borneo u. Sula-Inseln (Indien u. Sri Lanka selten)	From E Siberia south to Mongolia, N Korea and Burma Winter: India, Sri Lanka south to Borneo and Sula Islands (India, Sri Lanka rare)	46–51	♂ 344–367 ♀ 355–387	♂ 197–217 ♀ 211–240	♂ 265–325 ♀ –455	♂ 76–80 ♀ 81–88	(♂ 22–24 ♀ 25–27)
Circus buffoni (Gmelin, 1788) Langflügelweihe (Es scheint festzustehen, daß die brauneren Vögel Weibchen sind?)	Long-winged Harrier (adult birds with more brownish appearance probably are female- ?)	S. Amerika, v. Kolumbien, Trinidad u. Guayana, i. S bis Argentinien. Im W bis E Bolivien u. E Chile	S America, from Colombia, Trinidad and the Guianas south to Argentina, west to E Bolivia and E Chile	48–61	♂ 370–426 ♀ 403–484	245– 290	♂391,403,464 ♀ 580, 645	85– 92	
Circus maurus (Temminck, 1828) Mohrenweihe (mit zunehmendem Alter deutlicher Grauanflug auf Flügel und Schwanz)	Black Harrier (adults have longer silvery-grey areas on wings and tail)	Natal u. Kapland, Südafrikas	Natal and Cape-Province of S Africa	48–58	♂ 331–347 ♀ 363–370	230– 265		63– 71	18– 20

Plate 13

Circus c. cyaneus

♀ adult

juv.

♂ adult.

Circus c. hudsonius ♂ adult

♀ adult

Circus cinereus ♂ adult

♀ adult

Circus cinereus immat.

Circus macrourus

juv.

♀ adult

♂ adult

Circus pygargus ♂ adult

♀ adult

„dunkel" Circus pygargus

juv.

Circus melanoleucus

♀ adult

juv.

♂ adult

Circus buffoni ♀ adult

Circus buffoni ♂ adult

Circus buffoni „dunkel" adult

Circus maurus adult

immat.

Circus buffoni „dunkel" juv.

1974 F. Weick

Benennung	Nomenclature	Verbreitung	Distribution	Länge Length cm	Flügel Wing mm	Schwanz/Tail mm	Gewicht Weight g	Tarsus mm	Culmen mm () = mit Wachshaut with cere
Melierax metabates Heuglin, 1861 Dunkler Singhabicht	Dark Chanting Goshawk								
M. m. metabates Heuglin, 1861 (Oberschwanzdecken im Feld deutlich grauer als bei *canorus*)	(in field upper tail coverts appear clearly, greyer than in *canorus*)	Senegal, N Nigeria, E bis N Äthiopien, S bis Kenia u. Tanganjika	Senegal, N Nigeria, east to N Ethiopia, south to Kenya and Tanganyika		♂ 296–310 ♀ 310–330	♂ 206–213 ♀ 220–232	♂ 646, 695 ♀ 841, 852	86– 89	20– 21
M. m. theresae Meinertzhagen, 1939 (Nach Vaurie Synonym v. *metabates*)	(after Vaurie synonym of *metabates*)	SW Marokko	SW Marokko		♂ 288–297 ♀ 315–323				
M. m. neumanni Hartert, 1914 (ausgedehntere Fleckung auf Flügeldecken als *metabates*)	(vermiculations on wing coverts more extensive than in *metabates*)	N Sudan vom Tschad-See bis zum Blauen Nil u. Roten Meer	N Sudan, from Lake Chad to Blue Nile and Red Sea	43–51	♂ 300–310 ♀ –328				
M. m. ignoscens Friedmann, 1928 (farblich zwischen *metabates* u. *neumanni*)	(in colouring intermediate *metabates* and *neumanni*)	SW Arabien	South-western Arabia		♂ 278–290 ♀ 304–305		♂ 488, 511 ♀ 512–586		
M. m. mechowi Cabanis, 1882 (ungefleckte Flügeldecken u. Armschwingen, leuchtenderes Rot an Beinen u. auf Wachshaut)	(uniform grey unspeckled secondaries and wing coverts, brighter red on feet and cere)	Angola, Maputo N bis W u. S Tanganjika	Angola, Maputo north to W and S Tanganyika		♂ 295–310 ♀ –323				
Melierax canorus (Thunb., 1799) Heller Singhabicht	Pale Chanting Goshawk								
M. c. canorus (Thunb., 1799) (weiße Oberschwanzdecken, Unterseite feiner gezeichnet, große Flügeldecken u. Armschwingen, weißer als *poliopterus*)	(rump more finely barred below, whiter on wing coverts and secondaries than in *poliopterus*)	Südafrika (Matebele- u. Damaraland bis Kapland)	S Africa (from Matebele and Damaraland south to Cape-Province)	46–54	♂ 328–362 ♀ 360–392	228– 268		84– 100	18,5– 22
M. c. poliopterus Cabanis, 1868 (etwas dunkler auf Oberseite u. Armschwingen als *canorus*)	(rather darker above and on secondaries than in *canorus*)	E u. NE Afrika (Somalia bis Iringa, Tanganjika, Uganda)	E and NE Africa (Somalia to Iringa, Tanganyika, Uganda)		♂ 305–326 ♀ 325–340		♂ 514–581 ♀ 673–802		
Melierax gabar (Daudin, 1800) Gabarhabicht (dunkle Phase hat keinen weißen Bürzelfleck, Vögel die in Färbung zwischen Normal- u. Dunkel-Phase sind, ebenfalls bekannt)	Gabar Goshawk (dark phase without white rump, intermediates between melanistic and normal phase are known)	Afrika südl. einer Linie Senegal – N Äthiopien, bis SW Afrika, Oranje-Freistaat u. E Kapland. SE Arabien	Africa south of a line from Senegal to N Ethiopia, to SW Africa, Orange Free State and eastern Cape Province. SE Arabia	28–36	♂ 175–204 ♀ 186–215	♂ 150–165 ♀ 170–185	♂ 115–123 ♀ 167–168	♂ 42–50 ♀ 51–54	♂ 11,5– 14,5
Urotriorchis macrourus (Hartlaub, 1855) Langschwanzhabicht (extrem langer Stoß, länger als Kopf u. Rumpf zusammen)	African Long-tailed Hawk (very long tail, longer than head and body combined)	West- und Zentralafrika von Ghana, Kamerun bis Zaïre, W Uganda	W and Central Africa from Ghana, Cameroon to Zaïre, W Uganda	61	♂ 266–303 ♀ 293–310	♂ 305– ♀ 370		72– 78	
Megatriorchis doriae Salvadori u. D'Albertis, 1876 Neuguineahabicht (Jungvögel heller, weniger rostfarben an Oberseite, aber auf Unterseite kräftiger gefärbt, Fleckung verwaschener)	Doria's Goshawk (young birds paler, less rufous above, but more rufous below, less clearly barred)	Neuguinea	New Guinea	58–69	♂ 286 ♀ 321–348	♂ 254–255 ♀ 270–312		81– 96	(38) 23
Erythrotriorchis radiatus (Latham, 1801) Australhabicht (Jungvögel heller, an Ober- u. Unterseite aber kräftiger gefleckt, Stoß undeutlicher gebändert)	Red Goshawk (young birds paler below and above, more heavily streaked, tail less clearly banded)	NW Australien, Nord-Territorium, Queensland bis N Neusüdwales	NW Australia, N Territories, Queensland to northern New-South-Wales	51–58	♂ 355–372 ♀ 385–422	♂ 198–222 ♀ 235–268		74–87	(35)

Plate 14

Melierax gabar
adult   adult
                        „dunkel"

Melierax m.
mechowi
adult

Melierax m.
metabates
immat.   adult

Melierax m.
neumanni
adult

Melierax gabar
immat.

Melierax c.
poliopterus
adult

Melierax c.
canorus
adult   immat.

Urotriorchis
macrourus
adult   adult
                „dunkel"

Urotriorchis
macrourus
immat.

immat.

Erythrotriorchis
radiatus
adult

Megatriorchis doriae
adult   juv.

1974 F. Weick

Benennung	Nomenclature	Verbreitung	Distribution	Länge Length cm	Flügel Wing mm	Schwanz/Tail mm	Gewicht Weight g	Tarsus mm	Culmen mm () = mit Wachshaut with cere
Accipiter gentilis (Linnaeus, 1758) Habicht	Northern Goshawk								
A. g. gentilis (Linnaeus, 1758) (Oberseitenfärbung kann von gelbbraun bis dunkelbraun variieren)	(upper parts varying from yellow-brown to dark-brown)	Mittel- u. N Europa, i. E bis Wolga, Kaukasus u. N Iran i. S bis Marokko u. Kleinasien. In Großbritannien sehr selten	Central and N Europe, east to Volga, Caucasus and N Iran, south to Morocco and Asia Minor. Rare in Great Britain		♂ 300–342 ♀ 336–385	♂ 203–235 ♀ 243–270	♂ 571–1110 ♀ 820–2200	♂ 68–78 ♀ 78–87,5	♂ 20,5–24 ♀ 23–27,5
A. g. buteoides (Menzbier, 1882) (größer u. heller als *gentilis* m. deutl. Über-Augenstreif; weißliche Farbvariante)	(larger and paler grey than *gentilis* superciliary stripe more conspicuous, a whitish phase occurs)	Äußerstes N Skandinavien, Rußland südl. Onega-See, i. E bis zur Lena	Extreme N Scandinavia, Russia south of Lake Onega, east to Lena River		♂ 308–345 ♀ 340–388		♂ 870–1170 ♀ 1185–1850 Cn.Menzbier♀über2000)		
A. g. albidus (Menzbier, 1882) (Normalform noch heller als *buteoides* vor allem an Kopf u. Nacken. Weißliche Farbvariante häufiger als bei *buteoides*)	(normal-phase still paler than *buteoides*, whiter on head and nape, whitish birds more common than in *buteoides*)	NE Sibirien östl. des Gebietes v. *buteoides* i. S bis Kamtschatka	NE Siberia, east of the range of *buteoides*, south to Kamchatka		♂ 316–346 ♀ 370–388		♂ 894–1200 ♀ 1320, 1390		
A. g. arrigonii (Kleinschmidt, 1903) (etwas dunkler als *gentilis*, Unterseite dichter gebändert)	(rather darker above than *gentilis*, more heavily barred below!)	Korsika, Sardinien	Corsica and Sardinia	43–61	♂ 293–308 ♀ 335–347				
A. g. schvedowi (Menzbier, 1882) (ähnlich *arrigoni*, Oberseite mehr schiefergrau, Unterseite weniger stark gebändert)	(similar to *arrigonii*, above more slaty gray, less heavily barred below)	S E Rußland i. E bis Amur und Ussuriland, i. S bis Kirgizsteppe u. W China	SE Russia, east to Amur- and Ussuriland, south to Kirghiz-Steppes and W China		♂ 298–323 ♀ 330–362		♂ 556,600 1♀ 1000		
A. g. fujiyamae (Swann & Hartert, 1923) (kleiner u. etwas dunkler als *schvedowi*)	(similar to *schvedowi*; but smaller and some darker above)	Japan (Hondo)	Japan (Hondo)		3♂ 286–300 ♀323–339(Swann) 302–350(Kobayashi)	200–268		64–82	20–26
A. g. atricapillus (Wilson, 1812) (artliche Abtrennung v. *gentilis* scheint evtl. gerechtfertigt) (Rotäugig, dunkle, abgesetzte Kopfplatte, Unterseitenzeichnung in Flecken aufgelöst)	(may be a distinct species. Red eye, contrasting black cap, below without definite barring but finely stippled with grey and clear black shaft streaks)	N Amerika mit Ausnahme des äußersten Westens u. Südwestens	North America except extreme W and SW		♂ 308–330 ♀ 324–356		♂ 860 ♀ 1090–1290		
A. g. laingi (Taverner, 1940) (wie *atricapillus*, jedoch etwas dunkler)	(like *atricapillus* but rather darker)	Inseln der Küste v. Brit. Kolumbien (Vancouver u. Queen-Charlotte-Ins.)	Vancouver and Queen Charlotte Islands off coast of British Columbia		♂ 312 ♀ 332				
A. g. apache van Rossem, 1938 (wie *atricapillus*, Füße u. Gestalt kräftiger)	(like *atricapillus* but rather darker and with heavier feet)	NW Mexiko u. S Arizona sowie Neu-Mexiko	NW Mexico, S Arizona and New Mexico		♂ 344–354 ♀ 365–390				
Accipiter henstii (Schlegel, 1873) Hensthabicht (Unterseitenbänderung bis Kehle u. Zügel reichend)	Henst's Goshawk (closely barred below, barring extending to throat and lores)	Madagaskar (v. Meereshöhe bis ca. 1800 m.)	Madagascar (from sea level to 6000 feet)	48–58	♂ 276–282 ♀ 318–330	♂ 244–258 ♀ 288		81–100	(32)
Accipiter melanoleucus Smith, 1830 Trauerhabicht	Black and White Goshawk								
A. m. melanoleucus Smith, 1830 (schlanker als die bisherigen *Accipiter*-Arten, dunkelrote Augen)	(slimmer appearance than other „true goshawks", dark-red eyes)	E u. S Afrika i. W bis Gabun	E and S Africa, west to Gabon		♂ 287–295 ♀ 333–347	♂ 210–225 ♀ 253–267	♀ 780	73–90	18–24
A. m. temminckii (Hartlaub, 1855) (Habitus wie *melanoleucus*, jedoch kleiner)	(similar to *melanoleucus*, but smaller)	W Afrika v. Gabun bis Kap Verde	W Africa, from Gabon to Cape Verde	48–58	♂ 251–273 ♀ 290–310	♂ 190–203 ♀ 230–240			
Accipiter meyerianus (Sharpe, 1878) Papuahabicht Südseehabicht (grauer Anflug auf Bauch u. Flanken, weiße Hosen u. Unterschwanzdecken)	Meyer's Goshawk (greyish wash on white belly and sides, clear white thighs and under tail coverts)	Molukken (Ceramlaut, Ceram, Boano, Halmahera), Salomon Ins. (Kulanbangra, Guadalcanar), Neubritannien, Uatom, Japen, Neuguinea (1 ×)	Moluccas (Ceramlaut, Ceram, Boano, Halmahera), Solomons (Kulanbangra, Guadalcanal), New Britain, Uatom, Japen Island. One record New Guinea	51–61	♂ 295–315 ♀ 319–342	♂ 204,205 ♀ 227–239		71–74 78	25
Accipiter buergersi (Reichenow, 1914) Bürgershabicht (haselnußbraune Farbtöne auf Flügel, Skapularen, Rücken, Hosen, Flanken)	Bürger's Sparrow-Hawk (chestnut feather edgings on wing, scapulars, back, thighs and flanks)	E Neuguinea (selten)	Eastern New Guinea (rare)	48–58	♂ 288–295 ♀ 320–325	♂ 207–215 ♀ 229–250		♂ 70 ♀ 75	

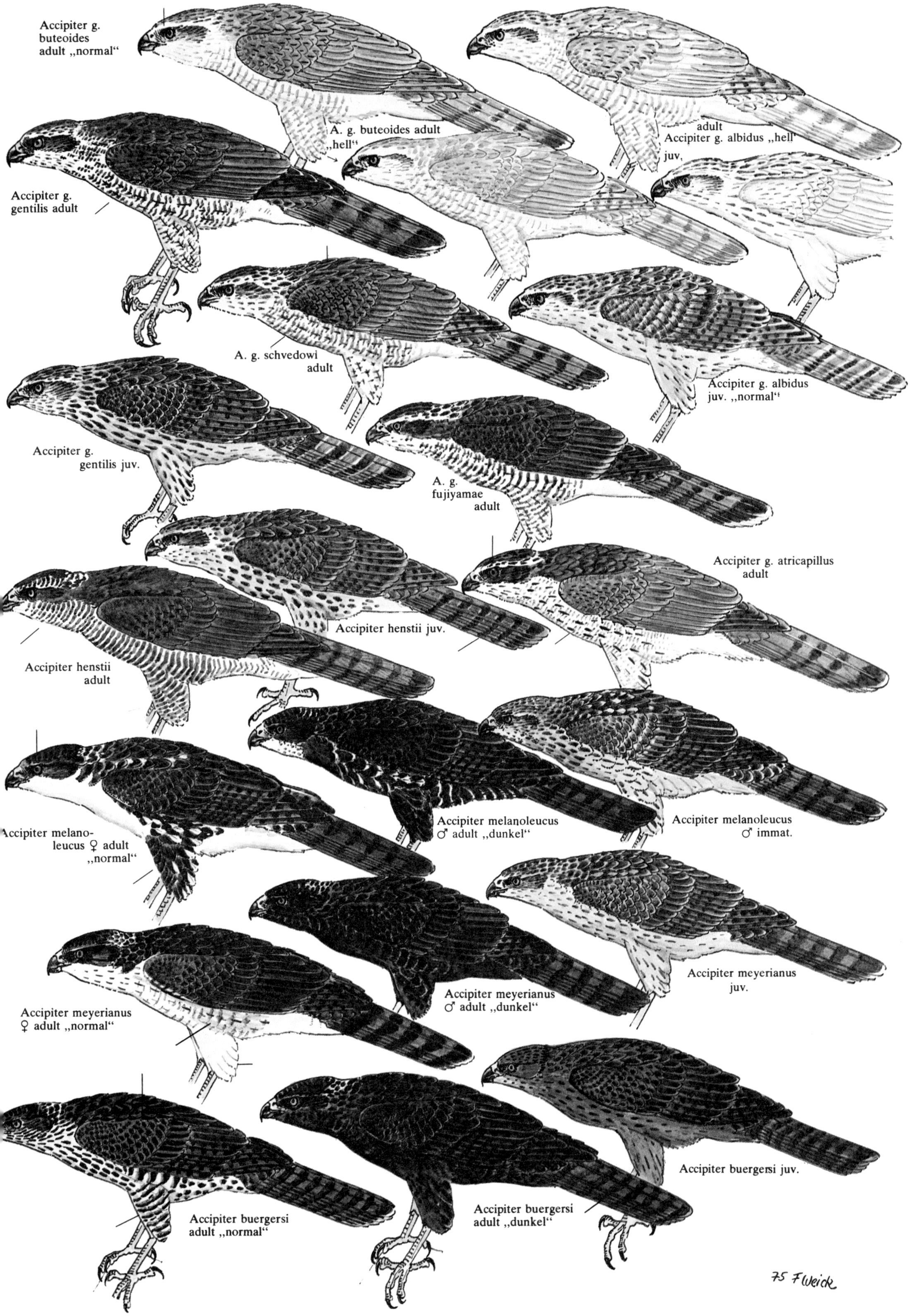

Plate 15

Accipiter g.
buteoides
adult „normal"

A. g. buteoides adult
„hell"

adult
Accipiter g. albidus „hell"

Accipiter g.
gentilis adult

juv.

A. g. schvedowi
adult

Accipiter g. albidus
juv. „normal"

Accipiter g.
gentilis juv.

A. g.
fujiyamae
adult

Accipiter g. atricapillus
adult

Accipiter henstii juv.

Accipiter henstii
adult

Accipiter melano-
leucus ♀ adult
„normal"

Accipiter melanoleucus
♂ adult „dunkel"

Accipiter melanoleucus
♂ immat.

Accipiter meyerianus
juv.

Accipiter meyerianus
♀ adult „normal"

Accipiter meyerianus
♂ adult „dunkel"

Accipiter buergersi juv.

Accipiter buergersi
adult „normal"

Accipiter buergersi
adult „dunkel"

75 F Weick

Benennung	Nomenclature	Verbreitung	Distribution	Länge Length cm	Flügel Wing mm	Schwanz/Tail mm	Gewicht Weight g	Tarsus mm	Culmen mm () = mit Wachshaut with cere
Accipiter ovampensis Gurney, 1875 Ovambosperber (Weiße Flecken auf Schwanz können auch schon bei Immaturvogel deutlich zu sehen sein.)	Ovampo Sparrowhawk (White tail-spots often visible already in immature-plumage.)	Afrika, v. Äthiopien bis Ghana u. südlich durch Kenia, Tanganjika bis NW Afrika u. Transvaal	Africa, from Ethiopia to Ghana and south through Kenya, Tanganyika to NW Africa and Transvaal	33–38	♂ 210–225 ♀ 245–253 (244 Gurney)	♂ 145–150 ♀ 160–190		43–52	13
Accipiter rufiventris A. Smith, 1830 = A. exilis (Temminck, 1830) Rotbrustsperber	Red-breasted Sparrowhawk			33–40				49–57	(22)
A. r. rufiventris A. Smith, 1830 (die rostfarbene bis rötl.-braune Unterseite ist kennzeichnend)	(in adult plumage the rufous or tawny undersurface is diagnostic)	Südafrika bis Zaïre, Uganda	South Africa to Zaire, Uganda		♂ 200–225 ♀ 230–245	♂ 155–162 ♀ 180–195			
A. r. perspicillaris (Rüppell, 1836) (größer u. dunkler als rufiventris)	(larger and darker than rufiventris)	Äthiopien	Ethiopia		♂ 192–200 ♀ –230				
Accipiter madagascariensis Smith, 1834 Madagaskarsperber (zeigt ähnl. Farbschema wie der größere A. henstii)	Madagascar Sparrowhawk (similar in colour pattern to the larger A. henstii)	Madagaskar, v. Meeresspiegel bis ca. 900 m Höhe	Madagascar from sea level to 3000 feet	29–38	♂ 168–198 ♀ 219–226	♂ 133–154 ♀ 174–187		♂ 48–55 ♀ 61–67	
Accipiter gularis (Temminck & Schlegel, 1845) Hondosperber (ohne den deutlichen Kehlstreif v. A. virgatus u. mit vier grauen Schwanzbinden)	Japanese Lesser Sparrowhawk (similar to A. virgatus but lacks the distinct median throat stripe and has four greyish tailbands)	Hondo (Japan), Riu-Kiu, Taiwan, E China, S Kurilen, Korea, Mandschurei, Winter: Burma, Malaya bis Indochina, Philippinen, W Indonesien, Sulawesi, Timor	Hondo (Japan), Riu Kius, Taiwan, E China, S Kuriles, Korea, Manchuria, Winter: Burma, Malaya to Indo-China, Philippines, W Indonesia, Sulawesi, Timor	23–30	♂ 156–187 ♀ 167–198	♂ 116–137 ♀ 138–143	♂ 92–142 ♀ 111–198	51–54	10–15
Accipiter virgatus (Temminck, 1822) Besrasperber	Besra Sparrowhawk								
A. v. virgatus (Temminck, 1822) (♂ auf Unterseite deutlich gesperbert)	(male below distinctly barred)	Java	Java		♂ 144–149,5 ♀ 168–179	♂ 107–119 ♀ 126–134		♂ 44–50 ♀ 50–58	10
A. v. affinis Hodgson, 1836 (ähnl. virgatus, jedoch noch deutlichere Unterseiten-Bänderung)	(similar to virgatus, but barring below still more distinct)	W Himalaja i. E bis Szechuan, E Siam, Kwangsi, Taiwan. Winter: Ind., Burma, Siam, Indochina	W Himalaya east to Szechuan, E Siam, Kwangsi, Taiwan, Winter: India, Burma, Siam, Indo-China		♂ 165–180 ♀ 197–218	♂ 123–135,5 ♀ 151–167		♂ 48,5–53 ♀ 54,5–61	(18–20) (22–24)
A. v. besra Jerdon, 1839 (etwas blassere Unterseitenfärbung als virgatus)	(rather paler below than virgatus)	Indien, südlich Bombay, Sri Lanka, Andamanen	India, from Bombay south, Sri Lanka, Andaman Islands		♂ 145–166 ♀ 182–189	♂ 112–119,5 ♀ 136–148		♂ 44–48 ♀ 46–55	
A. v. confusus Hartert, 1910 (bei ♂ Oberseite mehr bläulich, Unterseite nahezu ungebändert)	(male above more bluish, below nearly uniform rufous)	Philippinen, (m. Ausnahme v. Palawan)	Philippine Islands except Palawan	28–36	♂ 152–174 ♀ 175–185	♂ 121–124 ♀ 137–140	♂ 83–99 ♀ 131–140	♂ 50 ♀ 51–53	
A. v. rufotibialis Sharpe, 1887 (rotes Brustband u. rote Hosen, mehr in weinrote Farbtönung übergehend)	(breast rufous, thighs more vinaceous)	N Borneo (Mt. Kinabalu, Mt. Dulit, Kelabit Plateau)	N Borneo (Mt. Kinabalu, Mt. Dulit, Kelabit Plateau)		♂ 146–152,5 ♀ 172				
A. v. vanbemmeli Voous, 1950 (♂ auf Unterseite ausgedehnt rostbraun)	(male like rufotibialis, but still more rufous, barring less distinct)	Sumatra	Sumatra		♂146,5–160,5 ♀ 179–191				
Accipiter nanus (W. Blasius, 1897) Kleinsperber (lange Mittelzehe, weiße Hosen)	Celebes Little Sparrowhawk (male resembles A. rhodogaster but has white thighs and a long middle toe)	Sulawesi	Sulawesi	23–28	♂ 151–161 ♀ 164–182	♂ 109–119 ♀ 121–135		42–48	12,5
Accipiter rhodogaster (Schlegel, 1862) Rotbauchsperber	Vinous-breasted Sparrowhawk								
A. rh. rhodogaster (Schlegel, 1862) (♂ im Feld kaum v. nanus unterscheidbar, ♀ jedoch viel größer)	(♂ indistinguishable from A. nanus, but female is much bigger than that of nanus)	Sulawesi	Sulawesi		♂ 162–172 ♀ 201–209	♂ 115–122 ♀ 147–156		51–63	(20)
A. rh. butonensis, Voous, 1954 (Unterseite u. Kopfseiten heller)	(sides of head and under-surface paler than in nominate form)	Muna, Buton	Muna, Bhuton	28–33	♂ 165–175 ♀ 203–214		1♂ imm. 113 1♀ imm. 264		
A. rh. sulaensis (Schlegel, 1866) (Kopfseiten oft rostfarben überflogen)	(sides of head often washed with rufous)	Peling u. Sula	Peling and Sula		♂ 160 ♀ 175–185	♀ 147		♀ 55	(♀ 25)
Accipiter erythrauchen G. R. Gray, 1860 Molukkensperber, Graukehl-sperber	Moluccan Sparrowhawk								
A. e. erythrauchen G. R. Gray, 1860 (Unterseite oft stark grau überflogen)	(below often with a strong greyish wash)	Molukken (Batjan, Halmahera, Morotai, Obi)	Moluccas (Batjan, Halmahera, Morotai, Obi)		♂ 170 ♀ 193–208	♂ 137 ♀ 148–158		53–59	(♂ 26)
A. e. ceramensis (Schlegel, 1862) (Kopf u. Rücken dunkler, Unterseite grauer als bei erythrauchen)	(head and back blacker, below still greyer than erythrauchen)	Ceram u. Buru	Ceram and Buru	28–35	♀ 201–215	♀ 172	1♂ 156	♀ 61	♀ 19
Accipiter cirrhocephalus (Vieill. 1817) Kragensperber, Ringsperber	Collared Sparrowhawk								
A. c. cirrhocephalus (Vieillot, 1817) (rotbraunes Nackenband! ♀ kann mit A. fasciatus verwechselt werden, besonders mit A. f. didimus)	(collar generally rufous; always difficult to distinguish large female of ,cirrocephalus' from small male of A. fasciatus, especially A. f. didimus)	S Australien, Tasmanien	Southern Australia, Tasmania		♂ 195–219 ♀ 232–253	150–162	1♂ 125 1♀ 235	57–59	
A. c. quaesitandus Mathews, 1915 (Oberseite etwas fahler als Nomin.; Unterseite weniger deutl. gebändert)	(Paler above, less clearly barred below)	Halbinsel Kap-York u. N Australien	Cape York Peninsula and North Australia	25–33	♂ 194–209 ♀ 228–242				
A. c. rosselianus Mayr, 1940 (Oberseite dunkler als cirrhocephalus, m. einigen rostfarb. Federsäumen, Unterseite dunkler)	(above darker than cirrhocephalus, with some rufous feather-edges and deep chestnut below)	Louisiaden (Rossel-Insel)	Louisiades (Rossel Island)		214–219				
A. c. papuanus Rothschild & Hartert, 1913 (ähnl. rosselianus, Unterseite jedoch heller)	(similar to rosselianus, rather paler below)	Neuguinea, Waigeo, Salawati, Japen	New Guinea, Waigeu, Salawati, Japen		♂ 182–190 ♀ 204–220	♂ 132 ♀ 142		♂ 54	
Accipiter brachyurus (Ramsay, 1879) Kehlringsperber, Kurzschwanz-sperber (graue Unterseite gibt gutes Unterscheidungsmerkmal zu anderen kleinen Accipiter-Arten)	New Britain Sparrowhawk (greyish under-surface should be diagnostic from other little accipiters of this island)	Neubritannien	New Britain Island	28–33	♂ imm. 168 ♀ 202–205	♂ imm. 134 ♀ 139–148		54–63	

Plate 16

Accipiter
ovampensis

adult ♂
„normal"

♀
immat.

A. ovampensis ♂ adult-
„dunkel"

Accipiter r. rufiventris
♀ adult
♂ immat.

A.r. perspicilla-
ris ♂ adult

♂ adult

A. madagas-
cariensis adult
♂ ♀

A. mada-
gasca-
riensis
immat.

Accipiter gularis
adult
♂ ♀

A. gularis
immat.

immat
A. nanus
♂ adult

A. v.
rufotibi-
alis ♂
adult

A. v.
confusus
♂
adult

A. v.
vanbem-
meli ♂
adult

A. r. rhodo-
gaster
♀ immat ♂
adult

v.
gatus ♂
adult

A. v.
rufotibialis
♀ ad.

A. v.
confusus
♀ adult

← A. r. butonen-
sis
♂ adult

A. v.
virgatus
♀ immat.

♀
ad.

A. v.
besra
immat.
♀
adult

A. cirrhocephalus
♂ adult

← A. r.
sulaensis
♂ adult

← A. r.
rhodogaster
adult ♀

A. cirrho-
cephalus
♀immat
adult

♀ adult

A. brachyurus
♂ adult
„dunkel"

← Accipter e.
erythrauchen
♀ adult

← Acciter e.
ceramensis
♂ adult

A. brachyurus
♂ immat.

Accipiter e.
erythrauchen
♂ immat.

74 F Weick

Benennung	Nomenclature	Verbreitung	Distribution	Länge Length cm	Flügel Wing mm	Schwanz/Tail mm	Gewicht Weight g	Tarsus mm	Culmen mm () = mit Wachshaut with cere
Accipiter nisus (Linnaeus, 1758) Sperber	European Sparrowhawk								
A. n. nisus (Linnaeus, 1758) (♂♂ können auf Unterseite sehr unterschiedl. „Buntheit" zeigen)	(♂♂ below with different stronger or paler colouring)	Europa i. E bis SW Iran u. N Yennisei u. Ural, W bis Großbrit. u. Spanien	Europe, east to SW Iran, Yenisei and Ural, west to Great Britain and Iberian Peninsula		♂ 186–210 ♀ 223–248	♂ 135–154 ♀ 164–185	♂ 105–186 ♀ 192–310	♂ 48–56,5 ♀ 56–64	♂ 10,5–12,5 ♀ 13–15,3
A. n. punicus Erlanger, 1897 (heller u. etwas größer)	(paler and slightly larger than nisus)	Marokko, Algerien, Tunesien (S bis zum Hohen- u. Sahara-Atlas)	Morocco, Algeria, Tunisia (south to High Atlas)		♂ 203–214 ♀ 237–255				
A. n. granti Sharpe, 1890 (etwas dunkler u. etwas dichter gebändert)	(slightly darker, more heavily barred below than ‚nisus')	Madeira u. Kanarische Inseln (Palma, Gomera, Gr. Canaria, Teneriffa)	Madeira and Canaries (Palma, Gomera, Grand Canaria, Teneriffe)		♂ 186–198 ♀ 217–234				
A. n. wolterstorffi Kleinschmidt, 1901 (dunkler als granti und Unterseite mit breiter Bänderung)	(still darker and barring below wider than in granti)	Korsika, Sardinien	Corsica and Sardinia	28–38	♂ 181–196 ♀ 212–226				
A. n. nisosimilis (Tickell, 1833) (Habitus wie nisus, jedoch größer)	(similar to nisus, but larger)	Mittel- u. Ostsibirien, Ochotk-Meer. Winter: Korea, Japan, Indien, Burma	Central and E Siberia, Sea of Okhotsk. Winter: Korea, Japan, India, Burma		♂ 200–219 ♀ 239–260	♂ 145–161 ♀ 175–194		♂ 52–55 ♀ 60–65	♂ 11–12 ♀ 14–16
A. n. melaschistos Hume, 1869 (♂ Unterseite rostfarbener, Oberseite dunkler)	(♂ much darker above, much more rufous below)	Südzentralasiat. Gebirge, W bis Kaschmir. Winter: Burma	Southern Central-Asiatic-Mountains west to Kashmir. Winter: Burma		♂ 202–216 ♀ 241–260				
Accipiter striatus Vieillot, 1807 Eckschwanzsperber	Sharp-shinned Hawk								
A. s. velox (Wilson, 1812) (Schwanz eckig, gerade o. leicht ausgebuchtet)	(tail square or slightly notched)	Nordamerika, S bis S Arizona u. S Neu Mexico	North America, south to S Arizona and S New Mexico		♂ 161–178 ♀ 191–206	♂ 130–139 ♀ 149–162	♂ ⌀ 102 ♀ ⌀ 179	45–59	
A. s. perobscurus Snyder, 1938 (nur wenig dunkler als velox)	(slightly darker than velox)	Queen-Charlotte-Insel, Brit. Kolumbien u. evtl. benachb. Küste	Queen Charlotte Island, British Columbia and perhaps adjacent coastal areas		1♂ 174 1♀ 206				
A. s. suttoni van Rossem, 1939 (fahler als velox, m. einfarbigen „Hosen")	(paler than velox and uniform thighs)	S Arizona u. Neu-Mexiko S bis Veracruz u. Michoacan	Southern Arizona and New-Mexico south to Veracruz and Michoacan		♂ 170–192 ♀ 216–229	♂ 131–150 ♀ 165–177			
A. s. madrensis Storer, 1952 (wie suttoni, jedoch Iris gelb, Unterseite heller)	(like suttoni, but iris yellow and paler below)	Siefra Madre del Sur, Guerrero evtl. W Oaxaca	Sierra Madre del Sur, Guerrero and perhaps western Oaxaca		Maße ~ wie suttoni				
A. s. chionogaster (Kaup, 1851) (Unterseite weiß, Hosen beige, Oberseite dunkel)	(below white, thighs buff, above dark grey)	NW Chiapas, Guatemala, Honduras, El Salvador, Nicaragua	NW Chiapas, Guatemala, Honduras, El Salvador, Nicaragua	25–35	♂ 166–175 ♀ 198–209	♂ 130–135 ♀ 156–164		50–57	(♀ 20)
A. s. ventralis Sclater, 1866 (Hosen rostfarben, nicht beige)	(thighs more rufous than in chionogaster)	W Venezuela u. Anden v. Kolumbien bis W Bolivien	W Venezuela and Andes from Colombia to W Bolivia		♂ 152–178 ♀ 190–217	♂ 150– ♀ 188	1♂ 90 1♀ 219	50–56	(♀ 18)
A. s. erythronemius (Kaup, 1850) (Hosen u. Flanken rostfarben)	(thighs and mid-sides rufous)	E Bolivien, südl. Hälfte Brasiliens, Paraguay, Uruguay, N Argentinien,	E Bolivia, S Brazil, Paraguay, Uruguay, N Argentina		♂ 163–170 ♀ 190–195	♂ 145		♀ 50	(♀ 19)
A. s. striatus Vieillot, 1807 (ähnlich velox, doch Kopfseiten braunrot, Schwanz undeutl. gebändert)	(similar to velox, but sides of head russet)	Hispaniola	Hispaniola		♂ 141–153 ♀ 181–186				
A. s. fringilloides Vigors, 1828 (Kopfseiten mehr rostgelb)	(sides of head clearer rufous)	Kuba	Cuba		♂ 157 ♀ 178, 185	♂ 124		♂ 48	
A. s. venator Wetmore, 1914 (ähnl. striatus, jedoch mit deutl. schwarzen Schwanzbinden!)	(like striatus, but with more distinct, black tailbands)	Puerto Rico	Puerto Rico		♂ 145	♂ 122			
Accipiter erythropus (Hartlaub, 1855) Rotschenkelsperber	Red legged Sparrowhawk								
A. e. erythropus (Hartlaub, 1855) (weiße Oberschwanzdecken! Weiße Flecke auf Schwanz)	(white upper-tail coverts, white tailspots)	W Afrika v. Gambia–Kamerun, Kongo, Angola, Uganda,	W Africa from Gambia to Cameroon, Kongo, Angola, Uganda		♂ 145–152 ♀ 154–169	♂ 108 ♀ 118		43–45	(♂ 18)
A. e. zenkeri Reichenow, 1894 (Oberseite schwärzer, Unterseite mehr kastan.braun, selten deutlich gebändert)	(blacker above, below more chestnut, sometimes clearly barred)	E Nigeria u. Kamerun	E Nigeria and Cameroon	23–28	♂ 146–149 ♀ 174–180	♂ 115			
Accipiter minullus (Daudin, 1800) Zwergsperber (nicht so dunkel auf Oberseite wie erythropus, Unterseite deutlicher gespert)	African Little Sparrowhawk (less dark above than in erythropus, below more clearly barred)	E u. S Afrika v. Äthiopien bis Kapland	E and S Africa from Ethiopia to Cape Province	23–28	♂ 136–147 ♀ 156–168	105–117 130	♂ –83 ♀ –46	♂ 38–43	8– 12
Accipiter castanilius Bonaparte, 1853 Kastanienhabicht (-sperber)	Chestnut-bellied Sparrowhawk								
A. c. castanilius Bonaparte, 1853 (an intensiver rostbrauner Unterseite u. weißen Schwanzflecken v. den meisten tachiro-Formen zu unterscheiden)	(more chestnut colouring below and whiter tailspots distinguish castanilius from most subspecies of A. tachiro)	Nigeria bis VR Kongo, W Zaïre	Nigeria to W Congo, W Zaire	28–35	♂ 152–157 ♀ 174–183	♂ 130–140 ♀ 152–165		♂ 53	(♂ 21)
A. c. beniensis Lönnberg, 1917 (Habitus wie Nominatform, aber größer)	(similar to nominate-race, but larger)	E Zaïre	E Zaire		♂ 162–167 ♀ 188–190	♂ 146			
Accipiter tachiro (Daudin, 1800) Afrikahabicht	African Goshawk								
A. t. tachiro (Daudin, 1800) (im Feld sehr schwer v. castanilius zu unterscheiden)	(extremely difficult to distinguish in field from castanilius)	S Afrika im N bis S Angola, Simbabwe, Maputo	S Africa north to S Angola, Zimbabwe, Maputo		♂ 200–225 ♀ 240–257	♂ 168 ♀ –227		57–69	15–20
A. t. sparsimfasciatus (Reichw. 1895) (etwas dunkler auf Oberseite u. deutlicher gebändert auf Unterseite als tachiro, ohne weiße Schwanzflecke)	(slightly darker above and more clearly barred below, lacks white tail-spots)	E Afrika	E Africa		♂ 211 ♀ 252		2♀ 408, 509		
A. t. unduliventer (Rüppell, 1836) (noch dunkler an Ober- u. Unterseite als sparsimfasciatus mit weißen Schwanzflecken)	(still darker above and below than sparsimfasciatus, with white tailspots)	S u. N Äthiopien	S and N Ethiopia	35–43	♂ 184 ♀ 216				
A. t. canescens (Chapin, 1921) (Unterseite ohne Bänderung, Kehle hellgrau)	(below unbarred, throat pale grey)	N Zaïre	N Zaire		♂ 186 ♀ 226				
A. t. toussenelii (J. & E. Verreaux, 1855) (Kopf u. Hals deutl. grau, hellgraue Kehle.hebt sich deutl. von Brust ab)	(clearer grey on head and neck, white throat strongly contrasting with barred breast)	Gabun bis Niederguinea	Gabon and lower Guinea		♂ 183–201 ♀ 209–230	♂ 151–159 ♀ 182–196			
A. t. macroscelides (Hartlaub, 1855) (kleiner, dunkler u. mehr braunrot auf der Unterseite als toussenelii)	(smaller and darker, below more chestnut-barring than toussenelii)	Sierra Leone bis W Kamerun	Sierra Leone to W Cameroon		♂ 184–200 ♀ 210–213				
A. t. lopezi (Alexander, 1903) (Unterseite reichlich rotbraun u. intensiv gebändert, Oberseite dunkel, helle Schwanzflecke)	(richly barred chestnut below, above dusky, clear white tailspots)	Insel Fernando-Po	Fernando Po Island		♂ 182–189 ♀ 214–216	♂ 150 ♀ 190			

Plate 17

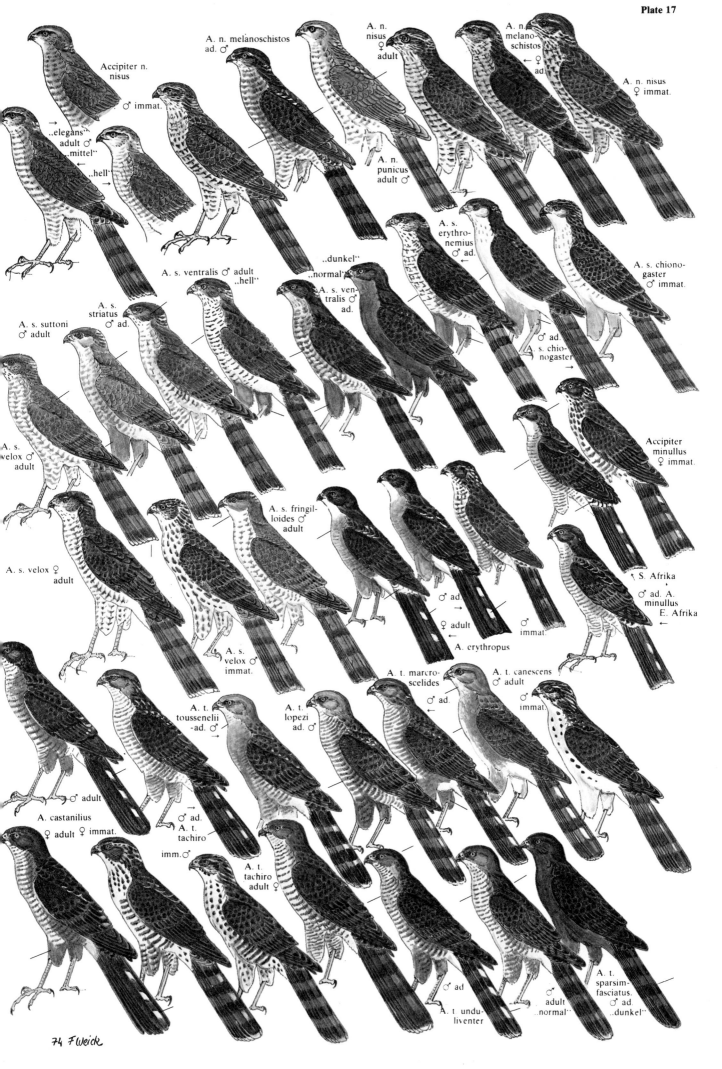

Accipiter n. nisus

..elegans" adult ..mittel" →

..hell" →

♂ immat.

A. n. melanoschistos ad. ♂

A. n. nisus ♀ adult

A. n. nisus ♀ immat.

A. n. melanoschistos ← ♀ ad.

A. n. punicus adult ♂

A. s. ventralis ♂ adult ..hell"

..dunkel"

..normal"

A. s. ventralis ♂ ad.

A. s. erythronemius ♂ ad.

A. s. chionogaster ♂ immat.

A. s. striatus ♂ ad.

♂ ad. A. s. chionogaster →

A. s. suttoni ♂ adult

A. s. velox ♂ adult

A. s. fringilloides ♂ adult

Accipiter minullus ♀ immat.

A. s. velox ♀ adult

A. s. velox ♂ immat.

♂ ad. →

♀ adult

A. erythropus

immat.

S. Afrika • ♂ ad. A. minullus E. Afrika

A. t. marcroscelides

♂ ad. ←

A. t. canescens ♂ adult

immat.

A. t. toussenelii -ad. ♂ →

A. t. lopezi ad. ♂

A. castanilius ♂ adult ♀ adult ♀ immat.

♂ adult

♂ ad. → A. t. tachiro

imm. ♂

A. t. tachiro adult ♀

♂ ad

A. t. unduliventer

♂ ad. ..normal"

A. t. sparsimfasciatus. ♂ ad. ..dunkel"

74 F. Weick

Benennung	Nomenclature	Verbreitung	Distribution	Länge Length cm	Flügel Wing mm	Schwanz/Tail mm	Gewicht Weight g	Tarsus mm	Culmen mm () = m Wachshal with ce
Accipiter poliocephalus G. R. Gray, 1858 Neuguinea Graukopfhabicht (graue Ober- u. weiße Unterseite bilden deutlichen Kontrast)	New-Guinea Grey-headed Goshawk (grey upperparts clearly contrasting with white underparts)	Neuguinea u. Nachbarinseln, Misool, Salawati, Waigeo, Batanta, Japen, Fergusson, Misima, Arus	New Guinea and surrounding islands: (Misol, Salawati, Waigeu, Batanta, Japen, Ferguson, Misima and Arus)	33–38	♂ 190–201 ♀ 203–217	♂ 146–149 ♀ 152–165	♂ 200–210 ♀ 225	♂ 54–62 ♀ 58	16 (♀ 32)
Accipiter princeps Mayr, 1934 Neubritannien Graukopfhabicht (Beleg eines immaturen Stückes fehlt)	New Britain Grey-headed Goshawk (immature-plumage unknown)	Durch 3 ad. Exemplare bekannt von Neubritannien	known from three specimen (adult) taken on New Britain	38–45	♂ 253,257 ♀ 285	♂ 183,186 ♀ 207		68–71	
Accipiter trinotatus Bonaparte, 1850 Fleckschwanzhabicht (extrem kurze Zehen und weiße Schwanzflecken kennzeichnen diese Art)	Spot-tailed Goshawk (extremely short toes and conspicuous white tailspots distinguish this species)	Sulawesi, Muna, Buton	Sulawesi, Muna and Buton islands	29–31	♂ 153–159 ♀ 158–172	♂ 124–129 ♀ 134–143		49–55	(19–22)
Accipiter soloënsis (Horsfield, 1821) Chinesenhabicht, Chinashikra (Unterseite mehr grau u. rostbraun überflogen als gebändert)	Grey Frog Hawk (Under-parts washed rather than barred with grey and rufous!)	Mittel-China u. Korea bis Szechuan u. S bis Kwangsi, Kwangtung, Taiwan. Winter: Philipp., Sulawesi, Malaya, Gr. Sunda-Ins., Molukken u. Waigeo	Central-China and Korea to Szechuan and south to Kwangsi, Kwangtung, Taiwan. Winter: Philippines, Sulawesi, Malaya, Great Sunda Islands, Moluccas and Waigeu	25–30	♂ 170–201 ♀ 187–209	♂ 120–132 ♀ 127–139	1♂ 140 1♀ 204	39–44	(17–19)
Accipiter badius (Gmelin, 1788) Shikra **A. b. badius (Gmelin, 1788)** (Schwanzbänderung unterscheidet diese Art gut v. A. nisus u. virgatus)	Shikra (lack of tailbands distinguish this species distinctly from A. nisus and virgatus)	S Indien, Sri Lanka	South-India, Sri Lanka		♂ 169–182 ♀ 186–207	♂ 129–134 ♀ 145–161		44–54	(♂ 19–2 (♀ 22,23
A. b. dussumieri (Temminck, 1824) (auf Ober- u. Unterseite heller als badius)	(above and below paler than badius)	Indien v. Kaschmir u. Sikkim S bis Mittel-Indien	India from Kashmir and Sikkim south to Central-India		♂ 173–206 ♀ 201–222	♂ 160		50–54	
A. b. cenchroides (Severtzow, 1873) (heller als badius u. dussumieri)	(paler than badius and dussumieri)	Transkaukasus E bis Tien-Shan u. Ferghana, S bis Syr Darya u. N Persien	Transcaucasia east to Tianshan and Ferghana, south to Syr Darya and N Persia	28–35	♂ 177–202 ♀ 205–230	♂ 165 ♀ 180	1♂ 193 1♀ 266	♀ 58	
A. b. poliopsis (Hume, 1874) (Kopf mehr grau als dussumieri)	(similar to dussumieri but clearer grey head)	Assam E bis Taiwan, i. S bis Indochina u. Tenasserim	Assam east to Taiwan, south to Indo-China and Tenasserim		♂ 176–203 ♀ 190–226				(♂ 19–22 (♀ 20–22
A. b. sphenurus (Rüppell, 1836) (Oberseite matter grau, Unterseite rostfarbener als asiat. Arten)	(above duller grey, more rufous below than Asiatic forms)	Afrika v. Gambia bis Äthiopien, S bis Mittel-Kongo u. Tanganjika. S Arabien	Africa from Gambia to Ethiopia south to Central Congo and Tanganyika, S Arabia		♂ 171–187 ♀ 188–200	♂ 145	1♂ imm. 162	♂ 45	(22)
A. b. polyzonöides Smith, 1838 (einige weiße Flecke auf Mantel u. Flügel)	(some white spots on wing and mantle)	S Tanganjika u. Kasai, S bis Kapland	S Tanganyika and Kasai, south to Cape-Province		♂ 165–184 ♀ 185–200	♂ 120 ♀ 150–155		♂ 40 ♀ 44–48	10–12
Accipiter butleri (Gurney, 1898) Nikobarenshikra **A. b. butleri (Gurney, 1898)** (Schwanz m. feiner Subterminalbinde, Unterseite fein gesperbert)	Nicobar Shikra (uniform coloured tail with narrow terminal-band, below, breast finely barred)	Car-Nikobar-Insel	Car-Nicobar Island	28–33	♂ 168–176 ♀ 180	♂ 134–140 ♀ 152		46–48	(22)
A. b. obsoletus (Richmond, 1902) (fahler als butleri, ohne rötl. Tönung an Oberbrust)	(paler, lacking reddish on breast as in butleri)	Katchal-Insel (S Nikobaren)	Katchal-Island (South-Nicobar)		♀ 192	♀ 157		♀ 52	(♀ 21,5)
Accipiter brevipes (Severtzow, 1850) Kurzfangsperber (durch graue Ohrdecken von A. nisus zu unterscheiden)	Levant Sparrowhawk (distinguished from A. nisus by grey cheeks!)	Balkan E bis S Rußland u. Astrachan, S bis Kleinasien. Winter: SW Persien, Syrien, Israel, Ägypt., manchmal bis S Sudan u. Tansania	Balkan east to S Russia and Astrakhan, south to Asia Minor. Winter: SW Persia, Syria, Israel, Egypt. Sometimes south to Sudan and Tanzania	33–38	♂ 210–228 ♀ 231–245	♂ 148–162 ♀ 155–170	♂ 150–195 ♀ 232	♂ 46–50,5 ♀ 50–53,5	♂ 12–13 ♀ 13,5–1
Accipiter francesii Smith, 1834 Francessperber **A. f. francesii Smith, 1834** (durch Unterseitenzeichnung gut v. A. madagascariensis zu unterscheiden)	France's Sparrowhawk (distinguished from A. madagascariensis by different colouring of under-surface)	Madagaskar	Madagascar		♂ 151–163 ♀ 166–188	♂ 140–150 ♀ 160–163		♂ 50 ♀ 51	(♂ 20)
A. f. griveaudi Benson, 1960 (mit stärker ausgeprägter Unterseitenbänderung)	(barring below more extensive and distinct)	Große Komoren-Insel	Grand Comoro	28–33	♂ 139–149 ♀ 167–171	♂ 104–116 ♀ 113–129			
A. f. pusillus (Gurney, 1875) (ohne lachsfarbenen Anflug d. Unterseite beim ♂)	(♂ lack salmon wash on under-surface)	Anjouan (Gr. Komore?) Selten!	Anjouan (Grand Comoro?) rare		♂ 135–149 ♀ 155–163	♂ 99–108 ♀ 113–125			
A. f. brutus (Schlegel, 1866) (♂ m. deutl. rotbrauner Unterseitenbänderung)	(barring below still more distinct than in other forms)	Majotte	Mayotte Island		♂ 137–143 ♀ 150–162	♂ 101–109 ♀ 118–128		♀ 48	
Accipiter trivirgatus (Temminck, 1824) Haubensperber **A. t. indicus (Hodgson, 1836)** (Größe, schlanke Gestalt u. Haube sind gute Kennzeichen)	Crested Goshawk (large size but slim appearance and crest arc good field marks to this species)	N Indien bis Kwangsi, Jünnan, Hainan	North-India to Kwangsi, Yunnan, Hainan		♂ 216–236 ♀ 232–262	♂ 168–195 ♀ 182–213		56–59	
A. t. layardi (Whistler & Kinnear, 1936) (stärkere Unterseitenzeichnung als indicus)	(more brightly coloured below than indicus)	Sri Lanka	Sri Lanka		♂ 183–190 ♀ 198–206	♂ 150–152 ♀ 157–168		♀ 50–53	(♂ 24–26) (♀ 27–28)
A. t. peninsulae Koelz, 1949 (♂ an Brust weniger rot als indicus)	(♂ with less reddish breast than indicus)	S Indien südl. v. Bombay	South-India, south of Bombay		♂ 196–211 ♀ 215–237	♂ 159–168 ♀ 169–180			(♂ 26–28' (♀ 29–31)
A. t. trivirgatus (Temminck, 1824) (hellere Unterseitenzeichnung als indicus)	(paler barring below than indicus)	Sumatra	Sumatra		♂ 197–205 ♀ 218–221				
A. t. javanicus Mayr, 1949 (Oberseite u. Kopf grauer, Haube kurz)	(head and upper-surface greyer, short crest)	Java	Java		♂ 191–202 ♀ 208–230	151–173		51–57	21–26
A. t. niasensis Mayr, 1949 (etwas dunkler u. kleiner als trivirgatus)	(slightly smaller and darker than trivirgatus)	Nias	Nias Islands	33–46	♂ 180–188 ♀ 207–217				
A. t. microstictus Mayr, 1949 (feinere Bänderung als trivirgatus auf der Unterseite)	(more finely barred below than trivirgatus)	Borneo	Borneo		♂ 191–200 ♀ 216–227				
A. t. palawanus Mayr, 1949 (♂ auf Unterseite viel kräftiger gezeichnet als microstictus)	(♂ similar to microstictus but more heavily barred below)	Palawan u. Natuna-Insel, Calamian-Ins.	Palawan, Natuna Islands (?) and Calamianes		♂ 189–195 ♀ 218,5–220,5				
A. t. extimus Mayr, 1945 (Unterseitenzeichnung sehr rostfarben)	(barring of underside more rufous)	Philippinen (Negros, Samar, Leyte u. Mindanao)	Philippines (Negros, Samar, Leyte and Mindanao)		♂ 182–193 ♀ 205–217	142–150		52–53	
A. t. castroi Manuel & Gilliard, 1952 (Rücken blauer als extimus u. mehr rotbraune Bänderung)	(similar to „extimus", but bluer back, below barring still more rufous)	Philippinen (Polillo Inseln)	Philippines (Pollilo Island)		♂ 184–190	♂ 148–160		♂ 54–55	
Accipiter griseiceps (Schlegel, 1862) Blaukopfsperber (Unterseite cremeweiß m. kräftigen Längsflecken)	Celebes Crested Goshawk (heavily streaked below on creamy-white ground)	Sulawesi, Muna, Buton, Togian	Sulawesi, Muna, Buton and Togian Islands	33–38	♂ 171–179 ♀ 182–206	♂ 133–147 ♀ 140–165	1♂ 212 1♀ 299	51–56	(♀ 31)

Plate 18

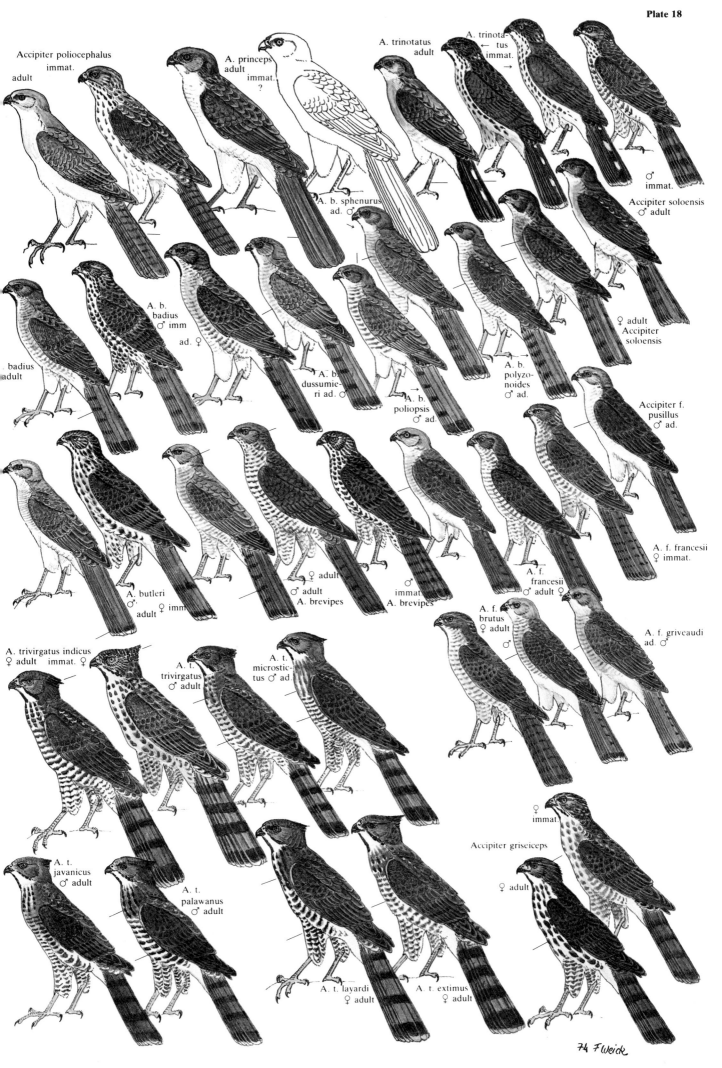

Accipiter poliocephalus
immat.
adult

A. princeps
adult
immat.
?

A. trinotatus adult

A. trinotatus immat.

♂
immat.

Accipiter soloensis
♂ adult

♀ adult
Accipiter soloensis

A. b. sphenurus ad. ♂

A. b.
badius
♂ imm
ad. ♀

A. b.
dussumieri ad. ♂

A. b.
poliopsis
♂ ad.

A. b.
polyzonoides
♂ ad.

badius
adult

Accipiter f.
pusillus
♂ ad.

A. butleri
♂
adult ♀ imm

♀ adult
♂ adult
A. brevipes

immat.
A. brevipes

A. f.
francesii
♂ adult ♀

A. f.
francesii
♀ immat.

A. f.
brutus
♀ adult

♂

A. f. griveaudi
ad. ♂

A. trivirgatus indicus
♀ adult   immat. ♀

A. t.
trivirgatus
♂ adult

A. t.
microstictus ♂ ad.

♀
immat.

Accipiter griseiceps

A. t.
javanicus
♂ adult

A. t.
palawanus
♂ adult

A. t. layardi
♀ adult

A. t. extimus
♀ adult

♀ adult

74 F.Weick

Benennung	Nomenclature	Verbreitung	Distribution	Länge Length cm	Flügel Wing mm	Schwanz/Tail mm	Gewicht Weight g	Tarsus mm	Culmen mm () = mit Wachshaut with cere
Accipiter melanochlamys (Salvadori, 1875) Schwarzmantelhabicht (kann in seinem Verbreitungsgebiet mit keinem anderen Greifvogel verwechselt werden)	Black-mantled Goshawk (impossible to confuse with any other bird of prey in this area)	Berge Neuguineas v. 1500–3300 m	Mountains of New Guinea from 4500–10 000 feet	33–38	♂ 221–227 ♀ 244–261	♂ 152–168 ♀ 185–207	♂imm172,225 1♀ 294	56–71	♂ 16 (♀ 28) ♀ 19
Accipiter imitator Hartert, 1926 Imitator- o. Trughabicht (viel kleiner als albogularis)	Imitator Sparrow-Hawk (Much smaller than albogularis)	Salomon-Inseln: Choiseul u. Isabel	Solomon Islands (Choiseul and Ysabel)	28–33	♂ imm 182 ♀ 197–208	1♂ imm 141 ♀ 149–163	♀ 225, 250	56–62	
Accipiter albogularis Gray, 1870 Weißkehlhabicht	Pied Goshawk, White-throated Goshawk								
A. a. woodfordi (Sharpe, 1888) (weißbauchige Individuen mit feiner Zeichnung an Hals- u. Brustseiten)	(specimen with white undersurface, sometimes with fine bars on neck and sides of chest)	Salomon-Ins. (Bougainville, Treasury, Shortlands, Choiseul, Florida, Isabel, Guadalcanar, Malaita)	Solomon Islands (Bougainville, Treasury, Shortlands, Choiseul, Florida, Ysabel, Malaita, Guadalcanal)		♂ 199–220 ♀ 243–263	♂ 148–156 ♀ 177–184		♂ 56–59 ♀ 62–72	
A. a. gilvus Mayr, 1945 (nur Immaturvogel unterscheidet sich v. woodfordi; Adultvogel ohne Kragen u. mit dunkler Phase)	(differs from woodfordi only in immatures; adult lacks collar and shows a dark phase)	Neugeorgien-Gruppe, Salomon Ins. (Vella Lavella, Kulambangra, Neu Georgia, Rendova)	New Georgia Group, Solomons (Vella Lavella, Kulambangra, New Georgia, Rendova)		2♂ 211 ♀ 247				
A. a. albogularis Gray, 1870 (Zeichnung der Kehlseiten schwarz verdüstert)	(sides of throat dusted black)	San-Cristobal-Gruppe, Salomon-Ins. (Ugi, St. Anna, San Cristobal)	San Cristobal Group, Solomons (Ugi, St. Anna, San Cristobal)	33–41	♂ 198–215 ♀ 243–254	1♀ 202	1♂ 250 1♀ 425	1♀ 67	(1♀ 34)
A. a. eichhorni Hartert, 1926 (Oberseite heller, Unterseitenzeichnung grau u. rötlich)	(upper-surface pale, markings on underside greyish vinaceous)	Insel Feni, östl. v. Neuirland	Feni Island, east of New Ireland		♂ 202–207 ♀ 232–244				
A. a. sharpei (Oustalet, 1877) (Oberseite dunkler, Unterseite ausgedehnter gebändert!)	(darker above, with more extensive vermiculations below)	Santa Cruz-Inseln	Santa Cruz Islands (Vanikoro, Utupua)		♂ 221–222 ♀ 239–255				
Accipiter haplochrous Sclater, 1859 Schwarzkehlhabicht (Schwanzbänderung)	New Caledonia Sparrow-hawk (tailbanding)	Neukaledonien	New Caledonia	35–41	♂ 195–202 ♀ 229–240	♂ 142–148 ♀ 175–177	♂ 181, 218 ♀ 281	55–61	
Accipiter rufitorques (Peale, 1848) Fidjihabicht (♂ mit blaugrauem Kopf u. blaß-weinrot überflogener Unterseite)	Fiji Goshawk (♂ with ashy grey head and vinous undersurface)	Fidji-Inseln (Viti Levu, Kandava, Taveuni, Ovalau, Bega, Vanua, Levu). Wahrscheinlich auch Insel Rotuma	Fiji Islands (Viti Levu, Kandava, Taveuni, Ovalau, Bega, Vanua, Levu, possibly Rotuma)	33–41	♂ 194–198 ♀ 232–242	♂ 135–140 ♀ 164–167 (180 Swann)		53–66	(21)
Accipter luteoschistaceus Rothschild & Hartert, 1926 Blaugrauhabicht (elfenbeinfarbene Unterseite, Farbe v. Fuß u. Wachshaut)	Blue and Grey Sparrow-hawk (below ivory to buff tinged, colour of legs and cere in adult)	Neubritannien	New Britain	31–38	♂ 185–194 ♀ 212	♂ 139–145 ♀ 166		57–64	
Accipiter henicogrammicus G. R. Gray, 1860 Molukkenhabicht (ohne Kragen, mit tief nußbrauner Unterseite)	Gray's Goshawk (without a collar, deep chestnut underside)	Molukken (Batjan, Halmahera, Morotai)	Moluccas (Batjan, Halmahera, Morotai)	38–48	♂ 218–228 ♀ 230–247	♂ 192–219 ♀ 219–230		♂ 66–68 ♀ 70–73	(♂ 32) (♀ 35)
Accipiter fasciatus (Vigors & Horsfield, 1827) Bänderhabicht	Australian Goshawk								
A. f. fasciatus (Vigors & Harsfield, 1827) (Oberseite tief sepiabraun m. rostbraunem Kragen)	(above deep sepia coloured with rufous halfcollar)	Australien, Tasmanien	Australia, Tasmania		♂ 255–278 ♀ 280–313	♂ 203–215 ♀ 240, 253	♀ 436–593	75–88	
A. f. didimus (Mathews, 1912) (kleiner u. durchweg heller)	(smaller, generally paler)	Küstengebiete Australiens, v. Cooktown, Kap York bis Derby, NW-Australien	Coastal areas of N W Australia		♂ 229–249 ♀ 263–297				
A. f. vigilax (Wetmore, 1926) (Habitus wie fasciatus, nur kleiner)	(similar to fasciatus, but smaller)	Neukaledonien, Loyalty-Inseln, Neue Hebriden	New Caledonia, Loyalty Islands, New Hebrides		♂ 236–253 ♀ 263–282				
A. f. polycryptus Rothschild & Hartert, 1914 (Unterseite mehr rötlichbraun als fasciatus)	(more reddish below than fasciatus)	E Neuguinea	Eastern New-Guinea		♂ 230–236 ♀ 256		♂185,215,269 ♀ ?	♂ 61	♂ 17
A. f. dogwa Rand, 1941 (Oberseits heller als polycryptus, Unterseits mit mehr Weiß, vor allem an Flanken u. Unterbauch)	(above paler than polycryptus, more whitish on flanks and abdomen)	S Neuguinea	Southern New Guinea		♂ 233 ♀ 245–256				
A. f. buruensis Stresemann, 1914 (sehr ähnlich didimus, etwas größer)	(resembles didimus, rather larger)	Buru (S-Molukken)	Buru (southern Moluccas)	33–51	♀ 259–270				
A. f. hellmayri Stresemann, 1922 (ähnlich dogwa, Unterseite noch mehr weiß)	(like dogwa, under-surface still whiter)	Timor, Samao, Alor	Timor, Samao, Alor		♂ 202–215 ♀ 240–255	♂ 151–163 ♀ 176–186		♀ 66	(♀ 20)
A. f. savu Mayr, 1941 (wie hellmayri, jedoch etwas heller an Unterseite mit schmaleren u. blasseren Querstreifen)	(similar to hellmayri, but paler below with narrower and paler barring)	Savu	Savu		♂ 220–222 ♀ 244–288	♂ 172 ♀ 188–191			
A. f. stresemanni Rensch, 1931 (Immaturvogel auf Unterseite mehr beigeweiß, viel Weiß auf d. Rücken)	(immatures more creamy or buffy-white below, more white flecks on back)	Djampea, Kalao, Bonerate, Madu, Tukang Besi.	Djampea, Kalao, Bonerate, Madu, Tukang Besi Islands		♂ 195–208 ♀ 234				
A. f. wallacei (Sharpe, 1874) (Unterseite dichter rötl. braun gebändert u. mit wenig weißgrauen Abzeichen)	(chest nearly uniform coloured and less barred with narrow greyish-white)	Lombok, Sumbawa, Flores, Sermata, Wetar, Damar, Moa, Letti	Lombok, Sumbawa, Flores, Sermata, Wetar, Damar, Moa, Letti		♂ 210 ♀ 237				
A. f. tjendanae Stresemann, 1925 (zwischen wallacei u. fasciatus!)	(intermediate in plumage between wallacei and fasciatus)	Sumba (kl. Sunda-Inseln)	Sumba (Lesser Sunda Island)		♂ 207–219 ♀ 247–255				
A. f. natalis (Lister, 1888) (ähnlich wallacei, aber größer)	(resembles wallacei but larger)	Weihnachtsinsel (Ind. Ozean) selten!	Christmas Island (Indian Ocean) rare!		♂ 217 ♀ 268	♂ 183 ♀ 220			

Plate 19

Accipiter melano-
chlamys
adult ♂ immat.

Accipiter imitator
adult „hell"
immat.

adult „normal"

♂ adult
Accipiter
haplochrous
♀ immat.

a. woodfordi
♀ adult
„normal"
ad. ♀
„Kragen"

A. a. woodfordi
♀ adult
„dunkel"

A. a. gilvus
♂ imm.

A. a. sharpei
♀ adult

A. a. eichhorni
♀ ad.

Accipiter a.
albogularis
♂ adult

a. woodfordi imm.
„normal" ♀
mat. ♂ „dunkel"

A. rufitorques
adult
imm.

A. luteoschistaceus
ad. ♂
imm.

A. f. wallacei
♂ ad.

♂ adult

A. henicogrammus
immat.

A. f. hellmayri
♀ adult

A. f.
hellmayri
♂ imm.

♂ adult
imm. ♀
A. f.
fasciatus

A. f.
didimus ♀
adult

A. f.
polycryptus

A. f.
dogwa
♂ ad.

Accipiter
f. natalis
adult

A. f.
stresemanni
♂ immat.

1975 wiik

Benennung	Nomenclature	Verbreitung	Distribution	Länge Length cm	Flügel Wing mm	Schwanz/Tail mm	Gewicht Weight g	Tarsus mm	Culmen mm () = mit Wachshaut with cere
Accipiter griseogularis (Gray, 1860) Graukehlhabicht	Grey-throated Goshawk								
A. g. mortyi Hartert, 1925 (deutl. Schwanzbänderung u. rotbraunes Nackenband)	(clear tailbanding and rufous collar!)	Insel Morotai (N Molukken)	Morotai Island (northern Moluccas)		1♂ 207 1♀ 251	1♂ 160 1♀ 197		1♂ 56 1♀ 68	
A. g. griseogularis (Gray, 1860) (Kehle grauer, Nackenband undeutlicher)	(greyer throat and less sharp collar)	Zentral-Molukken (Halmahera, Gobe, Ternate, Tidore, Batjan)	Central Moluccas (Halmahera, Gobe, Ternate, Tidore, Batjan)	43–48	♂ 218–225 ♀ 260–280				
A. g. obiensis Hartert, 1903 (Habitus wie mortyi, etwas kleiner)	(similar to mortyi, but rather smaller)	Insel Obi (S Molukken)	Obi Island (southern Moluccas)		♂ 200 ♀ 231–234	♀ 185			
Accipiter novaehollandiae (Gmelin, 1788) Weißer, Grauer o. Rotbrusthabicht	White, Grey or Vinous-chested Goshawk								
A. n. misoriensis (Salvadori, 1875) (Schwanz fein gebändert, Unterseite heller weinrot als hiogaster)	(tail faintly barred, below paler vinous-red than hiogaster)	Insel Biak	Biak Island		173–188	146		48	(24)
A. n. hiogaster (S. Müller, 1841) (Oberseite dunkler grau, Unterseite mehr rostbraun als misoriensis)	(above darker slate-grey, below darker chestnut than misoriensis)	Ceram, Saparua, Amboina, Kelang	Ceram, Saparua, Amboina, Kelang		♂ 180–195 ♀ 215–218	♀ 178		53–57	(31)
A. n. albiventris (Salvadori, 1875) (Schwanz ungebändert, Bauch, Hosen u. Unterschwanzdecken weiß, Halbkragen kann fehlen)	(uniform-coloured tail-feathers, belly, undertail coverts and thighs whitish or clear white, half-collar also may be absent)	Kei-Inseln	Kei Islands		♂ 185–200 ♀ 222–226	♀ 180		♀ 61	(29)
A. n. pallidiceps (Salvadori, 1879) (Kopf u. Hinterhals deutlich heller als die Rückenpartie)	(head and hind-neck pale grey and distinctly contrasting with grey back)	Buru-Inseln	Buru Islands		♂ 190 ♀ 232				
A. n. matthiae Mayr, 1945 (in Farbe wie dampieri, aber ohne Bänderung u. Unterschwanzdecken nicht weiß)	(similar to dampieri, but lack barring and white undertail covert)	St. Mathias-Inseln	St. Mathias Islands		♂ 199–202 ♀ 234	♂ 150 ♀ 180			
A. n. manusi Mayr, 1945 (fahler u. kleiner als lavongai)	(similar to lavongai, but paler and smaller)	Admiralty-Inseln (Manus, St. Miguel, Rambutye, Nauna)	Admiralty Islands (Manus, St. Miguel, Rambutye, Nauna)		♂ 198–213 ♀ 235–239				
A. n. lavongai Mayr, 1945 (ähnlich hiogaster, Schwanz ungebändert auf d. Oberseite)	(similar to hiogaster, but dark slate upper-surface of tailfeathers unbarred)	Neuhannover (= Lavongai Insel)	New Hanover (= Lavongai Island)		♂ 221–228 ♀ 254–260	♂ 153 ♀ 178–194			
A. n. pulchellus (Ramsay, 1881) (sehr hell, Kehle wenig deutlich von der restlichen Unterseite abgesetzt)	(very pale, throat less contrasting with breast)	Guadalcanar, Insel Florida, Cape Pitt	Guadalcanar, Florida Island, Cape Pitt		♂ 188–206 ♀ 215–222				
A. n. malaitae Mayr, 1931 (ähnl. bougainvillei, Unterseite manchmal fein gebändert)	(similar to bougainvillei, under-surface sometimes faintly barred)	Malaita-Inseln	Malaita Islands	33–51	1♂ 194 1♀ 237				
A. n. bougainvillei (Rothschild & Hartert, 1905) (kleiner, oberseits heller als rufoschistaceus)	(smaller than rufoschistaceus and paler above)	Bougainville- u. Faure-Inseln	Bougainville and Faure Islands		♂ 194–200 ♀ 212–219				
A. n. rufoschistaceus (Rothschild & Hartert, 1902) (groß, ungebänderter Schwanz u. Hosen)	(large size unbarred on tail and thighs)	Isabel, Choiseul, Treasury-Ins.	Ysabel, Choiseul, Treasury Islands		♂ 212–216 ♀ 240–251	♂ 182–185 ♀ 205–210		♂ 55 ♀ 62	
A. n. rubianae (Rothschild & Hartert, 1905) (dunkel auf Ober- u. Unterseite, Hosen m. feiner Zeichnung)	(dark on upper- and under-surface, thighs faintly barred)	Neugeorgia, Rendovo, Gizo, Vella Lavella	New Georgia, Rendovo, Gizo, Vella Lavella		♂ 195–200 ♀ 206–214				
A. n. sylvestris Wallace, 1863 (sehr hell, viel Weiß auf Skapularen u. Armschwingen)	(pale slate above with much white on scapulars and secondaries)	Sumbawa, Flores, Pantar, Alor	Sumbawa, Flores, Pantar, Alor		♂ 180–187 ♀ 200–208	♂ 146 ♀ 170		48–53	(25)
A. n. dampieri (Gurney, 1882) (Unterseite nahezu einfarbig mit wenig Querbänderung an Flanken, Unterschwanzdecken weiß)	(under-surface nearly uniform vinous-red some barrings on side, undertail coverts white)	Rook-Inseln, Neubritannien	Rook Islands, New Britain		♂ 188–197 ♀ 212–234	♂ 135–145 ♀ 155–176	♂ 175		
A. n. lihirensis Stresemann, 1933 (ähnliche Unterseitenzeichnung wie dampieri, weiße Bänderung auch am Bauch u. Unterschwanzdecken)	(similar to dampieri, but barred markings on under-surface extending to belly and undertail coverts)	Lihir Gruppe u. Tanga-Inseln	Lihir Group and Tanga Islands		♂ 212–232 ♀ 257–263	♂ 153–168 ♀ 184–198			
A. n. misulae Mayr, 1940 (angedeuteter „Kragen", Unterseitenzeichnung reicht bis zur Brust)	(with traces of a collar, below barring extending to breast)	Louisiaden-Gruppe	Louisiades Archipelago		♂ 234–241 ♀ 274–284				
A. n. leucosomus (Sharpe, 1874) (dunkle Farbphase selten; weiße Vögel dagegen etwa ein Drittel aller Individuen)	(Collar! below white with some rufous barring on belly, sides and thighs)	Neuguinea u. angrenz. Inseln	New Guinea and nearby islands		♂ 206–219 ♀ 239–250	♂ 150	1♀ 439	57	(28)
A. n. polionotus (Salvadori, 1890) (Kragen! Unterseite weiß mit wenigen rotbraunen Binden auf Bauch, Flanken, Hosen)	(Collar! below white with some rufous barring on belly, sides and thighs)	Barbar, Damar, Timorlaut u. Banda-Inseln	Babar, Damar, Timorlaut and Banda Islands		♂ 206,207 ♀ 227–241				
A. n. pallidimas Mayr, 1940 (Unterseite rotbraun mit weißer Querbänderung auf Bauch u. Flanken)	(below rufous or chestnut, obscurely barred on belly and thighs)	Ferguson- u. Goodenough-Inseln u. D'Entrecasteaux-Archipel	Ferguson and Goodenough Islands and D'Entrecasteaux Archipelago		♂ 218–232 ♀ 271–275				
A. n. novaehollandiae (Gmelin, 1788) (Tasmanische u. S E Austral. Vögel vorwiegend weiß, graue Vögel überwiegen in Inneraustralien)	(white individuals predominate in SE Australia and Tasmania, grey birds predominate in interior of Australia)	Australien, Tasmanien	Australia, Tasmania		♂ 251–272 ♀ 286–311	♂ 200 ♀ 225–240	♂ 430 ♀ 846,990	68–84	

Plate 20

Accipiter griseogularis mortyi ♀ adult ♀ imm.

A. g. griseogularis ♀ adult

A. n. misoriensis ♀ ad.

A. n. hiogaster ♂ ad.

A. n. pallidiceps ♀ ad.

A. n. lavongai ♂ adult

A. n. rubianae ad. ♀ imm. ♂

A. n. rufoschistaceus ♂ ad.

A. n. bougainvillei ♂ ad. immat.

Accipiter n. pulchellus ♀ adult

Accipiter n. misulae ♀ adult

A. n. pallidimas ♀ adult

A. n. albiventris ♀ ad.

Accipiter n. polionotus ♀ adult

A. n. dampieri ♀ adult

Accipiter n. lihirensis ♂ adult

A. n. sylvestris ♂ adult

immat.

A. n. leucosomus adult „normal"

Acc. n. novaehollandiae ♂ adult „hell"

♂ adult „normal"

A. n. novaehollandiae ♀ adult „normal" „hell" immat. „normal"

A. n. leucosomus adult „hell" „dunkel"

1974 Weick

Benennung	Nomenclature	Verbreitung	Distribution	Länge Length cm	Flügel Wing mm	Schwanz/Tail mm	Gewicht Weight g	Tarsus mm	Culmen mm () = mit Wachshaut with cere
Accipiter superciliosus (Linnaeus, 1766) Augenstreifsperber, Amerika Zwergsperber	Tiny Sparrow Hawk								
A. s. fontanieri Bonaparte, 1853 (dunkler Kopf deutlich v. hellerem Rücken abgesetzt)	(Darker on crown, clearly separated from paler back)	Nikaragua, W Kolumbien, Ekuador	Nicaragua, western Colombia and Ecuador	23–30	♂ 127–134 ♀ 148	♂ 84–89 ♀ 103		38–43	
A. s. superciliosus (Linnaeus, 1766) (etwas größer u. heller als *fontanieri*)	(Slightly larger and paler than *fontanieri*)	Trop. S Amerika, N bis Panama	Tropical South America, north to Panama		♂ 135–145 ♀ 160–167	♂ 99 ♀ 121		40–45	(15)
Accipiter collaris Sclater, 1860 Halbringsperber (im Feld durch kräftiger gebänderte Unterseite v. *superciliosus* zu unterscheiden)	American Collared Sparrowhawk (In the field the heavily barred undersurface should distinguish it from *A. superciliosus*)	Merida-Region Venezuelas; Kolumbien (Santa Marta, Tolima, Cauca, Valle), W Ekuador (Gualca, Nanegal)	Merida-Region of Venezuela; Colombia (Santa Marta, Tolima, Cauca, Valle). Western Ecuador at Nanegal and Gualca	28–31	♂ 148–162 ♀ 171–180	118–133		50	
Accipiter gundlachi Lawrence, 1860 Kubasperber (Kopfseiten grau, Brust hell graubraun, Unterseite viel weniger weiß als bei *cooperi*)	Gundlach's Hawk (Sides of head grey, chest pale greybrown, less flecked with white below than *cooperi*)	Kuba, Insel de Pinos, schon immer selten, jetzt wahrscheinlich ausgestorben	Cuba. Isle of Pines, rare generally; but now nearly extinct.	41–48	♂ 247–250 ♀ 268	♂ 197–205 ♀ 237		67–70 79	
Accipiter cooperi (Bonaparte, 1828) Rundschwanzsperber (Stoß gerundet! Alte ♂ ♂ können mit ♀ ♀ von *A. striatus* verwechselt werden, doch diese mit eckig-geradem od. ausgebuchtetem Stoß)	Cooper's Hawk (Tail rounded? Adult ♂ ♂ can be confused with female sharp-shinned Hawk, but these have a square or notched tail)	S Kanada, USA S bis Florida, Texas, NW Mexiko, Winter: bis Costa Rica, 1 × Kolumbien	Southern Canada, entire USA south to Florida, Texas, north western Mexico. In winter reaching Costa Rica and once Colombia	39–46	♂ 214–238 ♀ 247–278	♂ 181–211 ♀ 215–242	♂ ⌀ 380 ♀ 561	♂ 61–73 ♀ 66–76	(26)
Accipiter bicolor (Vieillot, 1817) Zweifarbsperber	Bicoloured Sparrow-hawk								
A. b. bicolor (Vieillot, 1817) (Altvogel mit weißgrauer Kehle, gesamte Unterseite sehr variabel hellgrau bis dunkel bleigrau, Hosen prächtig rostbraun)	(Adult with pale whitish grey throat, whole under-surface highly variable from pale grey to dark leaden grey, thighs bright rufous)	Yucatan, i. S. durch das nördl. Südamerika, Amazonien, trop. u. subtrop. Anden bis E Bolivien	Yucatan, south over northern South America, through Amazonia, tropics and subtropics of the Andes to eastern Bolivia	33–40	♂ 197–216 ♀ 228–253	♂ 172–180 ♀ 203–205	♂ 204–250 ♀ 342–454	56–69	(19)
A. b. fidens Bangs & Noble, 1918 (Habitus wie *bicolor*, aber größer)	(Similar to *A. b. bicolor*, but larger)	S Mexiko nördl. der Landenge v. Tehuantepec	Southern Mexico north of the Isthmus of Tehuantepe		♂ 219 ♀ 251, 260				
A. b. pileatus (Temminck, 1823) (Altvogel heller u. mit hellgrauem „Kragen". Immaturvögel mehr gefleckt)	(In adult paler than *bicolor* and with a pale grey collar. Immatures with more mottled appearance)	Brasilien, S von Amazonien	Brazil, south of Amazonia		♂ 203–216 ♀ 245–264				
A. b. guttifer Hellmayr, 1917 (Altvogel düsterer als *bicolor* u. *pileatus*, Unterseite teilweise gebändert. Jungvogel ähnlich dem v. *pileatus*)	(Adult darker than *bicolor* and *pileatus*, below partly barred. Young birds similar to *pileatus*)	Trop. Zone S Boliviens, N Argentinien, Chaco v. Paraguay	Tropical zone of southern Bolivia, northern Argentina and the Paraguayan Chaco		♂ 206–213 ♀ 247–265	♂ 172 ♀ 215		60–67	
A. b. chilensis Philippi & Landbeck, 1864 (Altvogel an Unterseite weiß mit graubrauner Bänderung, Kehle weiß od. weiß mit braunem Anflug)	(Adult below white flecked and barred with brownish-grey, throat white or white, tinged with lawny)	Anden Chiles u. Argentiniens vom Aconcagua bis Feuerland u. Staaten-Insel	Andes of Chile and Argentina from Aconcagua to Tierra del Fuego and Staten Island		♂ 203–219 ♀ 237–276	♂ 195 ♀ 207		♂ 64	
Accipiter poliogaster (Temminck, 1824) Graubauchhabicht (alte ♀ ♀ werden an Größe nur von echten Habichten übertroffen, die Fänge sind aber nicht so kräftig wie bei diesen)	Grey bellied Goshawk (Adult ♀ ♀ may be exceeded in size only by „true Goshawks", but has not so heavy feet)	S Amerika: E Ekuador, Peru, Bolivien, Kolumbien, Venezuela, Guayanas, Brasilien, Paraguay, Provinz Misiones in Argentinien. Überall selten	South America, eastern Ecuador, Peru, Bolivia, Colombia, Venezuela, Guaianas, Brazil, Paraguay. Misiones Province of Argentina. Rare everywhere	43–48	♂ 233–247 ♀ 271–277	♂ 168–176 ♀ 196–212		♂ 51–54 ♀ 58–60	(22 ♂) (26 ♀)

Plate 21

A. s. fontanieri ♂ ad.

A. s. superciliosus ♂ ad.

A. s. fontanieri ♀ immat. „normal" „rot"→

Accipiter collaris ♂ adult ♀ immat. „rot" „normal"

A. gundlachi ♂ adult imm. ♀

Accipiter bicolor bicolor ♂ adult „hell" „dunkel" ♂ immat. „hell" ♀ imm. „rot"

A. cooperi ad. ♀ imm.

A. bicolor pileatus ♂ adult ♂ imm. „hell" ♀ imm. „rot"

Accipiter cooperi ♂ adult

Accipiter poliogaster

Augenfarbe?

adult ♀

♂ adult

♂ imm.

A. bicolor chilensis ♂ adult

A. bicolor guttifer ♀ adult ♂ imm.

♂ adult

75 F. Weick

Benennung / Nomenclature		Verbreitung	Distribution	Länge Length cm	Flügel Wing mm	Schwanz/Tail mm	Gewicht Weight g	Tarsus mm	Culmen mm () = mit Wachshaut with cere
Butastur rufipennis (Sundevall, 1851) Heuschreckenbussard (rostbraune Farbtöne, weiße Kehle mit schwarzem Mittelstreif, dunkler Bürzel)	Grasshopper Buzzard Eagle (rufous-brown, with bright rufous wing patch, white throat with median black streak, rump dark)	Trop. Afrika, südl. d. Sahara von Senegal bis Somalia u. N Äthiopien, wandert bis Tanganjika	Tropical Africa, south of Sahara from Senegal to Somalia, N Ethiopia. Migrating as far as Tanganjika	36–41	♂ 290–311 ♀ 305–330	♂ 160–175 ♀ 172–182	♀ 305,408	♂ 55–58 ♀ 57–63	♂ 18 ♀ 19
Butastur liventer (Temminck, 1827) Rotflügelbussard (haselnußbraune Flügel u. Schwanz sowie helle Unterseite sind gute Kennzeichen.)	Rufous-winged Buzzard Eagle (chestnut coloured wings and tail and light under-surface are good field-marks)	Nieder Burma, Tenasserim, Thailand, S E Borneo, Java, Sulawesi, Sula- u. Banggai-Inseln	Lower Burma, Tenasserim, Thailand, south-eastern Borneo, Java. Sulawesi, Sula and Banggai Islands	38–43	♂ 261–275 ♀ 264–292	139 145		62– 66	28–31
Butastur teesa (Franklin, 1832) Weißaugenbussard (weiße Kehle m. schwarzem Streif, aufgehellter Flügelfleck, weißes Auge)	White-eyed Buzzard (white-throat with black streak, light wing-patch and a white eye)	NW Indien S bis Kerala, E bis Assam, Burma u. Tenasserim	North-western India, south to Kerala, east to Assam, Burma and Tenasserim	38–43	♂ 278–304 ♀ 294–314	♂ 151–180 ♀ 170–183		♂ 58–67 ♀ 61–68	(♂ 28–32) (♀ 29–32)
Butastur indicus (Gmelin, 1788) Graugesichtbussard (dunkler Kopf, weiße Kehle, Unterseite dicht gebändert)	Grey-faced Buzzard Eagle (dark head, white throat, strongly barred below)	Ussuriland, S Mandschurei, N China, Japan (Hondo). Winter: Indochina, Philippinen, N Sulawesi, seltener Tenasserim, Malaya, N Molukken (Waigeo, Salawati)	Ussuriland, S Manchuria, N China, Japan (Hondo). Winter: Indo-China, Philippines, N Sulawesi, Tenasserim (less common), Malayan Peninsula, N Moluccas (Waigeu, Salawati)	41–46	♂ 313–325 ♀ 322–347	♂ 182 ♀ 200	♂ 375–433	54– 65	19– 23
Kaupifalco monogrammicus (Temminck, 1824) Eidechsenbussard, Kehlstreifbussard	Lizard Buzzard								
K. m. monogrammicus (Temminck, 1824) (Weißer Bürzel u. weiße Schwanzbinden, sowie graue Oberseite sind gute Kennzeichen.)	(white rump, white tailbands and grey upper-surface are good field-marks)	Senegal u. Sudan bis Äthiopien u. Kenia	Senegal and Sudan to Ethiopia and Kenya	31–33	♂ 201–225 ♀ 222–240	♂ 130–136 ♀ 141–155		♂ 48–54 ♀ 53–55	(♂ 16– ♀ 18)
K. m. meridionalis (Hartlaub & Monteiro, 1860) (auf Unterseite etwas stärker quergebändert als monogrammicus)	(more strongly barred below than monogrammicus)	Südl. v. Kenia bis Angola, Malawi u. Damaraland, Natal	S Kenya to Angola, Malawi and Damaraland, Natal		♂ 210–228 ♀ 222–252		♀ 268,355		
Leucopternis schistacea (Sundevall, 1850) Schieferbussard (einzige weiße Schwanzbinde, sonst schiefergrau)	Slate coloured Hawk (tail with one white band in adult, otherwise entire slaty-black)	v. Venezuela (W Amazonas) E Anden b. Kolumbien, E Ecuador, E Peru, E Bolivien, Brasilien (Amazonien S v. Amazonas)	From Venezuela (Amazon) to E Colombia, E Ecuador, E Peru, E Bolivia, Brazil (Amazonia)	43–46	♂ 273–298 ♀ 290–304	♂ 185–190 ♀ 190–201	1♀ mager 1000	74– 85	
Leucopternis plumbea Salvin, 1872 Bleibussard (dunkler als schistacea, Adultvogel m. gebänderten Hosen)	Plumbeous Hawk (darker than schistacea, adult with whitish thigh-barring)	Pazif. Küste Kolumbiens, S bis W Ecuador u. äußerst. NW Peru, E Panama?	Pacific coast of Colombia, south to W Ecuador and extreme NW Peru, possibly E Panama?	38	♂ 221–238 ♀ 240–248	♂ 129– ♀ 145		65– 73	
Leucopternis princeps (Sclater, 1865) Sperberbussard	Barred Hawk								
L. p. princeps (Sclater, 1865) (Größe, schwarzweiße Bauch- u. Hosenbänderung)	(large size, belly and thighs barred black and white)	Costa Rica, W Panama, Kolumbien	Costa Rica, W Panama, Colombia	46–56	♂ 364–367 ♀ 380–388	♂ 210–223 ♀ 225–227		94– 104	(♀ 53)
L. p. zimmeri Friedmann, 1935 (Habitus wie princeps, kleiner)	(similar to princeps, but smaller)	Kolumbien u. N Ecuador	Colombia and northern Ecuador		♂ 350–352 ♀ 351–358				
Leucopternis melanops (Latham, 1790) Schwarzgesichtbussard (kontrastreiches Gefieder, schwarze Maske)	Black-faced Hawk (contrasting plumage, black face mask)	Guayanas, S Venezuela, S Kolumbien, N E Ecuador, Brasilien, N v. Amazonas	Guianas, S Venezuela, S Colombia, NE Ecuador, Brazil (north of Amazon)	41	♂ 205–220 ♀ 210–243	129– 152	♂ 297–317 ♀ 329–380	57– 66	(♂ 31) (♀ 35)
Leucopternis kuhli Bonaparte, 1850 Weißbrauenbussard (Immaturkleid unbekannt)	White-browed Hawk (immature-plumage unknown)	E-Peru, Brasilien S v. Amazonas	East-Peru, Brazil south of Amazon	38	♂ 207–212 ♀ 214–237	♂ 126–135 ♀ 131–157		59– 70	(♀ 35)
Leucopternis lacernulata (Temminck, 1827) Weißhalsbussard (Unterscheidet sich v. polionota durch Schwanzzeichnung)	White-necked Hawk (distinguished from polionota by different tail-banding)	S u. E Brasilien	South and East-Brazil	46–48	290– 315	175– 192		72– 81	(♀ 40)
Leucopternis semiplumbea Lawrence, 1861 Halbgrauer Bussard (dunkle Ober-, helle Unterseite)	Semiplumbeous Hawk (contrasting dark upper-and light under-surface)	Honduras, Nicaragua u. Costa Rica bis W Kolumbien u. NW Ecuador	Honduras, Nicaragua and Costa Rica to W Colombia and NW Ecuador	38	♂ 165–190 ♀ 183–208	♂ 127–137 ♀ 126–148		55– 66	(♀ 31)
Leucopternis albicollis (Latham, 1790) Weißbussard	White Hawk								
L. a. ghiesbreghti (Du Bus, 1845) („weißeste" Form, wenig schwarz am Auge, Flügel, Schwanz)	(whitest race, little black facemask, some black on primaries and tail)	S Mexiko bis Nicaragua	From S Mexico to Nicaragua		♂ 336–366 ♀ 362–388	♂ 221–235 ♀ 222–234	1♂ 652	80– 87	(♀ 45)
L. a. costaricensis Sclater, 1919 (ähnl. ghiesbreghti, Dunkel auf dem Flügel ausgedehnter)	(similar to ghiesbreghti, more extensive black markings on wing)	Honduras, Panama, N Kolumbien	Honduras, Panama, N Colombia	48–58	♂ 351 ♀ 362				
L. a. williaminae Meyer de Schauensee, 1950 (noch dunkler auf Flügel, Rücken, Schwanz, Schaftstriche am Kopf)	(still darker on wings, back, tail; shaft-streaks on head)	NW Kolumbien u. W Venezuela	NW Colombia and W Venezuela		♂ 347–357 ♀ 342–368				
L. a. albicollis (Latham, 1790) (Rücken, Flügel u. Schwanz weitgehend dunkel, weiße Endbinde am Schwanz)	(back, wings and tail generally dark, with narrow white terminal tail-band)	Venezuela, Guayanas, Trinidad S bis Südl. Amazonien u. Mato Grosso	Venezuela, Guianas, Trinidad south to S Amazonia and Mato Grosso		♂ 310–328 ♀ 346–365	♀ 228	2♂ 600,670 ♀ 780–855	♀ 82	
Leucopternis occidentalis Salvin, 1876 Graurückenbussard (weiße Unterseite u. nur 1 dunkles subterminales Band auf Schwanz)	Grey-backed Hawk (white under-surface, white tail with one subterminal band)	W Ecuador	W Ecuador	48	♂ 335–359 ♀ 370–373	♂ 200–204 ♀ 214–215		82– 85	
Leucopternis polionota (Kaup, 1847) Mantelbussard (von lacernulata u. albicollis durch Schwanzzeichnung zu unterscheiden)	Mantled Hawk (from lacernulata and albicollis distinguished by white terminal half of tail)	E u. S Brasilien, sowie die angrenzenden Gebiete Paraguays u. Argentiniens	E and S Brazil, and adjacent Paraguay and Argentina	48–53	♂ 358–380 ♀ 390–410	♂ 182 ♀ 228		86– 95	(♀ 43)

Plate 22

Butastur rufi-
pennis
adult
juv.

Butastur
liventer
adult
juv.

Butastur
teesa
adult
immat.

Butastur
indicus
ad.
immat.

Kaupifalco
a. meri-
onalis ad.

Kaupifalco
monogrammi-
cus
immat.

L. schistacea
ad.
immat.

L. plumbea
imm.
ad.

Leucopternis
princeps
adult

ifalco
mono-
micus
adult

Leucopternis
lacernulata
adult

immat.

imm.?

adult

L. kuhli

adult
immat.

immat.

Leucopternis melanops

. a. albicollis adult
immat.

Leucopternis
a. ghiesbreghti
adult
immat.

L. a.
costariciensis
adult

adult
immat.

Leucopternis semiplumbea

Leucopternis
a. williamae
adult

L.
polionota
- adult

adult
immat.
L. occidentalis

Benennung / Nomenclature	Verbreitung	Distribution	Länge Length cm	Flügel Wing mm	Schwanz/Tail mm	Gewicht Weight g	Tarsus mm	Culmen mm () = mit Wachshau with cere
Heterospizias meridionalis (Latham, 1790) Savannenbussard — Savannah Hawk				♂ 383–409 ♀ 393–415	♂ 196–207 ♀ 197–214	3♂ 785–1042 2♀ 921, 960	90–113	♂ (38)
H. m. meridionalis (Latham, 1790) (langbeinig, fuchsig gefärbt, weiße Schwanzbinde) (long legged, rufous-coloured, with white tailband)	E Panama, über das trop. S Amerika W bis Ecuador, E bis Peru u. Bolivien	E Panama to tropical S America, west to Ecuador, east to Peru and Bolivia						
H. m. australis Swann, 1921 (Oberseite dunkler, weniger grau a. Rücken) (darker above, less grey wash on back)	Z Argentinien	Central Argentina	51–61	♂ 415–417 ♀ 430–447				
Busarellus nigricollis (Latham, 1790) Fischbussard, Schwarzhalsbussard — Fishing Buzzard, Black-collared Hawk							72–89	♂ (47)
B. n. nigricollis (Latham, 1790) (Heller Kopf u. dunkler Kropffleck sind gute Kennzeichen.) (withish head and dark crop-patch are good field characters)	W Mexiko, M Amerika bis Guayanas, Brasilien, Peru, Venezuela, Kolumbien	W Mexico, Central America to Guianas, Brazil, Peru, Venezuela, Colombia	48–53	♂ 358–388 ♀ 380–405	♂ 157–182 ♀ 175–183	♂ 391–717 ♀ 580–829		
B. n. leucocephalus (Vieillot, 1816) (Kopf weißer, Gesamtkolorit etwas heller) (head clearer white, plumage slightly paler)	Paraguay u. N Argentinien	Paraguay and N Argentina		♂ 410–420 ♀ 425–445				
Parabuteo unicinctus (Temminck, 1824) Harris' o. Wüstenbussard — Bay-winged or Harris' Hawk								
P. u. harrisi (Audubon, 1837) (weißer Bürzel auch bei Immaturvogel) (white rump also in immature plumage)	S Texas südl. durch Mexiko (ohne NW) Mittelamerika bis W Ecuador u. N Peru	S Texas, south through Mexico (except NW) Central-America to W Ecuador and N Peru		♂ 310–352 ♀ 325–370	♂ 207–230 ♀ 213–243		80–92	
P. u. superior van Rossem, 1942 (wenig dunkler u. größer als *harrisi*) (slightly larger and darker than *harrisi*)	S E Kalifornien, SW Arizona, Nieder-Kalifornien, W-Mexiko	SE California, SW Arizona, Baja California, W Mexico	48–56	♂ 324–357 ♀ 351–388		♂ 634–877 ♀ 918–1203		
P. u. unicinctus (Temminck, 1824) (an Unterseite u. Hosen mehr weiß, etwas kleiner als *harrisi*) (underside and thighs more flecked and barred with white, markedly smaller than *harrisi*)	S Amerika bis S Chile, Mittel-Argentinien, Paraguay, i. E bis Venezuela u. Innerbrasilien	S America to S Chile, Central Argentina, Paraguay, east to Venezuela and interior of Brazil		♂ 295–332 ♀ 315–367	228–265		70–86	22–26
Buteogallus aequinoctialis (Gmelin, 1788) Krabbenbussard — Rufous Crab Hawk (Der dunkle Kopf u. die undeutlichere weiße Schwanzbinde sind gute Kennzeichen im Feld gegenüber *Heterospizias*) (in field, dark head and lesser distinct white tail-band, distinguish it from *Heterospizias*)	Guayana, Kolumbien, Brasilien, Paraguay	Guianas, Colombia, Brazil, Paraguay	41–48	♂ 310–316 ♀ 313–326	155–164	♂ 506–665 ♀ 725–945	76–81	♀ (44)
Buteogallus anthracinus (Lichtenstein, 1830) Schwarzer Krabbenbussard — Common Black Hawk								
B. a. anthracinus (Lichtenstein, 1830) (Bürzel mit wenig Weiß) (rump less whitish)	S USA, Mexiko bis Panama	Southern USA, Mexico to Panama	46–58	♂ 365–380 ♀ 375–405	♂ 192–228 ♀ 203–244	1♀ 945	74–107	♀ (45)
B. a. subtilis (Thayer & Bangs, 1905) (mehr rostbraun auf Handschwingen) (more rufous on primaries)	S Mexiko bis äußerst. NW Peru (Mangroven-Zone)	S Mexico to extreme NW Peru (mangrove zone)		♂ 330– ♀ 365				
B. a. gundlachi (Cabanis, 1854) (brauner als andere Formen, weißer Zügelstreif) (appears browner than other races, white malar stripe)	Kuba, Insel de Pinos	Cuba, Isle of Pines		♂ 340–365	♂ 206		♂ 92	♂ (38.5)
Buteogallus urubitinga (Gmelin, 1788) Schwarzbussard — Great Black Hawk								
B. u. ridgwayi (Gurney, 1884) (weißer Bürzel, Schwanzzeichnung, Färbung Schnabel, Wachshaut) (white rump; tail-banding; colour of cere and bill!)	Mexiko (S-Sinaloa Tamaulipas) bis Guatemala u. Costa Rica	Mexico (S Sinaloa, Tamaulipas) to Guatemala and Costa Rica		♂ 367–403 ♀ 363–417	♂ 226–274 ♀ 237–270	♂ 1010–1306 ♀ 1400	108–127	
B. u. urubitinga (Gmelin, 1788) (gesamte Schwanzwurzel weiß, Farbe Schnabel, Wachshaut) (entire base of tail white, colour of cere and bill!)	S. Amerika u. Venezuela u. Kolumbien bis Brasilien, Chile u. Argentinien	S America from Venezuela and Colombia to Brazil, Chile, Argentina	51–63	♂ 377–400 ♀ 383–440	♂ 230–260 ♀ 230–270	♂ 965–1306 ♀ 1355–1560	110–122	
Harpyhaliaëtus solitarius (Tschudi, 1844) Schwarzer Streitadler, Einsiedleradler — Black Solitary Eagle								
H. s. sheffleri van Rossem, 1948 (Habitus wie *solitarius*, etwas größer u. dunkler) (slightly larger and darker than *solitarius*)	S Sonora (Mexiko)	S Sonora (Mexico)	69–74	♂ 530 ♀ 552				
H. s. solitarius (Tschudi, 1844) (kurze Haube, kurzer Schwanz, Größe; größer u. kurzschwänziger als *B. urubitinga*) (short crest, larger size and shorter tailled than *B. urubitinga*)	Mexiko: südl. der Landenge v. Tehuantepec bis Venezuela, Kolumbien, Ecuador, Peru	Mexico south of Isthmus of Tehuantepec to Venezuela, Colombia, Ecuador, Peru		♂ 485–512 ♀ 520–525	♂ 218–234 ♀ 250–270		119–135	36–42
Harpyhaliaëtus coronatus (Vieillot, 1817) Streitadler, Kronenstreitadler — Crowned Solitary Eagle (längere Haube, heller u. grauer als *solitarius*, Schwanzzeichnung) (longer crest, paler and greyer than *solitarius*; tailbanding!)	E Bolivien, Paraguay, Brasilien bis N Patagonien	E Bolivia, Paraguay, Brazil to N Patagonia	74–81	♂ 527 ♀ –562	♂ 264 –315 (340 Swann)		130	♀ (75

Plate 23

Heterospizias m. meridionalis adult

immat.

H. m. australis adult

Busarellus n. nigricollis ad.

imm.

Busarellus n. leucocephalus adult

Parabuteo u. harrisi adult

juv.

Parabuteo u. unicinctus adult

juv.

Buteogallus aequi- noctialis

ad.

juv.

B. a. anthracinus ad.

juv.

B. a. subtilis ad.

B. a. gundlachi adult

Buteogallus u. ridgway adult

juv.

Harpyhaliaëtus coronatus

juv.

adult

Harpyhaliaëtus s. solitarius

adult

juv.

B. u. urubitinga

juv.

adult

F.Weick 1975

Tafel 24

Benennung	Nomenclature	Verbreitung	Distribution	Länge Length cm	Flügel Wing mm	Schwanz/Tail mm	Gewicht Weight g	Tarsus mm	Culmen mm () = mit Wachsha with cere
Geranoaëtus melanoleucus (Vieillot, 1819) Aguja, Blaubussard	Grey Eagle-Buzzard			56–78				106–113	
G. m. melanoleucus (Vieillot, 1819) (Bauch u. Hosen bei Adultvogel fast reinweiß)	(adult with almost unspotted belly and thighs)	E Argentinien, S-Brasilien, Uruguay, Paraguay	East-Argentina, South-Brazil, Uruguay, Paraguay		♂ 455–492 ♀ 520–575	♂ 200–216 ♀ 240–259 imm. 290	♂ 1670 ♀ 3170		
G. m. australis Swann, 1922 (Bauch u. Hosen dunkel gewellt, bei gleicher Größe wie melanoleucus)	(belly and thighs finely barred with blackish, size like melanoleucus)	Venezuela, Kolumbien, Ecuador, Peru, NW Argentinien bis Patagonien, Magellanstraße, Zentral-Chile	Venezuela, Colombia, Ecuador, Peru, NW Argentina, south to Patagonia, Straits of Magellan; Central-Chile						
Buteo nitidus (Latham, 1790) Graubussard, Zweibindenbussard	Grey Hawk, Mexican Goshawk								
B. n. plagiatus (Schlegel, 1862) (♀ auf Oberseite grauer, Unterseitenzeichnung grober)	(♀ on upper-surface darker grey, barring below more distinct)	S USA i. S bis NW Costa-Rica	Southern USA, south to NW Costa Rica		♂ 232–252 ♀ 254–259	♂ 146–163 ♀ 161–167	♂ 364, 434 ♀ 572, 655	67–75	(♂ 32)
B. n. costaricensis (Swann, 1922) (wie plagiatus, Oberseite etwas stärker gebänd.)	(similar to plagiatus, but upper-surface slightly more barred)	SW Costa-Rica S bis N Kolumbien u. W Ecuador	SW Costa-Rica south to N Colombia and W Ecuador		♂ 236–242 ♀ 241–250				
B. n. nitidus (Latham, 1790) (etwas heller als plagiatus)	(slightly paler than plagiatus)	Trinidad, Venezuela, E Ecuador, Guayanas, Amazonien	Trinidad, Venezuela, E Ecuador, the Guianas, Amazonia	38–43	♂ 248–267 ♀ 270–278		♂ 350–497 ♀ 320, 516 592	65–70	
B. n. pallidus (Todd, 1915) (heller als nitidus, Kopf u. Brust weißlich)	(paler than nitidus, head and breast whitish)	S Brasilien, E Bolivien, Paraguay, Nördl. Mittel-Argentinien	S Brazil, E Bolivia, Paraguay, northern Central Argentina		♂ 254 ♀ 264				
Buteo magnirostris (Gmelin, 1788) Großschnabelbussard, Wegebussard	Roadside-, Large-billed Hawk								
B. m. griseocauda Ridgway, 1873 (kann mit B. nitidus o. B. platypterus verwechselt werden)	(may be confused with B. nitidus or B. platypterus)	Mexiko (ohne Tabasco u. Yucatan) bis NW Costa-Rica, Chiriqui, Panama	Mexico (except Tabasco and Yucatan) to NW Costa-Rica, Chiriqui and Panama		♂ 218–249 ♀ 238–248	♂ 157–175 ♀ 175–178	♀ 291, 314	64–69	
B. m. conspectus (Peters, 1913) (auf d. Rücken heller grau)	(back lighter grey)	Yucatan, Tabasco (Mexiko) N Brit.-Honduras	Yucatan and Tabasco (Mexico) N British Honduras		♂ 219–226 ♀ 220–237		♂ 250, 269 ♀ 231, 318		
B. m. gracilis (Ridgway, 1885) (mehr Streifencharakter auf Unterseite, Hosen meist ungezeichnet bei Adultvogel)	(more streaky below, thighs uniform coloured)	Cozumel u. Holbox-Inseln vor Yucatan	Cozumel and Holbox Island off Yucatan		200–218		♂ 189 ♀ 217, 234		
B. m. sinushonduri Bond, 1936 (dunkler als griseocauda)	(darker than griseocauda)	Bonacca u. Ruatan-Inseln (Honduras)	Bonacca and Ruatan Islands (Honduras)		♂ 229– ♀ 231				
B. m. petulans van Rossem, 1935 = ruficauda (Sclater & Salvin, 1869) (rostbraun auf Handschwingen u. Schwanz)	(rufous on primaries and tailfeathers)	SW Costa Rica, Pazifik-Küste u. Inseln v. Panama bis Rio Tuyra	SW Costa-Rica, Pacific-coast and nearby islands from Panama to Rio Tyura		♂ 205–215 ♀ 220–234				
B. m. alius (Peters & Griscom, 1929) (ähnlich petulans, auf Flügel u. Schwanz heller rotbraun, Bauch stärker gebändert)	(similar to petulans, lighter rufous on primaries and tail, belly more strongly barred)	San Miguel, San Jose, Insel Pearl, Panama	San Miguel, San Jose, Pearl Island, Panama	28–35	207–226				
B. m. magnirostris (Gmelin, 1788) (Oberseite u. Schwanz zieml. grau getönt)	(upper-surface and tail grey)	Kolumbien, Ecuador, Venezuela, Guayana, N Brasilien	Colombia, Ecuador, Venezuela, Guianas, N Brazil		204–227	155–165	♂ 206–290 ♀ 257–350	62	♂ 17
B. m. occiduus (Bangs, 1911) (Oberseite u. Schwanz mehr braungetönt)	(more brownish wash on upper-surface and tail)	E Peru, äußerst. N Bolivien, W Brasilien	E Peru, extreme N Bolivia, W Brazil		204–223				
B. m. saturatus (Sclater & Salvin, 1876) (Kehle dunkel, Unterseite u. Schwanz mit viel Rostbraun)	(blackish throat, under-surface and tail-feathers with strong rufous wash)	Bolivien, Paraguay, W Argentinien	Bolivia, Paraguay, western Argentina		♀ bis 270				
B. m. nattereri (Sclater & Salvin, 1869) (ähnl. magnirostris, U Seite mehr rotbraun)	(similar to magnirostris, but underside more rufous)	NE Brasilien S bis Bahia	NE Brazil, south to Bahia		197–220 228–233		♂ 200, 250		
B. m. magniplumis (Bertoni, 1901) (Oberseite grauer als nattereri, Schwanz grau)	(above greyer than nattereri with grey-banded tail)	S Brasilien, Misiones. (Argentin.) u. angrenz. Paraguay	S Brazil, Misiones (Argentina), nearby parts of Paraguay		235–255				
B. m. pucherani (I. & E. Verreaux, 1855) (ähnl. saturatus, Brust u. Bauch heller u. feiner gezeichnet)	(similar to saturatus, but paler on chest and belly with narrower barring below)	E Argentinien (ohne Misiones) S bis Provinz Buenos Aires, Uruguay	E Argentina (except Misiones) south to Buenos-Aires Province; Uruguay		267–285				
Buteo leucorrhous (Quoy & Gaimard, 1824) Weißbürzelbussard (Kleinheit u. dunkles Gefieder sowie Schwanzbänderung sind gute Feldkennzeichen.)	Rufous-thighed Hawk (small size, dark plumage and tail-banding are good field marks)	Venezuela, Kolumbien bis Ecuador, Peru, NW Argentinien	Venezuela, Colombia to Ecuador, Peru, NW Argentina	35–38	206–252	136–171	♀ 389	57–64	
Buteo ridgwayi (Cory, 1883) Haitibussard (helle Kehle, helle Schwanzbinden)	Ridgway's Hawk (light throat and whitish tail-barring)	Hispaniola u. umliegende Inseln wie Gonave, Ile a Vache, Beata	Hispaniola and some off-lying islets as Gonave, Ile a Vache, Beata	28–35	♂ 210–235 ♀ 236–253	♂ 137–152 ♀ 149–163		60–69	
Buteo lineatus (Gmelin, 1788) Rotschulterbussard	Red-shouldered Hawk								
B. l. lineatus (Gmelin, 1788) (rostfarbene Brust u. weiße Schwanzbinden)	(rufous breast and white tail-bands)	E Nordamerika ohne Florida	Eastern North-America except Florida		♂ 309–346 ♀ 315–356	♂ 193–228 ♀ 207–237	♂ ∅ 550 ♀ ∅ 701	75–87	20–23
B. l. alleni Ridgway, 1885 (heller als lineatus)	(paler than lineatus)	Florida ohne Südspitze, E Texas	Florida except southern tip; E Texas		♂∅ 301 ♀∅ 316				
B. l. extimus Bangs, 1920 (wie alleni, aber kleiner u. noch heller)	(similar to alleni, but smaller and still paler)	Südl. Florida u. Keys	S Florida and Keys	41–51	♂ 270–283 ♀ 295–305	♂ 167–169		73	19
B. l. texanus Bishop, 1912 (lebhafter rostfarben an Ober- u. Unterseite)	(more richly coloured rufous below and above)	Texas S bis Tamaulipas, Mexiko	Texas south to Tamaulipas (Mexico)		♂ ∅ 309 ♀ ∅ 334	218			
B. l. elegans Cassin, 1855 (an Unterseite ähnl. texanus, Oberseite jedoch ähnl. lineatus)	(like texanus below, but upper-surface rufous like lineatus)	S Oregon bis N Niederkaliforn.	S Oregon to northern Baja California		♂ ∅ 299 ♀ ∅ 302				
Buteo platypterus (Vieillot, 1823) Breitflügelbussard	Broad-winged Hawk								
B. pl. platypterus (Vieillot, 1823) (dunkle Phase sehr selten)	(melanistic phase rare)	E Nordamerika, Winter: M Amerika bis Venezuela, Peru	Eastern N America; Winter: Central America to Venezuela, Peru		♂ 244–277 ♀ 265–296	♂ 148–174 ♀ 155–185	♂ ∅ 420 ♀ ∅ 490	57–66	
B. pl. cubanensis Burns, 1911 (ähnl. Nominatform Immaturkleid)	(adult similar to immature plumage of nominate)	Kuba	Cuba		♂ 250,256 ♀ 254,266				
B. pl. brunnescens Danford & Smyth, 1935 (nur in wenigen Exemplaren bekannt)	(known from a few specimens)	Puerto Rico	Puerto Rico		♀ 265				
B. pl. insulicola Riley, 1908 (heller u. kleiner als übrige Rassen)	(lighter and smaller than other forms)	Insel Antigua	Antigua Island	36–46	♂ 227				
B. pl rivierei Verril, 1905 (dunkler als Nominatform)	(darker than nominate form)	Dominica, Martinique, St. Lucia	Dominica, Martinique and St. Lucia						
B. pl. antillarum Clark, 1905 (wie rivierei, etwas fahler u. größer)	(similar to rivierei, slightly paler and larger)	Barbados, St. Vincent, Grenadines, Grenada, Tobago, Little Tobago	Barbados, St. Vincent, Grenadines, Grenada, Tobago, Little Tobago		♂ ∅ 260 ♀ ∅ 267				
Buteo brachyurus Vieillot, 1816 Kurzschwanzbussard	Short-tailed Hawk								
B. br. fuliginosus Sclater, 1858 (starker Kontrast von Ober- u. Unterseite)	(strong contrasting upper- and lowersurface)	N Amerika (S Florida) bis S Panama	North-America (S Florida) south to Panama		♂ 282–313 ♀ 326–336	♂ 142–167 ♀ 165–182	♂ imm 342	58–62	
B. br. brachyurus Vieillot, 1816 (nie mit rostfarbenen Halsseiten)	(never with rufous sides of neck)	S Amerika (Brasilien, Bolivien, Peru, Guayana, Venezuela) selten	South-America (Brazil, Bolivia, Peru, the Guianas, Venezuela), rare	38–43	♂ 275–297 ♀ 325	♂ 139–146 ♀ 157	♂ 450–470 ♀ 425–530		
Buteo albigula Philippi, 1899 Weißkehlbussard (Unterseitenzeichnung, Hosenzeichng. bei Adultvogel)	White-throated Hawk (note strong marking below and colour of thighs in adults)	Anden Kolumbiens u. Venezuelas, Chile, Peru, Ecuador	Andean parts of Colombia, Venezuela, Chile, Peru, Ecuador	38–43	♂ 272–287 ♀ 293,311 323, 327	♂ 157–177 ♀ 168–193	♀ imm 550		

Plate 24

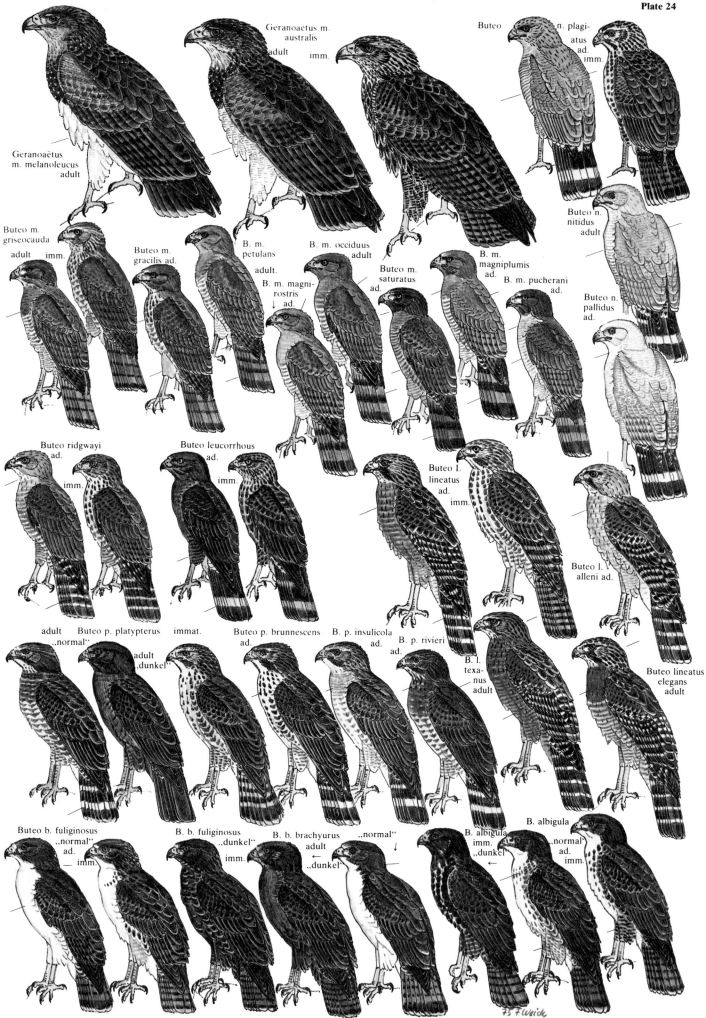

Geranoaëtus m. melanoleucus adult

Geranoaëtus m. australis adult imm.

Buteo n. plagiatus ad. imm.

Buteo n. nitidus adult

Buteo n. pallidus ad.

Buteo m. griseocauda adult imm.

Buteo m. gracilis ad.

B. m. petulans adult.

B. m. magnirostris ad.

B. m. occiduus adult

Buteo m. saturatus ad.

B. m. magniplumis ad.

B. m. pucherani ad.

Buteo ridgwayi ad. imm.

Buteo leucorrhous ad. imm.

Buteo l. lineatus ad. imm.

Buteo l. alleni ad.

adult Buteo p. platypterus immat.

Buteo p. brunnescens ad.

B. p. insulicola ad.

B. p. rivieri ad.

adult „normal" „dunkel"

B. l. texanus adult

Buteo lineatus elegans adult

Buteo b. fuliginosus „normal" ad. imm.

B. b. fuliginosus „dunkel"

B. b. brachyurus adult „dunkel"

„normal"

B. albigula imm. „dunkel"

B. albigula „normal" ad. imm.

75 F.Weick

Benennung	Nomenclature	Verbreitung	Distribution	Länge Length cm	Flügel Wing mm	Schwanz/Tail mm	Gewicht Weight g	Tarsus mm	Culmen mm () = mit Wachshaut with cere
Buteo swainsoni Bonaparte, 1838 Präriebussard (Bürzel u. Schwanzwurzel oft weißlich)	Swainson's Hawk (rump and base of tail often whitish!)	Westl. N Amerika von Alaska bis N Mexiko Winters: bis Argentinien	Western N America from Alaska to N Mexico. Winter: south to Argentina	46–53	♂ 362–406 ♀ 375–427	♂ 185–214 ♀ 194–234	♂ ⌀ 908 ♀ ⌀ 1069	62–76	
Buteo galapagoensis (Gould, 1837) Galapagosbussard (da der einzige Greifvogel auf Galapagos, leicht zu bestimmen)	Galapagos-Hawk (the only diurnal bird of prey in the Galapagos, indentification no problem)	Galapagos-Inseln	Galapagos Islands	48–56	♂ 365–395 ♀ 410–435	♂ 191–215 ♀ 222–243		70–89	♂ (44)
Buteo albicaudatus Vieillot, 1816 Weißschwanzbussard **B. a. hypospodius Gurney, 1876** (Kehle kann auch aufgehellt sein)	White tailed Hawk (throat also may be lighter)	Texas bis N Kolumbien u. W Venezuela	Texas south to N Colombia and W Venezuela		♂ 404–430 ♀ 423–450	♂ 194–207 ♀ 199–211		85–95	
B. a. colonus Berlepsch, 1892 (heller als *hypospodius* im Normalkleid, Kehle reinweiß)	(paler than *hypospodius* in normal-phase, throat clear white)	E Kolumbien bis Surinam u. die Inseln Trinidad, Aruba, Bonaire, Curaçao	E Colombia to Surinam and Islands of Trinidad, Aruba, Bonaire, Curaçao	59–61	♂ 375–400 ♀ 425–440		♂ 865 ♀ 1101		
B. a. albicaudatus Vieillot, 1816 (Kopf u. Skapularen dunkler, Flanken u. Hosen etwas deutlicher gezeichnet)	(head and mantle darker, sides and thighs rather clearly marked)	S Brasilien bis Uruguay, Paraguay, Argentinien u. Chile	S Brazil to Uruguay, Paraguay, Argentina, Chile		♂ 400–440 ♀ 440–480			86–95	♂ 37
Buteo polyosoma (Quoy & Gaimard, 1824) Rotrückenbussard **B. p. polyosoma (Quoy & Gaim. 1824)** (Beachte die variablen Kleider)	Red-backed Buzzard (look highly variable with many colour-phases)	Kolumbien, Chile, W u. Z. Argentinien, Patagonien, Feuerland. Falkland-Ins.	Colombia, Chile, W and Central Argentina, Patagonia, Tierra del Fuego, Falkland Islands	48–53	♂ 350–427 ♀ 374–450	190–210		78–90	
B. p. exsul Salvin, 1875 (ähnlich „normalem" ♂ von *polyosoma*, jedoch dunkler auf der Oberseite)	(like male of normal phase *polyosoma*, but much darker on upper-surface)	Mas Afuera-Insel, Chile	Mas Afuera Island. Chile		380–430	203–223		90–95	♂ 245 ♀ 250
Buteo poecilochrous Gurney, 1879 Gurneybussard (im Feld vom Rotrückenbussard meist nicht zu unterscheiden)	Gurney's Buzzard (scarcely distinguishable from Red-backed Buzzard in field)	Hochanden v. S W Kolumbien bis N Chile u. NW Argentinien	Higher levels of Andes from SW Colombia to N Chile and NW Argentina	51–56	♂ 423–473 ♀ 445–478	215–250		88–102	
Buteo albonotatus Kaup, 1847 Bänderschwanzbussard, Schwarz-streifbussard (wird manchmal mit Truthahngeier verwechselt, dessen Flügelhaltung u. Flugstil er kopiert)	Zone-tailed Hawk (sometimes confused with Turkey-Vulture which it perhaps mimics)	SW Grenze der USA, Mexiko mit Niederkalifornien, Guatemala, Nicaragua, Costa Rica, Peru, Bolivien, Paraguay, Brasilien, Surinam, Trinidad	South-western boarder of USA, Mexico with Lower California, Guatemala, Nicaragua, Costa Rica, Peru, Bolivia, Paraguay, Surinam, Trinidad	46–53	♂ 367–393 ♀ 409–448 (♀ 455 Boliv.) (♀460 NWPeru)	♂ 216–223 ♀ 223–235	♂ 565	67–78	

Plate 25

Buteo swainsoni
ad. „normal"   ad. „dunkel"   ad. „rot"

Buteo swainsoni
immat. „normal"   immat. „rot" o. „dunkel"

Buteo galapagoensis
adult   immat.

Buteo a.
hypospodius
adult   immat.

Buteo a.
colonus
ad. „normal"   „dunkel" ad.

Buteo a.
albicaudatus
adult

Buteo p.
polyosoma
„normal"

adult ♂[1]
„dunkel"

Buteo p.
polyosoma
adult ♂
„dunkel-
rotrückig"
♀ adult
„normal"[1]

juv. „normal"

Buteo p.
polyosoma
♀ adult
„dunkel"

Buteo p. polyosoma
juv. „dunkel"

Buteo polyosoma
exsul
♀ adult

Buteo poecilochrous

♀ adult
„normal"

immat.
„normal"

immat.
„dunkel"

[1] diese Färbungstypen
kommen auch bei dem
etwas größeren B. poe-
cilochrous vor!
these colour-types are also
present in the rather larger
B. poecilochrous!

Buteo albonotatus
adult

immat.

75 Fuisk

Tafel 26

Benennung	Nomenclature	Verbreitung	Distribution	Länge Length cm	Flügel Wing mm	Schwanz/Tail mm	Gewicht Weight g	Tarsus mm	Culmen mm () = mit Wachshaut with cere
Buteo solitarius Peale, 1848 Hawaiibussard (Vögel mit weißem Kopf u. Unterseite selten)	Hawaian Hawk (adult birds with white bead and under-surface rare)	Hawaii	Hawaii Island	38–43	♂264–278 ♀ 288–308	♂ 152–159 ♀ 162–171		71– 88	
Buteo ventralis Gould, 1837 Patagonienbussard (Gesamtkolorit dunkler als bei *jamaicensis*, Schwanz gebändert)	Patagonian Red tailed Buzzard (darker in plumage, than *jamaicensis*, tail of adult clearly barred)	S Chile u. Argentinien bis zur Magellan-straße	South-Chile and Argentina to Straits of Magellan	48–53	♂ 351–369 ♀ 370–427 (–450)	♂ 195–238 ♀ 196–241	1♀ 1135	♀ 84	
Buteo jamaicensis (Gmelin, 1788) Rotschwanzbussard	Red-tailed Hawk								
B. j. borealis (Gmelin, 1788) (Schwanz des Immaturvogels kann auch bräunlich sein)	(immature birds also with brownish tail-feathers)	E Nordamerika i. W bis „Plains" ohne Florida, Winter bis Zentral-Mexiko,	Eastern N America west to plains, except Florida. Winter: South to Central Mexico		♂ 337–396 ♀ 370–427	♂ 197–240 ♀ 215–254	♂ ∅ 1028 ♀ ∅ 1224	77– 93	♂ 24–27 ♀ 25–29
B. j. calurus Cassin, 1855 (Vögel mit weniger roter Unterseite sind meist stärker gezeichnet als *borealis*)	(birds with less rufous wash below are more strongly barred than in *borealis*)	Westl. Nordamerika v. Mittl. Yukon bis W Spitze der „Gr. Plains". Guadaluppe	Western N America from Middle Yukon to western part of Great Plains; Guadalupe Island		♂ 358–404 ♀ 386–428				
B. j. harlani (Audubon, 1830) (nur Schwanzfärbung zur Feldbestimmung)	(for field-identification, look at tail-colouring)	N Alberta, Brit. Kolumbien i. E bis Küste u. S Alaska. Winter: Arkansas u. Nachbarstaaten	N Alberta, British Columbia, east to coast and S Alaska. Winter: Arkansas and adjacent states		♂ 365–390 ♀ 390–430				
B. j. alascensis Grinnell, 1909 (Färbung wie *borealis*, etwas kleiner)	(similar to *borealis*, but rather smaller)	SE Alaska bis Ins. Queen-Charlotte	SE Alaska to Queen Charlotte Island		♂ 334–362 ♀ 358–370				
B. j. krideri Hoopes, 1873 (helle Prärieform, Schwanz meist weiß)	(pale prairie-form, tail almost white)	Südl. Prärieprovinzen Kanadas bis Colorado u. Nebraska	Southern prairie-provinces of Canada to Colorado and Nebraska		♂ 352–400 ♀ 393–432				
B. j. fuertesi Sutton & Van Tyne, 1935 (ähnlich *calurus*, Unterseite jedoch immer heller)	(similar to *calurus*, but under-surface always much paler)	S Texas, Neu-Mexiko u. Nordmexiko	S Texas, New Mexico, N Mexico	51–58	♂ 385–402 ♀ 425–436				
B. j. hadropus Storer, 1962 (wie *calurus*, kleiner, Rücken weniger gefleckt)	(similar to *calurus*, smaller, back less mottled)	Berge Mexikos v. Ialisco bis Landenge v. Tehuantepec	Mountains of Mexico from Ialisco to Isthmus of Tehuantepec		♂ 379				
B. j. kemsiesi Oberholser, 1959 (heller als *calurus*, Brust ungefleckt)	(paler than *calurus*, with unspotted or barred breast)	Berge v. Oaxaca (Mexiko) bis Nicaragua	Mountains of Oaxaca (Mexico) to Nicaragua		♂ 357–380 ♀ 381–405				
B. j. costaricensis Ridgway, 1874 (Bauch u. Hosen weitgehend ungezeichnet rostrot)	(belly and thighs rich uniform rufous)	Berge von Costa Rica u. W Panama	Mountains of Costa Rica and W Panama		♂ 368–377 ♀ 392–410				
B. j. socorroensis Nelson, 1898 (helle Form ähnl. *calurus*, starke Fänge)	(light race similar to pale *calurus*, legs and feet more powerful)	Insel Socorro (Mexiko)	Socorro Island (Mexico)		♂ 368–390 ♀ 415–418				
B. j. fumosus Nelson, 1898 (dunkler als *socorroensis*, Hosen stark gebändert)	(darker than *socorroensis*, strongly barred thighs)	Tres-Marias-Inseln (Mexiko)	Tres Marias-Islands (Mexico)		♂ 368, 370 1 ♀ 395				
B. j. umbrinus Bangs, 1901 (Schwanzzeichnung)	(tailbarring)	Florida u. Bahamas	Florida and Bahamas		♂ 398–400 ♀ 373–432				
B. j. solitudinis Barbour, 1935 (ähnlich *umbrinus*, aber kleiner)	(similar to *umbrinus* but smaller)	Kuba u. Insel de Pinos	Cuba and Isle of Pines		2 ♂ 357, 382 2 ♀ 397, 412				
B. j. jamaicensis (Gmelin, 1788) (Unterseitenzeichnung)	(barring and mottling of under-surface)	Jamaica, Hispaniola, Puerto Rico, Virgin-Inseln	Jamaica, Hispaniola, Puerto Rico, Virgin Islands		♂ 330–339 ♀ 350–371				
Buteo buteo (Linnaeus, 1758) Mäusebussard	Common Buzzard								
B. b. buteo (Linnaeus, 1758) (Gefieder schier endlos variabel, jedoch generell mit weniger Rotbraun als die folgenden Rassen)	(plumage highly variable, but generally less rufous than following races)	Atlantische Inseln u. Europa i. E bis Finnland, Rumänien, Kl. Asien	Atlantic Islands and Continental Europe east to Finland, Rumania, Asia Minor		♂ 350–418 ♀ 375–432 (440)	♂ 196–223 ♀ 201–236	♂ 535–985 ♀ 700–1200	70–82	♂ 20–23, ♀ 217–25
B. b. vulpinus (Gloger, 1833) (viel mehr Rotbraun im Gefieder als *buteo*, vor allem Schwanzfärbung)	(plumage much more rufous than in *buteo*, especially the tail)	N u. E Europa, Sibirien E bis Yennisei S bis Altai, Kentei u. Tienshan. Winter: Arabien, E. u. S Afrika	N and E Europe, Siberia east to Yenisei, south to Altai, Kentei and Tianshan. Winter: Arabia, E and S Africa to Cape		♂ 335–377 ♀ 358–397	♂ 170–200 ♀ 175–209	♂ 560–675 ♀ 710–1175	69– 82	19– 25
B. b. menetriesi Bogdanov, 1879 (Schwanz u. Unterseite oft weniger rotbraun als *vulpinus*, mit stärkerer Fleckenzeichnung)	(tail and under-surface often less rufous but more heavily spotted than *vulpinus*)	Kaukasus, Elburs	Caucasus, Elburz	48–56	♂ 351–397 ♀ 372–413				
B. b. japonicus (Temminck & Schlegel, 1844) (Untergrundfärbung m. viel Ockergelb, beachte Schwanzfarbe u. Zeichnung)	(below with much ochre-yellow ground-colour, look at tail-colour and marking)	Sibirien (E v. *vulpinus*) bis Japan, S bis Tibet, Sikiang, Szechwan. Winter: Indien, Burma, Indochina	Siberia (east of *vulpinus*-areal) to Japan, south to Tibet, Sikang, Szechwan Winter: India, Burma, Indo-China		♂ 362–400 ♀ 370–408	191– 235	♂ 630–810 ♀ 515–970	64– 77	20– 26
B. b. tojoshimai Momiyama, 1927 (ähnl. *japonicus*, jedoch deutlich heller u. kleiner, Flügelschnitt stärker gerundet)	(like *japonicus*, but much smaller and paler, more rounded wings)	Sieben Inseln v. Izu u. Bonin-Inseln	Seven Islands of Izu and Bonin Islands		♂ 341–356 ♀ 356–375				
Buteo oreophilus Hartert & Neumann, 1914 Gebirgsbussard	African Mountain Buzzard								
B. o. oreophilus Hartert u. Neumann, 1914 (ähnl. *Buteo buteo*, jedoch kleiner, Unterseite mehr gefleckt als gebändert)	(similar to *Buteo buteo*, but smaller, below more heavily spotted not barred!)	Äthiopien – E Afrika – Natal	Ethiopia – E Africa – Natal		♂ 332–336 ♀ 345–356	♂ 174–183 ♀ 180–196		61– 72	21– 23
B. o. trizonatus Rudebeck, 1957 (Oberseite mehr rostbraun, Unterseite lichter als *oreophilus*)	(upper-surface much more rufous, below paler than *oreophilus*)	Kapland i. N bis Natal	Cape Province north to Natal	41–46	♂ 318–352 ♀ 330–362				
Buteo brachypterus Hartlaub, 1860 Madagaskarbussard (Unterseitenzeichnung mit viel Weiß, sonst ähnlich Gebirgsbussard, kann nicht verwechselt werden, da einzige *Buteo*-Art Madagaskars!)	Madagascar Buzzard (below more marked with white, similar to Mountain Buzzard, but cannot be confused, the only *Buteo* on Madagascar)	Madagaskar v. Meereshöhe bis 1800 m	Madagascar, from sea level to 6000 feet	41–46	♂ 290–336 ♀ 293–346	♂ 164–196 ♀ 169–194		♂ 62–82 ♀ 64–82	♂ 21–

Plate 26

Buteo solitarius
adult „hell"
adult „normal"
adult „dunkel"

Buteo solitarius
immat.
„hell"
„dunkel"

Buteo ventralis
„dunkel" adult
„normal"
immat.

Buteo jam. borealis ad.
immat.

B. j. harlani → adult

B. j. calurus adult.

B. j. fuertesi adult

B. j. kriderii adult

B. j. costari-ciensis ad

B. j. umbrinus adult

Buteo buteo buteo

„dunkel" adult „intermed."

„intermed." immat. „dunkel" →

Buteo j. jamaicensis adult

adult ←„hell"→

immat. „hell"

B. buteo japonicus adult

B. buteo vul-pinus adult ← →

Buteo brachypterus adult   imm.

Buteo o. oreophilus ad. imm.

B. o. trizonatus adult

- B. buteo menetriesi adult

75 F Weick

Benennung	Nomenclature	Verbreitung	Distribution	Länge Length cm	Flügel Wing mm	Schwanz/Tail mm	Gewicht Weight g	Tarsus mm	Culmen mm () = mit Wachshaut with cere
Buteo lagopus (Pontoppidan, 1763) Rauhfußbussard **B. l. lagopus (Pontoppidan, 1763)** (Brustband, Schwanzzeichnung, Lauf-befiederung)	Rough-legged Buzzard (chestband, typical tailbanding, feathe-red tarsus)	N Europa u. W Sibirien v. der Arkt. Küste i. S bis Norwegen, N u. W Schweden, Finnland, Rußland, i. E bis Jenissei.	N Europe and W Siberia, from arctic coast south to Norway N and W Sweden, Finland, Russian Karelia, east to Yenisei. Winter: south to Central Europe, Caucasus, Kazakstan, Russian Turkestan, south to Syr Darya and Tianshan		(385) ♂ 400–438 ♀ 420–468	200–229 226–255	♂ 709–990 ♀ 783–1152	65–72,5 72–77	19,5–22 22–23,8
B. l. menzbieri, Dementiev, 1951 (meist weniger stark gestreift u. mit weniger ausgeprägter Schwanzbinde)	(usually less heavily streaked, chestband less distinct)	Sibirien v. Jenissei E bis NE Sibirien. Winter: Turkestan, Mandschurei, Ussuriland, N China, Korea, Japan	Siberia from Yenisei east to N E Siberia; Winter: Turkestan, Manchuria, Ussuriland, N China, Korea, Japan	51–61	♂ 408–450 ♀ 434–470	218– 252	♂ 1290–1377 ♀ 1239–1430	60– 74	20– 25
B. l. kamschatkensis, Dementiev 1931 (dunkles Gefieder schwärzer, helles weißer als bei menzbieri)	(dark parts of plumage blacker, lighter part white than in menzbieri)	Kamschatka, Küste der Ochotsk. See, N Kurilen, Aleuten, S W Alaska? Winter: Ussuri, S Kurilen, Hokkaido	Kamschatka, coastal range of sea of Okhotsk, N Kuriles, Aleutians, S W Alaska? Winter: Ussuriland, S Kuriles, Hokkaido		♂ 420–445 ♀ 447–483		♂ 900 ♀ 1050,1209		
B. l. sancti-johannis (Gmelin, 1788) (dunkler als die anderen Rassen, beige Farbtöne)	(darker and more uniformly coloured than other races, more buff tinged)	N Amerika, v. Alaska bis Labrador, SE Quebec, Neufundland	North America from Alaska to Labrador, SE Quebec, Newfoundland		♂ 392–410 ♀ 400–445		♂ Ø 822 ♀ Ø 1080		
Buteo rufinus (Cretschmar, 1827) Adlerbussard **B. r. rufinus (Cretschmar, 1827)** (spärliche Schwanzzeichnung, heller Bürzel)	Long-legged Buzzard (tail almost plain ore less barred, light rump)	S E Europa, Kleinasien, Zentral-Asien	South-eastern Europe, Asia Minor, Central Asia		♂ 405–451 ♀ 433–490	♂ 224–240 ♀ 240–289	♂ 590–1281 ♀ 1147–1543	♂ 83–92 ♀ 86–95	♂ 24–26 ♀ 26,5–29
B. r. cirtensis (Levaillant jr., 1850) (Habitus wie rufinus, jedoch erheblich kleiner)	(similar to rufinus, but distinctly smaller)	N Afrika v. Marokko bis Agypten, Sinai Halbinsel	North Africa from Morocco to Egypt, Sinai Peninsula	56–66	♂ 345–384 ♀ 360–425				
Buteo hemilasius Temminck & Schlegel, 1844 Hochlandbussard (heller Kopf, Schwanz hell und schwach gebändert)	Upland Buzzard (pale head, tail light and sparsely barred)	Zentralasien v. Mandschurei u. Kansu W bis E Altai, Tienshan, S bis Tibet Winter: N Indien, Burma, Z China, Korea	Central Asia from Manchuria and Kansu west to E Altai, Tianshan, south to Tibet. Winter: N-India, Burma, Central-China, Korea	61–69	♂ 429–480 ♀ 485–510	♂ 255–278 ♀ 282	♂ 950–1400 ♀ 970–2050	81– 90 (95?)	♂ (43)24– ♀ (47)29
Buteo regalis (G. R. Gray, 1844) Königsrauhfußbussard (groß, Schwanzzeichnung, rostfarbene Hosen bilden bei Adultvög. guten Kontrast zu hellem Bauch, Lauf teilweise befiedert)	Ferruginous Hawk (large size; rufous thighs in adult birds contrasting with light belly, tarsus partly feathered)	N Amerika v. E Washington, S Alberta, S Saskatschewan u. S W Manitoba S bis E Oregon, Nevada, Neu-Mexiko, NW Texas u. W Oklahoma. Winter: bis N Mexiko u. Niederkalifornien	North America: from eastern Washington, S Alberta, S Saskatchewan and SW Manitoba, south to E Oregon, Nevada, New Mexico, NW Texas and W Oklahoma Winter: to Baja California and N Mexico	61–66	♂ 421–440 ♀ 427–450 (460 Swann)	♂ 231–246 ♀ 239–252 (272 Swann)		81– 92	♀ (48)
Buteo auguralis Salvadori, 1865 Afrikanischer Rot-schwanzbussard (roter Schwanz, dunkle Vorderbrust u. gefleckte Hinterbrust)	African Red-tailed Buzzard (red tail, dark chest and spotted breast)	W u. Zentral-Afrika, v. S W Äthiopien bis Sierra Leone u. S bis Angola	West- and Central-Africa, from S W Ethiopia to Sierra Leone and south to Angola	41–46	329–377	178–205		77–82	
Buteo rufofuscus (Forster, 1798) Schakalbussard **B. r. rufofuscus (Forster, 1798)** (Roter Schwanz, kontrastreiche Gefiederfärbung)	Jackal or Augur Buzzard (tail reddish, body plumage with strongly contrasting colours)	S Afrika (Transvaal bis Kapland)	South Africa (from Transvaal to Cape Province)		♂ 393–410 ♀ 423–444	180– 220	♀ 1530	76– 85	24– 30
B. r. augur (Rüppell, 1836) (Dunkel oder schwarzweiß, Schwanz rot)	(all black or black and white; red tail)	E Afrika (Äthiopien bis Angola u. Simbabwe)	East Africa (Ethiopia to Angola and Zimbabwe)	48–56	♂ 384–415 ♀ 435–466	♂ 220 ♀ 228	♂ 880–1160 ♀ 1097–1303	80– 92	♂ 38
B. r. archeri W. Sclater, 1918 (mehr rostbraun auf der Oberseite als die anderen Rassen)	(more rufous feather edgings above, more rufous below, than in other races)	N Somaliland	N Somalia		379–436	♂ 195		♂ 85	

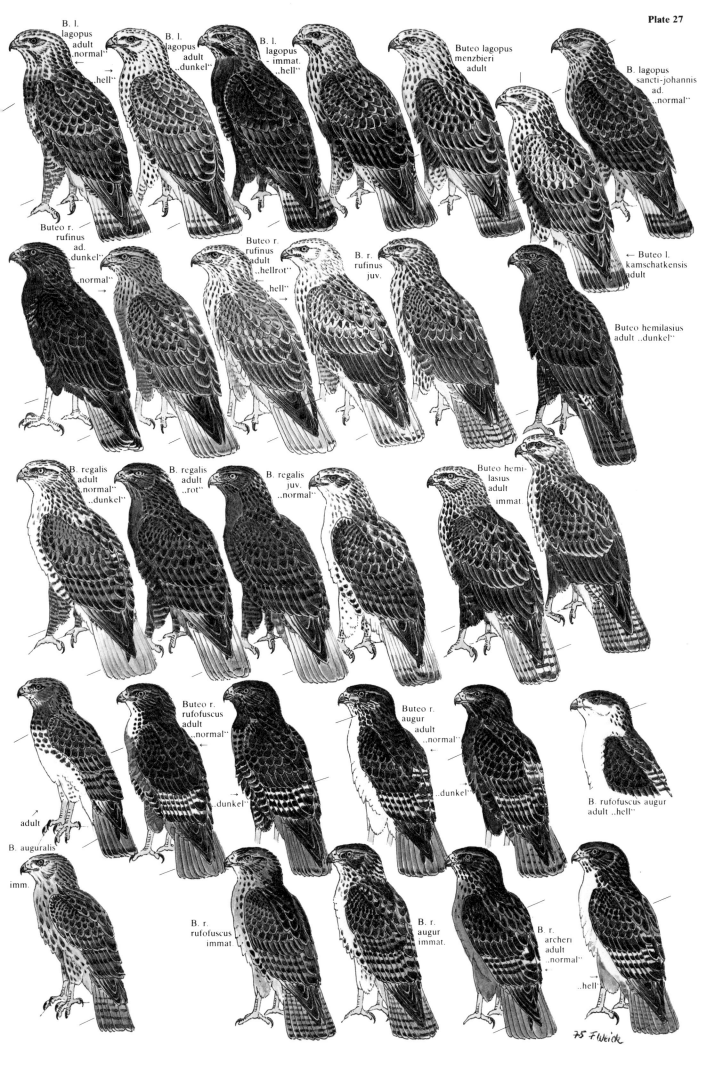

Plate 27

B. l. lagopus adult „normal"

„hell"

B. l. lagopus adult „dunkel"

B. l. lagopus - immat. „hell"

Buteo lagopus menzbieri adult

B. lagopus sancti-johannis ad. „normal"

← Buteo l. kamschatkensis adult

Buteo r. rufinus ad. „dunkel"

„normal"

Buteo r. rufinus adult „hellrot"

„hell"

B. r. rufinus juv.

Buteo hemilasius adult „dunkel"

B. regalis adult „normal" „dunkel"

B. regalis adult „rot"

B. regalis juv. „normal"

Buteo hemi-lasius adult immat.

adult

B. auguralis

imm.

Buteo r. rufofuscus adult „normal"

„dunkel"

Buteo r. augur adult „normal"

„dunkel"

B. rufofuscus augur adult „hell"

B. r. rufofuscus immat.

B. r. augur immat.

B. r. archeri adult „normal"

„hell"

75 F.Weick

Benennung / Nomenclature		Verbreitung	Distribution	Länge Length cm	Flügel Wing mm	Schwanz/Tail mm	Gewicht Weight g	Tarsus mm	Culmen mm () = mit Wachshaut with cere
Morphnus guianensis (Daudin, 1800) Würgadler (sehr langschwänzig; Kopf erscheint durch die lange Haube ziemlich groß)	Guiana Crested Eagle (very long-tailed, head appears large with long crest)	Von Honduras bis N Paraguay, Peru, Bolivien u. Argentinien (Misiones)	From Honduras to N Paraguay and Argentina (Misiones)	81–91	♂ 430–449 ♀ 425–481 (500)	♂ 360–385 ♀ 390–430	1♀ 1750	103–118	40
Harpia harpyja (Linnaeus, 1758) Harpieadler, Harpyie (Größe; Doppelhaube; kurze, breite Flügel; langer Schwanz)	Harpy Eagle (huge size, double-crest; short, rounded wings, long tail)	S Mexiko südlich bis E Bolivien, S Brasilien u. N Argentinien	S Mexico south to E Bolivia, S Brazil and N Argentina	91–110	♂ 543–580 ♀ 583–610	♂ 372–412 ♀ 417–420	♂ 4000–4600 ♀ 6000–9000 (L. H. Brown)	114–130	(73)
Harpyopsis novaeguineae Salvadori, 1875 Neuguineawürgadler (langer Schwanz; zieml. kurze runde Flügel; dicker Kopf, Farbe der Fänge von braungrau bis mattorange)	New Guinea Harpy-Eagle (long tail, rather short wings, big head colour of feet varying from brownish-grey to dull-orange)	Neuguinea	New Guinea	76–86	♂ 368–442 ♀ 450–494	♂ 364–393 ♀ 410–435		123–145	♂ 45 (62)
Pitheocophaga jefferyi Ogilvie-Grant, 1896 Affenadler (extrem hoher u. schmaler Schnabel; Lanzettschopf; langer Schwanz; Flügel breit u. gerundet; helle Unterseite, dunkle Oberseite)	Philippine Monkey-eating Eagle (extremely high and compressed bill, crown of lengthened, lanceolate feathers, long tail, wings broad and rounded, pale underside contrasting with dark upper-surface)	Philippinen: Luzon, Leyte, Samar, Mindanao (jetzt in wenigen Exempl. nur noch auf Luzon u. Mindanao)	Philippines: Luzon, Leyte, Samar, Mindanao (but now only in a few specimen on Luzon and Mindanao)	86–102	574–612	420–453 (465 Mearns)	♂ 4040–4650 ♀ ?	122–131	38 (51 hoch)
Stephanoaëtus coronatus Linnaeus, 1766 Kronenadler (♀♀ mit kürzerer Haube, dunklerer Brust, im Fluge langsamerer Flügelschlag als ♂♂, auffällig kurzflügelig u. langschwänzig)	Crowned Eagle (♀♀ with shorter crest, heavier barring on breast, and in flight slower wing beats than ♂♂, short-winged, longtailed)	West u. Zentral-Afrika (Ghana bis Uganda) bis Angola, S Afrika (Kapland)	W and Central Africa (Ghana to Uganda) to Angola, S Africa (Cape Province)	81–99	♂ 445–490 ♀ 500–532	♂ 300–330 ♀ 325–405	♂ 2800–4100 ♀ 3175–4700	85–103	37–43
Oroaëtus isidori (Des Murs, 1845) Glanzhaubenadler (Gefieder- u. Schwanzzeichnung, breite Flügel u. breiter Schwanz)	Isidor's Eagle (look at typical plumage and tail pattern, very broad wings and a broad tail)	Merida, Anden Venezuelas bis Bolivien u. W Argentinien	Merida, Andes of Bolivia and W Argentina	63–74	♂ 463–488 ♀ 508–528	♂ 283.300 ♀ 329.335		110–120	(♀ 63)
Polemaëtus bellicosus (Daudin, 1800) Kampfadler (♀♀ mit stärkerer Brust- u. Bauchfleckung als ♂♂, rundere Haube, langflügelig u. kurzschwänzig)	Martial Eagle (♀♀ with heavier spotting on breast and belly than ♂♂, rather shorter and more rounded crest, long-winged and short-tailed)	Afrika südl. Sahara v. Senegal bis Somalia u. S bis Kapland	Africa south of Sahara, from Senegal to Somalia and south to Cape Province	81–96	♂ 560–610 ♀ 605–675	♂ 273–280 ♀ 280–320 (355 Swann)	♂ 3800 ♀ 5924–6200	♂ 97–118 ♀ 114–130	40.5–49

Plate 28

Morphnus
guianensis ad.
"normal"

Morphnus
guianensis
"normal"
immat.   juv.
2. Jahr

Harpyopsis
novaeguineae
adult
            immat.

Harpia harpyja
immat.

juv.

Harpia
harpyja ad.

Pithecophaga
jefferyi
adult & immat.?

Stephanoaëtus
coronatus
juv.

Oroaëtus
isidori
adult

♂
adult

Polemaëtus bellicosus
♀ adult

juv.

S. coronatus
adult
♂   ♀

Oroaëtus
isidori
juv.
    sub-
    adult

75 F. Weick

Benennung	Nomenclature	Verbreitung	Distribution	Länge Length cm	Flügel Wing mm	Schwanz/Tail mm	Gewicht Weight g	Tarsus mm	Culmen mm () = mit Wachshaut with cere
Spizaëtus ornatus (Daudin, 1800) Prachthaubenadler	Ornate Hawk Eagle								
S. o. vicarius Friedmann, 1935 (lange Haube, Hosenzeichnung)	(long crest, barred thighs)	Mexiko, Panama, W Kolumbien u. W Ecuador	Mexico, Panama, W Colombia and W Ecuador		♂ 338–349 ♀ 353–388	♂ 244–268 ♀ 266–290	♂ 964–1004 ♀ 1389, 1400, 1607	87–100	
S. o. ornatus (Daudin, 1800) (heller als *vicarius*, vor allem an Kopf u. Stoß)	(paler than *vicarius*, usually on head and tail)	Kolumbien u. Ecuador bis Nord-Argentinien u. Paraguay	From Colombia and Ecuador to N Argentina and Paraguay	61–66	♂ 312 ♀ –381		♂ 835–1004		♂ 28,5– ♀ 32
Spizaëtus tyrannus (Wied, 1820) Tyrannenhaubenadler	Black Hawk Eagle								
S. t. serus Friedmann, 1950 (Altvögel mit sehr dunkler Unterseite)	(underside of adults very dark)	Zentral-Mexiko bis E Peru	Central Mexico to E Peru	63–71	♂ 354–394 ♀ 353–445	♂ 289–325 ♀ 289–386	♂ 904 ♀ 1092, 1123	81– 95	♂ 28– ♀ 30
S. t. tyrannus (Wied, 1820) (dunkler, weniger Weiß an Hosen, Unterschwanzdecken u. Flanken als *serus*)	(darker than *serus*, less white on thighs, flanks and lower tail-coverts)	E u. S Brasilien, Argentinien (Misiones)	East and South Brazil, Argentina (Misiones)		♂ 362–422 ♀ 428–460 (480)				
Spizaëtus alboniger (Blyth, 1845) Blythhaubenadler, Traueradler (Immaturvogel durch Schwanzzeichnung v. *nanus* unterschieden)	Mountain or Blyth's Hawk Eagle (immature may be distinguished from those of *nanus* by tail-banding)	S Burma (Tenasserim) SW Thailand, S Laos, Sumatra, Malaya, Mentawai-Ins. (N Pagi), Borneo	S Burma (Tenasserim) SW Thailand, S Laos, Sumatra, Malaya, Pagi, Borneo	51–58	♂ 280–323 ♀ 330–352	♂ 221–241 ♀ 240–252		81– 90	♀ 35
Spizaëtus nipalensis (Hodgson, 1836) Nepalhaubenadler	Hodgson's or Feather-toed Hawk Eagle								
S. n. nipalensis (Hodgson, 1836) (Größe, kurze Flügel, langer runder Schwanz)	(large size, short wings, long rounded tail)	Asiat. Festland S v. Himalaja. Von Kaschmir E bis SE China. Winter: Indien, Hainan, Taiwan	Asia (continental) south of the Himalayas. From Kashmir east to SE China Winter: India, Hainan, Taiwan		♂ 419–465 ♀ 445–508	283– 298		♂ 100 ♀ 108	(38– 45)
S. n. orientalis Temminck & Schlegel, 1844 (größer, heller u. m. kürzerer Haube als *nipalensis*)	(larger and paler than in *nipalensis*, with very short crest)	Japan	Japan	66–86	♂ 470–518 ♀ 500–540	325 395	♂ 2500 ♀ 3500	♂ 104– ♀ 126	32– 38
S. n. kelaarti Legge, 1878 (Vor allem Unterseite heller als *nipalensis*)	(under-surface rather paler than in *nipalensis*)	Sri Lanka, Kerala, Nilgiris, W Mysore	Sri-Lanka, Kerala, Nilgiri, W Mysore		♂ 398–453 ♀ 403–473	♂ 261–		98,5– 109	(♀ 42)
Spizaëtus bartelsi Stresemann, 1924 Javahaubenadler (Unterseite deutlich heller als bei *nanus*)	Java Hawk Eagle (barring on underside distinctly paler than in *nanus*)	W Java (selten)	Western Java (rare)	56–61	♂ 358 2 ♀ 371/372	♂ 247 ♀ imm 199		74– 80	27
Spizaëtus nanus Wallace, 1868 Zwerghaubenadler	Wallace's Hawk Eagle								
S. n. nanus Wallace, 1868 (kann nur durch Schwanzzeichnung v. subadultem *S. alboniger*, durch dichtere Unterseitenbänderung v. immaturem *alboniger* unterschieden werden)	(distinguished from subadult *S. alboniger* by tail-barring, from immature *alboniger* by heavier barring on underside)	Malaya, Borneo, Sumatra u. W Sumatra-Inseln	Malaya, Borneo, Sumatra and W Sumatran Islands		♂ 297–316 ♀ 307–321	♂ 215–232 ♀ 227–240		♂ 78 ♀ 78	
S. n. stresemanni Amadon, 1953 (nur Immaturvogel bekannt)	(only known in immature plumage)	Insel Nias	Nias Island	46–51	2 imm 282, 300	203			
Spizaëtus philippensis Gould, 1863 Philippinenhaubenadler (durch kürzere Haube u. braunere Unterseite v. *S. cirrhatus* unterscheidbar)	Philippine Hawk Eagle (distinguished from *S. cirrhatus* by crest and browner lower-surface)	Philippinen, einschl. Palawan	Philippines including Palawan	64–69	♂ imm 326 ♂ 330–350 ♀ 396 ♀ imm 353	♂ imm 260 ♂ 284– 290	♀ 1168	90– 100	♀ (45)
Spizaëtus lanceolatus Temminck & Schlegel, 1844 Celebeshaubenadler (Sehr kurze Haube. Rotbraune Brust kontrastiert deutlich mit weiß u. dunkelbraun gebändertem Bauch.)	Celebes Hawk Eagle (very short crest, chestnut breast strongly contrasting with white and dark-brown barred belly)	Sulawesi u. vorgelagerte Inseln Butan, Muna, Peling u. Sula-Gruppe	Sulawesi and off-lying islands of Buton, Muna, Peling and Sula group	56–64	♂ 350, 357 ♀ 382–414	230– 280		85– 95	(♀ 42)
Spizaëtus cirrhatus (Gmelin, 1788) Veränderlicher Haubenadler	Changeable Hawk Eagle								
S. c. cirrhatus (Gmelin, 1788) (Immaturvögel ähneln sehr den Jungen von *S. nipalensis* u. sind daher ziemlich schwer zu bestimmen.)	(Immatures similar to the youngs of *S. nipalensis* and so quite difficult to distinguish in the field)	Indien S der Ganges-Tiefebene, W Bengalen	India south of Gangetic plains, W Bengal		♂ 405–442 ♀ 448–462	280– 300 (322 Swann)		102 110	(♂ 44)
S. c. limnaetus (Horsfield, 1821) (Haubenlos, dunkle Phase mit einheitl. Schwanzfärbung u. breiter Subterminalbinde)	(crestless, dark phase: uniform tail with one terminal band)	N Indien (Vorberge d. Himalaya) SW bis Malaya, Java, Sumatra, Borneo, Philippinen	N India (Himalayan foothills) southwest to Malaya, Java, Sumatra, Borneo, Philippines	56–81	♂ 380–430 ♀ 405–462	♂ 240– ♀ 267, 278	♀ 1360–1810	100– 103	(♂ 39–) (♀ 44)
S. c. ceylanensis (Gmelin, 1788) (kleiner, heller u. mit 4 Schwanzbinden)	(smaller; paler and with four tail-bands)	Sri Lanka, S Kerala	Sri Lanka, S Kerala		351– –383	229– 266		90– 96	(35– 39)
S. c. andamanensis Tytler, 1865 (ähnl. dunkler Form v. *limnaetus*, kurze Haube)	(similar to melanistic phase of *limnaetus*, short crest)	Andamanen	Andaman Islands		♂ 330–355 ♀ 358, 366 377 (1 ♂ 375)				37– 38
S. c. floris (Hartert, 1898) (Größe, Unterseite nahezu reinweiß, haubenlos)	(large size, crestless, below nearly pure white)	Flores u. Sumbawa	Sumbawa and Flores		485– 495				
S. c. vanheurni Junge, 1936 (sehr klein, haubenlos)	(very small size, crestless)	Simalur-Inseln	Simalur Islands		♂ 312 ♀ 329–337				

Plate 29

S. o. vicarius adult

immat.

S. o. ornatus adult

S. t. serus adult

immat.

S. t. tyrannus adult

Sp. alboniger adult

Spizaëtus n. nipalensis imm.

adult

S. nipalensis orientalis adult

S. n. kelaarti adult

S. alboniger immat

S. alboniger subadult

Spizaëtus bartelsi

adult

immat.

S. n. nanus adult

imm.

S. nanus stresemanni imm.

immat. S. philippensis ad.

S. c. floris ad.

S. lanceolatus adult

Spizaëtus lanceolatus immat.

S. c. limnaetus adult „dunkel"

normal

imm.

S. c. cirrhatus ad.

Spizaëtus c. vanheurni adult

S. cirrhatus ceylanensis adult

75 F.Weick

Benennung	Nomenclature	Verbreitung	Distribution	Länge Length cm	Flügel Wing mm	Schwanz/Tail mm	Gewicht Weight g	Tarsus mm	Culmen mm () = mit Wachshaut with cere
Spizaëtus africanus (Cassin, 1865) Schwarzachseladler (kurz- u. rundflügelig; langschwänzig. weiße Unterseite)	Cassin's Hawk-eagle (contrasting white under-surface. short, rounded wings. very long tail)	W Afrika v. E Kongo bis Uganda (Bwamba), Gabun bis Togoland u. Zaïre (Katanga bis Uele)	W Africa, from E Congo to Uganda (Bwamba) Gabon to Togo and Zaïre (Katanga to Uele)	56–61	330–341 (381 Bannerman)	211–234 (262 Bannerman)		70–84	27
Lophaëtus occipitalis (Daudin, 1800) Schopfadler (Dunkles Gefieder u. sehr langer Schopf machen ihn unverwechselbar.)	Long-crested Eagle (all dark plumage and very long crest make it unmistikable)	Afrika, S der Sahara, Senegal bis Äthiopien u. S bis Kapland	Africa south of Sahara. Senegal to Ethiopia and south to Cape-Province	51–56	♂ 350–376 ♀ 370–408	♂ 192–200 ♀ 215–250	♂ 912–1363 ♀ 1367–1523	♂ 92–97 ♀ 95–100	♂ 27–28 ♀ 29–30
Spizastur melanoleucus (Vieillot, 1816) Schwarzweißhaubenadler (Schwarzweißer Habitus u. dunkler Schopf sind gute Feldkennzeichen.)	Black and White Hawk-eagle (black and white appearance and sharply contrasting crest identify this small eagle)	Von S u. E Mexiko über den größten Teil des trop. S Amerika östl. der Zentral Anden bis E Peru, Paraguay u. Misiones in Argentinien	From S and E Mexico through most tropical S America east of Central Andes to E Peru, Paraguay and Argentina (Misiones)	53–61	♂ 340–386 ♀ 394–423	♂ 230–245 ♀ 230–253	2♂ 750.780	72–99	(♂ 38)
Hieraaëtus kienerii (Geoffroy, 1835) Rotbauchadler, Indienzwergadler **H. k. kienerii (Geoffroy, 1835)** (Kontrastreiche Zeichnung sind beim Altvogel gute Kennzeichen.)	Chestnut-bellied Hawk-eagle (in adult bird. strongly contrasting plumage pattern are characteristic)	Indien, Sri Lanka, E Himalaja v. Nepal, Sikkim bis E Assam, Bangladesh, S Indien v. Goa u. Mysore bis Kerala; Malaya	India and Sri Lanka, E Himalayas from Nepal, Sikkim to E Assam, Bangladesh, S India, Malaya		♂ 380–394 ♀ 395–433	♂ 204–211 ♀ 216–242		73–76 79–82	(33–35 ♂) (35–37 ♀)
H. k. formosus (Stresemann, 1924) (Oberseite viel schwärzer u. ohne die Brauntöne von *kienerii*)	(blacker above, lacking brownish wash of *kienerii*)	Sumatra. Java. Borneo. Sulawesi. Kl. Sunda Inseln bis Sumbawa. Philippinen	Sumatra. Java. Borneo. Sulawesi. Lesser Sunda Islands. to Sumbawa. Philippines	48–61	♂ 324–340 ♀ 360–382		1♂ 732		
Hieraaëtus dubius (Smith, 1830) Afrika- o. Ayres' Zwergadler (Heller Überaugstreif, weißer Schulterfleck u. etwas dunkleres Unterseitenkolorit sind Unterschiede zu *spilogaster*.)	Ayres' Hawk-eagle (white eyebrow, white spot at base of wing, much darker, more heavily barred a. spotted underside distinguish it from *spilogaster*)	Afrika, S der Sahara (Äthiopien u. Nigeria bis Kapland)	Africa south of Sahara (Ethiopia and Nigeria south to Cape Province)	48–53	♂ 326–345 ♀ 360–420	♂ 175 ♀ 205–223	1♂ 714 2♀ 879. 940	56–78	20,5–26
Hieraaëtus morphnoides (Gould, 1841) Australienzwergadler **H. m. morphnoides (Gould, 1841)** (Haube deutlicher als bei *pennatus*)	Little Eagle (more distinctly crested than *pennatus*)	Australien (ohne Tasmanien)	Australia (except Tasmania)	43–56	♂ 334–345 ♀ 370–402	♂ 180–189 ♀ 205–219	♂ 900–1105 ♀ schwerer	58–71	
H. m. weiskei (Reichenow, 1900) (Oberseite dunkler, Unterseite mit breiteren Schaftstrichen als Nominatform)	(darker above, below with broader shaft-streaks)	Neuguinea	New Guinea		♂ 308–317 ♀ 327–342	♂ 177 ♀ 195	imm 483	♂ 56	
Hieraaëtus pennatus (Gmelin, 1788) Zwergadler (weißer Schulterfleck oft weitgehend verdeckt)	Booted Eagle (white shoulder-patch often hard to see)	N Afrika, S Europa (Spanien u. Portugal) bis Syrien, Iran, N Afghanistan, NW Indien, i. N bis Transkaspien u. Russ. Turkestan, S Asien bis Kentei. Brutvogel in S Afrika (Kap Kawoo). Winter: bis Afrika, Indien, Burma u. Malaya	N Africa, S Europe (Spain and Portugal) to Syria, Iran, N Afghanistan, NW India, north to Transcaspia and Russian Turkestan, S Asia to Kentei. Also breeds S Africa (Cape Kawoo). Winter: to Africa, India, Burma and Malaya	48–63	♂ 347–412 ♀ 355–435	♂ 187–202 ♀ 196–230	♂ 595–770 ♀ 840–1145	♂ 56–64 ♀ 63–78	21–24 24–26
Hieraaëtus fasciatus (Vieillot, 1822) Habichtsadler **H. f. fasciatus (Vieillot, 1822)** (Ziemlich kurzflügelig u. langschwänzig. Die dunkle Oberseite bildet scharfen Kontrast zur hellen Unterseite.)	Bonelli's Eagle (rather shortwinged and longtailed. dark upper-side contrasts strongly with almost white underside)	NW Afrika, S Europa E bis Kleinasien, Iran, N Irak, Beluchistan, Afghanistan, S Transkaspien, Russ. Turkestan, Indien, Burma, E China. Winter: Ägypten, W Arabien	NW Africa, S Europe east to Asia Minor, Iran, N Iraq, Baluchistan, Afghanistan, S Transcaspia, Russian Turkestan, India, Burma, E China. Winter: Egypt, W Arabia		♂ 450–520 ♀ 452–560	♂ 240–266 ♀ 253–292	♂ juv.1500–2160 ♂ 1712– ♀ 2386	♂ 93–109 ♀ 99–110	30–35 ♂ 32–36 ♀
H. f. renschii Stresemann, 1932 (kleiner als *fasciatus*; Hosen gefleckt u. gesperbert)	(smaller than *fasciatus*, thighs barred and spotted)	Kleine Sunda-Inseln	Lesser Sunda Islands	66–79	♂ 444–452 ♀ 493				
H. f. spilogaster (Bonaparte, 1850) (Oberseite schwärzer, Unterseite weißer als bei *fasciatus*)	(above much blacker, under-surface whiter than in *fasciatus*)	Afrika, S der Sahara bis Kapland	Africa, south of Sahara to Cape-Province		♂ 412–448 ♀ 435–465	255–290	♂ 1221 ♀ 1441–1662	90–100	♂ 30–32 ♀ 32,5–34,5

Plate 30

Spizaëtus
africanus
adult
immat.

Lophaëtus
occipitalis
adult
immat.

Spizastur
melanoleucus
adult
immat.

Hieraaëtus
dubius
adult
„dunkel"
immat.
„normal"

Hieraaëtus k.
kienerii
adult
immat.

H. kienerii
formosus
adult

Hieraaëtus
dubius
adult
„normal"

Hieraaëtus
pennatus
adult
„normal"
„dunkel"

H. pennatus
immat.
„dunkel"
„normal"

Hieraaëtus m.
weiskei
adult

Hieraaëtus m.
morphnoides
adult „normal"

H. m. morph-
noides
imm.
„normal"
ad
„dun-
kel"

immat.

Hieraaëtus f. fasciatus

adult

♂
♀
H. f.
spilogaster
adult

Hieraaëtus f.
renschii
adult

H. f.
spilogaster
juv.
juv.

75 F. Weick

Benennung	Nomenclature	Verbreitung	Distribution	Länge Length cm	Flügel Wing mm	Schwanz/Tail mm	Gewicht Weight g	Tarsus mm	Culmen mm () = mit Wachshaut with cere
Aquila wahlbergi Sundevall, 1851 Silberadler (normale Phase braun, sehr variabel; helle Phase seltener, etwa 1:10)	Wahlberg's Eagle (plumage normally brown, variable; pale phase individuals uncommon)	Afrika v. N Äthiopien, Gambia S bis N Kapland	Africa, from N Ethiopia, Gambia south to Cape-Province	56–61	♂ 400–435 ♀ 435–445	♂ 215–230 ♀ 235–250	♂ 437–845	♂ 71–76 ♀ 79–82	♂ 24–26,5 ♀ 27–29
Aquila rapax (Temminck, 1828) Raubadler, Steppenadler	Tawny or Steppe Eagle								
A. r. rapax (Temminck, 1828) (Gefiedervariation von fahl hellrostfarben bis nahezu schwarzbraun)	(plumage very variable in colour from pale rufous and whitish to almost brownish-black)	Süd-Afrika, S v. Kenia, Rutschuru-Steppe u. Katanga	South-Africa, south of Kenya to Rutchuru plains and Katanga		♂ 485–540 ♀ 525–565	245– 295	2♂1849,1954 2♀ 1572,2378	73– 92	36– 44
A. r. belisarius (Levaillant jr., 1849) (keine rostfarbenen Töne im Gefieder)	(lack rufous colour in plumage)	N Afrika v. Marokko bis Äthiopien, S bis Nigeria	North Africa, from Morocco to Ethiopia south to Nigeria		♂ 473–535 ♀ 500–555		1♂ 2004		
A. r. vindhiana Franklin, 1831 (meist ungebänderter Schwanz im Adultkleid)	(tail nearly uniform coloured in adult)	Belutschistan, Afghanistan, Indien bis E Bengalen u. Assam, N Burma, selten Thailand u. nördl. N Vietnam	Baluchistan, Afghanistan, India to E Bengal and Assam, N Burma, rarely in Thailand and northern N Vietnam		♂ 480–535 ♀ 510–560	♂ 242–258 ♀ 242–285		♂ 80–87 ♀ 84–91	♂ (48–51) ♀ (48–56)
A. r. orientalis Cabanis, 1854 (genérell dunkleres u. einfarbigeres Adultgefieder; Immaturgefieder sehr unterschiedlich zur rapax-Gruppe)	(generally darker and more uniform in adult plumage than rapax or belisarius; immature-plumage very different to rapax-group)	E Europa u. Zentral-Asien i E bis S Sibirien u. Kirgisensteppe. Winter: Afrika S bis Transvaal	E Europe and Central Asia, east to S Siberia and Kirghiz-Steppes. Winter: Africa S to Transvaal	66–81	♂ 503–569 ♀ 525–607	♂ 232–258 ♀ 260–279	3♂ 2.262–2700 3♀ 2274–4850	♂ 84–100 ♀ 92–108	♂ 37–43 ♀38–44,5
A. r. nipalensis Hodgson, 1833 (noch dunkler als orientalis, Immaturvögel sehr ähnlich orientalis)	(still darker in plumage than orientalis but immature birds much similar)	von Aralsteppe bis Transbaikal und Mongolei. Winter: bis Indien	From steppes between Aral and Transbaikalia to Mongolia. Winter: India		♂ 540–610 ♀ 600–650	♂ 250–290	♂ 2520–3500 ♀ 2300–4850	♂ 85–96 ♀ 92–98	♂ (50–56) ♀ (56–58)
Aquila clanga Pallas, 1811 Schelladler (mehr weiß o. gelblich am Bürzel als A. rapax u. A. pomarina)	Greater Spotted Eagle (more white or yellowish on upper tail coverts, than A. rapax and A. pomarina)	E Europa v. Rumänien u. Ostpreußen (Polen) N bis S Finnland, Baltische Staaten, Sibirien bis Amur, N Persien, Belutschistan, NW Indien. Winter: S Europa, NE Afrika, Kl. Asien, N Indien, S China	E Europe, from Rumania and E Prussia (Poland) north to S Finland, Baltic-States, Siberia to Amurland. N Persia, Baluchistan, NW India. Winter: S Europe, NE Africa, Asia Minor, N India, S China	66–74	(468) ♂ 485–530 ♀ 515–560	♂ 218–253 ♀ 230–272	♂ 1600–2000 ♀ 2150–3200	(85) 91,5–106 (110)	♂ 27–33 ♀ 31,7–38.7
Aquila pomarina Ch. L. Brehm, 1831 Schreiadler	Lesser Spotted Eagle								
A. p. pomarina Ch. L. Brehm, 1831 (Im Felde fast unmöglich vom Schelladler zu unterscheiden)	(nearly impossible to distinguish from A. clanga in field)	Norddeutsche Tiefebene, Polen, baltische Sowjetrepubl. bis Balkan, Griechenland, asiat. Türkei, Kaukasien. Winter: Naher Osten, Irak, Ägypten, N Sudan, S Zentral-Afrika, gelegentl. Z Europa	N Germany, Poland and Baltic Sovjet-Republic to Balkan Peninsula, Greece, asiatic Turkey and Caucasus Winter: Near East, Iraq, Egypt to N Sudan, S Central Africa, sometimes Central Europe		♂ 436–493 ♀ 475–505	♂ 198–237 ♀ 216–260	♂ 1053 1509 ♀ 1195–2160	♂ 82–97 ♀ 81–100	♂ 26.5–3 ♀ 27–34
A. p. hastata (Lesson, 1834) (Langläufiger, Immaturvogel zeigt nur geringe Fleckenbildung)	(longer-legged, in immature plumage white spots on wing coverts nearly absent)	Indische Ebenen. Winter: S Burma	Plains of India. Winter: Southern Burma	61–69	♂ 470–505 ♀ 493–508	♂ 230–248 ♀ 240–?		♂ 90–104 ♀ 102–?	(♂ 40–43) (♀ 48–52)
Aquila heliaca Savigny, 1809 Kaiseradler	Imperial Eagle								
A. h. heliaca Savigny, 1809 (Unterseite der Immaturvögel bis zu Unterbauch u. Flanken gestreift)	(in immature-plumage, the under-surface is streaked on abdomen and sides)	S Europa v. Griechenland, S Rußland, S Asien bis Zentral-Sibirien, SW Transbaikalien, Mongolei, Zypern, N. Iran, Israel, W Tianshan, N Tibet, NW Indien. Winter: Ägypten, Sudan, NE Afrika, S bis N Äthiopien, Kenia, Indien, SE China, N Indochina, Korea, Japan	S Europe from Greece, S Russia, S Asia to Central Siberia, SW Transbaikalia and Mongolia. South to Cyprus, Israel, N Iran, W Tianshan, N Tibet, NW India Winter: Egypt, Sudan, NE Africa south to N Ethiopia, Kenya, India, SE China, N Indo China, Korea, Japan		♂ 554–610 ♀ 610–665	♂ 244–310 ♀ 276–330	♂ 2600 3170 ♀ 2800–3965	♂ 85–110 ♀ 97–116	♂ 40–44 ♀ 41,5–48
A. h. adalberti Ch. L. Brehm, 1861 (Evtl. eigene Art) (Oberseite der Immaturvögel mehr roströtlich, Unterseite nur bis zur Brust gestreift)	(Possibly an independent species) (upper surface in immature-plumage more reddish, below only streaked on breast)	Spanien (selten, weniger als 60 Brutpaare) Vorkommen N. Marokko erloschen (B. U. Meyburg)	Spain (rare, lesser than 60 pairs) N Morocco extinct. (B. U. Meyburg)	79–84	♂ 560–590 ♀ –640	♂ 305 ♀ 322		♂ 96 ♀ 100	

Plate 31

Aquila wahlbergi
adult „normal"
immat.
adult „dunkel"

Aquila r. rapax
adult „hell" adult „dunkel"

Aquila r. rapax
immat. „hell"

Aquila r. rapax
immat. „dunkel"

Aquila rapax
belisarius
adult „hell"

Aquila rapax
vindhiana ad.
„hell"

← Aquila rapax
orientalis adult

A. r. orientalis
← immat.

Aquila rapax
nipalensis adult

Aquila clanga
immat.

immat.
Aquila h. heliaca
adult

Aquila clanga
← „normal" adult
→
„hell"

Aquila p. pomarina
adult immat.

Aquila heliaca
adalberti
imm.
adult

A. pomarina
hastata
immat.

75 F. Weick

Benennung	Nomenclature	Verbreitung	Distribution	Länge Length cm	Flügel Wing mm	Schwanz/Tail mm	Gewicht Weight g	Tarsus mm	Culmen mm () = mit Wachshaut with cere
Aquila gurneyi G. R. Gray, 1860 Gurneyadler, Molukkenadler (Langer, gerundeter Schwanz, an *Spizaëtus* o. *Harpyopsis* erinnernd; Gefieder aber sehr dunkel)	Gurney's Eagle (long, rounded tail and short wings, resembles *Spizaëtus* or *Harpyopsis*; but plumage very dark)	N Molukken (Morotai, Halmahera, Ternate, Batjan) Aru-Inseln, W-Papua-Inseln (Waigeo, Salawati, Misool), Japen, Neuguinea, Goudenough	N Moluccas (Morotai, Halmahera, Ternate, Batjan). Aru Islands. western Papuan Islands (Waigeu, Salawati, Misool) Japen Island. New Guinea. Goodenough Island	66–76	♂ 510–520 ♀ 530–568	♂ 316–347 ♀ 340–365	♀ imm. 3060	♂ 90–105 ♀ 100–110	
Aquila verreauxii Lesson, 1830 Kaffernadler (Altvogel am schwarzen Gefieder m. weißen Abzeichen leicht ansprechbar. Immaturvögel mit kontrastierenden Ohrdecken)	Verreaux's or Black Eagle (adults are unmistakable by their coal black plumage with white backmarking. Immature bird with contrasting ear coverts!)	Afrika, S der Sahara v. Sudan u. Somalia bis Kapland, 1 × Israel	Africa, south of Sahara from Sudan and Somalia to Cape-Province. Recorded Israel	81–89	♂ 565–595 ♀ 590–640	315–360	♂ 3600 ♀ 3686–5779	105–110	42–47.5
Aquila chrysaëtos (Linnaeus, 1758) Steinadler	Golden Eagle								
A. ch. chrysaëtos (Linnaeus, 1758) (Größe, Nackenfärbung) (Immaturvögel sind durch viel Weiß an Schwanzwurzel gut unterscheidbar.)	(large size, golden nape contrasting with dark brown colours) Immature birds are distinguishable by large white area at base of tail)	Europa, lokal (ohne Spanien) bis W Sibirien	Europe, locally (except Spain) to W Siberia		♂ 570–670 ♀ 625–725	290–332 328–365	♂ 3250–4440 ♀ 3750–6665	♂ 102–117 ♀ 106–120	♂ 36.3–42 ♀ 43.1–46.
A. ch. homeyeri Severtzov, 1888 (kleiner, dunkler, mit stumpferen Gefiederfarben!)	(smaller, darker, duller in plumage)	Spanien, N Afrika, Balearen, Kleinasien S bis Sinai-Halbinsel u. Arabien	Spain. North Africa. Balearic Islands, Asia Minor, south to Sinai Peninsula and Arabia		♂ 550–615 ♀ 600–705				
A. ch. daphanes Severtzov, 1872 (Alt- u. Jungvogel dunkler als *chrysaëtos*, Hinterkopf weniger „golden")	(adult and immature with darker plumage than *chrysaëtos*, lanceolate neck feathers less golden)	Russ. Turkestan, E bis Mandschurei, SW China, S bis Himalaya	Russian Turkestan east to Manchuria and SW China, south to the Himalayas	76–102	♂ 600–680 ♀ 660–720	♂ 315–335 ♀ 350–365	♂ 4000–4400 ♀ 4250–6500	♂ 89–95 ♀ 95–105	
A. ch. canadensis (Linnaeus, 1758) (Noch dunkler als *daphanea*; Färbung v. Laufbefiederung u. Vorderkopf)	(still darker than *daphanea*, colour of feathered tarsus and crown)	E u. NE Sibirien, S bis zum Ochotskischen Meer, Altai u. Nord-Mongolei, N Amerika v. Alaska bis Mexiko	E and NE Siberia, south to Sea of Okhotsk. Altai and N Mongolia, N America from Alaska to Mexico		♂ 555–655 ♀ 610–705		♂ 3300–5800 ♀ 3650–6100		
A. ch. japonica Severtzov, 1888 (Ähnlich *canadensis*, jedoch mit mehr Weiß an Lauf u. Schwanzinnenfahnen!)	(similar to *canadensis*, but with more white on feathered tarsus and inner web of tail quills)	Korea, Japan (Hondo), (Hokkaido?), S Kurilen, Kyushu	Korea. Japan (Hondo, Hokkaido?) S Kuriles. Kyushu		♂ 573–595 ♀ 630–655	310–347 (Kobayashi)		96–107	38–44
Aquila audax (Latham, 1801) Keilschwanzadler **A. a. audax (Latham, 1801)** (keilförmiger Schwanz, großer, kräftiger Schnabel)	Wedge-tailed Eagle (wedge-shaped tail; heavy, powerful bill)	Australien, evtl. Irrgast auf Neuguinea	Australia, perhaps accidentally to New Guinea	86–102	♂ 570–667 ♀ 600–667	♂ 420–457 ♀ 430–464	2495–4536 (evtl. über 5000, Fleay)	103	
A. a. fleayi Condon & Amadon, 1954 (Nackenfedern heller, Flügeldecken heller, Klauen stärker als bei Nominatform)	(Nape-feathers paler, shoulder lighter, rather heavier claws than nominateform)	Tasmanien	Tasmania		*etwa gleiche Maße wie „audax", jedoch kräftigere Krallen*				
Ictinaëtus malayensis (Temminck, 1822) Malaienadler **I. m. malayensis (Temm., 1822)** (Habitus wie *perniger*, jedoch kleiner)	Indian Black Eagle (similar to *perniger*, but smaller)	Burma, Malaya, Asiat. Festland bis Fokien, E Indien, Java, Sumatra, Borneo, Sulawesi, Sula-Inseln	Burma, Malaya, continental Asia to Fokien. East India, Java, Sumatra, Borneo, Sulawesi, Sula Islands		♂ 488–510 ♀ 525				
I. m. perniger (Hodgson, 1836) (langflüglig, langschwänzig, Altvogel vorwiegend schwarz, schlank)	(slender body, long wings and long tail, plumage all black in adult)	Indien, E bis Assam, Sri Lanka	India east to Assam. Sri Lanka	69–81	♂ 520–547 ♀ 538–600	♂ 285–326 ♀ –382		♂ 69–73 ♀ 81–88.5	♂ (37–43 ♀ (–46)

Plate 32

Aquila gurneyi
immat.
adult

Aquila verreauxii immat.
adult

A. chrysaëtos
homeyeri
adult

Aquila c.
chrysaëtos
ad. „hell"

Aquila c. chrysaëtos
immat.

adult
„normal"

Aquila c. chrysaëtos
adult

Aquila chrysaëtos
daphanea
adult

Aquila chrysaëtos
japonica
adult

Aquila c.
canadensis adult

Aquila a.
fleayi
adult

immat.

Aquila a.
audax

adult

juv.

Ictinaëtus m. perniger
immat.

Ictinaëtus malayensis perniger
adult

75 F. Weick

Benennung	Nomenclature	Verbreitung	Distribution	Länge Length cm	Flügel Wing mm	Schwanz/Tail mm	Gewicht Weight g	Tarsus mm	Culmen mm () = mit Wachshaut with cere
Daptrius ater Vieillot, 1816 Gelbkehlkarakara (bunte Hautteile; Weiß auf der Schwanzwurzel)	Yellow-throated Caracara (coloured skin on face and throat; white on basal twothirds of tail)	S Venezuela, Guayanas, Kolumbien E der Anden, E Ecuador, E Peru, Bolivien, Brasilien i. S bis Mato Grosso u. Maranhao	S Venezuela, Guianas, Colombia east of Andes, E Ecuador, E Peru, Bolivia, Brazil south to Mato Grosso and Maranhao	41–46	300–324	190–203	♂ 330 ♀ 348–445	54–60	(37)
Daptrius americanus (Boddaert, 1783) Rotkehlkarakara (bunte Hautteile; weißer Bauch u. Hosen)	Redthroated Caracara (coloured skin; abdomen and thighs white)			41–61					
Daptrius a. guatemalensis (Swann, 1921) (etwas größer als *americanus*)	(slightly larger than *americanus*)	S Mexiko, Guatemala bis Panama	S Mexiko, Gutamala to Panama		♂ 351–364 ♀ 357–368	♂ 237–264 ♀ 243–268	♂ ♀ 677	52– –60	
Daptrius a. americanus (Bodd., 1783) (Habitus bei allen Rassen gleich)	(plumage in all forms similar)	Nördl. S Amerika, v. Guayana, Venezuela, Surinam bis N Brasilien	Northern S America, from Guiana, Venezuela, Surinam to N Brazil		♂318–354 ♀ 347–360		♂ 570 ♀ 560–586		
Daptrius a. formosus (Latham, 1790) (größer u. schwerer als *guatemalensis*)	(size larger than *guatemalensis*)	S u. E Brasilien (Sao Paulo, Mato Grosso)	SandE Brazil (Sao Paulo, Mato Grosso)		♂ 365–376 ♀ 373–398		♂ ♀ –275	♂ ♀ 770	
Phalcoboenus carunculatus Des Murs, 1853 Karunkelkarakara (Immaturvogel lebhafter gefärbt als bei *megalopterus* u. *albogularis*)	Carunculated Caracara (immature bird more richly coloured than in *megalopterus* and *albogularis*)	Anden v. Ecuador u. S W Kolumbien	Andes of Ecuador and SW Colombia	48–53	379–391	203–206		83–93	(56)
Phalcoboenus megalopterus (Meyen, 1834) Bergkarakara (Flügeldecken beim Immaturvogel heller als bei *carunculatus* u. *albogularis*)	Mountain Caracara (shoulders lighter, with more white tips to feathers in immatures, than in *carunculatus* and *albogularis*)	Anden Perus u. Boliviens, NW Argentinien, N Chile	Andes of Peru and Bolivia. NW Argentina, N Chile	48–53	376–409	193–225	♂ 795	78–83	38
Phalcoboenus albogularis Gould, 1837 Weißkehlkarakara (Immaturvogel an Oberseite tiefbraun)	White-throated Caracara (immature bird above dark brown)	Chile u. Argentinien bis Feuerland	Chile and Argentina to Tierra del Fuego	48–53	♂ 368–377 ♀ 372–395	♂ 215 ♀ 214–235		78– 81	28
Phalcoboenus australis (Gmelin, 1788) Forsterkarakara, Falklandkarakara (Dunkle Färbung, Schenkelfärbung)	Forster's Caracara, Johnny Rook (dark colouring, rufous thighs)	Falklandinseln u. kleine Inseln Feuerlands	Falkland islands and small islands in Tierra del Fuego	58–63	♂ 403–406 ♀ 423	242–245	♂ 1 187	83–86	(48)
Polyborus lutosus Ridgway, 1876 † Guadalupekarakara (Eventuell konspezifisch mit *P. plancus*)	Guadalupe Caracara (Perhaps conspecific with *P. plancus*)	Insel Guadalupe vor Niederkalifornien. Ausgestorben seit etwa 1905	Guadalupe Island, off Baja California: Extinct about 1905		381–418	260–286		83–92	32–35
Polyborus plancus (Miller, 1777) Karakara, Schopfkarakara	Common Caracara								
P. pl. auduboni Cassin, 1865 (schwarze Federhaube; buntes Gesicht; gebändertes u. gestreiftes Gefieder)	(black crest, coloured face, barred and streaked plumage)	N Amerika bis W Panama, Kuba u. Insel de Pinos	N America to W Panama, Cuba, Isle of Pines		♂ 370–418 ♀ 373–408	223– 254		81– 94	
P. pl. pallidus Nelson, 1898 (wie *auduboni*, aber kleiner, heller)	(like *auduboni*, but smaller and paler)	Tres-Marias-Inseln	Tres Marias Islands		♂ 355– ♀ 375				
P. pl. cheriway (Jacquin, 1784) (dunkle Gefiederteile viel schwärzer, Brust u. Bauchzeichnung)	(dark areas of plumage blacker, markings on both chest and belly)	E Panama, Nördl. S Amerika bis Peru u. Amazonas, Niederländ. Westindien	E Panama, northern S America to Peru and Amazon, Netherlands West Indies	51–66	♂ 365– ♀ 400				
P. pl. plancus (Miller, 1777) (Rücken-, Brust- u. Unterschwanzdeckenzeichnung)	(Marking on back, chest and under-tail coverts)	Südl. S Amerika von Peru bis Feuerland, Falklandinseln	Southern S America from Peru to Tierra del Fuego. Falklands Islands		♂ 365–415 ♀ 393–450		♀ 830–1585	96	(52)
Milvago chimango (Vieillot, 1816) Chimango	Chimango								
M. ch. chimango (Vieillot, 1816) (mit Immaturvögeln der Gattung *Phalcoboenus* verwechselbar)	(may be confused with immature birds of genus *Phalcoboenus*)	Paraguay, Uruguay bis Argentinien u. N Chile	Paraguay, Uruguay to Argentina and N Chile	38–41	280–329	178–193		60–64	25
M. ch. temucoensis W. Sclater, 1918 (dunkler, m. stärkerer Zeichnung als bei *chimango*)	(darker, more heavily marked than *chimango*)	S Chile, Feuerland, Kap-Horn-Inseln	South Chile, Tierra del Fuego, Cape Horn Islands		280–293				
Milvago chimachima (Vieillot, 1816) Gelbkopfkarakara, Chimachima	Yellow-headed Caracara								
M. ch. chimachima (Viill. 1816) (kontrastreiches Gefieder, deutlichere Schwanzzeichnung als *chimango*)	(strongly contrasting plumage, trail more sharply barred than in *chimango*)	Panama u. Ins. Pearl S bis E Peru u. Bolivien, Uruguay, Paraguay u. N Argent.	Panama and Pearl Island south to E Peru and Bolivia, Uruguay, Paraguay and N Argentina	38–46	♂ 280–298 ♀ 295–306	♂ –204 ♀ –211	} ♂ 277–335 ♀ 307–364	52– 61	
M. ch. strigilata (Spix, 1824) (helle Gefiederteile, viel weißer als bei Nominatform)	(light plumage areas much whiter than in nominate race)	N E Brasilien	North-eastern Brazil		♂ 265 ♀ 278–290	♂ 181– ♀ 190–			

Plate 33

adult
Daptrius ater
immat.

immat.
Daptrius americanus
adult

Milvago c.
temucoensis adult

immat.

Milvago c.
chimango
adult

Milvago chimachima
strigilata
adult

Phalcoboenus
carunculatus
juv.

adult

immat.
Phalcoboenus
megalopterus
adult

Milvago c.
chimachima
juv.

adult

Phalcoboenus
albogularis
immat.

P. albogularis
ad.

P.
australis
adult
← subad.
4. Jahr

3. Jahr
imm.

Phalcoboenus
australis
juv.
→

immat.
Polyborus
lutosus†
ad.

Polyborus p.
plancus
adult

immat.

Polyborus plancus
auduboni
adult

Polyborus p.
cheriway
adult

75 F. Weick

Benennung	Nomenclature	Verbreitung	Distribution	Länge Length cm	Flügel Wing mm	Schwanz/Tail mm	Gewicht Weight g	Tarsus mm	Culmen mm () = mit Wachshaut with cere
Herpetotheres cachinnans (Linnaeus, 1758) Lachfalke	Laughing Falcon								
H. c. cachinnans (Linnaeus, 1758) (durch dicken Kopf, Maske u. Gefiederfärbung unverwechselbar)	(big head, facial mask and plumage colours make it unmistakable)	Mexiko S bis E Bolivien, N Argentinien, Paraguay u. S Brasilien	Mexico south to E Bolivia, N Argentina, Paraguay and S Brazil	43–51	♂ 262–307 ♀ 255–305	♂ 187–232 ♀ 188–242	♂ 408–597 ♀ 590, 655	58–77	
H. c. fulvescens Chapman, 1915 (tiefere Gelbtönung auf Kopf, Unterseite u. Schwanz)	(deeper in colour on head, under-surface and tail)	Pazif. Küste v. Panama, Kolumbien, Ecuador bis N Peru	Pacific coast from Panama and Colombia south to N Peru		250–260				
Micrastur ruficollis (Vieillot, 1817) Gebänderter Waldfalke, Sperberwaldfalke	Barred Forest Falcon								
M. r. guerilla Cassin, 1848 (Beachte das variable Immaturkleid.)	(immatures extremely variable: look at plumage variations)	Mexiko bis Nicaragua	Mexico to Nicaragua		♂ 165–178 ♀ 176–180	♂ 160–187 ♀ 180–186	♂ 162	53–58	(25)
M. r. interstes Bangs, 1907 (Altvogel etwas dunkler, Jungvogel an Unterseite etwas stärker gezeichnet)	(adult rather darker, immatures more strongly marked below)	Costa Rica bis W Kolumbien u. Ecuador	Costa Rica to W Colombia and Ecuador		♂ 160–170 ♀ 171–179	♂ 157–166 ♀ 161–168	⌀ 190	56–58,5	18–21
M. r. zonothorax (Cabanis, 1865) (Rücken kann schiefergrau o. braungrau sein.)	(back may be slategrey or greyish-brown)	N Venezuela, E Kolumbien	N Venezuela and E Colombia		♂ 170–178 ♀ 181–190	♀ 181		♀ 60	(26)
M. r. ruficollis (Vieillot, 1817) (Beachte zwei verschiedene Phasen.)	(look for two colour-phases)	Von Brasilien S des Amazonas bis Misiones (Argentinien) u. Paraguay	Brazil south of Amazon to Misiones (Argentina) and Paragua		♂ 165–175 ♀ 170–195	♂ 170 ♀ 175	♀ 195	♂ 53 ♀ 64	♂ 15 ♀ 19
M. r. olrogi Amadon, 1964 (Oberseite dunkler bei der rostbraunen Phase)	(in rufous phase upperside darker)	NW Argentinien	NW Argentina	31–38	♂ 186 ♀ 190–199				
M. r. gilvicollis (Vieillot, 1817) (Grautöne, weiße Unterseite)	(grey colouring, white belly)	Amazonien, Guayanas, S Venezuela	Amazonia. Guianas, S Venezuela		♂ 169–180 ♀ 180–190		♂ 181	♀ 63	♀ (25)
M. r. pelzelni Ridgway, 1875 (wie gilvicollis, aber größer)	(similar to gilvicollis, but larger)	Quellflüsse des Amazonas in Brasilien u. E Peru	Headwaters of Amazon in Brazil and E Peru		♂ 180–190 ♀ 190–200				
Micrastur plumbeus W Sclater, 1918 Bleiwaldfalke (kurzer Schwanz m. einer Binde)	Sclater's Forest Falcon (rather short tail with single band)	W Kolumbien u. NW Ecuador (selten)	W Colombia and NW Ecuador (rare)	31–36	166–178	125–140		56–58	15
Micrastur mirandollei (Schlegel, 1862) Schieferrückenwaldfalke (drei weiße Schwanzbinden)	Slaty-backed Forest Falcon (three white tailbands)	E Costa-Rica bis E Peru, i. E. bis Guayana, Brasilien (selten)	E Costa Rica to E Peru, east to Guianas and Brazil (rare)	43–46	♂ 216–237 ♀ 220–235 (248 Swann)	♂ 182–200 ♀ 187–200		74–81	♀ (32)
Micrastur buckleyi Swann, 1919 Traylorwaldfalke (viel kleiner als F. semitorquatus m. drei Schwanzbinden)	Traylor's Forest Falcon (smaller than F. semitorquatus, three tailbands)	Bekannt durch ca. 10 Exempl. Ecuador u. NE Peru	Known from ten specimens, Ecuador and NE Peru	41–46	♂ 209–219 ♀ 217	♂ 215–235 ♀ 230		55–65	
Micrastur semitorquatus (Vieillot, 1817) Halsringwaldfalke, Kappenwaldfalke	Collared Forest Falcon								
M. s. naso (Lesson, 1842) (Größe, langer Schwanz, kurze Flügel)	(large size, long tail, short wings)	Mexiko u. Mittelamerika S an der Pazif. Küste bis NW Peru	Mexico and Central America south on Pacific slope to NW Peru	46–61	♂ 256–275 ♀ 265–285	♂ 260–300 ♀ 270–300	♂ 511–642 ♀ 660–750	78–87	
M. s. semitorquatus (Vieillot, 1817) (in allen Kleidern etwas heller)	(paler in all plumages)	E Kolumbien, Venezuela, Guayana bis Peru, Bolivien, Paraguay u. Argentinien	E Colombia, Venezuela, Guianas, to Peru, Bolivia, Paraguay and Argentina		♂ 230–263 ♀ 270–275		♂ 467–511 ♀ 556–750		♂ (35)

Plate 34

Micrastur ruficollis guerilla

adult ♂

adult ♀ immat. "hell"

immat. "gelbbraun"

adult
→
H. c. cachinnans immat

adult
→
H. c. fulvescens

M. ruficollis interstes ad. ♀ imm.

Micrastur ruficollis gilvicollis ♂ ad. immat.

M. r. olrogi ad. "rot"

M. r. ruficollis ad. "rot" "weiß-kehlig"

M. r. zonothorax ad.

Micrastur plumbeus adult immat.

Micrastur mirandollei immat. adult

Micrastur buckleyi adult ♂ immat.

adult ♀

Micrastur s. naso immat. "hell" "dunkel"

"gelbbraun"

"hell"

Micrastur s. semitorquatus adult "gelbbraun"

Micrastur s. naso adult "hell"

"gelb-braun"

Micrastur s. naso adult "dunkel" ←

1975 F. Weick.

Benennung / Nomenclature		Verbreitung	Distribution	Länge Length cm	Flügel Wing mm	Schwanz/Tail mm	Gewicht Weight g	Tarsus mm	Culmen mm () = mit Wachshaut with cere
Spiziapteryx circumcinctus (Kaup, 1852)									
Tropfenzwergfalke	Spot-winged Falconet	W u. N Argentinien	W and N Argentina	28–31	♂ 155–160 ♀ 167–174	131– 150		35– 40	(19)
(weißer Bürzel, kurze, runde Flügel)	(white rump; short, rounded wings)								
Polihierax semitorquatus (A. Smith, 1836)									
Halsbandzwergfalke	African Pygmy Falcon								
P. s. semitorquatus (A. Smith, 1836)		S Afrika v. Angola, S Tanganjika bis Oranje Fluß, Lesotho	S Africa from Angola, S Tanganyika to Orange-River, Lesotho	19–24	♂ 110–119 ♀ 110–119	69– 74		24– 28	10– 10.5
(Farbe der Wachshaut u. Beine)	(colour of cere and legs)								
P. s. castanotus (Heuglin, 1860)		E Afrika. Somalia. Sudan	E Africa. Somalia. Sudan		♂ 112– ♀ 131		44– 72		
(dunkler u. bunter gefärbt)	(darker and more richly coloured)								
Polihierax insignis Walden, 1872									
Langschwanzzwergfalke	Fielden's Falconet								
P. i. insignis Walden, 1872		Oberes Burma	Upper Burma		♂ 138–143 ♀ 148	♂ 118–124 ♀ 129–132		34– 38	(21)
(Graufärbung u. Kleinheit)	(smallness. appearing grey)								
P. i. cinereiceps Stuart Baker, 1927	(♂ darker on back. contrasting with pale head)	Tenasserim. Laos. Indochina	Tenasserim. Laos. Indo-China	25–28	♂ 139–145 ♀ 143–147				
(Rücken dunkler, mehr Kontrast zu Kopf, ♂)									
P. i. harmandi (Oustalet, 1876)	(Kopf des ♂ noch heller mit reduz. Schaftstrichen)	Bas Laos, Süd-Annam, China	Bas Laos. South Annam. China		♂ 140–141 ♀ 143–147				
(Kopf des ♂ noch heller mit reduz. Schaftstrichen)	(head of ♂ still lighter coloured. shaft-streaks reduced)								
Microhierax caerulescens (Linnaeus, 1758)									
Indienzwergfalke, Rotschenkel Z.	Red-legged Falconet								
M. c. caerulescens (Linnaeus, 1758)	(Very small size, about that of a sparrow)	Indien i. E bis Assam (S bis Cachar)	India east to Assam, south to Cachar	14–19	♂ 91–106 ♀ 100–112	♂ 58–64 ♀ 64–67		♂ 20–22 ♀ ~25	♂ 11–12 ♀ 12–13
(klein, etwa sperlingsgroß)									
M. c. burmanicus Swann, 1920	(broader white nape-band, lighter below, very small size)	Burma, Shan-Staaten. Thailand, Siam. Kambodscha. S Annam	Burma, Shan-States, Thailand, Siam, Cambodia, S Annam		♂ 91–99 ♀ 104–109				
(breitere weiße Nackenzone, Unterseite heller)									
Microhierax fringillarius (Drapiez, 1824)									
Malaienzwergfalke, Schwarz-schenkelzwergfalke	Black-legged Falconet	S Tenasserim. Malaya. Sumatra. Borneo. Java. Bali	S Tenasserim. Malaya. Sumatra. Borneo. Java. Bali	14–15,5	♂ 89–103 ♀ 93–105	♂ 49–55 ♀ 51.5–60.5		18– 22	10– 12
(ohne den breiten weißen Überaugstreif u. Nackenband, etwa sperlingsgroß)	(lacks pronounced white eye-stripe and nape-band, very small size)								
Microhierax latifrons Sharpe, 1879									
Borneozwergfalke	Bornean Falconet	N W Borneo	NW Borneo	16	91–102	48–59		19–23	
(ohne weiße Schwanzflecke, etwa sperlingsgroß)	(lacks white tail-spotting, very small size)								
Microhierax erythrogonys (Vigors, 1831)									
Philippinenzwergfalke	Philippine Falconet	Philippinen (Luzon. Mindanao. Mindoro. Bohol. Samar. Cebu Negros)	Philippines (Luzon. Mindanao. Mindoro. Bohol. Samar. Cebu Negros)	15,5–18	♂ 102–118 ♀ 108–122	62.5– 70	♂ 40.47	20– 23	
(ohne weiße Stirn, etwa sperlingsgroß)	(lacks white forehead, very small size)								
Microhierax melanoleucos (Blyth, 1843)									
Weißstirnzwergfalke	Pied Falconet	Assam. SE China. Laos. N Annam	Assam. SE China. Haut Laos. N Annam	15,5–18	♂ 108–116 ♀ 111–121	65– 74		♂ 20–25 ♀ 27	♂ (14) ♀ (14–15)
(ohne braunen Anflug auf Gefieder. etwa sperlingsgroß)	(plumage with no trace of chestnut)								
Falco naumanni Fleischer, 1818									
Rötelfalke	Lesser Kestrel	Europa v. Spanien bis Kiew, Charkow, untere Wolga, Sibirien, NW Afrika. Kleinasien, Persien, Turkestan. Winter: Afrika, Indien	Europe from Spain to Kiev, Charkow, lower Volga, Siberia, NW Africa, Asia Minor, Persia, Turkestan Winter: Africa, India	28–31	♂ 223–247 ♀ 226–246	♂ 133–148 ♀ 139–155	♂ 92–172 ♀ 138–208	♂ 29.5–33 ♀ 30–31.5	♂ 12–15 ♀ 11.5–15
(Rücken des ♂ ungefleckt, schlanker als F. tinnunculus)	(back of male unspotted, more slender than F. tinnunculus)								
Falco rupicoloides A. Smith, 1830									
Weißaugenfalke	Greater or White-eyed Kestrel								
F. r. rupicoloides A. Smith, 1830	(♂ and ♀ with grey rump and tail)	S Transvaal N bis Tansania u. Angola	S Transvaal north to Tanzania and Angola		♂ 260–283 ♀ 272–290	148– 177		40– 46	(15– 18)
(grauer Bürzel u. Schwanz)									
F. r. arthuri (Gurney, 1884)	(slightly smaller than rupicoloides)	N Tansania u. Kenia N evtl. bis Rudolf-See	N Tanzania and Kenya north probably to Lake Rudolf		♂ 245–251 ♀ 248–257		♂ 165–192 ♀ 193.207		
(etwas kleiner als rupicoloides)									
F. r. fieldi (Elliot, 1897)	(much paler, straw-colour, than in rupicoloides)	Somalia. u. N Kenia evtl. bis Marsabit u. Rudolf-See	Somalia and N Kenya probably to Marsabit and Lake Rudolf	33–35,5	♂ 236–245 ♀ 247–252				
(viel heller, gelber als rupicoloides)									
Falco alopex (Heuglin, 1861)									
Fuchsfalke	Fox Kestrel	Ghana bis Sudan. S Äthiopien, Kenia	From Ghana to Sudan. S Ethiopia and Kenya	36–38	♂ 266–293 ♀ 269–308	♂ 180–212 ♀ 181–210		♂ 43–44 ♀ 43–45	15– 18
(überall fuchsrot, Größe)	(entire plumage foxy-red. rather large sized)								
Falco sparverius Linnaeus, 1758									
Buntfalke	American Kestrel or Sparrow-Hawk								
F. s. sparverius Linnaeus, 1758	(The only New World species of kestrels)	N Amerika S bis Süd-Karolina. Guerrero v. Nord-Niederkalifornien. Winter: S bis Mexiko. Panama.	N America. south to S Carolina. Guerrero and N Lower California. Winter: S to Mexico. Panama		♂ 174–198 ♀ 178–207	♂ 116–142 ♀ 119–142	♂ ⌀ 109 ♀ ⌀ 119	34– 42	15
(einzige Rüttelfalkenart der neuen Welt)									
F. s. paulus (Howe u. King, 1902)	(♂ more richly coloured. less spotted)	S Karolina bis Florida u. S Alabama	Carolina to Florida and Alabama		♂ 165–180 ♀ 175–186	♂ 110–122 ♀ 112–120			
(♂ etwas bunter u. weniger gefleckt)									
F. s. peninsularis Mearns, 1892	(very pale above and below)	S Niederkalifornien u. gegenüberlieg. Küsten v. Sonora u. Sinaloa (Mexiko)	S Lower California and opposite coasts to Sonora and Sinaloa (Mexico)		♂ 163–178 ♀ 170–181				
(Ober- u. Unterseite sehr hell)									
F. s. tropicalis (Griscom, 1930)	(♂ dark, without brown crown-patch)	Chiapas, Mex.. Guatemala, N Honduras	Chiapas. Mexico. Guatemala. N Honduras		♂ 171–175 ♀ 180–185	♂ 117–125 ♀ 124–128			
(♂ dunkel ohne braunen Kronenfleck)									
F. s. sparveroides Vigors, 1827	(look for both colour phases)	Kuba. Insel de Pinos. S-Bahamas	Cuba. Isle of Pines. S Bahamas		♂ 168–180 ♀ 174–189	♂ 114–126 ♀ 118–130			
(Beachte zwei Farbphasen.)									
F. s. dominicensis Gmelin, 1788	(pale-coloured; only female has shaft-streaks below)	Hispaniola u. umlieg. Inseln	Hispaniola and surrounding islets	23–31	♂ 180–194 ♀ 180–195				
(sehr hell, ♀ an Unterseite nur Schaftstriche)									
F. s. caribearum Gmelin, 1788	(♂ dark, heavily spotted below, tail with black shafts)	Puerto Rico, Virgin-Ins. u. Kleine Antillen	Puerto Rico. Virgin Islands, Lesser Antilles		♂ 160–172 ♀ 160–178	♂ 115–126 ♀ 121–138			
(♂ dunkel, Unterseite stark gefleckt, Schwanzfedern m. schwarzen Schäften)									
F. s. brevipennis (Berlepsch, 1892)	(similar to caribearum, black marking reduced, shoulders lighter grey)	Niederl. Westindien ohne Bonaire	Netherlands West Indies. except Bonaire		♂ 160–169 ♀ 169–182				
(ähnl. caribearum, aber Flecke reduziert, Flügeldecken heller grau)									
F. s. isabellinus Swainson, 1837	(very pale form)	Guayana, E Venezuela, Insel Margarita u. oberer Rio Branco, Brasilien	Guianas. E Venezuela. Margarita Island. upper Rio Branco, Brazil		♂ 172–182 ♀ 185–187				
(sehr fahle Färbung)									
F. s. ochraceus (Cory, 1915)	(more richly coloured below)	N W Venezuela, E Kolumbien	NW Venezuela. E Colombia.		♂ 168–192				
(kräftige Unterseitenfärbung)									
F. s. aequatorialis Means, 1892	(more strongly coloured than ochraceus, sides spotted in male)	Kolumbien (nahe Kauka-Tal) u. Ecuador	Colombia (near Kauka Valley) and Ecuador.		♂ 182–200 ♀ 195–209	♂ 125–145 ♀ 128–138			
(kräftiger gefärbt als ochraceus, Flanken gefleckt)									
F. s. peruvianus (Cory, 1915)	(similar to cinnamominus, but smaller)	SW Ecuador, Peru u. N Chile	SW Ecuador, Peru and N Chile		♂ 175–185 ♀ 181–190	♂ 129–138 ♀ 131–140			
(ähnl. cinnamominus, aber kleiner)									
F. s. cinnamominus Swainson, 1837	(back strongly barred)	SE Peru, S durch Chile u. Argentinien bis Feuerland, Bolivien. Paraguay, Uruguay	SE Peru. south through Chile and Argentina to Tierra del Fuego. Bolivia. Paraguay. Uruguay		♂ 183–200 ♀ 192–212	♂ 122–134 ♀ 129–149			
(Rücken stark gefleckt)									
F. s. fernandensis (Chapman, 1915)	(similar to cinnamominus, but underside deeply coloured)	Insel Mas-Tierra u. Juan Fernandes-Gruppe	Mas-Tierra Island, Juan-Fernandez Group		♂ 186–192 ♀ 199–203	♂ 129–135 ♀ 134–140			
(ähnl. cinnamominus, Unterseite kräftiger gefärbt)									
F. s. cearac (Cory, 1915)	(like cinnamominus, but smaller)	Brasilianisches Tafelland	Tableland of Brazil		♂ 172–189 ♀ 182–195	♂ 122–133 ♀ 123–132			
(ähnlich cinnamominus, aber kleiner)									

Plate 35

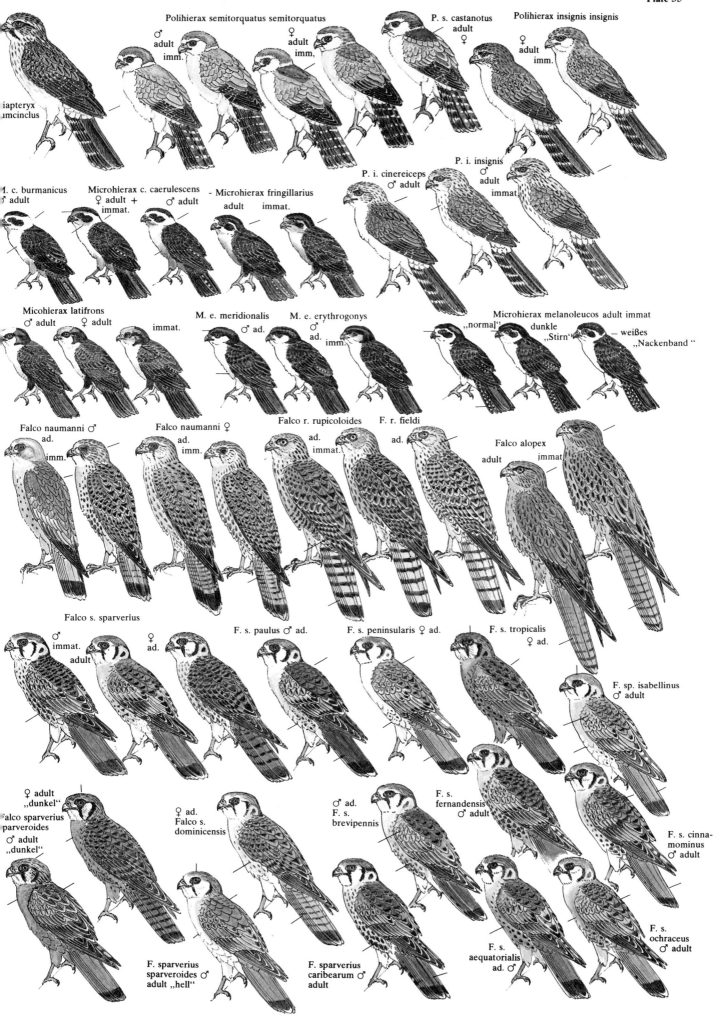

Polihierax semitorquatus semitorquatus
♂ adult
imm.
♀ adult
imm.
P. s. castanotus adult ♀
Polihierax insignis insignis
♀ adult imm.

iapteryx
imcinclus

P. i. cinereiceps ♂ adult
P. i. insignis ♂ adult immat.

M. c. burmanicus ♂ adult
Microhierax c. caerulescens ♀ adult + immat.
♂ adult
- Microhierax fringillarius adult immat.

Micohierax latifrons ♂ adult ♀ adult immat.
M. e. meridionalis ♂ ad.
M. e. erythrogonys ♂ ad. imm.
Microhierax melanoleucos adult immat
„normal" dunkle „Stirn" – weißes „Nackenband"

Falco naumanni ♂ ad. imm.
Falco naumanni ♀ ad. imm.
Falco r. rupicoloides ad. immat.
F. r. fieldi ad.
Falco alopex adult immat

Falco s. sparverius
♂ immat. adult
♀ ad.
F. s. paulus ♂ ad.
F. s. peninsularis ♀ ad.
F. s. tropicalis ♀ ad.
F. sp. isabellinus ♂ adult

♀ adult „dunkel"
alco sparverius parveroides ♂ adult „dunkel"
♀ ad. Falco s. dominicensis
♂ ad. F. s. brevipennis
F. s. fernandensis ♂ adult
F. s. cinnamominus ♂ adult

F. sparverius sparveroides ♂ adult „hell"
F. sparverius caribearum ♂ adult
F. s. aequatorialis ad. ♂
F. s. ochraceus ♂ adult

Benennung / Nomenclature	Verbreitung	Distribution	Länge Length cm	Flügel Wing mm	Schwanz/Tail mm	Gewicht Weight g	Tarsus mm	Culmen mm () = mit Wachshaut / with cere
Falco tinnunculus Linnaeus, 1758 Turmfalke — Common Kestrel								
F. t. tinnunculus Linnaeus, 1758 (♂ von *F. naumanni* durch helleren u. gefleckten Rücken, ♀ u. juv. durch stärkere Unterseitenzeichnung unterschieden) (♂ distinguished from *F. naumanni* by paler chestnut and spotted back, ♀ and juv. by more heavily spotted and streaked undersurface)	Europa, NW Afrika u. Asien S bis N Arabien, Persien, Belutschistan, Ladakh. W Himalaja, Tibet, Gobi, Yakutien, Amur, Ussuri. Winter: Afrika, S bis Tansania u. Malawi, Indien, Sri Lanka, Burma	Europe. NW Africa and Asia south to N Arabia. Persia. Baluchistan. Ladakh. W Himalaya. Tibet. Gobi. Yakutia. Amurregion. Ussuriland Winter: Africa south to Tanzania. Malawi, India. Sri Lanka. Burma		♂ 230–266 ♀ 235–275	♂ 150–174 ♀ 152–188	♂ 113–230 ♀ 154–283	♂ 37–43 ♀ 37.5–47	♂ 12.5–17 ♀ 13–17
F. t. interstinctus Mc. Clelland, 1839 (Oberseite kräftiger rotbraun u. intensiver gefleckt) (above darker chestnut and more heavily spotted)	Kaschmir bis Ladakh, Mandschurei, Korea, Japan, N China, Kansu, Sikiang Winter: Indien, Burma, Malaya, Thailand, Indochina, Hainan, Philippinen	Kashmir to Ladakh, Manchuria, Korea, Japan, N China, Kansu, Sikang. Winter: India, Burma, Malaya, Thailand, Indo-China, Hainan, Philippines		♂ 221–263 ♀ 245–267	♂ 153–169 ♀ 179,183	♂ 170–210 ♀ 122–202	♂ 37– ♀ 41–45	13– 15
F. t. objurgatus (Stuart Baker, 1927) (noch dunkler als *interstinctus*, Schwanz leicht gezeichnet) (still more dark chestnut than *interstinctus*, tail less marked)	S Indien v. Mysore u. Nelliampathy-Hügeln bis Sri Lanka	S India from Mysore and Nelliampathy hills to Sri Lanka		♂ 221–242 ♀ 234–258	♂ 147–163 ♀ 155–175			16–17
F. t. rupicolaeformis (Ch. L. Brehm, 1855) (♂ Kopffärbung) (colouring of males head)	Ägypten u. S Arabien. Winter: N Äthiopien	Egypt and South Arabia. Winter: N Ethiopia		♂ 223–247 ♀ 230–250				
F. t. archeri Hartert & Neumann, 1932 (♀ etwas heller, Schwanz stärker gebändert als bei *tinnunculus*) (♀ rather pale, tail with heavier barring than *tinnunculus*)	Somalia u. Küste Kenias S bis Lamu; Insel Socotra	Somalia and coastal Kenya south to Lamu, Socotra Island	31–35	♂ 218–229 ♀ 233–242	♂ 140–155 ♀ 141–152			
F. t. rufescens Swainson, 1837 (sehr dunkel, intensiv gebändert u. gefleckt, Kopf- u. Schwanzzeichnung) (very dark, heavily spotted and barred, markings on head and tail)	Afrika, südl. der Sahara, v. Ober-Guinea E bis Äthiopien u. von Kamerun u. N Angola bis S Tansania	Africa south of Sahara from Upper Guinea east to Ethiopia and from Cameroon and N Angola east to S Tanzania		♂ 223–227 ♀ 233–258	♂ 142–152 ♀ 165			
F. t. rupicolus Daudin, 1800 (♀ Kopfzeichnung) (head-marking of ♀)	S Afrika v. S Tansania u. N Angola bis Kapland	South Africa from S Tanzania and N Angola, south to Cape Province		♂ 217–248 ♀ 240–258				
F. t. canariensis (Koenig, 1890) (etwas dunkler als *tinnunculus* u. stärker gefleckt) (rather darker and more heavily spotted than *tinnunculus*)	Madeira u. Westl. Kanaren	Madeira and Western Canary Islands		♂ 213–230 ♀ 226–240				
F. t. dacotiae Hartert, 1913 (♀ an Kopfseiten heller, an Unterseite lebhafter gefärbt als Nominatform u. *archeri*) (♀ paler on cheeks, below brighter coloured than nominate form and *archeri*)	E Kanaren u. Lanzarote	Eastern Canary Islands and Lanzarote		♂ 210–233 ♀ 225–250				
F. t. neglectus Schlegel, 1873 (dunkelste Inselform, dunkler als *canariensis*) (darkest of island-forms, darker than *canariensis*)	Nördl. Kapverd. Inseln	Northern Cape Verde Islands		♂ 190–212 ♀ 203–217				
F. t. alexandri Bourne, 1955 („bunter", jedoch weniger stark gefleckt als *neglectus*) (more richly coloured but less heavily barred than *neglectus*)	Südl. Kapverd. Inseln	Southern Cape Verde Islands		♂ 209–229 ♀ 224–238				
Falco newtoni (Gurney, 1862) Madagaskarfalke — Madagascar or Aldabra Kestrel								
F. n. newtoni Gurney, 1863 (zwei Farbphasen) (two colour-phases)	Madagaskar	Madagascar		♂ 180–195 ♀ 188–203	♂ 110–130 ♀ 115–131		32– 40	♀ (19)
F. n. aldabranus Grote, 1928 (♀ oft mit reinweißer Unterseite) (female often with all white under-side)	Aldabra, Irrgast a. d. Komoren (Anjouan)	Aldabra Island straying to Comoro (Anjouan)	25–28	♂ 170–183 ♀ 177–185				
Falco punctatus Temminck, 1821 Mauritiusfalke — Mauritius Kestrel (einzige Kleinfalkenart auf Mauritius) (the single species of Kestrel on Mauritius)	Mauritius, äußerst selten (10–15 Exemplare)	Mauritius, very rare (10–15 specimen)	28–33	♂ 168–182 ♀ 183–192	♂ 126–135 ♀ 139		38– 45	(17.7)
Falco araea (Oberholser, 1917) Seychellenfalke — Seychelles Kestrel (einzige Falkenart auf den Seychellen) (the single species of Kestrel on Seychelles)	Seychellen (Mahé, Praslin) selten	Seychelles Islands (Mahe, Praslin) rare	23–25	♂ 146–151 ♀ 152–156	♂ 105–110 ♀ 103–115		32– 37	
Falco moluccensis (Bonaparte, 1850) Molukkenfalke — Moluccan Kestrel								
F. m. moluccensis (Bonap. 1850) (von *F. cenchroides* durch dunklere Färbung u. stärkere Fleckung unterschieden) (distinguished from *F. cenchroides* by darker chestnut and heavier markings)	Amboina. Ceram u. Buru. Obi. Halmahera. Ternate-Tidore. Batja. Morotai	Amboina. Ceram and Buru. Obi. Halmahera. Ternate-Tidore. Batja. Morotai		♂ 220–233 ♀ 228–250		145	♂ 42 ♀ 41	♂ (17.7)
F. m. timorensis Mayr, 1941 (heller, weniger intensiv gefleckt) (paler, less heavily barred above)	Timor, S W Inseln, Tanimbar-Inseln (Timorlaut)	Timor. Southwest Islands. Tenimber Islands		♂ 207–224 ♀ 221–232				
F. m. microbalia (Oberholser, 1917) (dunkler als *timorensis*, mehr Grau auf Wangen u. Ohrdecken) (darker than *timorensis*, greyer on cheeks and ear coverts)	Insel Solombo-Besar, Kl. Sunda-Inseln von Lombok bis Alor, Sulawesi, Buton, Tukong Besi u. Kaloa-Djampea-Inseln	Solombo-Besar Island. Lesser Sunda Islands from Lombok to Alor. Sulawesi. Buton. Tukong Besi and Kaloa Djampea Islands	28–33	♂ 205–233 ♀ 228–234		145	40	14.5
F. m. renschii Siebers, 1930 (ähnl. *timorensis*, aber stärker gefleckt) (similar to *timorensis*, but more heavily spotted)	Sumba-Inseln	Sumba Islands		♂ 228–233 ♀ 236				
F. m. javensis Mayr, 1941 (ähnl. *renschii*, U-Seite mehr rotbraun) (similar to *renschii*, below darker rufous)	Java. Bali. Nusa-Penida. Kangean	Java. Bali. Nusa Penida. Kangean		219–233				
Falco cenchroides Vigors & Horsfield, 1827 Australienrüttelfalke — Australian or Nankeen Kestrel								
F. c. cenchroides Vig. & Horsf., 1827 (Schwanz mit einziger Binde) (tail with single bar)	Australien. Tasmanien	Australia. Tasmania	28–31	♂ 236–255 ♀ 255–275	♂ 147 ♀ 157	♀ 273	♂ 38 ♀ 38.1	♂ 17.7 ♀ 19
F. c. baru Rand, 1940 (♂ mehr grau an Kopf u. Schwanz, etwas dunkler) (♂ greyer on head and tail. some darker)	Neuguinea (Winter: bis Kl. Sunda-Inseln u. Java)	New Guinea (Winter: to Lesser Sunda Islands and Java)		♂ 254–262 ♀ 269				
Falco ardosiaceus Vieillot, 1823 Graufalke — Grey Kestrel (Im Sitzen fallen die kürzeren Flügel gegenüber *F. concolor* auf.) (When perched, wing relatively shorter than in *F. concolor*.)	Afrika S der Sahara v. Senegal bis N Äthiopien u. S bis S Tansania	Africa south of Sahara from Senegal to N Ethiopia and south to South-Tanzania	33–35	♂ 205–232 ♀ 235–251	♂ 128–152 ♀ 150–164		♂ 38–45 ♀ 40–47	16–18 17–20
Falco dickinsoni P. L. Sclater, 1864 Dickinsonfalke — Dickinson's Kestrel Schwarzrückenfalke (Heller Kopf bildet starken Kontrast zum schwarzen Rücken.) (pale head contrasting with dark wings and back)	Afrika v. Tansania S bis Maputo, W bis Angola, Pemba Insel	Africa from Tanzania south to Maputo, and west to Angola, Pemba Island	28–31	♂ 210– ♀ 236	130– 150		35– 38	16– 17
Falco zoniventris Peters, 1854 Madagaskargraufalke — Madagascar Banded Kestrel (Habitus ähnelt keinem anderen Kleinfalken Madagaskars.) (It is unlike any other common small falcon on Madagascar)	Madagaskar	Madagascar	31–33	♂ 211–223 ♀ 219–234	♂ 138–143 ♀ 144–152		34– 39	(25.4)
Falco vespertinus Linnaeus, 1766 Rotfußfalke — Red-footed Falcon								
F. v. vespertinus Linnaeus, 1766 (Immat. ♂ kann mit Baumfalke verwechselt werden.) (immature males may be confused with Hobby)	E Europa N bis Schweden u. Archangelsk i. W bis Ungarn. i. E bis W Sibirien u. Baikalsee. Kl. Asien. Winter: Afrika	Eastern Europe north to Sweden and Archangelsk, west to Hungary, east to W Siberia and Lake Baikal. Asia Minor. Winter: Africa		♂ 230–262 ♀ 235–253	♂ 119–135 ♀ 122–138	♂ 115–160 ♀ 150–197	♂ 24–30.5 ♀ 28–30.5	♂ 11–13 ♀ 11–13.6
F. v. amurensis Radde, 1863 (Brust u. Bauch heller als ♂ *vespertinus*) (chest and belly paler than ♂ *vespertinus*)	E Sibirien u. N China, N Korea Winter: S Afrika, Namibia, Arabien, Indien	E Siberia and N China, N Korea. Winter: S Africa, Namibia, Arabia, India	28–31	♂ 218–245 ♀ 225–242	124– 131	♂ 97–155 ♀ 111–188	28– 33	(16–18)

Plate 36

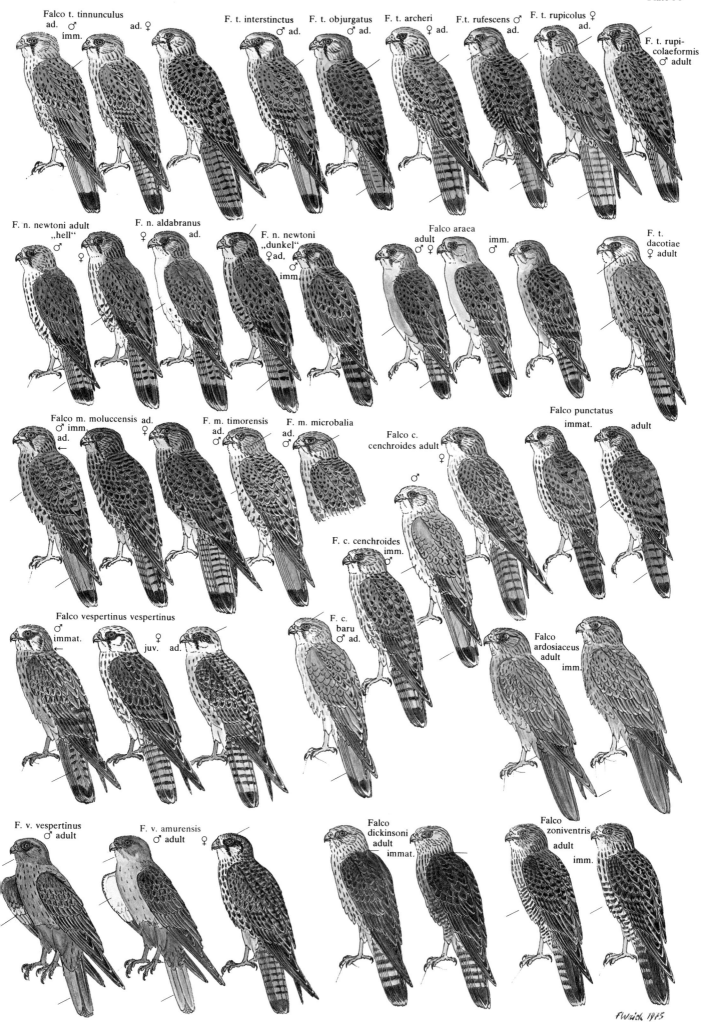

Falco t. tinnunculus
ad. ♂
imm.
ad. ♀

F. t. interstinctus
♂ ad.

F. t. objurgatus
♂ ad.

F. t. archeri
♀ ad.

F.t. rufescens ♂
ad.

F. t. rupicolus ♀
ad.

F. t. rupi-
colaeformis
♂ adult

F. n. newtoni adult
„hell"
♂
♀

F. n. aldabranus
♀
ad.

F. n. newtoni
„dunkel"
♀ ad.
♂
imm.

Falco araea
adult
♂♀
imm.
♂

F. t.
dacotiae
♀ adult

Falco m. moluccensis ad.
♂ imm.
ad.
♀

F. m. timorensis
ad.
♂

F. m. microbalia
ad.
♂

Falco c.
cenchroides adult
♂

Falco punctatus
immat.
adult

F. c. cenchroides
imm.
♂

Falco vespertinus vespertinus
♂
immat.
juv.
ad.
♀

F. c.
baru
♂ ad.

Falco
ardosiaceus
adult
imm.

F. v. vespertinus
♂ adult

F. v. amurensis
♂ adult
♀

Falco
dickinsoni
adult
immat.

Falco
zoniventris
adult
imm.

fWeick 1975

Benennung	Nomenclature	Verbreitung	Distribution	Länge Length cm	Flügel Wing mm	Schwanz/Tail mm	Gewicht Weight g	Tarsus mm	Culmen mm () = mit Wachshaut with cere
Falco chicquera Daudin, 1800 Rotkopfmerlin	Turumti or Red-headed Falcon								
F. ch. chicquera Daudin, 1800 (Roter Kopf bildet starken Kontrast zu Rücken u. Unterseite.)	(note red head contrasting strongly with back and lower-parts)	Indien, südlich vom Himalaya	India south of the Himalayas	28–36	♂ 190–207 ♀ 220–232	♂ 124–137 ♀ 148–156		♂ 35–40 ♀ 38–44	♂ (19–24) ♀ (25)
F. ch. ruficollis Swainson, 1837 (Oberseiten- u. Schwanzzeichnung)	(marking of upper-surface and tailbanding)	Afrika, nördl. des Sambesi u. südlich der Sahara	Africa north of Zambezi river and south of Sahara		♂ 192–218 ♀ 212–236		♀ 257		
F. ch. horsbrughi Gunning & Roberts, 1911 (Habitus wie *ruficollis*, etwas größer)	(similar to *ruficollis* but larger)	Afrika, südlich des Sambesi	Africa south of Zambezi river		♂ 203–227 ♀ 230–240	134– 165		38– 40	13,5– 15,5
Falco columbarius Linnaeus, 1758 Merlin	Pigeon Hawk, Merlin								
F. c. aesalon Tustall, 1771 (kleiner, gedrungener Körper, breite Flügel)	(small, compact body; broad, less pointed wings)	Europa, v. Färöer bis N Rußland, W Sibirien bis zum Jenissei	Europe from the Faeroes to N Russia and W Siberia as far as Yenisei		♂ 192–210 ♀ 210–233	♂ 114–127 ♀ 124–141	♂ 150–215 ♀ 187–255	♂ 35–38,5 ♀ 37–40	♂ 11,8–13 ♀ 12,8–15
F. c. subaesalon Ch. L. Brehm, 1827 (Habitus wie *aesalon*, größer)	(similar to *aesalon*, but larger)	Island, gelegentl. Färöer u. Shetlandinseln Winter: S bis Großbritannien u. Belgien	Iceland, occasional Faeroes and Shetland Islands Winter: South to Great Britain and Belgium		♂ 204–214 ♀ 220–238				
F. c. insignis (Clark, 1907) (durchweg heller u. größer als *aesalon*)	(gererally paler and rather larger than *aesalon*)	Zentral-Sibirien u. E Sibirien bis Kolyma. Winter: bis N Indien, Japan, Korea	Central Siberia and E Siberia to Kolyma-River Winter: to N India. Japan. Korea		♂ 199–211 ♀ 218–231	♂ 117–129 ♀ 131–138	♂ 164,190 ♀ 155–205	♂ 34–39 ♀ 37–39	♂ 12–15 ♀ 15–16
F. c. pallidus Suschkin, 1900 (♂ u. ♀, lighter paler, but also slightly größer als *insignis*)	(♂ and ♀, lighter paler, but also slightly larger than *insignis*)	Kirgisistan u. SW Sibirien E bis West-Altai. Winter: Transkaukasien, Irak, Afghanistan u. N Indien	Kirghiz and S W Siberia, east to W Altai. Winter: Transcaucasia, Iraq, Afghanistan, N India		♂ 202–214 ♀ 208–235		♂ 166–188 ♀ 224–261		
F. c. lymani Bangs, 1913 (ähnl. *insignis*, aber dunkler)	(similar to *insignis*, but darker)	E Altai, Tianshan, S W Transbaikalien, Tarbagatai, Winter: bis Chines. Turkestan. Tsaidan. N Kansu	E Altai, Tian Shan, SW Transbaikalia and Tarbagatai Winter: to Chinese Turkestan, Tsaidan and N Kansu	25–33	♂ 221–242 ♀ 241–263				
F. c. columbarius Linnaeus, 1758 (Dunkler als *aesalon* u. viel stärker gezeichnet, mehr weiß auf Flügeln u. Schwanz)	(darker than *aesalon* and more strongly barred, whiter on wings and tail)	N Kalifornien, Brit. Kolumbien u. E Saskatschewan, N bis NW Alaska, E Kanada, Neufundland Winter: Texas. Louisiana. Mexiko. Venezuela. Ecuador	N California, British Columbia and E Saskatchewan. North to NW Alaska, E Canada and Newfoundland Winter: Texas. Louisiana. W Indies. Mexico. Venezuela. Ecuador.		♂ 182–200 ♀ 193–215		♂ 162		
F. c. richardsoni Ridgway, 1871 (heller als *columbarius*)	(paler than *columbarius*)	USA (Great Plains v. Alberta u. Saskatschewan bis Wyoming u. Dakota) Winter: S bis Colorado. Neumexiko. W Texas	USA (Great Plains from Central Alberta and Saskatchewan to Wyoming and Dakota. Winter: South to Colorado. New Mexico. W Texas)		♂ 195–203 ♀ 210–228				
F. c. suckleyi Ridgway, 1873 (dunkelste Rasse, Oberseite nahezu schwarz)	(darkest race. nearly black above)	Westl. Britisch-Kolumbien, Küsteninseln von Süd-Alaska Winter: bis N Kalifornien	Western British Columbia. Island on coast off S Alaska Winter: South to N California		♂ 186–197 ♀ 207–215				
Falco subbuteo Linnaeus, 1758 Baumfalke	European Hobby								
F. s. subbuteo Linnaeus, 1758 (schlank, lang- u. spitzflügelig)	(slender, with long, pointed wings)	Europa, N Afrika, Asien E bis Kaschmir. Turkestan, SW Transbaikalien. NO Sibirien, Kamtschatka. Kurilen. Hokkaido	Europe, N Africa, Asia east to Kashmir. Turkestan, SW Transbaikalia, NE Siberia, Kamchatka, Kurile Islands and Hokkaido	31–35	♂ 238–272 ♀ 255–286	♂ 116–140 ♀ 125–142	♂ 131–222 ♀ 141–325	♂ 32–36 ♀ 33–37,5	♂ 11–14,5 ♀ 11,5–15,5
F. s. streichi Hartert & Neumann, 1907 (Habitus wie *subbuteo*, aber kleiner)	(similar to *subbuteo*, but smaller)	China, v. Tsingling-Bergen bis Shan-Staaten, Jünnan, SE China, Laos	China, from Tsingling mountains south to Shan-States. Yunnan, SE China and Laos		♂ 232–253 ♀ 251–257				
Falco cuvieri A. Smith, 1830 Afrikabaumfalke (Unterseite mit mehr Rostbraun als *F. subbuteo*)	African Hobby (below more chestnut than *F. subbuteo*)	Afrika, südlich der Sahara	Africa south of the Sahara	25–31	♂ 208–243 ♀ 230–254	108– 125		30– 35	12– 14
Falco severus Horsfield, 1821 Indienbaumfalke	Oriental Hobby								
F. s. severus Horsfield, 1821 (Oberseite dunkler als *F. subbuteo*, Unterseite ungestreift)	(upper-surface darker than *F. subbuteo*, underside unstreaked)	Asiat. Kontinent, v. Himalaya bis Assam, Indochina, Sunda-Inseln, Philippinen	Continental Asia, from the Himalayas to Assam. Indo China. Sunda Islands. Philippines	28–33	♂ 211–219 ♀ 221–248	♂ 94–95 ♀ 105–112	♂ 183 ♀ 249	30– 34	(17– 19)
F. s. papuanus Meyer & Wiglesworth, 1893 (Oberseite, auch Schwanz, nahezu schwarz)	(upperside including tail nearly black)	Sulawesi, bis Salomoninseln	Islands from Sulawesi to the Solomons		♂ 215–220 ♀ 228–240	♂ 97–100 ♀ 101–111	♂ 168, 183 ♀ 192,225,249	29– 35.5	
Falco longipennis Swainson, 1837 Australienbaumfalke	Little Falcon, Australian Hobby								
F. l. longipennis Swainson, 1837 (Schwanzzeichnung, Nackenfärbung)	(tail-barring, nape-colouring)	S E u. S W Australien, Tasmanien, Bass-Straße. Winter: Neuguinea, Bismarckarchipel, Molukken	S E and S W Australia, Tasmania. Bass Strait. Winter: New Guinea. New Britain. Kei Islands, Kalao Tua, Moluccas	28–33	♂ 230–245 ♀ 242–272	♂ 128 ♀ 137	♀ 260	34– 37	
F. l. murchisonianus Mathews, 1912 (an Ober- u. Unterseite viel heller, Kopf u. Backen m. braun auf Krone rostfarben)	(above and below much paler. head and cheeks brown. crown washed rufous)	N Australien, Winter: dasselbe Gebiet wie Nominatform.	N Australia. In Winter same region as nominate race.		♂ 235–248 ♀ 245–278		♀ 247–420		(20– 21)
Falco eleonorae Gené, 1839 Eleonorenfalke (Stirn, Kinn, Kehle bei dunklen Vögeln manchmal aufgehellt)	Eleonora's Falcon (dark birds sometimes with whitish forehead, chin and throat)	Mittelmeerraum v. E Kanaren bis Zypern. Winter: Madagaskar	Mediterranean region from E Canary--Islands to Cyprus. Winter: Madagascar	33–38	♂ 300–335 ♀ 310–366	175– 195		37– 39	15–
Falco concolor Temminck, 1825 Schieferfalke (im Normalkleid heller als melanistischer Eleonorenfalke, im „dunklen" Kleid nahezu schwarz)	Sooty Falcon (in normal-phase paler than melanistic *F. eleonorae* in dark-phase nearly uniform black)	Von Libyen bis Rotes Meer, Nichtbrüter Küste E Afrikas, Madagaskar manchmal Mauritius, Sudan, Viktoriasee	From Libya to Red Sea area. In non-breeding-season chiefly coastal areas of E Africa and Madagascar straggling to Mauritius. Sometimes Sudan and Lake Victoria area	31–33	♂ 258–264 ♀ 284–292	♂ 136– ♀ 150		34– 35	(22– 24)
Falco rufigularis Daudin, 1800 Fledermausfalke	Bat Falcon								
F. r. rufigularis Daudin, 1800 (trotz Kleinheit oft m. *F. deiroleucos* im Felde verwechselt)	(though his small size, often confused with *F. deiroleucos* in field)	Südl. Mittelamerika S bis Ecuador, E Peru, Bolivien, Paraguay, N Argentinien, Trinidad	Southern Central America south to Ecuador, E Peru, Bolivia, Paraguay, N Argentina, Trinidad	23–31	♂ 173–197 ♀ 209–229	♂ 88–102 ♀ 103–118	♂ 108–148 ♀ 177–242	32– 39	
F. r. petrophilus van Rossem & Hachisuka, 1937 (Oberseite mehr schiefergrau, rostfarbene Teile viel blasser)	(upper-side more slaty-grey. rufous parts much paler)	W Mexiko (S-Sonora u. Sinaloa)	W Mexico (South Sonora and Sinaloa)		♂ 192 ♀ 224,228				
Falco femoralis Temminck, 1823 Aplomadofalke	Aplomado Falcon								
F. f. septentrionalis Todd, 1916 (Kopf-, Mittelbauch- u. Flankenzeichnung)	(note markings on head, vent and sides)	SW USA u. Mexiko (Guatemala?)	SW USA and Mexico (Guatemala?)		♂ 248–267 ♀ 272–303	♂ 172–193 ♀ 192–207	♂ 235 ♀ 271–305	48– 60	
F. f. femoralis Temminck, 1823 (Oberseite mehr braungrau als blauish-grau)	(above more brownish-grey than blu-ish-grey)	Südamerika S bis Patagonien (Tiefland)	S America. south to Patagonia (lower altitudes)	33–43	♂ 230–254 ♀ 261–282				
F. f. pichinchae Chapman, 1925 (Größe etwa wie *septentrionalis*, dunkelste Rasse, dunkle Bauchzone ausgedehnter)	(size as *septentrionalis*, darkest race, black ventral area more extended)	Südamerika, Anden v. Kolumbien bis Chile, NW Argentinien	S America. Andes from Colombia to Chile and NW Argentina		♂ ? ♀ 290–295	♀ 205–210			

Plate 37

F. c. chicquera ad. imm.

F. chicquera ruficollis ad. imm.

F. c. aesalon adult ♂

F. c. subaesalon ♀ adult

F. c. aesalon ♂ imm. ♀ ad.

F. c. suckleyi ad. ♀

F. c. columbarius ♀ imm. ♂ ad.

F. c. pallidus ♀ imm. ad.

F. c. insignis ♂ adult

Falco s. subbuteo ad. ♀ imm. ♂

Falco cuvieri ad. imm.

F. s. severus ad. imm.

F. s. papuanus ad.

immat.
F. l. longipennis adult

Falco eleonorae ad. „dunkel"
♀♂

Falco eleonorae adult
„hell"
♀ „hell"

imm. „hell"
Falco eleonorae imm. „dunkel"

„hell" adult
Falco concolor ad. „dunkel"

Falco concolor immat.

F. l. murchisonianus adult

F. f. pichinchae adult

F. f. femoralis adult.
F. f. septentrionalis immat.

F. f. septentrionalis ad.

F. r. rufigularis adult imm.

Falco r. petrophilus adult

1975 Fwewk

Benennung	Nomenclature	Verbreitung	Distribution	Länge Length cm	Flügel Wing mm	Schwanz/Tail mm	Gewicht Weight g	Tarsus mm	Culmen mm () = mit Wachshaut with cere
Falco berigora Vigors u. Horsfield, 1827 Habichtsfalke	Brown Hawk								
F. b. berigora Vigors u. Horsf., 1827 (langer Schwanz u. lange Beine, Farbe d. Wachshaut u. Fänge)	(note long tail, long legs, colour of cere and feet)	Australien (feuchtere Gebiete)	Australia (humid parts)		♂ 319–355 ♀ 350–397	205– 230	♂ 387–512 ♀ 505–635	70– 75	(♂ 28) (♀ 28)
F. b. centralis (Mathews, 1916) (im „Normal"- u. „Dunkel"-Kleid heller als *berigora*)	(normal- and melanistic phase are paler than in *berigora*)	Australien (trockeneres Inland)	Australia (drier interior)	38–46	315– 374				
F. b. novaeguineae (Meyer, 1894) (weniger gefleckt als die anderen Rassen, einschließlich der äußersten 6 Handschwingen, deutliche Schaftstriche an Ober- u. Unterseite)	(less spotted than other races, including the first six primaries, but conspicuous black shaft streaks above and below)	Neuguinea, Dampier- u. Manam-Inseln	New Guinea, Dampier- and Manam Islands		324– 381	184– 233			
Falco novaezeelandiae Gmelin, 1788 Neuseelandfalke (im Normalkleid deutl. Bartstreif u. rotbraune Hosen, im melan. Kleid Kinn u. Kehle hell)	New Zealand Falcon, Quail Hawk (normal-phase with conspicuous moustachial stripe and rufous thighs, in melanistic-phase chin and throat whitish)	Neuseeland	New Zealand	38–46	♂ 230–260 ♀ 246–305	♂ 164–195 ♀ 195–229		♂ 55–58 ♀ 60–62	(♂ 31) (♀ 32)
Falco hypoleucos Gould, 1841 Bleifalke (in seinem Verbreitungsgebiet unverwechselbar mit anderen Falken)	Grey Falcon (cannot be confused in its habitat with any other falcon)	Australien (trockenere Gebiete)	Australia (drier areas)	31–41	♂ 268–302 ♀ 315–338	♂ 138–170 ♀ 156–185		41– 45	(25)
Falco subniger Gray, 1843 Australfalke, Rußfalke (kann nur mit „dunklem" F. berigora verwechselt werden, doch dieser mit deutlich längerem Schwanz)	Black Falcon (can only be confused with the dark phases of *F. berigora*, which have a distinctly longer tail)	Australien (ohne Gebiete m. größeren Niederschl.)	Australia (excluding wetter areas)	43–48	♂ 363–374 ♀ 391–415	♂ 206–222 ♀ 223–247	♂ 597,607 ♀ 670	♂ 50 ♀ 57	(♂ 31) (♀ 32)
Falco jugger, Gray, 1834 Laggarfalke (mittlere Schwanzfedern einfarbig, Unterseite bei Altvogel m. wenigen Flecken, dunkle Flanken, kräftige Kopffärbung)	Laggar-Falcon (uniform central feather, adult less spotted on under-surface, dusky on sides, richly-coloured head)	Belutschistan, Indien bis Assam u. Zentral-Burma, südl. v. den Himalaya-Vorbergen bis W Madras. Afghanistan? Russisch-Turkestan?	Baluchistan, India to Assam and Central Burma south to the foothills of Himalaya to W Madras. Afghanistan? Russian Turkestan?	38–43	♂ 305–335 ♀ 323–370	♂ 164–183 ♀ 169–210	♀ 755	46–54	(25–33)
Falco biarmicus Temminck, 1825 Lanner, Feldeggsfalke	Lanner Falcon								
F. b. biarmicus Temminck, 1825 (meist kräftigere Backenstreifen als Saker, Altvögel mit sparsam gefleckter, rosa Unterseite)	(moustachial stripes slightly more distinct than in Saker Falcon; below pinkish, sparsely spotted in adult)	Südafrika, v. Kapland bis Angola, Katanga u. Kenia i. N	S Africa from Cape Province to Angola, Katanga and Kenya in north		♂ 308–332 ♀ 340–360	♂ 160–178 ♀ 185–210	551– 583	♂ 46–55 ♀ 45–53	(1♂ 30)
F. b. abyssinicus Neumann, 1904 (Unterseite stärker gezeichnet, Oberseite u. Schwanzbinden dunkler u. kräftiger)	(more heavily marked above, below more strongly marked darker, with dark subterminal tail-band; generally darker)	Afrika, südlich der Sahara von N Athiopien, N Nigeria u. Ghana bis Uganda u. Zaire (Uele)	Africa south of Sahara, from N Ethiopia, N Nigeria and Ghana to Uganda and Zaire (Uele)		♂ 318–333 ♀ 353–387				
F. b. tanypterus Schlegel, 1844 (Brust gefleckt, aber mehr fahl-beige als rotbraune Grundfärbung der Unterseite)	(spotted breast pale buff rather rufous coloured)	Ägypten, Nil-Tal, Sinai-Halbinsel, Arabien, Irak	Egypt, Nile Valley, Sinai, Arabia, Iraq	38–46	♂ 314–338 ♀ 352–375				
F. b. erlangeri Kleinschmidt, 1901 (Noch heller als *tanypterus*, Oberkopf meist wenig gezeichnet)	(still paler than *tanypterus*; crown usually unspotted)	N W Afrika, v. Marokko bis Tunesien, S bis Span. Sahara u. N Mauretanien	NW Africa from Morocco to Tunisia south to Spanish Sahara and N Mauretania		♂ 308–324 ♀ 338–360				
F. b. feldeggii Schlegel, 1843 (ziemlich dunkel u. kräftig gezeichnet, Oberseite bläulich überflogen)	(with rather darker and more heavily marked, upper side more bluish-tinged)	Italien, Sizilien, Griechenland, Jugoslawien, Albanien, Kleinasien u. Armenien	Italy, Sicily, Greece, Yugoslavia, Albania, Asia-Minor and Armenia		♂ 308–335 ♀ 345–375	♂ 175–195 ♀ 185–224	♂ 500–600 ♀ 700–900	♂ 44–53 ♀ 52–57	

Plate 38

F. b. berigora "hell" adult ♀ immat.

F. b. berigora "dunkel" ♂ adult

Falco novae-zeelandiae ♂ adult imm. ♀ "hell" "hell"

Falco b. centralis ♂ adult

F. berigora novaegui-neae ♂ adult

Falco novae-zeelandiae ♂ adult "dunkel"

Falco hypoleucos immat. adult

Falco subniger adult immat.

♂ adult

F. jugger ♀ immat.

F. biarmicus tanypterus immat.

F. biarmicus biarmicus immat. adult

- Falco biarmicus feldeggii adult

F. biarmicus abyssinicus adult

F. biarmicus tanypterus adult

F. biarmicus erlangeri adult

1975 F.Weick.

75 F.Weick

Benennung	Nomenclature	Verbreitung	Distribution	Länge Length cm	Flügel Wing mm	Schwanz/Tail mm	Gewicht Weight g	Tarsus mm	Culmen mm () = mit Wachshaut with cere
Falco mexicanus Schlegel, 1843 Präriefalke (Helle Vögel können durchaus mit Gerfalken verwechselt werden, im Normalkleid jedoch durch stärker gefleckte Unterseite v. diesen zu unterscheiden. Brauner u. heller als Wanderfalke)	Prairie Falcon (Pale birds may easily be confused with Gyrfalcons, but normally can be identified by smaller size, more spotted. Paler and browner than the Peregrine-Falcon!)	Nordamerika von Brit.-Kolumbien, N Alberta u. Saskatchewan u. westl. Norddakota S bis Niederkalifornien, Mexiko, südl. Arizona, Neu-Mexiko u. N Texas	N America from British Columbia, N Alberta. Saskatchewan and W Dakota south to Lower California, Mexico, S Arizona, New Mexico and N Texas	41–48	♂ 289–328 ♀ 331–357	♂ 159–179 ♀ 185–201	♀ 801–811	50–64	(♀ 35)
Falco cherrug Gray, 1834 Saker, Würgfalke	Saker Falcon								
F. ch. cherrug Gray, 1834 (Größe, Brauntönung, Schwanzfleckung u. schwacher Backenstreif sind Feldkennzeichen.)	(Size, brownish-looking appearance, tail spots and an indistinct moustachial stripe are good field-characters)	Von Wolga bis Steppe von Minussinsk; Winter: NW Indien, Sudan	From the Volga River to the steppes of Minussinsk; Winter: NW India. Sudan	46–58	♂ 336–372 ♀ 375–423	♂ 190–200 ♀ 207–235	♂ 730–750 ♀ 1000–1300	50–58	♂ 20 (26–27) ♀ 25
F. ch. cyanopus Thienemann, 1846 (Altvogel viel dunkler an Kopf u. Oberseite, Unterseite viel stärker gestreift)	(adult much darker on head and upper-surface, below more heavily streaked)	Böhmen bis Wolga	Bohemia to Volga River		♂ 345–368 ♀ 381–415	♂ 179–200 ♀ 200–230	♂ 820–950 ♀ 970–1300	♂ 52–57 ♀ 54–61	♂ 20–23 ♀ 23–26
F. ch. saceroides (Bianchi, 1907) (Ockergelbe Querzeichnung, graublauer Anflug)	(above ochre-barred; bluish-grey wash)	Kirgisensteppe bis Sajan, Altai, Tarbagatai, NW Mongolei Winter: Persien, Afghanistan bis W China	Kirghiz-steppe to Sajan, Altai, Tarbagatai, NW Mongolia Winter: Persia, Afghanistan to W China						
F. ch. coatsi Dementiev, 1945 (noch bunter u. daher kontrastreichere Oberseitenfärbung als saceroides)	(more richly coloured and therefore more contrasting above than saceroides)	Tien-Shan u. westwärts bis NE Iran	From Tian Shan west to NE Iran				evtl. nur Farbphasen, dann alles Synonyme von *F. ch. milvipes* (siehe auch Vaurie: Birds of Pal. Fauna, pt. I. p 210–214)		
F. ch. hendersoni Hume, 1871 (ziegelrote Querzeichnung, Unterseitenzeichnung)	(above more reddish; below barred)	Pamir u. Himalaya bis Kansu	Highland of Pamir and from the Himalayas to Kansu				Possibly only colour-phases, then all names are synonymes of *milvipes* (also see Vaurie, Birds of Palearct. Fauna, pt. I p 210–214)		
F. ch. milvipes Jerdon, 1871 (incl. altaicus-Typ) (Normalkleid intermediär zwischen saceroides u. hendersoni. Altaicus-Typ kann dunklem cyanopus o. dunklem F. rusticolus sehr ähneln.)	(plumage normally intermediate between saceroides and hendersoni. Altaicus-type may be like a dusky F. ch. cyanopus or a dusky F. rusticolus)	Mongolei, Südtransbaikalien, W Mandschurei Winter: W Pakistan, NW Indien	Mongolia, S Transbaicalia. W Manchuria Winter: W Pakistan, NW India		♂ 341–380 ♀ 374–435	188–236	♂ 735	50–60	(25–27)
Falco rusticolus Linnaeus, 1758 Gerfalke, Jagdfalke (Drei variable, jedoch gut gegeneinander abgrenzbare Farbphasen, deren Häufigkeit sehr stark u. weitgehend klimaparallel variiert. In borealen u. subarkt. Gebieten dominieren o. gibt es fast ausschließlich „dunkle" Vögel. In niederarktischen Gebieten dominiert die graue Phase. In hocharktischen Gebieten ist die weiße Phase überwiegend. Die dunkelsten Vögel kommen im östlichen Nordamerika vor, die dunklen Individuen Skandinaviens sind etwas heller. Vögel der grauen Phase werden in der Paläarktis von W nach E, in der Nearktis von E nach W heller. Vögel der weißen Phase sind in Ostsibirien oft blasser u. spärlicher gezeichnet als grönländische. Die kleinsten Individuen leben in Skandinavien u. Alaska, die größten in Südgrönland und Ostsibirien. Auch adulte Vögel können blaue o. blaugraue Flügel haben.)	Gyrfalcon (Three main, but varying colour types, varying extensively related to climatic conditions occur. In boreal and sub-arctic regions dark birds predominate; in lower arctic regions grey types predominate; and in high-arctic regions white types predominate. The darkest individuals recur in E North America; dark Scandinavian Gyrfalcons are slightly paler. Grey-type birds become paler in the Palearctic from West to East and in the Nearctic from East to West. White-type birds in E Siberia are often paler and less clearly marked than those from Greenland. The smallest individuals come from Scandinavia and Alaska, the largest from S Greenland and E Siberia. Legs and feet can be blue or bluish-grey even among the adults)	Zirkumpolar: Arktisches Europa, Asien u. N Amerika, Grönland, Island. Klimat. bedingte Wanderungen S bis N USA, W Europa, Zentralrußl. usw.	Circumpolar: Arctic Europe, Asia and N America, Greenland, Iceland Winter migrant south to N USA, W Europe, Central Russia a.s.o.	51–58	♂ 340–406 ♀ 370–426	♂ 190–225 ♀ 207–265	♂ 960–1300 ♀ 1400–2100	50–71	20.5–29

Plate 39

Falco mexicanus

adult
„hell"

immat.

„normal"

Falco c. cherrug
♀ adult ♂ imm.

♂
normal
F. c. milvipes
adult.
„altaicus-
Typ" ♀

F. c.
„coatsi"
ad. ♀

F. ch. cyanopus
adult

♀ =
„sacer-
oides"
Fort-
schritts-
kleid

F. c.
„hendersoni"
♂ ad.

F. rusticolus
♀ immat.
„grau-
weiß"

F. rusticolus
„obsoletus"
♂ ♀
ad. imm.

F. rusticolus
„weiß"
♂ ad. ♀ ad

„weiß" immat.

F. rusticolus
„grau-weiß"
♀ ad.

F. rusticolus
„weiß-grau"
♂ ad.

♂ immat.

F. rusticolus
„weiß-grau"
ad. ♂

1975 F. Weick

Benennung	Nomenclature	Verbreitung	Distribution	Länge Length cm	Flügel Wing mm	Schwanz/Tail mm	Gewicht Weight g	Tarsus mm	Culmen mm () = mit Wachshaut with cere
Falco deiroleucus Temminck, 1825 Rotbrustfalke (Orangene Halsseiten u. Unterseitenfärbung sowie Stoßflecken sind gute Unterschiede zu *Falco peregrinus subsp..*)	Orange-breasted Falcon (The orange sides of neck and undersurface as well as tailpots are good distinctions from *Falco peregrinus subsp.*)	Mexiko, M Amerika (Panama u. Trinidad), Südamerika östl. der Anden bis Peru, N Argentinien, Paraguay	Mexico, Central America (Panama and Trinidad) and South America east of the Andes, to Peru, northern Argentina and Paraguay	33–38	♂ 231–253 ♀ 275–287	♂ 128 ♀ 139–141	2 ♂ 338, 340 4 ♀ 550–654	43–56	
Falco fasciinucha Reichenow & Neumann, 1895 Taitafalke (Helles Kinn, blaugrauer Stoß u. Bürzel sowie Nackenzeichnung sind gute Unterschiede zu dem Baumfalken!)	Taita Falcon (White chin, bluish-grey tail and rump and rufous nape-patches distinguish it from Hobby Falcons)	Sehr selten, E- u. Z.-Afrika (Äthiopien bis Sambesi)	Eastern and Central Africa (Ethiopia to Zambesi river). Very rare	28–33	203–237	1 ♂ 78 > 80?			16
Falco kreyenborgi Kleinschmidt, 1929 Kleinschmidtfalke (Ähnelt in der Gefiederzeichnung mehr dem Wüstenfalken als einem *F. peregrinus*, Handschwingen u. Fußproportionen unterscheiden ihn vom Gerfalken)	Kleinschmidt's Falcon (Resembles the Barbary Falcon more than a Peregrine, proportions of primaries and feet are different to Gyrfalcons)	Bekannt durch 3 Exempl. v. Punta Arenas (Chile) u. 2 immat. Vögeln aus Feuerland u. N Patagonien. Brütet evtl. auf Inseln südlich von Feuerland u. zieht i. Winter weiter nördlich?	Known on three individuals of Punta Arenas (Chile) and two immature birds recorded from Tierra del Fuego and northern Patagonia. Probably breeds on islands south of Tierra del Fuego moving northward in winter?	38–43	♂ 296–305 (incl. juv.) ♀ 333	♂ 146–155 (incl. juv.) ♀ 170		♂ 45–49 ♀ 54	
Falco peregrinus Tunstall, 1771 Wanderfalke	Peregrine Falcon, Duck Hawk								
F. p. peregrinus Tunst., 1771 (♀ oft dunkler auf dem Unterrücken u. auf Unterseite bis zur Vorderbrust mit Tropfenflecken)	(Female often darker on lower back and rump, below dropshaped markings up to upper-breast)	Europa i. E bis N Rußland u. S bis Mittelmeer u. Kaukasus	Europe east to north Russia and south to Mediterranean and Caucasus	36–48	♂ 289–334 ♀ 339–375	♂ 127–160 ♀ 155–185	♂ 550–660 ♀ 740–1120	♂ 45–51 ♀ 50–55,5	♂ 17,5–2 ♀ 21–24
F. p. calidus Latham, 1790 (durchschnittlich heller auf Oberseite, spärlicher gefleckt auf Unterseite, schmaler Bartstreif, weiße Wangen)	(Averaging paler above, below more sparsely spotted, moustachial stripe more extensive, cheeks white)	N Rußland, Lappland, N Sibirien, bis 76° nördl. Breite u. bis E der Lena. Winter: Europa u. Asien zwischen 36–40° N, aber auch bis Afrika u. Neuguinea!	North Russia, Lapponia, northern Siberia, as far north as 76° N and as far east as the Lena. Winter: Migrant in Europe and Asia between 36–40° N, but also in Africa and New Guinea!		♂ 305–333 ♀ 350–378		♂ 588–740 ♀ 825–1333		
F. p. japonensis Gmelin, 1788 (dunkel, Unterseite kontrastreicher als Nominalform, Bauch gelblich-rötlich, Flanken grau)	(Dark bars on underside contrast strongly with ground colour, belly darker buff, grey on sides)	Von E Sibirien bis Kurilen, Winter Japan, Riu Kiu, Formosa	East Siberia to Kurile Islands. Winters in Japan, Riu Kiu and Formosa		♂ 296–329 ♀ 350–372	1 ♂ 135–145 ♀ 181	1 ♂ 500	♂ 49–51 ♀ 55	(♂ 25–26 (♀ 27–30)
F. p. anatum Bonaparte, 1838 (Unterseite lebhaft ockerrötlich u. spärlich gezeichnet, starker Bartstreif)	(Below with more rufous, less spotted below than *peregrinus*, large moustachial stripe)	Labrador, E Grönland, Alaska u. z. südl. Niederkalifornien. Winter: M u. S Amerika bis Chile.	Labrador, eastern Greenland, Alaska south to southern Lower California. Winter in Central and South-America south to Chile.		♂ 290–355 ♀ 342–378		♂ 510–719 ♀ 851–1223		
F. p. pealei Ridgway, 1874 (verhältnismäßig längerer u. breiterer Stoß)	(Proportionally longer and broader tailed)	Nordpazif. Küstengebiete Nordamerikas, Aleuten, Kommandeur-Inseln.	North Pacific Coast of North America. Aleutians and Commandeur Islands		♂ 305–340 ♀ 356–387		♂ 810–1058 ♀ 1244–1597		
F. p. tundrius White, 1968 (Arctic Tundra Falcon) (Habitus ähnlich *calidus*, kleiner u. leichter als *anatum*)	(Resembles *calidus*, smaller and lighter than *anatum*)	Von Beringstraße bis nördl. Baffin-Insel. Südl. etwa bis 65° N	From Bering-Strait to northern Baffin Island. South to about 65° N		♂ 308 ♀ 352		♂ 633 ♀ 961		
F. p. cassini Sharpe, 1873 (dunkler als Nominalform, schwarze Kopfseiten, stärkere Unterseitenzeichnung)	(Darker than *peregrinus*, sides of head black and with large clear markings below)	Chile, Südpatagonien, Feuerland u. Falklandinseln	Chile, south Patagonia, Tierra del Fuego and Falkland Islands		♂ 292–328 ♀ 334–355				
F. p. fruitii Momiyama, 1927 (wie kleiner *pealei*. Stoß jedoch dunkler u. weniger deutlich gebändert)	(Like a small *pealei* but tail less clearly barred)	Vulkaninseln SE v. Japan. Bonininseln?	Volcano Islands SE of Japan. Probably Bonin Islands		♂ 307–319 ♀ 356–368				
F. p. brookei Sharpe, 1873 (oft rotbraun auf Krone u. am Nacken, Unterseite oft rosa überflogen, stark gefleckt)	(Often traces of rufous in crown and on nape, below often with strong pinky wash and heavy spotting)	Mittelmeergebiet (Haupts. Küsten) von S Spanien u. N Marokko, E bis Kaukasus, Kl.-Asien	Mediterranean area (especially on coast), southern Spain and northern Morocco, E to Caucasus, Asia Minor		♂ 280–312 ♀ 306–355		1 ♂ 445 ♀ bis 920		
F. p. madens Ripley & Watson, 1963 (viel Braun auf „Krone" und Nacken, unregelmäßigen „Kragen" bildend, Oberseite braun überflogen, Unterseite ockergelb überflogen)	Much brown on crown and nape producing an irregular collar, above with brown wash, below tinged buff to tawny)	Kap Verde	Cape Verde Islands		♂ 315–320 ♀ 340				
F. p. minor Schlegel, 1844 (zieml. dunkel, Oberkopf, Bartstreif fast schwarz)	(Rather dark, on head and moustachial stripe nearly black)	Afrika südl. der Sahara u. Ghana E bis N Äthiopien u. S bis Kapland	Africa south of Sahara from Ghana to N Ethiopia and south to Cape Province.		♂ 265–311 ♀ 297–325				
F. p. radama Hartlaub, 1861 (Oberseite noch schwärzer als *minor*, Unterseitenzeichnung sehr scharf)	(Above darker than *minor*, barrings below strongly contrasting)	Madagaskar u. Komoren	Madagascar and Comoro Islands		♂ 265–288 ♀ 310–325				
F. p. peregrinator Sundevall, 1837 (Südindische Vögel unterseits viel lebhafter gefärbt als solche v. Südchina u. Vietnam.)	(Individuals of southern India have stronger rufous or chestnut wash than birds of South China and Vietnam on underside)	Indien, Ceylon E bis S China, evtl. Formosa	India, Ceylon (Sri Lanka) east to South China, possibly Formosa		♂ 265–302 ♀ 312–345	♂ 128–162	♂ 562	♂ 48–50	(♂ 25–2 (♀ 28–29)
F. p. ernesti Sharpe, 1894 (dunkelste Unterart, Oberseite schwarz m. grauen Säumen, Bartstreif zu Dreieck ausgedehnt, Unterseite tief graublau, rötlich überflogen)	(Darkest race, above black edged grey, the whole head and cheeks black, moustachial stripe becomes triangle, underside deep bluish grey tinged with rufous)	Indonesien, Philippinen, Neuguinea u. angrenz. Inseln	Indonesia, Philippines, New Guinea and adjacent Islands		♂ 272–298 ♀ 315–342				
F. p. nesiotes Mayr, 1941 (Oberseite u. Bartstreif ähnlich *ernesti*, Unterseite jedoch ähnl. *macropus*)	(Above and moustachial stripe similar to *ernesti*, underside however like *macropus*)	Tanna-Insel, Neue Hebriden, Beaupré Insel, Loyalty-Inseln, Neukaledonien u. evtl. Fidji-Inseln	Tanna Island, New Hebrides, Beaupré Island, New Caledonia and possibly to Fiji		♂ 283–295 ♀ 321–327				
F. p. macropus Swainson, 1838 (schwarze Kopfseiten, Oberseite ziemlich hell)	(Sides of head black, upper surface rather light)	Australien ohne den Südwesten. Tasmanien	Australia, except the southwest. Tasmania		♂ 270–300 ♀ 305–348				
F. p. submelanogenys Mathews, 1912 (Oberseite wie *macropus*, Unterseite ähnelt jedoch *peregrinator*)	(Above as in *macropus*, but under-surface like *peregrinator*)	S W Australien	South-western Australia		♂ 270–294 ♀ 321–344		1 ♂ 424 1 ♀ 964		
F. pelegrinoides Temminck, 1829 Wüstenfalke	Barbary Falcon Shaheen								
F. p. pelegrinoides Temminck, 1829 (Langflügliger u. rundschwänziger als *peregrinus*)	(Longer wings and more rounded tail than *peregrinus*)	Nubien u. N Afrika bis Süd-Atlas und Atlantik-Küste S Marokkos	Nubia and North Africa to southern Atlas and Atlantic coast in south Morocco	34–44	♂ 260–293 ♀ 282–332		1 ♀ 610		
F. p. babylonicus Sclater, 1861 (stärker entwickeltes Nackenband, Kopf erscheint oft ganz rostrot. Die hellen Vögel sind aus d. Iran, Afghanistan und Belutschistan, die dunkelsten aus Ostturkestan u. d. Westmongolei)	(Stronger nape-band, crown and nape allmost all rufous. The palest birds are from Iran, Afghanistan and Baluchistan, the darkest from eastern Turkestan and western Mongolia)	Asien, v. Irak u. E Persien E bis Mongolei. Winter: Indien	Asia, from Iraq and east Persia east to Mongolia. Winters in India		♂ 274–310 ♀ 312–348	♂ 126–135 ♀ 151–158	♂ 330–398 ♀ 513–765 (930 Hume)	♂ 45–46 ♀ 53–55	(♂ 23–2 (♀ 26–28)

Plate 40

Falco fasciinucha
ad. imm.

Falco
deiroleucus
ad. imm.

Falco kreyenborgi
ad.
imm.

imm.
F. p.
pelegrinoi-
des
adult

F. p. peregrinus
♂ adult

♂ adult

F. p. japonensis
♂ ad.

F. p.
babilonicus

♂ ad.
„hell"

F. p.
peregrinus
♂ imm.

F. p.
brookei
♂ ad.

F. p.
babilonicus
♀ ad.
„dunkel"

F. p.
brookei
♂ adult
„normal"

F. p.
anatum
♂ imm.
adult

♂ ad.
F. p.
pealei
imm. ♀

F. p.
calidus
♂ ad.

♀ imm

F. p.
cassini
♂ adult

F. p.
tundrius
♂ ad.

F. p.
radama
♂ ad.

Falco p.
fruitii
♂ ad.

F. p.
madens
♂ ad.

F. p.
nesiotes
♂ adult

adult
„hell"

F. p.
submelanogenys
ad. ♀

Falco p.
macropus
♀ ad.

F. p.
ernesti
♂ ad.

F. p.
minor
♂ adult

F. p.
peregrina-
tor. ♀
ad.
„normal"

75 F. Weick

Verzeichnis der wissenschaftlichen Namen   Index of scientific names

Gattungsnamen sind groß geschrieben. Die in Klammern stehenden Gattungsnamen sind Synonyme, dahinter steht der jetzt gebräuchliche Name. Der Name der Unterart (Subspezies) wird nur mit dem Gattungsnamen zusammen zitiert: z. B. Falco peregrinus anatum als anatum, Falco. Die Ziffern hinter den Namen geben die Tafelnummer an.

Generic names begin with a capital letter. Those in brackets are synonyms, followed by the name in correct use. Names of subspecies are listed only with the generic names e. g. Falco peregrinus anatum as = anatum, Falco. The figures next the names give the plate number.

Micrastur semitorquatus

Verzeichnis der deutschen Namen   Index of German names

Milvus milvus

Index of English names   Verzeichnis der englischen Namen

Elanus caeruleus

Literaturverzeichnis Annotated bibliography

Ali, S. (1945): The Birds of Kutch. London, Oxford.
Ali, S. (1946): The Book of Indian Birds. Bombay.
Ali, S. (1949): Indian Hill Birds. London, Oxford.
Ali, S. (1953): The Birds of Travancore and Cochin. London, Oxford.
Ali, S. (1962): The Birds of Sikkim. London.
Ali, S. (1969): The Birds of Kerala. London. (2nd edit. of „The Birds of Travancore etc.").
Ali, S. & Ripley, S. D. (1968): Handbook of the Birds of India and Pakistan. Vol. 1. Bombay, London, New York.
Allen, R. P. (1961): Birds of the Caribbean. New York.
Allous, B. E. (1953): The Avifauna of Iraq. Baghdad.
Amadon, D. (1933): Remarks on the Asiatic Hawk-eagles of the Genus *Spizaëtus*. Ibis. 95. London.
American Ornithologist's Union Checklist Committee. (1957): Check List of North America. Birds 5th edition. Ithaca N. Y.
Audubon, J. J. (Reprint 1965): The Birds of America. New York.
Austin, O. L. jr. (1948): The Birds of Korea. Bull. Mus. Comp. Zool. 101 Nr. 1.
Austin, O. L. jr. & Kuroda, N. (1953): The Birds of Japan. Bull. Mus. Comp. Zool. 109.pp.277–639.
Austin, O. L. jr. (1963): Die Vögel der Welt. München, Zürich.

Baker, E. C. S. (1928): Fauna of British India. Birds. Vol. V. London.
Bannermann, D. A. (1930–51): The Birds of tropical West Africa. London.
Bannermann, D. A. (1953): The Birds of West- and Equatorial-Africa Vol. I. London.
Bannermann, D. A. (1953): The Birds of the British Isles. Vol. V. Edinburgh.
Bannermann, D. A. & Bannermann W. M. (1958): Birds of Cyprus. Edinburgh, London.
Bannermann, D. A. & Bannermann W. M. (1965): A History of the Birds of Madeira. Edinburgh.
Bannermann, D. A. & Bannermann, W. M. (1966): A History of the Birds of Azores. Edinburgh, London.
Bannermann, D. A. & Bannermann W. M. (1968): History of the Birds of the Cape Verde Islands. Edinburgh.
Bates, G. L. (1930): Handbook of Birds of West Africa. London.
Bates, R. S. P. & Lowther, E. H. N. (1952): Breeding Birds of Kashmir. London.
Baumgart, W. (1974): Über die Ausbildung heller und dunkler Phasen bei Greifvögeln. Der Falke Nr. 11. pp 376–383.
Bemmel van, A. C. V. & Voous, K. H. (1954): On the Birds of the islands of Muna and Buton, SE. Celebes. Treubia 21 pp. 27–104.
Benson, C. W. (1960): Birds of the Comoro Islands. Ibis 1036. pp. 5–106. London.
Bent, A. C. (1931, 32): Life Histories of North American Birds of Prey. 2 Vols. Bull. US. Nat. Mus. New York.
Berlioz, J. (1946): Oiseaux de la Réunion. Paris.
Berndt, R. & Meise, W. (1959–66): Naturgeschichte der Vögel. 3 Vols. Stuttgart.
Bijleveld, M. (1974): Birds of Prey in Europe. London.
Blake, G. R. (1953): Birds of Mexico. Chicago.
Blanford, W. T. (1895): The Fauna of British India, Ceylon and Burma. Vol. III Birds. London.

Bond, J. (1971): Birds of the West Indies. New York, London. (Reprint).
Brown, L. H. (1955): Eagles. London.
Brown, L. H. (1970) (a): African Birds of Prey. London.
Brown, L. H. (1970) (b): Eagles. London.
Brown, L. H. (1976) (a): British Birds of Prey. London.
Brown, L. H. (1976) (b): Birds of Prey, their biology and ecology. Feltham.
Brown, L. H. (1976) (c): Eagles of the World. Newton Abbot.
Brown, L. H. & Amadon, D. (1969): Eagles, Hawks and Falcons of the World. 2 vols. Feltham.
Brown, P. E. (1964): Birds of prey. London.
Brudenell-Bruce, P. G. C. (1975): The birds of New Providence and the Bahama Islands. London.
Brüll, H. (1962): Die Greifvögel im Niederwildrevier. München.
Brüll, H. (1964): Das Leben deutscher Greifvögel. Ihre Bedeutung in der Landschaft. Stuttgart.
Bruun, B., Singer, A., König, C. (1973): Die Vögel Deutschlands und Europas in Farbe. Stuttgart (2 nd. ed.).

Cain, A. J., Galbraith, I. C. (1956): Birds of the Salomon Islands. Ibis 98. London.
Caldwell, H. R. & John, C. (1931): South China Birds. Shanghai.
Cave, F. O. & Macdonald, J. D. (1955): Birds of Sudan.
Cayley, N. W. (1932, 1st ed. 1971 reprint): What Bird is that? A Guide to the Birds of Australia. Sydney.
Collins, H. H. jr. (1959): Complete Field Guide to American Wildlife (East, Central, North).
Condon, H. T. & Amadon, D. (1954): Taxonomic notes on Australian hawks. Rec. South Austral. Mus. 11 pp. 189–246.
Conover, B. (1946): Notes on some Neotropical Hawks. Fieldiana Zool. 31, pp. 39–45. Chicago.
Coomans de Ruiter, L. (1947): Birds of prey of Celebes. Limosa 20 (213–229).
Craighead, J. J. & F. C. (1956): Hawks, owls and wildlife. Washington. (1969. N.Y.).
Curry-Lindahl, K. (1959–63): Våra Fåglar i Norden 4 vols. Stockholm.

Das Reader's Digest Buch der Vogelwelt Mitteleuropas. (1973): Stuttgart, Zürich, Wien.
Deignan, H. G. (1945): The Birds of Northern Thailand. Bull. Uni-Nat. Mus. 186.
Delacour, J. (1966): Guide des oiseaux de la Nouvelle Calédonie et de ses dépendences. Neuchâtel.
Delacour, J. & Mayr, E. (1946): Birds of the Philippines. New York.
Delacour, J. & Mayr, E. (1971): Birds of Malaysia. New York.
Dementiev, G. P. (1960): Der Gerfalke. Neue Brehm-Bücherei (264) Wittenberg-Lutherstadt.
Dementiev, G. P. & Gladkov, N. A. (1954): The Birds of the Soviet Union. Moskau.

Eisenmann, E. (1955): „The Species of Middle American Birds". Trans. Linn. Soc. New York.
Engelmann, F. (1928): Die Raubvögel Europas. Naturgeschichte, Kulturgeschichte und Falknerei. Neudamm.
Erlanger, C. v. (1898): Beiträge zur Avifauna Tunesiens. Journ. Ornith. 46. Berlin.

Etchécopar, R. D. & Hüe, F. (1967): The Birds of North Africa. (Engl. P. A. D. Hollom). Edinburgh, London.

Fehringer, O. (1926) (1956 repr.): Vögel Mitteleuropas. Vol. 2. Heidelberg.

Fischer, W. (1959) (1973 repr.): Die Seeadler. Neue Brehm Bücherei (221) Wittenberg-Lutherstadt.

Fischer, W. (1963): Die Geier. Neue Brehm Bücherei (311) Wittenberg-Lutherstadt.

Fischer, W. (1967): Der Wanderfalke. Neue Brehm Bücherei (380) Wittenberg-Lutherstadt.

Fischer, W. (1973): Die Greifvögel der Erde. Der Falke. Nr. 3 pp. 78–87. Berlin.

Fischer, W. (1976): Stein-, Kaffern- und Keilschwanzadler. Neue Brehm Bücherei (500). Wittenberg-Lutherstadt.

Friedman, H., Griscom, L., Moor, R. T. (1950): Distributional Check-List of the Birds of Mexico. Pac. Coast. Avif. Nr. 29. Berkeley.

Frieling, H. (1960): Was fliegt denn da? Stuttgart.

Géroudet, P. (1947) (1965 repr.): La vie des oiseaux. Les rapaces. Neuchâtel/Paris.

Gill, E. L. (1970): A first Guide to the South-African Birds. Cape Town.

Glenister, A. G. (1971): The birds of the Malay Peninsula, Singapore and Penang. London.

Glutz v. Blotzheim, U. N. (1962): Die Brutvögel der Schweiz. Aarau.

Glutz v. Blotzheim, U. N., Bauer, K. M., Bezzel, E. (1971): Handbuch der Vögel Mitteleuropas. Vol. IV Frankfurt/M.

Goodall, J. D., Johnson, A. W. & Philippi, R. A. (1951): Los Aves de Chile. Buenos Aires.

Gray, G. R. (1859): List of New Caledonian Birds. London.

Gore, M. E. J. & Won Byong-Oh. (1971): The Birds of Korea. Seoul.

Grossman, M. L. & Hamlet, J. (1964): Birds of Prey of the World. London.

Harris, M. (1974): A Field Guide to the Birds of Galapagos. London.

Hartert, E. (1903–1922): Die Vögel der paläarktischen Fauna. Vol. 2. Berlin.

Hartert, E. & Steinbacher, J. (1932–38): dto. Ergänzungsband. Berlin.

Hartlaub, G. (1877): Die Vögel Madagaskars und der benachbarten Inselgruppen. Halle.

Haverschmidt, F. (1968): Birds of Surinam. Edinburgh, London.

Hege, W. & Kapherr, E.v. (1933): Deutsche Raubvögel. Weimar.

Heim de Balsac, H. & Mayaud, N. (1962): Les oiseaux du nord-ouest de l'Afrique. Paris.

Heinroth, O. & M. (1924–28) und (1937): Die Vögel Mitteleuropas. Bd. II und IV.

Heinzel, H., Fitter, R., Parslow, J. (1972): Pareys Vogelbuch. Hamburg, Berlin.

Hellmayr, C. E. (1914): Die Avifauna von Timor. Stuttgart.

Hennicke, C. R. (1903): Die Raubvögel Mitteleuropas. Gera-Untermhaus.

Henry, G. M. (1955): A Guide to the Birds of Ceylon. London.

Herklots, G. A. C. (1961): The Birds of Trinidad and Tobago. London.

Hiraldo F., Delibes M. & Calderon J. (1976): Sobre el status taxonómico del águila imperial ibérica. Doñana, Acta Vertebrata 3 (2), 171–182.

Holman, F. C., (1947): Birds of Gold Coast. Ibis 89 (623–650).

Hollom, P. A. D. (1952) (1972 repr.): The Popular Handbook of British Birds. 1. vol. London.

Holmström, C. T. Henrici, P. Rosenberg, G. Söderberg, R. (1944): Våra Fåglar i Norden. Del. II Stockholm.

Holstein, V. (1944): Hvespevagen, *Pernis p. avivorus* (L.) Kopenhagen.

Holstein, V. (1956): Musvagen, *Buteo b. buteo* (L.). Kopenhagen.

Iredale, T. (1956): Birds of New Guinea. Melbourne. 2 Vols.

Johnson, A. W. (1965–67): The Birds of Chile and adjacent Region of Argentina etc. 2 Vols. Buenos Aires.

King, B. F. & Dickinson, E. C. (1975): A Field Guide to the Birds of South East Asia. London.

Kleinschmidt, O. (1901): Der Formenkreis *Hierofalco* und die Stellung der ungarischen Würgfalken zu denselben. Aquila VIII Budapest.

Kleinschmidt, O. (1912–37): *Falco Peregrinus*. I und II. Berajah, Zoographia infinita. Halle.

Kleinschmidt, O. (1922–23): *Falco Palumbarius*. Berajah, Zoographia infinita. Halle.

Kleinschmidt, O. (1923): *Falco Nisus*. Berajah, Zoographia infinita. Halle.

Kleinschmidt, O. (1923–37): Die Realgattung *Hierofalco* I–IV, Berajah, Zoographia infinita. Halle.

Kleinschmidt, O. (1935) und (1940): Die Formenrassen der deutschen Habichte. Falco 34.

Kleinschmidt, O. (1958) (2. edit.): Raubvögel und Eulen der Heimat. Wittenberg-Lutherstadt.

Kobayashi, K. (1965): Birds of Japan. Osaka.

Koenig, A. (1936): Die Vögel am Nil. 2. Band (Die Raubvögel). Bonn.

Koepcke, M. (1964): Les Aves del Departamento de Lima. Lima.

Kramer, V. (1955): Habicht und Sperber. Neue Brehm Bücherei (158). Wittenberg-Lutherstadt.

Kuroda, W. (1933–36): Birds of the islands of Java. Vol. 2. Tokyo.

La Touche, J. D. D. (1931–34): A Handbook of Birds of Eastern China. Vol. 2. London.

Leach, J. A. (1958): 9th. edit. An Australian Bird Book.

Lloyd, G. & D. (1971): Greifvögel und Eulen. Stuttgart.

Mackworth-Praed, C. W. & Grant, C. H. B. (1957): Birds of Eastern and North-eastern Africa. Vol. I. London.

Mackworth-Praed, C. W. & Grant, C. H. B. (1962): Birds of the Southern Third of Africa. Vol. I. London.

Mackworth-Praed, C. W. & Grant, C. H. B. (1970): Birds of West Central and Western Africa. Vol. I. London.

Makatsch, R. (1953): Der schwarze Milan. Neue Brehm-Bücherei (100) Wittenberg-Lutherstadt.

Marle van, J. G. & Voous, K. H. jr. (1946): The endemic Sparrow-hawks of Celebes. Limosa 19 pp. 15–23.

Mathew, G. M. & Iredale, T. (1921): A Manual of the Birds of Australia. London.

May, J. B. (1935): The hawks of North America. Nat. Audubon Soc. New York.

Mayr, E. (1940): On the Birds of the Loyalty Islands. Am. Mus. Novit. Nr. 1057 New York.

Mayr, E. (1941): List of New Guinea Birds. The Am. Mus. of Nat. History New York.

Mayr, E. (1945): Notes on the Birds of Northern Melanesia. Amer. Mus. Novit. Nr. 1294 New York.

Mayr, E. (1945): Birds of the Southern Pacific. New York.

Mayr, E. & Gilliard, E. T. (1954): Birds of the Central New Guinea. Bull. Am. Mus. Nat. Hist. 103 pp. 311–374.

Mebs, Th. (1964): Greifvögel Europas und die Grundzüge der Falknerei. Stuttgart.

Mebs, Th. & Fischer, W. (1976): Die Greifvögel der Erde. Barmstedt.

Meinertzhagen, R. (1930): Nicoll's Birds of Egypt. Vol. 1. London.

Meinertzhagen, R. (1954): Birds of Arabia. London.

Meinertzhagen, R. (1959): Pirates and Predators. Edinburgh.

Meise, W. (1939): Über die Schlangenadler der Gattung *Spilornis* Gray. Journ. f. Ornith. 87 pp. 65–74.

Melde, M. (1960): Der Mäusebussard. Neue Brehm-Bücherei (185) Wittenberg-Lutherstadt.

Meyburg, B.-U. (1970): Die Biologie des Schreiadlers. Deutscher Falkenorden 69: 32–66.

Meyburg, B.-U. (1975): On the biology of the Spanish Imperial Eagle. Ardeola. Vol. 21: 245–283.

Meyburg, B.-U. (1976): Status, Bedrohung und Schutz der Greifvögel (Falconiformes) in Westspanien. Angewandte Ornithologie Bd. 5, Nr. 1: 13–31.

Meyer, A. B. & Wigglesworth, L. W. (1898): The Birds of Celebes. Berlin.

Meyer, P. O. (1934): Seltene Vögel auf Neubritannien. Journ. f. Ornith. 82. Berlin.

Meyer, de Schauensee, R. (1964): Birds of Colombia. Philadelphia.

Meyer, de Schauensee, R. (1966): The Species of Birds of South America, with their Distribution. Narberth-Pensilv.

Meyer, de Schauensee, R. (1971): A quide to the Birds of South America. Edinburgh.

Milon, P. J. Petter, J. Randriansolo, G. (1973): Fauna de Madagascar. Oiseaux.

Moll, K. H. (1962): Der Fischadler. Neue Brehm-Bücherei (308). Wittenberg-Lutherstadt.

Münch, H. (1955): Der Wespenbussard. Neue Brehm-Bücherei (151) Wittenberg-Lutherstadt.

Munro, G. C. (1944): Birds of Hawaii, Honolulu.

Naumann, J. F. (1905): Neuaufl. Naturgeschichte der Vögel Mitteleuropas. Vol. V.

Niethammer, G. (1937–42): Handbuch der deutschen Vogelkunde. Vol. I. Leipzig.

Oliver, W. R. B. (1930) (1952 2nd edit.): New Zealand birds. Wellington/N. Z.

Parkes, K. C. (1958): Specific relationship in the genus *Elanus*. Condor 60. pp 139–140. Berkeley.

Peeters, H. J. (1963): Über die Waldfalken. Journal f. Ornith. 104 pp. 357–364.

Penny, M. (1974): A field Guide to the Birds of the Seychelles and outlaying Islands. London.

Peters, J. L. (1931 & 1979): Check list of Birds of the World. Vol. 1. Cambridge, Mass.

Peterson, R. T. (1949): How to know the Birds. New York.

Peterson, R. T. (1961): A Field Guide to the Birds. Boston.

Peterson, R. T. (1961): A Field Guide to the Western Birds. Boston.

Peterson, R. T. (1963): A Field Guide to the Birds of Texas. Boston.

Peterson, R. T. & Chalif, E. L. (1973): A Field Guide to the Mexican Birds. Boston.

Peterson, R. T. & Mountfort, G. & Hollom, P. A. D. (1954, 1973 repr.): Die Vögel Europas. Hamburg.

Piechocki, R. (1970): Der Turmfalke. Neue Brehm-Bücherei (116). Wittenberg-Lutherstadt.

Porter, R. F., Willis, J., Christensen, S., Nielsen, B. P. (1974): Flight Indentification of European Raptors. Berkhamsted.

Rand, A. L. & Rabor, D. S. (1960): Birds of the Philippine Islands. Chicago.

Rand, A. L. & Gilliard E. T. (1967): Handbook of New Guinea Birds. London.

Reichenow, A. (1894): Die Vögel Deutsch-Ostafrikas. Berlin.

Reichenow, A. (1913): Die Vögel. Vol. 1. Stuttgart.

Richmond, W. K. (1954): British birds of prey. London.

Ridgway, R. & Friedman, H. (1950): Birds of North and Middle America. US. Nat. Museum Bull. 50/XI.

Rieck, W. (1954): Der Seeadler. Der Falke 1. Nr. 4.

Ripley, S. Dillon (1944): The bird Fauna of the West Sumatran Islands. Bull. of the Mus. Comp. Zool. at Harvard Coll. 94 pp 307–430. Cambridge.

Roberts, A. (1957): 2nd. ed. The Birds of South Africa. London.

Rutgers, E. (1966–1970): Ein Vogelparadies in Farben. Europ. Vögel. Vol. 1 Gorssel.

Rutgers, E. (1966–1970): Ein Vogelparadies in Farben. Vogelwelt Asiens. Vol. 1. Gorssel.

Rutgers, E. (1966–1970): Ein Vogelparadies in Farben. Austral. Vogelwelt. Vol. 1. Gorssel.

Rutgers, E. (1966–1970): Ein Vogelparadies in Farben. Vogelwelt v. Neuguinea. Vol. 1. Gorssel.

Serventy, D. L. & Whittell, H. M. (1962): Birds of Western Australia. 3rd. ed. Perth.

Slater, P. (1971): A Field Guide to the Australian Birds. Non Passerines. Vol. 1. Edinburgh.

Smith, K. D. (1965): The birds of Morocco. Ibis. 107 (493–526).

Smythies, B. E. (1940) new. edit.: The Birds of Burma. Edinburgh.

Smythies, B. E. (1960): The Birds of Borneo. London.

Snyder, O. E. (1966): The Birds of Guyana. Salem.

Steinbacher, I. (1962): Beiträge zur Kenntnis der Vögel von Paraguay. Frankfurt/M.

Storer, R. W. (1952): Variation in the Resident Sharpshinned Hawks of Mexico. Condor 54. Berkeley.

Stresemann, E. (1927–34): Handbuch der Zoologie. Bd. 7. Aves. (2. Hälfte). Berlin, Leipzig.

Stresemann, E. (1938): *Spizaëtus alboniger* (Blyth) und *Spizaëtus nanus* Wallace . . . Journ. f. Ornith. 86 pp. 425–431.

Stresemann, E. (1939): Die Vögel von Celebes. Journ. f. Ornith. 87.

Stresemann, E. (1946): Die Vögel von Celebes. Journ. f. Ornith. 88.

Stresemann, E. (1959): Die Gliederung der Schlangenadlergattung *Spilornis*. Vierteljahresschrift der Naturf. Gesellsch. Zürich 104. pp. 208–213.

Stresemann, E. (1959): *Buteo albigula* Philippi ... Journ. f. Ornith. 93 pp. 144–153.

Stresemann, E. & Stresemann, V. (1960): Die Handschwingenmauser der Tagraubvögel. Journ. f. Ornith. 101 pp. 373–403.

Sutton, G. M. (1951): Mexican Birds. Oklahoma.

Sutton, G. (1944): The kites of the Genus *Ictinia*. Wilson Bull. 56 pp. 3–8.

Swann, H. K. & Wetmore, A. (1924–1945): A Monograph of the Birds of Prey. 2 Vols. London.

Taverner, P. A. (1934): Birds of Canada. Canad. Dep. Mines Bull. Nr. 72.

Traylor, M. A. jr. (1948): New Birds from Peru and Ecuador. Fieldiana 31. pp. 195–200.

Trommer, G. (1974): Die Greifvögel. Stuttgart.

Vaurie, Ch. (1959–1965): The Birds of the Palearctic Fauna. Non Passeriformes. London.

Vaurie, Ch. & Amodon, D. (1962): Notes on the Honey-Buzzards of Eastern Asia. Amer. Mus. Novit. 2111. New York.

Verheyen, R. (1959): Révision de la systématique des Falconiformes. Bull. Inst. roy. Sa. not. Belg. 35 No. 37.

Voous, K. H. (1957): The Birds of Aruba, Curaçao and Bonaire. The Hague.

Voous, K. H. (1960): Atlas of European Birds. London.

Wendland, V. (1959): Schrei- und Schelladler. Neue Brehm-Bücherei (236). Wittenberg-Lutherstadt.

Wenzel, F. Ottens, H. W. (1963): Das Bilderbuch der Vögel. Taggreife etc. Hannover.

Wetmore, A. (1964): A revision of ... genus *Cathartes*. Smith. Mis. Coll. 146 Nr. 6 pp. 1–18.

Whistler, H. (1949): Popular Handbook of Indian Birds. Vol. II. London.

Wigglesworth, L. W. (1892): Aves Polynesia. Berlin.

Williams, J. G. (1971): Säugetiere und seltene Vögel in den Nationalparks Ostafrikas. Hamburg/Berlin.

Williams, J. G. (1973): Die Vögel Ost- und Zentralafrikas. Hamburg/Berlin.

Wink, M., Wink, C., Ristow D. (1978): Biologie des Eleonorenfalken. Journ. f. Ornith. 119, pp 421–428.

Witherby, H. F. et. al. (1947): Handbook of British Birds. Vol. II London.

Wolfe, L. R. (1938): Birds of central Luzon. Auk. 55 (198–224).

Wolfe, L. R. (1950): Birds of Korea. Auk. 67 (433–455).

Wolters, H. E. (1975/76): Die Vogelarten der Erde. 1. + 2. Lieferung. Hamburg/Berlin.

Wüst, W. (1970): Die Brutvögel Mitteleuropas. München.

Yamashina, Y. (1931): Die Vögel der Kurilen. Journ. f. Orn. 79 Berlin.

Yamashina, Y. (1961): Birds in Japan. A field guide. Tokyo.

Accipiter gentilis